ANCIENT INDIAN TRADITION & MYTHOLOGY

Translated by
A BOARD OF SCHOLARS

Edited by
Prof. J.L. SHASTRI

VOLUME 13

ANCIENT INDIAN TRADITION AND MYTHOLOGY SERIES

[PURĀṆAS IN TRANSLATION]

Volumes Released

ŚIVA 1-4
LIṄGA 5-6
BHĀGAVATA 7-11
GARUḌA 12-14
NĀRADA 15-19
KŪRMA 20-21
BRAHMĀṆḌA 22-26
AGNI 27-30
VARĀHA 33-36
VĀYU 37-38
PADMA 39-48
SKANDA, PARTS I-XXI, 49-69
VĀMANA 72-73

Volumes Under Preparation

SKANDA, PARTS XXII-XXIII, 70-71
BHAVIṢYA
BRAHMAVAIVARTA
DEVĪBHĀGAVATA
KĀLIKĀ
MĀRKAṆḌEYA
MATSYA
VIṢṆU
VIṢṆUDHARMOTTARA

THE GARUḌA-PURĀṆA

Translated and Annotated by

A BOARD OF SCHOLARS

PART II

MOTILAL BANARSIDASS PUBLISHERS
PRIVATE LIMITED • DELHI

Reprint: Delhi, 1991, 1996, 2003, 2009
First Edition: Delhi, 1979

ISBN: 978-81-208-0345-9

MOTILAL BANARSIDASS
41 U.A. Bungalow Road, Jawahar Nagar, Delhi 110 007
8 Mahalaxmi Chamber, 22 Bhulabhai Desai Road, Mumbai 400 026
203 Royapettah High Road, Mylapore, Chennai 600 004
236, 9th Main III Block, Jayanagar, Bangalore 560 011
Sanas Plaza, 1302 Baji Rao Road, Pune 411 002
8 Camac Street, Kolkata 700 017
Ashok Rajpath, Patna 800 004
Chowk, Varanasi 221 001

UNESCO COLLECTION OF REPRESENTATIVE WORKS—*Indian Series*
This book has been accepted in the Indian Translation Series of the UNESCO Collection of Representative Works, jointly sponsored by the United Nations Educational, Scientific and Cultural Organization (UNESCO) and the Government of India

PRINTED IN INDIA

By Jainendra Prakash Jain at Shri Jainendra Press,
A-45 Naraina, Phase-I, New Delhi 110 028
and Published by Narendra Prakash Jain for
Motilal Banarsidass Publishers Private Limited,
Bungalow Road, Delhi 110 007

PUBLISHER'S NOTE

The purest gems lie hidden in the bottom of the ocean or in the depth of rocks. One has to dive into the ocean or delve into the rocks to find them out. Similarly, truth lies concealed in the language which with the passage of time has become obsolete. Man has to learn that language before he discovers that truth.

But he has neither the means nor the leisure to embark on that course. We have, therefore, planned to help him acquire knowledge by an easier course. We have started the series of Ancient Indian Tradition and Mythology in English Translation. Our goal is to universalize knowledge through the most popular international medium of expression. The publication of the Purāṇas in English Translation is a step towards that goal.

PREFACE

The present Volume contains the *Garuḍa Purāṇa*, Part II (Chapters 147-240 of Ācārakāṇḍa and Chapters 1-20 of Dharma-Kāṇḍa) in English translation. It is the thirteenth in the series of fifty Volumes on *Ancient Indian Tradition and Mythology.*

The project of the series was envisaged and financed in 1970 by late Lala Sundarlal Jain, the veteran enterprizer in the field of Oriental Publication and the leading partner Messrs Motilal Banarsidass. Hitherto thirteen Volumes of the Series, including the present one, (that is, four Vols. of the *Śiva Purāṇa*, two Vols. of the *Liṅga Purāṇa*, five Vols. of the *Bhāgavata Purāṇa* and two Vols. of the *Garuḍa Purāṇa*) have been published and released for sale.

The *Garuḍa Purāṇa* is normally classified as a Vaiṣṇava Purāṇa, but, in fact, this Purāṇa is non-sectarian and cosmopolitan in character. Its encyclopedic nature is reflected in the treatment of multifarious or miscellaneous subjects such as Medicine, Astrology, Palmistry, Metrics, Philosophy in addition to the legitimate topics of a Purāṇa. This variety of topics, the section on medicine in particular, needed elucidation—a task which could not be accomplished by a mere translation. Hence the provision has been made for the footnotes. What is missing in the footnotes will be found in the Glossary appended to the Third Part, at the beginning of Index. Thereby, the reader will not be disappointed for want of a footnote. Introduction and Abbreviations, since they are included in Part I, are not repeated here.

Acknowledgment of Obligations

It is our pleasant duty to put on record our sincere gratitude to Dr. S. K. Chatterjee, Dr. V. Raghavan, Dr. R. N. Dandekar, Shri R.K. Kripalani and the authorities of the UNESCO for their kind encouragement and valuable help which render this work more useful to scholars than it would otherwise have been. We must also thank Shri T. V. Parameswar Iyer for his valuable spade-work which lightened our labour, especially in the initial stage.

—Editor

CONTENTS

PART II

Ācāra (Karma) Kāṇḍa (continued from AITM Vol. 12)

Dharma (Preta) Kāṇḍa

Chapters

CHAPTER ONE HUNDRED AND FORTYSEVEN[1]

Diseases

Dhanvantari said:

1. I shall expl-in the pathology of fevers for a thorough understanding of all types of fevers. The infuriated Rudra at the destruction of sacrifice of Dakṣa cast a fiery look from his third eye in the forehead from whence fever originated. In the medical sience it is known as Rogapati (lord of diseases); Pāpmā (sin), Mṛtyurāja (king of death); Aśana (the devourer) Antaka (the finisher).

2-3. It is caused by unhygienic misconduct, it produces delirium, unconsciousness and harassing rise in temperature. This cruel affliction is found in all sorts of animals and even in inanimate objects. In elephants it is called Pākala[2] or Kūṭapākala or Hastivātajvara: In horses Abhitāpa. In dogs Alarka. In clouds Indramada. In water Nīlika. In herbs Jyotis (fluorescence). In soils Ūṣara (saline and barren).

4. In the fever due to derangement of Kapha the indications are hiccough, Vomiting sensation, Catarrh, stiffness and rigidity of the body, coldness of the skin and pain in every limb.

5. As days pass, these symptoms are seen operating and increasing. Non-application of proper remedies or application of contrary remedies may aggravate them.

6-7. The characteristic symptoms in Āmajvara[3] (in fever due to constipation) are:—Loss of appetite, indigestion, rigidity of the body, lethargy, burning sensation in the heart, a reverse or relapse, drowsiness and lassitude, abdominal

1. The chapter mentions the names of fevers which attack elephants, horses, dogs, cloud, water, herbs and earth.

2. Pākala is a fever which attacks elephants. This is tenfold. Kūṭapākala is the deadliest of all fevers and kills elephants at once. For detail see ch. 9 of the *Hastyāyurveda* of Pālakāpya.

3. GP mentions fever with or without constipation and the fever *sannipāta* caused by the disturbance of the three humours.

bruises, ill functioning of the humours, salivation, hiccough, loss of hunger, moistness in the mouth tasting sweet, a transparent glossiness of the skin, temperature, heaviness of limbs, profuse urination and neither digestion nor exhaustion.

8. In the Nirāmajvara (fever without constipation) there is emaciation due to hunger, a lightness is felt in the limbs, abatement of temperature and relapse in eight days are the symptoms. When there is the admixture of different types of fever the characteristic symptoms of every one are seen.

9. The Vāyu principle in combination with the principle of Pitta brings about a type of fever when the following symptoms are seen: Headache, swooning, vomiting, burning sensation in the body, parchedness of throat and mouth, aching in the joints, insomnia, agitation, horripilation, yawn and perpetual prattle.

10. In the fever due to the derangement of both Śleṣmā (phlegm) and Vāyu (gas) the symptoms are: fall of temperature, loss of appetite, pain in the joints, headache, difficulty in breathing, frequent coughs, discoloration of the skin, pallid face, sluggishness, chillness, sensation of darkness, whirling of the head and lassitude.

11. In the fever due to the derangement of both Śleṣmā and Pitta humours the symptoms are:—chillness, rigidity, profuse perspiration, burning sensation, unsteadiness, thirst, coughing, vomiting of bile and phlegm, stupefaction, drowsiness and bitter salivation.

12. When all the deranged humours combine in producing a fever it is called Sannipāta Jvara or Abhinyāsa Jvara. where the symptoms mentioned before are present. In addition to these there are other symptoms such as:—Burning sensation and chillness in alternation, vertigo sleeping in the day and wakefulness at night.

13. The patient either sleeps always or does not sleep at all; sometimes he perspires profusely or never at all. He sings, dances nnd laughs. Natural functions of the body cease.

14. Eyes become red hot, sunk in the sockets and full of tears. The eyelids droop down. There is pain in the calves, sides, joints, head and in the bones. Dizziness is felt.

15. Ringing in the ears with acute pain, great chilliness or no chilliness at all alternately; the tongue appears burnt and rough. The joints seem to crackle and appear loose and heavy.

16. Blood-streaked bilious matter is vomited, the head begins to roll and toss. Excessive thirst is experienced; The rooms appear to be dark and brownish red and ringlets appear before the eyes.

17. Pain is felt in the heart. Loose motions or coming bit by bit. Chilliness of the face, debility, loss of voice, and delirium.

18. Development of the humours, a long drowsiness, a diffused croaking sound in the throat. These are the indications in Sannipāta Jvara known as Abhinyāsa Jvara also. The Ojas or vitality in the body becomes fully spent.

19. The gaseous humour (Vāyu) being held at the throat the bilious principle suppressed within tries to come out due to its expansive nature. Hence the eyes appear yellowish in colour in a patient of Sannipāta Jvara.

20. The Sannipāta jvara wherein the doṣas become excessively aggravated and the gastric function is impaired is incurable. Other types of Sannipāta fevers can be cured with great difficulty.

21. There is another type of Sannipāta jvara where the Pitta humour remains aloof and produces burning sensation in the skin or in the viscera either before or after (the onset of fever).

22-23. In the Sannipāta Jvara due to Vāyu and Kapha the chillness, burning sensation, etc, are felt more acute. When Kapha in fluid state is dried up by the pitta and when pitta subsides later, swooning, intoxication and thirst result. If there is burning sensation at the beginning and somnolence and lassitude in the end, vomiting is the result.

24. The Āgantu (i.e casual fever due to extraneous causes) fever is of four types (1) due to hurt or blow, (2) due to contact, (3) due to curse, (4) due to black magic. If there is fever, due to burns or scalds it comes under the class Abhighātaja i.e the first type.

25. If there is fever due to exhaustion, the wind principle contaminates the blood. There is pallor, pain and rise in temperature and swelling too.

26. Malignant planets, narcotics, poisons, anger, fright, sorrow and love may cause fever. This may be classified under the casual type but the special characteristics will be spasmodic laughter and cries.

27. In the fever due to inhalation of drugs and narcotics, fainting, headache, vomiting and sneezing are the special symptoms. The fever due to poison generates swooning, dysentery, darkness and discoloration of the skin, burning sensation and vertigo.

28. The fever due to anger has the special symptoms of tremulousness and headache; that due to fright and grief is signified by perpetual prattle.

29. The fever due to lust and love is marked by dizziness, loss of taste for food, burning sensation, extreme shyness, loss of sleep and absence of firmness of mind and courage.

30. In the fever due to adverse planets as in the Sannipāta Jvara both the gaseous and bilious principles are aggravated.

31. The fevers due to curse and black magic are considered to be very terrible and unbearable. The *mantras* and incantations of black magic excite the victim and harass him.

32. Here and there in the body eruptions appear. The patient feels giddy. There is burning sensation and swooning in the end. The fever rises every day.

33-34. Such are eight[1] types of fever. In brief, they are of two kinds, viz. physical and mental; mild and virulent; internal and external; Prākṛta (Natural i.e Seasonal) and Vaikṛta (unnatural or sporadic) ; curable and incurable or mature and immature. In the former, the fever is in the body and in the latter it is in the mind.

35-36. When Vāyu principle is in combination with Kapha principle there will be chilliness. There will be burn-

1. Besides the eightfold division of fever, there is a twofold division of six kinds, viz *śārīra-mānasa*, *saumya-tīkṣṇa*, *antar-bahir āśraya*, *prākṛta-vaikṛta* *sādhya-asādhya*, and sāma-nirāmaya.

ing sensation if it is in combination with Pitta. A mixture of these two when the doṣas are mixed. If the fever is within, the disorder and deterioration is internal and there will be constipation. In the case of external fever there may be loose motions. The fever is curable.

37. In the rainy season a fever due to the derangement of Vāyu is Prākṛta; still this is generally incurable. Fevers due to the derangement of the other two in the rainy season are Vaikṛta and definitely incurable.

38. In the Autumn a fever due to derangement of Pitta is Prākṛta, otherwise it is Vaikṛta.

39-40. In the spring, a fever due to the derangement of Kapha is Prākṛta, otherwise it is Vaikṛta. All Vaikṛta fevers are incurable. Vāyu deranged in the rainy season causes fever with the combination of Pitta and Kapha. Pitta deranged in autumn causes fever with the support of kapha. Due to its nature and discharge there is no danger in fasting. Kapha deranged in Spring causes fever with the support of Vāyu and Pitta.

In strong persons with less defects fever does not cause much harm and hence is curable. If the doṣas are all altogether aggravated it is incurable.

41. The characteristic sign of an Āmajvara is immature virulence of fever), low functioning of the gastric fire, excessive urination, nonfunctioning of the digestive and excretory systems and loss of hunger.

42. The characteristic sign of a Pacyamāna (or ripening or maturing) fever is virulence of fever, excessive thirst, prattling and delirium, rapid breathing, vertigo, loose motions and acute pain.

43. Since digestion is possible by the removal of the Āma matter, a seven days fast is recommended in this case. Jvaras are classified into five taking into consideration the extent of derangement in the malas (humours), the periodicity or the season of attack and the comparative strength or weakness of the patient or the exciting factors.

44. Generally when there is a combination of many factors these fevers are produced. They are Santata, (remittent) Satata, (intermittent), Anyedyu (appearing on every

other day), Tṛtīyaka (tertian) Caturthaka (occurring once in four days).

45-46. The doṣas pervading the ducts and vessels carrying the seven dhātus, urine and faeces distress the entire body and get aggravated on equal sight (?) etc. The Rasas or secretions are strong or weighty due to the special characteristics of the body. Always they make the fever unbearable, having no antagonist.

47. It may alleviate the doṣas, fever, heat or the dhātus by means of purity or impurity.

48. Generally it reaches the limit either for complete abatement or for finishing (the patient) in seven, ten or twelve days in the case of Vāyu, Pitta and Kapha respectively.

49. This is Agniveśa's[1] opinion. According to Hārīta the crucial days are twice seven (fourteen), ninth and eleventh This is the line of demarcation for the three doṣas either for abatement or for finishing the patient.

50-51. Based on purity or impurity the duration of the attack may be more. If lean persons contract disease and do not observe rules of diet and conduct, even a slight aggravation of the deranged doṣa, strengthened by the support of other exciting factors may become fatal.

52. The doṣa increasing or decreasing irregularly will cause fever in its own time.

53. The doṣas being weakened, the fever subsides due to the powerful antidotes (by way of medicines) and its subtle form gets merged in the secretions.

54. With the absorption of fever emaciation, pallor and sluggishness vanish and its spreading in the whole of the body is checked since the dilation of the excretory vessels helps them to be thrown out through natural outlets.

55. The Santata is remittent fever. The Satata (intermittent) is contrary to it since its beginning is irregular though it becomes acute during the night.

1. The Purāṇa's reference to Agniveśa and Hārīta in chapters on Āyurveda indicates that the āyurvedic section of the Purāṇa is based on authority and is therefore authentic.

56. Generally, the morbid humour getting mingled in blood produces the Satata type of fever. The Anyedyu type of fever comes at the time of the juncture of day and night.

57. In this fever, vessels containing fleshy matter and fat substance are contaminated. Due to the combined action of Pitta and Vāyu there is pain in the head. Due to Kapha and Pitta there is pain in the Trika (Spine).

58. Pain in the back is due to the combined action of Vāyu and Kapha. This fever subsides for a day in the middle. In the fever Caturthaka the fat, marrow and the bones are contaminated by the Doṣas.

59. The Caturthaka fever confined to marrow alone manifests twice a day. Due to Kapha affection there is pain in the knee-joint, and calves, while affected by Vāyu the head also aches in the beginning.

60. The Caturthaka-viparyaya fever confined to bones and marrow continues for three days and subsides on the fourth day.

61. The derangement of the humours aggravated by unsuitable diet and activities being matured due to non-elimination) the patient must be compelled to fast for seven days.

62. The mind and the bodily functions of the patient are affected by the fever. This Caturthaka fever is incurable because it has entered deep into the ducts of Dhātus (the seven primary constituent elements of the body), and the doṣas have risen up all simultaneously and attained equal heights of virulence.

63-67. In the case of all these subtle attacks of fever the deranged humour traverses slowly along the vessels of blood, etc and since it takes a long time to cover the whole body it does not harass the body much. But if medication ceases the fever may be acute and nighty paroxysms of pyrexia may be witnessed. As the physical strength of the patient becomes less and less, the fever slowly permeates the whole of the Rasa constituents of the body. Then the doṣa (deranged humour or diathesis) becomes aggravated sooner or later resulting in high fever.

68. Just as a seed in the soil when watered well does not take time to sprout so also the seeds of doṣas sprout into fever.

69. Just as poison taken in becomes virulent and fatal so also the doṣas getting strength from other factors become aggravated.

70. Thus, the fevers Viṣama, Satata, etc. function. The characteristic symptoms when the fever is confined to Rasa constituent of the body (Lymph):—Disquietude (or sea sickness), heaviness, dejection, shooting pain in the limbs, yawning, loss of taste, vomiting sensation, difficulty in breathing, etc.

71. When the fever permeates the blood, the symptoms are:—Spitting of blood, excessive thirst, appearance of coarse hot eruptions on the skin, red patches, burning sensation, vertigo, intoxication and prattling delirium.

72-74. When the fever is restricted to the flesh, the symptoms are thirst, fatigue, defiled splendour, an internal burning sensation, dizziness, appearance of darkness, fetidness and jerky movements of the limbs. When the fever has permeated the fat, the symptoms are perspiration, excessive thirst, vomiting, foul smell and irritability. When the fever penetrates the bone the symptoms are delirium, exhaustion, loss of taste and appetite and pain in the bones.

75. When the fever permeates the marrow the symptoms are the functioning of the doṣas, dyspnea (difficulty in breathing), convulsive movements of the limbs, croaking sound in the throat, burning sensation within, chilliness outside, deep sighs and hiccough.

76. When the fever permeates the semen virile, the symptoms are appearance of darkness, splitting of the vulnerable joints, numbness of the penis, and death when seminal egress takes place.

77. These five types of Caturthaka Viparyaya fever are more and more difficult to treat as enumerated above. The Pralepaka type of fever exhibits the symptoms of delirium, chilliness, low temperature and heaviness of the limbs. One feels as if one's body is coated with phlegm.

78. The Aṅgabalāśaka (Devourer of the strength of limbs) type of fever exhibits the symptoms of low temperature,

coarseness or stiffness of the body, numbness of limbs and difficulty in walking. Phlegm will be profusely manifested.

79. If the wine passed is of the colour of the cut piece of turmeric the fever is called Hāridraka (yellow fever?). It is fatal.

80. Where the patient is deficient in Pitta and, Kapha and Vāyu are equally dominant there is no fever during the day but there is fever at night. This type is called Rātrijvara or Paurvarātrika.

81. The onset of fever is at nightfall since due to the action of Vāyu the body gets dried up in the Kapha content either by means of exercise or due to the action of Sun's rays.

82. When Kapha and pitta are in the abdomen the upper part of the body remains cold but the lower part remains warm.

83. But when Kapha goes lower down, the Pitta remaining in the upper region, the body is felt warm and the lower part chill (at the hands and feet).

84. The fever confined to the lymph and blood vessels can be cured. So also the fever that is restricted to flesh and fat. But the fever affecting bones and marrow is incurable. At the onset of fever the different limbs are discoloured rendered pallid.

85. The patient attacked by fever sometimes becomes unconscious. He has an appearance of an angry man. He evacuates hot mucuous and bilious matter very frequently.

86. The characteristic signs of a patient freed from fever are lightness of body and exhaustion; delusion and heat disappear, some eruptions in the mouth, freedom from pain, natural functioning of the sense organs, perspiration, sneezing, mind at rest, appetite and itching sensation on the head.

CHAPTER ONE HUNDRED AND FORTYEIGHT

Diseases

Dhanvantari said :

1-2. I shall explain the pathology of Raktapitta (Bilious Haemorrhage). The deranged pitta contaminates the blood. The cause of derangement is the excessive intake of such articles of food as are bile-provoking in character e.g. the grains of Kodrava and Uddālaka. Too hot, bitter, pungent, sour, saline and thirst—inducing foodstuffs also have the similar effect.

3-4. This mixture of bile and blood has the colour, smell etc of the blood. Hence, in Āyurvedic parlance it is known as Rakta. It comes out of blood vessels, spleen and liver.

5-7. The onset of this haemorrhage is indicated by various symptoms :—Heaviness of the head, non relish for food, desire to eat cold things, a smoky vision, sour vomiting, nausea, hiccough, gasping for breath, vertigo, fatigue, allergy to red colour, fishy smell in the mouth when the fever abates, reddish, yellow and green colour in the eyes, inability to distinguish the colours of blue, red and yellow and dreams of madness.

8. The deranged and contaminated blood comes out through nose, eyes, mouth and ears when it flows up or through penis, vagina or anus when it flows down. It comes out of the roots of hair also all over the body.

9. The egress of bilious blood when it flows up can be cured by means of purgatives. In the case of pitta also it is better to purge it out rather than arrest it with medication.

10. Purging cleans the system where Kapha persists. Astringent, sweet and Kapha producing drugs can be used in cleansing the system.

11-12. Or drugs of pungent, bitter and astringent nature naturally generating phlegm can be used. If the haemorrhage takes a downward course and the patient appears to die, emetics are to be used. If the patient is given a little medicine to curb the pitta and then the emetics are applied he will have strength regained.

13. Astringent and sweet things are alone good for him. If there is concerted action of both Kapha and Vāyu on the deranged pitta it is incurable.

14. If the flow of blood is upward (regressing) it is unbearable and medication is ineffective. Purging then becomes impossible in his case.

15. In Raktapitta cases of Pratiloma type (upward flow), purging and emetic are the only remedies.

16-17. But when all the humours are deranged emetic alone is advisable. It should be known that like Śiva's dart the disease is fatal since many unfavourable symptoms and disorders are observed from the beginning. If cure is effected it is good.

CHAPTER ONE HUNDRED AND FORTYNINE

Diseases

Dhanvantari said :

1. Since cough runs its course quickly I shall explain it now. There are five types of cough (1) due to Vāyu (2) due to Pitta (3) due to Kapha (4) due to internal wounds (5) due to Consumption.

2. All these coughs are more and more powerful in the order enumerated above. If neglected, they will end in consumption. A sure sign of their onset is irritation in the throat and allergy to food.

3-6. The cough generated due to the derangement of Vāyu exhibits the symptoms of dryness in the ear cavity and parchedness of throat and mouth. The wind coursing through the lower parts of the body suddenly rushes up, reaches the chest and then presses against the larynx. The agitated wind fills the ducts and vessels and the limbs are as though thrown up. It seems to uproot the eyes from their sockets. With a subdued sound it affects the sides and is passed out of the throat with a sound of a broken bell-metal vessel. It produces pain in the chest, sides, thighs and head. Agitation and fainting may be seen. Aphonia (inability to speak) and dry cough also will be observed. While coughing, shooting pain is felt and loud sound is heard and the patient's body has horripilation too. By spitting out a lump of dry kapha with great deal of difficulty he feels a bit relieved.

7-9. The cough generated by the derangement of pitta humour exhibits the following symptoms :—Yellow colour in the eyes, bitter taste in the mouth, rise in temperature, vertigo, vomiting of bilious blood, thirst, loss of speech, clouded vision, inebriety and appearance of fiery rings at the time of coughing.

The cough generated by the derangement of Kapha produces a light pain in the chest, and head as well as numbness and heaviness in the cardiac region : The throat appears to be choked with a sticky lump of Kapha. There is cold in the nostrils as well as vomiting sensation with distaste for food. Horripilation is also observed.

10-12. Fights, exercises, etc, carelessly indulged in, beyond one's capacity may cause internal wounds in the chest cavity and aggravate the Vāyu humour which accompanied by the aggravated Pitta humour makes the kapha also aggravated. The kapha gets mixed with blood and then knotted. It may be yellow or dark in colour. The patient coughs and spits out the dry Kapha lump with an excruciating pain as if the chest is breaking asunder. He feels as if he is being pierced with a number of needles.

13-14. He feels as if he is being speared through. Pain is felt in the joints with fever, thirst, gasping for breathing, loss of voice and shivering. Attempting to speak he simply coos like a dove feeling pain at the sides. He spits or vomits Kapha. His digestion is impaired, strength decreases and pallor sets in.

15. In the debilitated state he passes urine with blood. There is dyspnea (difficulty to breathe) lumbago and back pain. The deranged Vāyu then upsets all the Dhātus and makes a Kṣatakāsa patient a patient of Rājayakṣma (Phthisis).

16. He coughs and spits out kapha a fetid pus like yellow and greenish red mucous matter.

17. When he tries to sleep he feels as if he is being afflicted with pain. The heart seems to be roasted. Suddenly he

evinces a liking for a hot or cold thing by turns. Insatiety in meals and debility also follow.

18. The face suddenly becomes bright and glossy with eyes shining brilliantly. With this all, the symptoms of the wasting disease are manifested.

19. This is the nature of cough born of consumption that destroys the bodies of already debilitated persons. In strong men this as well as the cough due to wounds can be cured if they are in the preliminary stage.

20-21. By careful treatment these ailments and others in the case of old men too can be eradicated. Cough, dyspnea, phthisis, nausea, aphonia and other ailments if neglected are aggravated and so they must be eradicated quickly.

CHAPTER ONE HUNDRED AND FIFTY

Diseases

Dhanvantari said :

1. I shall now mention the pathology of Śvāsa Roga (Dyspnea) or difficulty in breathing. When cough becomes chronic it becomes dyspnea or it may be due to those factors that aggravate the humours.

2. It may result from Āmātisāra (mucous dysentery), vomiting, toxins, and jaundice fever. Exposure to dust, smoke, gusts of wind and snowmelted water and violent attack on vulnerable joints may also cause dyspnea.

3-4. Śvāsa roga is of five types (1) Kṣudraka (minor) (2) Tamaka (3) Chinna (4) Mahān and (5) Ūrdhva. Vāyu that spreads all round when prevented by Kapha turns round and courses through the passages of vital airs, water ducts and food canals spoiling them. It comes to the cardiac region and produces the illness of breath in the abdomen.

5-8. Its premonitory symptoms are pain in the chest and sides, the adverse direction of the breath, constipation, splitting of the temples and exhaustion due to overeating. The aggravated wind turns back through the ducts aggravating the kapha and produces the difficult breathing called Kṣudra. It grips the head, neck and cardiac region and produces pain at the sides. It generates hiccough with a wheezing round attended with catarrhal paroxysm. It makes the breath speedily,taken distress the vital breath but the patient gets slight relief after spitting it out.

9. Lying down he feels difficulty in breathing but in sitting he feels relief. If he looks up he finds the forehead perspire and he suffers acute pain.

10. Gasping frequently and finding the lips parched the patient longs for hot drink with slight shivering. This (Tamaka) Śvāsa becomes aggravated when it rains or when chill east wind flows or Kapha-producing food is taken.

11. Tamaka type of dyspnea is curable only in a strong person. If there is acute fever and fainting it will never subside by cold application.

12. The patient of Mahā Śvāsa breathes hard and feels pain due to the splitting of the vulnerable joints. He perspires and swoons. He has constipation. Burning sensation is felt in the abdomen.

13. He keeps the eyes facing down. The eyes seem to rove. One of the eyes appears tinged with glossy red glitter. The mouth is dry. He prattles dejectedly. He is unconscious and there is pallor in the face.

14. He breathes hard with great noise if lifted up bodily, like an ox in rut.

15. He has no sensation or awareness. The eyes and face wear a confused look. Urine and faeces do not pass out. He is speechless.

16. The patient of Ūrdhvaśvāsa is unable to breathe out though he takes in long drawn breaths. He has acute pain at the temples and the head. His throat is parched.

17. The mouth and ears appear to be stuffed with mucous Kapha matter. Distressed by the aggravated Vāyu he looks up rolling it all round as if in confusion.

18. When the vulnerable joints are being split he groans with his speech checked (unable to speak). All these ailments can be cured if the symptoms are not very manifest or pronounced. If they are pronounced they are fatal indeed.

CHAPTER ONE HUNDRED AND FIFTYONE

Diseases

Dhanvantari said :

1. O Suśruta, listen, I shall describe the causes of the illness Hiccough. Its preliminary stage is due to dyspnea. The different types of hiccough have their own nature as the differentiating factor.

2-3. Hiccough is of five types (1) Bhakṣyodbhavā (originating from diet) (2) Kṣudrā (Insignificant) (3) Yamalā (The twin-natured) (4) Mahatī (great, acute) (5) Gambhīrā (grave). The first type is caused by hasty eating of coarse pungent unwholesome food stuffs injudiciously. The usual onset is along with the evening meal and beverage when the Vāyu is aggravated with the food and the drink. A low sound is produced.

4. By exertion the Vāyu principle gets excited and produces the Kṣudrā hiccough.

5. It originates from the root of the clavicle. Its paroxysm is not virulent.

6. The Kṣudrā hiccough is aggravated by exertion and becomes mild on taking food. The next type of hiccough (yamalā) rises in couples and is slow in its action.

7. It culminates in the face shaking the head and neck violently. It is called Yamalā (Twin-natured) hiccough.

8. Delirium, vomiting, dysentery, distortion of the eyes and yawning are the symptoms which are very pronounced at the advanced stage.

9-10. The symptoms in the acute type of hiccough (Mahatī) are—the eyebrows droop down and the temples sunk, the eyes turn towards the ears, the body is benumbed, speech is impaired, power of memory fails and unconsciousness results. The vulnerable joints are split, the spinal column is bent down.

11-12. The Gambhīrā (grave) type of hiccough rises from the abdomen or navel just like the previous one, but is attended with great pain, loud sound, severe violence and high potency. It induces a wide yawning and jerky movements of the limbs. This is curable if carefully treated.

13-15. The first two types shall be avoided as also the hiccough where all the symptoms are pronounced. As a general rule, in the cases of old men, persons of impaired digestion and accumulated undigested matter within, persons indulging too much in sexual exercise, invalids and starving emaciated persons, all ailments are fatal unless attended to quickly. Hiccough and dyspnea are definitely fatal.

CHAPTER ONE HUNDRED AND FIFTYTWO

Diseases

Dhanvantari said :—

1. Now I shall explain the pathology of Yakṣmaroga (pulmonary consumption). It is a sequel to many ailments and precursor to many others.

2. It is mentioned by many terms Rājayakṣmā (King-Consumption), Kṣaya (Consumption), Śoṣa (withering up), Rogarāṭ (king of ailments). Stars, Moon, brahmins and kings were supposed to have suffered from this formerly. Hence it is called Rājayakṣmā.

3. It is called Kṣaya (wasting disease) because the body is wasted, medicine is wasted (ineffective), and it is the culmination of Kṣaya (consumption). It is called Śoṣa because it dries up the lymph and other secretions of the system. It is called Rogarāṭ because it is the king of all ailments.

4. There are four main causes for this: (1) Sāhasa, Rash feats of strength and overexercise, (2) Vegasaṁrodha, suppression of natural propulsions of the body such as passing of urine, evacuating the bowels, etc., (3) Śukrajaḥ snehasaṁkṣayaḥ, wasting of semen, vitality and albuminous substances in the body, (4) Annapānavidhityāga (abandonment of the rules of diet and regimen.

5-6. The principle of Vāyu gets aggravated by the causes mentioned before, scatters pitta and useless accumulations in the body, kapha, etc. and permeates the ducts, channels and joints of the body. Then it affects the nerves either by closing the openings of the ducts or dilating them too much. It then produces great pain in the cardiac region in the middle, above, below or at the sides.

7. Many indications of its onset can be observed. Cold, high rise in temperature, salivation, sweet taste in the mouth, glossiness of the body and loss of appetite.

8. An eager desire to walk and take food and drink. The patient finds impurity even in clean things. He supposes that a fly, a blade of grass, a bit of hair, etc. has fallen in his dish or cup.

9. Hiccough and disquietude, vomiting, non-relish of food, weakening even without bath.

10. A bright white colour in the hands, thighs, chest, feet, face, stomach and the eyes. A shooting pain in the arms and the tongue, a feeling of abhorrence over the body.

11. A liking for women, wine and meat and an unreasonable disgust immediately and giddiness.

12. The nails, hair and bones grow rapidly. The patient dreams of the attack or fall of chameleon, serpent, monkey and birds and beasts of prey.

13. He sees in dreams that he climbs or steps on hair, bones, husks, ashes, etc. He sees deserted villages, ponds and tanks drying up brilliant comets and stars in the sky or forest fire with burning trees.

14-15. There are eleven specific symptoms in the pulmonary consumption :—Catarrh, dyspnea, cough, loss of voice, headache, nonrelish for food, updrawn breath, emaciation, vomiting, fever and pain (in the viscera, while standing, at the sides, while getting up from bed, and at the joints.

16. The distressing features are a breaking pain at the throat, yawning, severe pressure felt in the limbs, spitting out (bloody mucous substances), impaired gastric functions and foul smell in the mouth.

17-18. Due to the aggravation of Vāyu there is pain in the head and sides with a severe pressure of limbs. Constriction of the throat and aphonia are also due to the Vāyu. The aggravated pitta causes a burning sensation int he shoulders, hands, and feet, dysentery, vomiting of blood, foul smell in the mouth, fever and inebriety. The excited kapha produces non-relish of food, vomiting, cough and a sense of heaviness in one half of the body.

19-20. Watery discharge from the lips, cold, dyspnea, aphonia and impaired gastric function are also due to kapha. As a result of impaired digestion, the humours are further excited and anasarca(śotha)and a clammy coating of kapha shuts up the openings of the ducts. Further production of the dhātus ceases and the burning sensation increases bringing mental anguish. There are other distressing features also.

21. The food taken in by phthisis patient undergoes acidity in the stomach along with the lymph and other secretions), hence the diet does not nourish his limbs.

22. The lymph does not generate blood in him, although some flesh is put. In this benumbed state he remains emaciated.

23. Even if all the symptoms are not present, an emaciated person with his six sense organs impaired must be given up as incurable; but if the person is otherwise (i.e not emaciated) he can be cured.

24. Due to the several and combined actions of the deranged humours the fat becomes wasted and aphonia sets in. The voice becomes feeble, coarse and tremulous.

25. The deranged Vāyu makes the body lose its glossiness and warmth as well as produces a colour like that of an awn of barley in the throat. Due to Pitta there is burning sensation in the throat and palate.

26. Due to Kapha there is a peculiar wheezing sound in the throat and it seems as if there is some sticky mucuous substance there. The consumption starts with all the symptoms.

27. Vertigo and darkness of vision and other characteristics of kapha also are present. The patients are incurable and even if only a few symptoms are present the emaciated patient shall be avoided.

CHAPTER ONE HUNDRED AND FIFTYTHREE

Diseases

Dhanvantari said :

1. Suśruta, I shall now describe the pathology of Arocaka (Non-relish for food). Three types of Arocaka are caused by the three humours severally situated in the tongue and the heart.

2. Fourth type of Arocaka is caused by all the three in combination. Fifth type of Arocaka is caused by the dejection of the mind. If wind is the cause, the mouth has an astringent taste. If Pitta is the cause, it has a bitter taste. If Kapha is the cause, a sweet taste is experienced.

3. Just as everything is tasteless at the time of sorrow and anger so also in all the five types of Arocaka, food is tasteless due to the vomiting sensation on account of the deranged humour.

4. The Udāna vāyu flings up the deranged humours resting beneath the mouth and they give rise to a saline taste with watery oozings in the mouth. Hence non relish for food.

5. It pains the umbilical region and the back; the food taken is cast to the sides. The patient vomits, bit by bit, small lumps of frothy astringent matter.

6. Due to the action of vāyu there is an eructation with loud sound that dries up the mouth. Hiccough with hoarseness of voice is also observed.

7. If the attack is by the deranged pitta the patient vomits something like saline water mixed with blood. It is sometimes greenish yellow in colour, bitter and pungent in taste. Thirst, fainting and a burning sensation in the body are the further characteristics.

8. If kapha is the cause, a thick glossy yellowish honey-like mucous of excessively saline taste is vomited with watery discharge and horripilation.

9. Patients having swelling in the mouth, with sweet taste, pain and disquietude in the sinews and hiccough are to be considered having all symptoms and are to be given up as incurable.

10. To him seeing anything or hearing any sound is hateful. If the sickness is due to the food being contaminated by germs, the symptoms are colic (śūla), shivering and disquietude aggravated by vāyu, etc.

CHAPTER ONE HUNDRED AND FIFTYFOUR

Diseases

Dhanvantari said :

1. O Suśruta, now I shall explain the cause and pathology of Hṛdroga, (Ailment of the heart) etc. They are of five types, one due to germs and the other four due to the three humours severally or in combination.

2. If the cause is Vāyu, a feeling of emptiness is observed. The patient eats much and cries. The heart is benumbed, seems to break asunder and dries up; dizziness is experienced.

3. Suddenly, the patient is dejected, feels grief and is frightened. He cannot bear to hear the least sound. He shivers and faints as a result. There is difficulty in breathing and sleeplessness.

4. As a result of the attack of Pitta the symptoms are thirst, exhaustion, burning sensation, perspiration, eructation with acidity, vomiting of acid or bilious matter, fever and cloudy vision.

5. If deranged kapha causes Hṛdroga the heart becomes numbed, the digestion is impaired, the face is distorted; hiccough, pain in the bone, spitting of mucous matter, drowsiness, lassitude, fever non relish of food are observed.

6. If the ailment of the heart is caused by the combined action of all the three doṣas all the different symptoms are observed. If the ailment is due to germs the symptoms are :— blackish yellow colour in the eyes, dizziness and dark vision, cardiac oedema, disquietude, itching sensation in the limbs and expectoration of kapha.

7. The patient thinks that his heart is being sawn with scissors. This ailment shall be treated in the early stages, otherwise it is fatal.

8. Thirst may be caused by Vāta, Pitta or Kapha. Debility is caused by their combination. A sixth variety of Hṛdroga is caused by contact with the persons who are sick. The exciting factors may be Vāta and Pitta.

9. In all these ailments it is their aggravation that brings about spasmodic jerks in all the limbs, palpitation, agitation, and burning sensation in the heart and fainting through the withering up of all the dhātus.

10. Thirst arises as a result of the drying up of the root of the tongue, throat, lungs, palate and the water-carrying vessels. This is a common characteristic symptom of all kinds of Hṛdroga.

11-12. Parchedness of the mouth, insatiable thirst for water, hatred for food, weakness in voice, difficulty in putting out the tongue due to the roughness of throat, palate and the lips, prattling in delirium, mental aberration and eructation are also the symptoms in Hṛdroga.

13-16. The derangement of Vāyu causes emaciation, dejection of spirit, dizziness of the head, breaking pain at the temples, impaired sense of smell, loss of juiciness in the mouth, dullness of hearing, insomnia and general debility. The derangement of the Pitta brings about slight increase in the acidity, fainting, bitterness in the mouth, redness in the eyes, perpetual drying up of the body and burning sensation and a feeling as of fumes escape through the skin. The aggravated Kapha obstructs the Vāyu in the water-carrying vessels. The ducts with the accumulated Kapha absorb the heat as in the case of mud. The throat appears to be pierced with the awn of barley. Sleepiness with a sweet taste in the mouth is experienced. A continuous sluggishness felt in the head, lassitude, vomiting, nonrelish for food and indigestion—these symptoms are in brief brought about by all humours in combination.

17. Blood is obstructed due to the accumulation of mucous and undigested matter thus causing the aggravation of

both Vāyu and Pitta. So the patient while experiencing intense heat experiences an unbearable chillness.

18. If thirst obstructs the humour in the viscera the ailment is definitely caused by Pitta. The aching pain caused by drinking too much water is due to the digestion and dilution of albuminous content.

19. The thirst generated by taking in greasy, pungent, acid and saline stuffs is due to Kapha. The thirst due to the loss of lymph and other secretions is an indication of onset of consumption;

20. The thirst generated by the admixture of atrophy, fainting and fever with other chronic ailments is called Upasargātmikā (foreboding evil)

CHAPTER ONE HUNDRED AND FIFTYFIVE

Diseases

Dhanvantari said :

1. I shall explain the pathology of Madātyaya (distemper due to inebriation) as mentioned by sages. Wine is sharp, acid, dry, parchifying and light and induces quickness in sexual intercourse.

2. It pervades even the minutest capillaries of the system but its effect on the fat is just opposite. The qualities of sharpness etc. mentioned by the sages have disturbing effect on the mind.

3. Excessively drunk, wines and spirits are fatal. With their qualities of sharpness, etc. they destroy the vitality of the addict and bring about sluggishness.

4. Exciting the sense organs wine upsets the mind. On taking it for the first time or second time it may have an exciting and exhilarating effect on the drinker.

5-6. The fool carried away by indecision and uncertainty considers it pleasing. A king who becomes an addict to wine becomes unbridled like an unchecked serpent. There is nothing that he will not do in his inebriation : Wine is the source of unspeakable mischiefs and supports wickedness.

7-9. It is the sole guide of wretchedness that has a hundred paths leading to it. Bereft of all energetic actions the addict in the third stage of inebriety may yearn for wine always. The sinful wretch has now come to a stage worse than death. He cannot distinguish between righteousness and evil, pleasure and pain, honour and dishonour, and wholesome and unwholesome. Withered up and deluded, highly pleased at times and dejected at other he loses his power of memory and falls unconscious. Well built strong persons of gluttonous habits may not become too intoxicated after drinking wine over a heavy meal.

10. The ailment of inebriety may be caused by the three humours—Vāyu, Pitta and Kapha severally or in combination. Unconsciousness and pain in the heart characterize all varieties.

11-13. Thirst engendered by frequent loose motions, mild dejection, fever and nonrelish for food, constipation, darkness of vision, hiccough, difficulty in breathing sleeplessness, excessive perspiration, obstruction of ordure (Viṣṭhambha), intumescence, and mental agitation too characterize all types of inebriety. The patient is in a dreamy state and does not speak when addressed. Due to the attack of Pitta there is a burning sensation, fever and perspiration, fainting and a continuous palpitation of the heart. Due to the action of Kapha there is vomiting, disquietude, sleepiness and Udaragaurava (Tympanites—heaviness in the stomach due to gas trouble).

14-15. In the ailment of inebriation due to the action of all humours in combination all the symptoms can be observed. Those who knowingly take to wine become victims thereof and lose the power of thinking and mental disorders set in. Everything is pleasing to them whether a chip of wood or an article of food. They do not differentiate between them. Due to the action of Vāyu many of these symptoms occur. The patient spits out mucous matters of phlegm and experiences parchedness of throat and somnolence.

16. He does not brook sounds. His sound is distracted. He feels Rheumatic pain all over the body. His heart and throat

are effected. He falls into fainting fits. He gasps for breath. Excessive thirst, nausea and fever also oppress him.

17. A person who controls himself and intelligently refrains from drinking wine, is never afflicted by any disorder whether physical or mental.

18-19. Deluded persons of irascible temperament indulging in injudicious diet suffer from the three disorders of inebriation, epileptic fits and abject prostration more and more powerful in the order of enumeration. This is due to the obstruction of ducts carrying fat, blood and other lymphatic secretions. Inebriation is caused by the derangement of all the humours, impure blood, and presence of wine and toxic matter in the system.

20. In the ailment of inebriation due to the derangement of Vāyu, the patient becomes anaemic and all brightness of complexion vanishes. The body assumes a coarse dark reddish hue. The patient becomes deceitful in behaviour and fickle-minded.

21. The intoxicated person becomes irritable and quarrelsome due to the affliction of Pitta and his body assumes a reddish yellow hue. The affliction of Kapha is responsible for the symptoms of somnolence, loose irrelevant talks or when the patient appears to be in a trance .

22-26. The combined action of all the doṣas brings about all the above symptoms as well as obstruction of the circulation of blood and paralysis of the limbs. If the patient exhibits a loathsome desire or fails to recognize familiar voices it is an indication of derangement of Pitta. He may be exhausted utterly and go to deep sleep but the body may be shaking vigorously : The signs of an affliction of Vāyu must be carefully noted. The inebriated patient may either see the sky red, blue and black or without seeing anything sink in darkness. He may regain consciousness immediately but may experience pain in the cardiac region, a shivering sensation and vertigo. In epileptic fits brought about by derangement of Vāyu the patient has hiccough and brownish red colour of the skin. Afflicted by Pitta the patient, seeing the sky red and yellow, may sink into swoon. When he wakes up he perspires profusely and is oppressed with excessive thirst and a burning sensation. During the fit a portion of the body may be yellow and the other blue. His eyes may be red, yellow or crimson.

27-28. In Kapha affliction the epileptic patient sees the sky enveloped with clouds as it were, sinks into a deep coma and regains consciousness very late. He complains of disquietness in the cardiac region. There is salivation. Heavy and benumbed in limbs he falls in a thud like a goat in the unconscious state. In the combined action of all the doṣas it appears like an Apasmāra (epilepsy).

29-30. He falls down motionlessly and does not have any frightful convulsive movements of limbs. In the ailment of mada, mūrcchā, the morbid humours spread themselves out and become calm without medication when the patient sinks into prostration. Speech, body and the mind do not function properly but he does not lose strength.

31. Patients who fall down in prostration, fall like logs of wood, no better than dead but with risk of death.

32. If the treatment is not immediately carried out he may die like a person in a deep sea full of crocodiles.

33. A person in prostration (like the person in the sea) should be immediately taken out of it. A person suffering from inebriation may be irritated or pleased, it is certain.

34-35. Used judiciously wine relieves persons of worries, otherwise leads him to hell. It gives ability to work, helps the natural functions, and blesses with beauty. Judicious use of wine is like that of nectar.

CHAPTER ONE HUNDRED AND FIFTYSIX

Diseases

Dhanvantari said:

1-3. O Suśruta, I shall explain the pathology of Arśas (Piles) ailments. Among the condylomatous (pinlike) growths in the flesh those that obstruct the anus are called Arśas. The deranged humour defiling the skin, flesh and the fat makes many shoots of flesh of diverse shapes in the region of the rectum. They are called Arśas (Piles). In brief, they are of two types sahaja (congenital) and Anantarottha (postnatal).

4. The passage of the rectum is five and a half Aṅgulas long. There, dry stone-like lumps three and a half aṅgulas long grow.

5-6. Blood vessels passing through the entrails come to these lumps and split open. Hence, within an aṅgula from without, bleeding occurs in the region of these condylomatous growths. Hair about one and a half aṅgulas in length grow beyond them. In the congenital type of piles the cause is the discomfort of the child in the womb.

7. The creation of the seeds of piles is due to the misdeeds of the parents. Curse of gods also may be the cause. In the piles due to the combined action of the doṣas it is the food taken in that creates the seeds.

8. All ailments congenital in nature are incurable. The piles of congenital type are rough, ugly looking, pointing inward and pale, yellow in colour. The disorders brought about by them are dreadful.

9. Piles are of six types when caused by doṣas after the birth. The three different doṣas severally or their combinations in twos make up the six varieties. The dry piles are due to Vāyu and Kapha and the wet ones due to Pitta.

10. When more and more faces accumulate in the gastric fire that reduces the food taken before into faeces, if the person indulges in excessive sexual intercourse the doṣas become aggravated.

11-14. The Apāna Vāyu (genito-urinary illiac nerve force) becomes aggravated due to various such causes as:—drinking in a fitful state, taking in hard indigestible foodstuffs, frequent rubbing of the belly, eyes and throat with the palms, contact with very chill water, continuous riding for a long time, suppression of natural urges and evacuating them with difficulty, dysentery, constipation, pulling things and in woman miscarriage and painful labour.

15-16. When the Apāna becomes excited the faeces get obstructed in the flexus of the rectum and condylomatous growths occur on their knotty joints. Its indications are low gastric function, obstruction to the removal of ordure, pain in the bones and calves of the legs, vertigo, burning sensation in the eyes, intumascence and either loose motions or constipation.

17. Obstructed from the front, the wind moves about below the umbilicus and when the patient breathes with difficulty it comes out with blood.

18. A rumbling sound in the entrails, eructation, profuse belching of saline stuff, excessive urination, scanty faeces, non-inclination to take food, vertigo, sour taste in the mouth.

19. Pain in the head, back and chest, lassitude, yearning for sensuous pleasures, anger due to frustration or neglect of service by others are also observed.

20. Sometimes the symptoms give rise to the suspicion of other ailments such as diarrhoea, wasting disease, jaundice, enlargement of the spleen and dropsy. All these diseases increase when piles begin to grow.

21. When the Apāna returns, it is obstructed by these growths and so it aggravates other vital airs moving among the sense organs and parts of the whole body.

22. Then it produces a parched condition in the seats of Pitta, Kapha, urine and faeces and obstructs the gastric fire. Then usually all the piles grow.

23. The patient becomes lean, his enthusiasm and jolly spirit vanishes; he becomes dejected, emaciated, pallid in face, and appears like a worm eaten tree, sapless and devoid of shade.

24-25. All the disorders mentioned in Yakṣmā (Pulmonary consumption) distress him. They give rise to acute pain in the vulnerable joints, Cough, excessive thirst, dryness in the mouth, dyspnea, catarrh, lassitude, aching pain in the limbs, nausea, sneezing, intumescence, fever, debility, deafness, rigidity and the disease gravel—all these torment him.

26. Completely emaciated, with voice broken, he sinks into a trance and frequently spits. He does not show any inclination to take food. He has pain in all joints, bones, chest, navel, anus and the thigh joints. A kind of bilious matter begins to ooze out of the anus. It resembles water with which meat has been washed.

27. Some of these piles are dry but others are found to suppurate and burst; they are caused by Pitta and are of the colour of turmeric.

28. These piles generated by aggravated Vāyu are dry and rough. They are faded, reddish or brownish in colour and uneven.

29. They are of unequal sizes and shapes, curved, sharp-pointed with their external ends cracked and severed. They resemble the fruits of Bimba Kharjūra[1], Karkandhu[2] and Karpāsa[3] seed.

30. Some of them resemble Kadamba flowers, and some those of the white mustard. Acute pain in the head, sides, shoulders, calves, thighs, thigh joints, etc. is felt.

31. Sneezing, eructation, obstruction to the removal of ordure, catching pain in the heart and non relish for food, cough, dryspnea, impaired function of the digestive system, ringing noise in the ears and vertigo are further symptoms.

32. A patient distressed with these disorders passes stools with great difficulty. It is scanty. A loud sound is produced while evacuating the slimy frothy stuff.

33. The skin, nail, faeces, urine, eyes and face are black in colour. Chronic enlargement of the spleen, drooping and globular tumours (Aṣṭhīlā) occur.

34. The condylomatous growths of piles due to the derangement of Pitta are bluish in colour at the opening and red, yellow and black otherwise. They exude bloody, watery stuff through their small tips. They smell like raw meat. They are soft to the touch and hang loosely.

35. Some of them resemble the tongue of a parrot, split liver or the mouth of a leech. Burning sensation, fever and perspiration, thirst, epileptic fits, non-relish for food and loss of sense are the symptoms at the time of suppuration.

36. The faeces are hot, liquid in form, bluish, reddish and yellow in colour and undigested. The piles are thick in the middle like barley grain. The skin, nail etc are green or yellow in colour.

1. Phoenix dactylifer or p. acaulis (Refer *GVDB* p. 131).
2. Zizyphus nummularia.
3. Glossypium barbadens.

37. If Kapha be the cause the piles are deep rooted, thick, less painful, white in colour, of decaying appearance, glossy, globular in shape and unyielding.

38. Lubricious, rigid, smooth and mild they produce an itching sensation and the patient finds it pleasant to handle them and scratch them. Some of them are like the bamboo shoots or the seed of the jack fruit or the teat of a cow.

39. There is catching pain at the thigh joints, rectum, bladder and navel. Dyspnea, cough, disquietude in the cardiac region, salivatiou non-relish of food and catarrh are the symptoms.

40. Strangury (difficulty in passing urine), sluggishness of head, shivering chilliness are experienced. Impotency, impaired gastric function, vomiting and all the disorders in undigested state are also found in the patient.

41. The faeces come out in profusion. They have the colour of suet. They contain mucous kapha matter. The piles do not crack nor do they bleed. Skin, etc., have grey colour and are glossy.

42. In the piles caused by the combined action of all doṣas all the symptoms can be observed. If they are caused by the impurity of blood such symptoms as are in the Pittaja type can be observed.

43. They resemble the shoots of Vaṭa or Guñjā berries or coral. The faeces are hard and hot and contaminated.

44. If the motions are many the blood gushes out suddenly. The skin of the patient is like that of a frog. He suffers all disorders due to the deficiency of blood.

45-47. The patient loses the colour of his complexion, strength and mental gaiety. His vitality is impaired. His sense organs do not function properly. By taking hard foodstuffs dehydrating the faeces, like Mudga[1], Kodrava[2], Jambīra[3], bamboo shoots, Bengal gram, etc., the wind becomes aggravated in the region of the rectum and obstructs the ducts flowing down and dries up the waste matter.

1. Phaseolus radiatus
2. Paspalum screbiculatum.
3. An Allium species (Refer *GVDB*. p. 164).

48. It absorbs the moisture of faeces and urine and makes them thick with disastrous consequences. As a result of it acute pain in the viscera, back, cardiac region and the sides results.

49. Tympanites, Ascites, accumulation of faeces, colic, pain in the bladder and intumescence in the cheeks are likely to follow.

50. The deranged Vāyu taking an upward course causes vomiting, non-relish for food and fever. Palpitation of the heart, diarrhoea, suppression of urine and dysentery are also caused.

51. Deafness, dyspnea, acute headache, consumption, catarrh, faecal disorder, thirst, enlargement of the spleen dropsy, etc., follow.

52. All these caused by the derangement of Vāyu are terrific. Piles bring about even death.

53. Piles grow in the rectum of those persons whose viscera are attacked by Vāyu even without the exciting factors. The congenital piles as well as those that grow in the inner grove of the rectum are incurable. If the digestive power is maintained palliation is the only alternative.

54. Growths of condylomatous nature caused by any two of the doṣas in combination and those in the second flexus are incurable if left untreated for a year.

55. Those piles that grow in the external groove as well as those caused by a single doṣa can be easily cured if they are of recent origin.

56. Condylomatous growths are said to grow on the penis, etc., as well as in the navel too. They are like the Gaṇḍūpada (the pillow footed worm or Earthworm) and are lubricious and soft.

57. The wind Vyāna in combination with Kapha brings about growth of piles on the outer skin like nails rough to the touch and firm. They are called Carmakīla.

58. The roughness and piercing nature of the piles is due to Vāyu; the blackness at the top is due to Pitta; and their glossiness, knotty nature and colouration are due to Kapha.

59. An intelligent man must exert himself in quelling the piles quickly. Otherwise they may lead to graver disorders and asitis.

CHAPTER ONE HUNDRED AND FIFTYSEVEN

Diseases

Dhanvantari said:

1. O Suśruta, I shall explain the pathology of dysentery and diarrhoea. They are of six types, the doṣas severally and in combination produce four varieties and fear and sorrow produce two types.

2-3. Dysentery is usually caused by drinking too much of water. The Vāyu becomes aggravated due to the injudicious intake of dry foods, fatty stuffs, fried things, gingelly seed cakes, shoots and germinated sprouts and inordinate quantities of wine, day-sleep, worms and suppression of natural urges for excretion.

4. The aggravated Vāyu causes the downward rush of the blood extinguishing the gastric fire. Then it permeates the inner chamber of food and faeces and liquefies the waste matter.

5. The indication of its imminent onset is an acute pain in the chest, rectum and viscera, perspiration all over the body and constipation.

6. Distention of the abdomen, indigestion and absence of fever are due to Vāyu. The patient passes scanty faeces without any sound but with constant interruptions.

7. The waste matter is hard, turbid, frothy and knotty. A burning sensation in the fleshy region of the rectum is felt. The lubricious surface is cut up. There is a prolapse in the constricted anus. The patient gasps for breath and has horripilation all over the body.

8-10. In the pittaja type diarrhoea the waste matter is yellow, black, turmeric coloured and grass coloured with blood mixed with it. It has a fetid smell. The patient has a burning sensation, excessive thirst and epileptic fits. If the cause is kapha there is an acute pain in the anus with burning sensation. The waste matter is thick, slimy and scanty in a continuous flow. If the three doṣas in combination cause diarrhoea, all the symptoms and particularly horripilation, severe pain, and heaviness in bladder, belly and anus are observed. The patient loses sense and thinks what he has done as not done.

11. If extreme fright agitates the mind the patient passes stool even as he lies down. The Vāyu liquefies it and it passes out in warm jets.

12. If extreme agony causes diarrhoea the symptoms are as in Vātaja and Pittaja types. In brief, diarrhoea can be divided into two (1) Sāma or with mucous and (2) Nirāma or without mucous.

13. In the Sāma type the waste matter emits fetid smell. There is swelling, obstruction to the passage of ordure, and salivation. The opposite characteristics are observed in Nirāma type. Due to Kapha none sinks.

14. Atisāra (diarrhoea) not given careful attention may lead to Grahaṇī (acute dysentery) by taking in articles of food bringing about the quenching of gestric fire.

15. Atisāra is so called because there is plenty (Ati) of evacuation (Sāra) of digested Sāma or Nirāma waste matter. Hence, it is very active and virulent naturally. If Sāma is undigested it becomes shattered; if digested it does not become Pakva (fully ripe and digested).

16. A chronic Atisāra with the accumulations leads to Grahaṇī disorder which is of four types, the three doṣas severally and collectively being the cause.

17-21. The general symptoms of the onset of Grahaṇī are :—exhaustion of the limbs, purification of the body with delay (delayed evacuation), a little salivation, draught in the mouth, non relish for food, thirst, vertigo, binding pain in the abdomen, vomiting and ringing in the ears. Some of these symptoms are also seen :—Weakness and emaciation of the body, acute Tamaka fever, epileptic fits, numbness in the head and thighs, intumescence in hands and feet, drowsiness, parchedness of the palate due to the action of the wind, darkness of vision, noisy echo in the ears, pain in the sides, thighs, thigh joints, neck, etc. and acute cholera.

22. In weak patients the symptoms are very pronounced, hunger and thirst greatly oppressing them. There is inflation of belly during the process of digestion or on the completion of the same. After taking meal the patient gets some relief.

23. In the Vātaja type of Grahaṇī the following indications can be seen. Palpitation of the heart, enlargement of the spleen, piles, jaundice, loss of sense, passing of either loose or hard lumpy dry waste matter with froth and loud report, gasping for breath and hiccough. The motion is frequent.

24. In the Pittaja type of Grahaṇī the waste matter is either yellow or bluish yellow and liquid in nature. Acid eruptions, burning sensation in the heart and throat, nonrelish for food and excessive thirst are also seen.

25-27. Difficulty in digestion, painful motion, vomiting, non-relish for food, burning sensation in the mouth, frequent spitting, cough, disquietude and catarrh, sensation of bulkiness in the heart, distension and heaviness of abdomen, eructation with defiled sweetness, lassitude, horripilation, etc. are the specific features of the Kaphaja type. The waste matter is thick split up and charged with mucous matter. Even if the patient is not lean he feels weak. In the Sannipātaja Grahaṇī all the symptoms are observed.

28-29. The first three types are very disorderly. All the symptoms mentioned before are observed in Grahaṇī too. Eight ailments are called Mahārogas (great illnesses). They are incurable. They are :—Rheumating gravel in urine (or stone in bladder), leprosy, epilepsy, dropsy, gonorrhoea, piles and Grahaṇī.

CHAPTER ONE HUNDRED AND FIFTYEIGHT

Diseases

Dhanvantari said :

1-3. Now I shall explain the pathology of Mūtrāghāta (suppression of urine or strangury), Suśruta, please listen. The urinary bladder, its top or outlet, the penis, the hip, the scrotum and the rectum, all these are covered by a single peritoneum and are situated in the pelvic cavity. Though the bladder is placed with its face down it is continuously filled with urinary secretions through the ducts carrying them and always exuding them. Doṣas entering these secretions produce twenty diseases.

4-5. Strangury and diabetes affect the vulnerable joints of the pelvis containing the bladder, thigh joints and the penis. In the Vātaja type the urine is scanty and emitted constantly with the greatest pain. In the Pittaja type it is yellow giving rise to pain and burning sensation. In the Kaphaja type it is red. The patient feels heaviness in the bladder and penis. Intumescence is also found there.

6-7. The urinary discharge is lubricious or tawny in colour in a combined action of all doṣas. When the deranged Vāyu turns the face of the bladder and dries it up the urine is charged with Pitta, Kapha or semen and a terrible gravel is formed like a lump of Gorocanā which is a limb of the pitta matter.

8. In all cases the deranged Kapha is an exciting factor in Aśmarī. Its premonitory symptoms are :—Inflammation of the urinary bladder and excruciating pain all round it in that region.

9. The urine gets obstructed in the bladder. There is difficulty in passing urine. There is fever and nonrelish for food. The general indications are pain in the umbilical region, foreskin of the prepuce and the top of the urinary bladder, etc.

10. When there is obstruction in the passage by the gravel the micturition is delayed and painful. If the patient

passes urine after a long retention the urine is clear and crystal coloured and he feels great pain.

11. If it is excited it comes out with blood and fleshy matter. There is pain in the passage. In the Vāyuja concretion of urine the patient grinds his teeth and shakes violently.

12. The patient feels that something stops the urine and afflicts the navel, he evacuates the bowel with a gaseous discharge and urinates in drops frequently.

13. The Aśmarī is tough and dark in colour. It appears to be studded with thorns. Pitta brings about a burning sensation in the bladder. It appears hot as if being cooked.

14. The concretions appear like the stones of Bhallātaka fruit red, yellow and white in colour. Due to the affliction of Kapha the bladder appears to be inflicted upon and is heavy and cool to the touch.

15. In infants the Aśmarī is large, glossy and honey-coloured or white. Many children are affected by it.

16-17. Since they have not grown large or fully developed they can be extracted easily. The Śukrāśmarī or concretion in semen is generated by suppression of emission and it is dreadful. The aggravated vāyu collects and dries up the semen unreleased or dislodged from it soriginal seat within the scrotum. It is then called Śukrāśmarī.

18. It produces a painful swelling in the bladder and micturition is very painful. The semen secreted becomes dry if there are Śukrāśmarī formations.

19. An attack of fever or chronic cough makes the urinary concretions into Śarkarā (gravel). The internal Vāyu splits and crushes these concretions and sends them out along with the urine. If the Vāyu takes an averse course they lie within the bladder and mature.

20. The aggravated Vāyu may make the top of the bladder let out urine. Sometimes it may obstruct the flow of urine and from its seat it may generate pain.

21. It may cover up the bladder or lifting it, it may scatter it about, then a great pain is felt with throbbings and irritation.

22. When the bladder is thus afflicted the urine may

come out in drops. The continuous flow is obstructed; this disease is called Vātavasti.

23. It is difficult to be cured. The second one is still more difficult to be cured. The powerful Vāyu comes in between the path of faeces and the bladder.

24. It generates a kind of thick knotty round raised concretions called Vātāṣṭhilā (Globular seed like concretions caused by Vāyu.) They are found both in the faeces and in the urine.

25-26. A sickness called Vātakuṇḍalikā is produced when semen is retained for a long time without emission. The deranged Vāyu lies within the bladder in a coil and gives great pain. It whirls after obstructing the urine. There is rigidity, heaviness and convolution in the bladder. Urine is passed out bit by bit.

27-28. The urine being obstructed does not pass out completely. After the passage of urine there is a slight pain. When the Vāyu is obstructed by the collection of urine it returns to the umbilical region or lower abdomen and produces pain. There is no distension but due to loss of strength faeces are collected and obstructed.

29-30. Urine may enter the abdominal passage by the pressure of wind and stay in the bladder or umbilical region and flow out gradually. It may or may not be painful. It is without cessation. Its residue is dried up.

31. Inside the bladder near its entrance there is a knotty small firm concretion like gravel. It is called Mūtragranthi.

32. Sometimes a man in his sexual intercourse may not discharge semen immediately although it might have been dislodged from its seat. This is due to the action of Vāyu. But when he begins to urinate the semen may come out either before or after urination.

33. The urine then appears like water washing down ashes. The stuff is called Mūtraśukram (Spermatorrhoea) Sometimes weak persons or those of harsh nature are afflicted by Vāyu when passing stools.

34. The faecal matter may get into the urinary tract and hence the urine drop may have the smell of faeces. This is called Mūtravighāta.

35-36. The Vâyu aggravated by Pitta, physical exercises, excessive intake of sharp acid food stuffs and inflammation may generate a burning sensation in the urinary bladder and urine mixed with blood or blood alone comes out in hot jets. It is called Uṣṇavāta.

37. Pitta and Vāyu in the urinary bladder of a constitutionally parched up person or thoroughly weary man may cause deficiency of urine accompanied by pain and burning sensation. The ailment is called Mūtrakṣaya.

38-40. If either kapha or pitta or both are affected by Vāyu the passage of urine is very painful. It is a thick fluid yellow, red or white in colour. There is a burning sensation. It may have the colour of bile or powdered conch shell. It may be dry in some cases. It may have all the colours too. The ailment is called Mūtrasāda. Thus all ailments in the context of urination have been explained in detail.

CHAPTER ONE HUNDRED AND FIFTYNINE

Diseases

Dhanvantari said :

1. I shall now explain the pathology of Pramehas (Diabetes), please listen O Suśruta. Diabetes consists of twenty varieties. Ten are caused by Kapha, six are caused by Pitta and four are caused by Vāyu. Fat, urine and phlegm are the seats of disorders.

2. A patient of Hāridrameha passes hot faeces and urine having the colour of turmeric and smelling like saw flesh. A patient of Māñjiṣṭhameha passes urine like the water with which Indian madder is washed (yellowish red).

3. A patient of Raktameha discharges flesh smelling hot saline red urine. A patient of Vasāmeha frequently discharges urine mixed with fat and having the colour of fat.

4-5. A patient of Majjāmeha passess urine charged with marrow and resembling marrow. A patient of Hastimeha discharges a continuous copious flow of urine containing slimy mucous matter.

6. A patient of Madhumeha discharges urine like honey. It is of two types.

7-9. When the Vāyu gets aggravated due to deficiency of dhātus and its path is obstructed by the doṣas the patient begins to exhibit the symptoms and without any apparent reason he shows signs of amelioration and aggravation by turns. It then becomes incurable. All pramehas, neglected at the outset, turn into Madhumeha in course of time.

All those cases of Prameha where the excretions are sweet like honey can be classified under Madhumeha.

10. The common disorders in the Pramehas caused by Kapha are indigestion, nonrelish for food, vomiting, somnolence, cough and catarrh.

11. The characteristic symptoms in Meha caused by deranged Pitta are:—Pricking pain in the bladder and urethra, bursting of the scrotum, fever, burning sensation in the body, thirst, sour eructations, epilepsy and loose bowels.

12. The Vāyu afflicted person exhibits the following symptoms :—Udāvarta (Prolapsus of the anus), shivering, pain in the heart, morbid longing (for bitter and astringent food-stuffs), Colic, sleeplessness withering up, dyspnea and cough.

13. Ten types of abscesses caused by the neglect of Prameha are :—(1) Śarāvikā (2) Kacchapikā (3) Jvālinī (4) Vinatā (5) Alajī (6) Masūrikā (7) Sarṣapikā (8) Putriṇī (9) Vidārikā and (10) Vidradhi.

14. The main cause is food stuff, sweat, sour, saline, oily, heavy, lubricious and cold in combination with Kapha.

15. Newly harvested grains, wine, dal soup, gravy, jaggery and milkproducts in excess cause sharing the bed or seat as a patient may also cause the same.

16. The defiled Kapha located in the urinary bladder first defiles the body, secretions like sweat, and the fat and flesh. Then it produces Pramehas.

17. The Kapha makes the blood mixed with urine when Kapha etc. are exhausted. When Kapha subsides Vāyu brings the dhatus to the bladder.

18. The curability or otherwise and the necessity to wait in the case of Pramehas shall be decided by understanding the underlying cause. If the doṣas are eliminated the disease can be cured, if they are aggravated the sickness persists.

19. The general characteristic of all Pramehas is copious urination turbid in nature. By the combination of doṣas different disorders are observed. The different types of Prameha are classified according to the colour of the urine.

20. The patient of Udakameha (Polyuria) passes clear copiouscool odourless urine like water. It is slightly lubricious and turbid.

21-22. The patient of Ikṣumeha discharges excessively sweet wine, like sugar-cane juice. The patient of Sāndrameha (Chyluria) passes thick urine resembling state rice gruel.

23. The patient of Surāmeha passes urine like wine transparent at the surface but leaving a sediment at the bottom. The patient of Piṣṭameha passes copious urine white-like pasted rice. He has horripilation at the time of urination.

24. The patient of Śukrameha (Spermatorrhoea) passes une highly charged with semen resembling it in colour. The patient of Sikatāmeha passes urine with sediments like grains of sand.

25. The patient of Śītameha passes copious urine cold and sweet. The patient of Śanairmeha passes urine slowly in broken jets. The patient of Lālāmeha passes slimy, shreddy urine like saliva.

26. The patient of Kṣārameha passes urine alkaline in character in smell, colour, taste and touch. The patient of Nīlameha passes bluish urine and the patient of Kālameha passes urine black like ink.

27. Abscesses usually occur in vulnerable joints and fleshy portions in the body. An abscess elevated at the extremities and dipped in the centre, producing no discharges nor giving any pain is called Śarāvikā since it resembles a saucer in shape.

28. An abscess giving a burning sensation and resembling the back of a tortoise shall be known Kacchapikā by

scholars. The abscess large in size and blue in colour is called Vinatā.

29. At the time of its incubation the abscess Jvālinī gives excruciating pain and a burning sensation. The abscess Alajī is terrible. It is either red or white and is surrounded by blisters.

30. An abscess resembling a Masūra dāla (lentil seed) is called Masūrikā. Small clusters of abscesses resembling mustard seeds in the tongue are called Sarṣapikā. They are very painful. They suppurate too.

31. The abscess Putriṇī is of various sizes. Some are large, some small and some very minute. The abscess Vidārikā is hard and round like the bulbous root of Vidārī (an esculent tuber).

32. An abscess with the characteristics of Vidradhi (Erysipelas) is called Vidradhikā. The abscesses Putriṇī and Vidārikā give intolerable pain and are fatty.

33. Many other abscesses occurring suddenly due to the deranged Pitta are less fatty. Their virulence is in accordance with the aggravation of the doṣas.

34. In a patient of defiled fat these abscesses occur even without Prameha. They are not recognized as long as the colour is not clearly developed.

35. Without the characteristic symptoms of Prameha if a patient passes urine red in colour or resembling the washings of turmeric he is a victim of Raktapitta (urethral haemorrhage).

36-37. Perspiration, foul smell in the limbs, lassitude and looseness in the limbs, inclination to lie down, sleep, or take food, burning sensation in the chest, eyes, tongue and ears, thickness of the tips hair and nails and their profuse growth, fondness for cool things, parchedness in the throat and palate, taste of sweetness in the mouth, burning sensation in hands and feet, all these are the symptoms indicating the onset of Prameha. Ants move about in the urine of the patient.

38. Thirst and sweetness of urine and similar disorders of various forms occur when the illness progresses. When the symptoms are full the type occurs. When the other dosas subside the Vātaja type may occur.

39. Prameha caused by Pitta and Kapha exhibits the entire symptoms simultaneously and that caused by sexual indulgence exhibits them gradually. Pittaja Prameha can be checked or alleviated. If the Prameha is not fully developed it can be cured.

CHAPTER ONE HUNDRED AND SIXTY

Diseases

Dhanvantari said:

1-3. I shall now describe the pathology of Vidradhi (Erysipelas) and Gulma (Intumescence), please listen O Suśruta. If stale or very hot, dry, coarse and parchifying foodstuffs are taken, or if abnormal activities are indulged in, if hard and uneven beds are used the blood becomes vitiated. Then it vitiates the skin, flesh, fat and bones and takes refuge in the abdominal cavity and produces intumescence inside and outside the body. It gives excruciating pain. It may be elongated or circular in shape. This is called Vidradhi.

4. The doṣas either severally or in combination produce on the surface of the body on different limbs knotty intumescences due to exuding contaminated blood.

5. Inside, they are in the form of inflammations very terrible, deep seated and exuding. They grow like anthills. They impair digestion.

6. They usually occur in the umbilical region, urinary bladder, liver, spleen lungs, heart, abdomen and the thigh joints. When there is palpitation of the heart they give excruciating pain.

7. At the time of incubation it is black in colour and at the time of ripening or suppurating it becomes red. It is irregular information: It brings in loss of consciousness, vertigo, constipation, suppression of urine and noisiness in movement.

8. In the pittaja type it is red, copper coloured or black producing thirst, fainting, fever and burning sensation. In the

kaphaja type it quickly incubates and suppurates. A little greyish in colour it gives an itching sensation.

9. Shivering, chillness to touch, numbness of the affected part, yawning, nonrelish for food and heaviness are the symptoms. The Sannipātaja type is slow in growth and does not suppurate. It is irregular in formation.

10 Looseness of the bowels is the common characteristic of both the external and the internal vidradhi. It assumes a black colour, surrounded by blisters and is attended with an intolerable burning pain and fever.

11. The external abscess due to contaminated blood is a sign of Pitta. Such abscess in the internal regions is peculiar to women. There is another Vidradhi due to wounds with a weapon, or hitting with something.

12. The blood originating from the wound is tossed by the Vāyu and it aggravates pitta and produces a vidradhi of grave disorders exhibiting the symptoms of both Pitta and contaminated blood.

13. Difference in the disorder is due to the difference in the seat of the abscess. If puffing up is the disorder in an abscess in the umbilical region that in the bladder is strangury.

14. An abscess in the spleen will cause difficulty in inhaling and exhaling and excessive thirst. An abscess in the lungs produces constriction in the throat. An abscess in the heart produces pain all over the body.

15. An abscess in the abdomen or its side produces loss of sense, *Tamaka Śvāsa* (a peculiar dyspnea) and digging pain in the heart.

16. If there is an abscess in the thigh joints internally or externally or in the hips or on the back the pain will be in the sides and the wind will be obstructed at the rectum.

17. The state of incubation, that of ripening and that of fully ripened tumour in the inside are to be known as very like those of any swelling. An internal abscess occurring above the umbilical region sends out the exudation after suppuration through the mouth and the others through the anus.

18. In a vidradhi formation in rectum mouth or umbilical region the doṣa can be known from its suppuration. A sannipātaja vidradhi shows alteration from its seat.

19. The Vidradhi in the umbilical region or in the urinary bladder, externally or internally when ripe, bursts. That which is fully grown suppurates but under-developed is infested with disorders.

20. Sinful wicked women suffer from internal abscesses when the child in the womb dies; an inflammation occurs there very thick.

21. An abscess on the breasts of women has all the characteristics of an external abscess. The blood in women is very subtle. Hence small girls do not suffer from internal abscess.

22-23. An aggravated but obstructed Vāyu in its path generally causes swellings. From the region between scrotum and the thigh joints it reaches the nerve vessel passing beyond the testicles and oppresses it. Thus it causes its swelling and a vitiation of the fat in the locality. It is called Vṛddhi (Hydrocela). It is of seven types.

24. Due to the affliction of Vāyu, in the case of Vṛddhi whether external or internal there is excessive micturition. The swelling becomes inflated, parched and rough to the touch accompanied by a burning sensation.

25. Due to the affliction of Pitta the swelling resembles a ripe Udumbara fruit (Ficus Indica) attended with heat, burning sensation and suppuration. Due to the affliction of Kapha the swelling is heavy, glossy and slightly painful. It produces an itching sensation.

26. Due to the affliction of contaminated blood, the swelling becomes compact, dark in colour and covered with bulbous eruptions on its surface. All the symptoms of Pittaja Vṛddhi are present. Due to the action of fat defiled by Kapha the Vṛddhi is soft and rounded like a palm fruit.

27. This ailment is called Mūtraja Vṛddhi as the patient habitually suppresses the passage of urine. There are no hair on the swelling. It is soft and quiet but is disturbed on movement.

28. Plunging into chill water, and taking in foodstuffs aggravating the Vāyu produces strangury and ringlike markings beneath the scrotum.

29-30. Suppression of faeces and passage of urine and

abnormal activities of the limbs causes the aggravation of the Vāyu that affects the virility of the patient and takes the blood downwards. This causes knotty swelling in the thigh joints.

31. Neglected at the outset this Vṛddhi turns into Gulma (enlarged spleen, etc.) and produces in its wake many disorders like distension, etc. Firmly pressed it goes in with a sound but comes out swelling again.

32. The Rakta Vṛddhi is incurable. Vāta Vṛddhi continues in the same size with a network of coarse blue and red veins like a window covered with a woollen net.

33. There are seven types of Vṛddhi due to the doṣas severally and combined in diverse ways and the eighth one happens in women due to the contamination of menstrual blood.

34. Fever, dysentery, fainting, vomiting, chillness and hunger make even a strong man emaciated.

35. The patient who takes boiled rice and drinks too much or fasts or takes bath is soon overwhelmed with fits of fainting.

36. Without resorting to emollient or diaphoretic measures, drying up measures shall be used or those measures provoking free flow of blood shall be used whether the patient is free from defiled doṣas or not.

37-38. In the case of the Vātaja Vidradhi the wind and the defiled matter can be eliminated separately or collectively. The Vāyu mixed with blood passing through the ducts obstructs their upward or downward passage and produces pain. The swelling Gulma can be felt by the hand in a knotty globular shape. It feels a little hot.

39. The Vāyu lodged in the abdomen becomes hard and coarse due to fasting or obstruction to the passage by Kapha and waste matter.

40. The aggravated Vāyu continuing in its own locatious acts independently, while located in the seat of any other doṣa it is dependent on that doṣa. The consolidated lump of kapha in combination with dirt occupying the bladder, umbilical region, thoracic cavity and sides is called Gulma.

41. In the Vātaja type of gulma, headache, fever, inflammation of the spleen, rumbling sound in the entrails, a pricking pain in the limbs, loose motions, and difficult painful urination are the symptoms.

42. There is swelling (Śotha or Anasarca) in the limbs, mouth or in the feet, impaired gastric function, parchedness and black colour of the skin etc. due to the fickleness of Vāyu.

43. Like a blind man groping about rolling his eyeballs without realising the place where he is, the gulma rolls about as if a number of ants have covered it. It throbs.

44. Due to Pitta, burning sensation is felt. There are acid eructations, epileptic fits, loose motions, sweating thirst, chlorosis (Hāridrya) and swellings all over the body.

45. The deranged kapha is aggravated or diminishes and scorches its seat. There is rigidity due to kapha, non relish for food, a feeling of exhaustion, heaviness of head and fever.

46. Obesity, lassitude, disquietude whiteness or blackness of skin etc. are observed. The swelling becomes hard and fixed and the patient has steady sleep for a short while.

47. Inflammations caused by two doṣas in combination affecting their own respective seats and exhibiting their own symptoms prove fatal.

48-49. Rakta gulma (ovarian tumour) found only in women is caused by all doṣas and exhibits severe pain and burning sensation. It suppurates quickly. It is hard and raised and is incurable. If a woman suffering from uterine trouble exposes herself to gusts of wind during her menstrual period the Vāyu principle gets aggravated.

50. It obstructs the passage of menstrual flow of blood which collecting in the abdominal cavity produces symptoms of pregnancy.

51. Disquietude, milk in the breasts, craving desire for various foodstuffs etc. as in pregnancy and waywardness are also seen. In combination with Vāyu, Pitta accumulates in the vaginal passage.

52. The blood is too collected there. All the symptoms of Vātaja and Pittaja gulmas are observed. In the womb the seat of blood there is acute pain.

53. There is vaginal discharge with fetid smell and

lencorrhoea with pain. Enlarged spleen also appears like pregnancy sometimes. All these are due to unnatural desire for sexual intercourse.

54. It suppurates slowly and the vidradhi does not grow again. If that is contaminated with impure blood it suppurates quickly.

55-56. Since it gives a burning sensation quickly it is called Vidradhi. If a gulma occurs on another gulma there is burning sensation and pain in the spleen. Digestion is impaired, colour of complexion is faded and strength diminishes. The natural urges are suppressed. If the previous symptoms are not present the symptoms of an external abscess are present. There is not much pain in the viscera or the limbs.

57. Pallour, cough, bulging out of the abdomen, rumbling sound in the abdomen with excruciating pain and distension are also present.

58. The wind is obstructed above and below. It is called Ānāha. If there is the outcome of thick seed-like thing with knotty grips it is called Aṣṭhīlā.

59. When the Vāyu originating from the stomach gives rise to an excruciating pain and all other symptoms too are present it is called Pratyaṣṭhīlā.

60-61. Profuse eructation, suppression of faeces, insatiation, rumbling sound in the entrails, severe distension, inability to digest, etc. are the symptoms of an imminent Gulma.

CHAPTER ONE HUNDRED AND SIXTYONE

Diseases

Dhanvantari said :—

1. I shall explain the pathology of Udara (Ascites, dropsy, flatulence) O Suśruta, please listen. All ailments affect the man of impaired digestion. The more so in the case of Udaras.

2. Due to the accumulation of waste matter many ailments such as indigestion etc. are produced. The Vāyus going up or down when obstructed make the Pravāhiṇi (the ducts of the digestive system) in-operative.

3 The Prāṇa vāyus defile the Apāna vāyus and incarcerate them in the inter spaces of flesh and skin after producing the inflammation of the abdomen. Udara ailment is of eight types.

4. The different doṣas severally and in combination give rise to four. The spleen, the thigh joints, wounds and fluid watery substances are the four other causes giving rise to four types of Udara. People affected by Udara have dry palate and lips. The hands, feet and the abdomen pain very much.

5. Inability to move about, deficiency in strength, inability to eat, distension of the abdomen—all these are symptoms of the onset. Patients look like ghost.

6. Appetite is lost, distaste for everything is experienced. At the time of digestion a burning sensation is felt. He who is not particularly mindful of taking food after digestion is injudicious in his diet.

7. His strength diminishes, limbs become emaciated, even a slight activity makes him breathe hard, he shirks work: he is dejected; he becomes lean.

8. Pain in the bladder joints always, fever and indigestion even after a light meal, loss of strength etc. occur in a Jaṭhararogin (a patient of Ascites).

9. Free somnolence and lassitude, loose motions bit by bit, burning sensation, intumescence, distension in the entrails — all these are to be found in an Udara roga due to watery accumulation (serous fluid).

10. Patients of Ascites due to serous fluid definitely die and they need not be bewailed. A rumbling sound is heard inside the belly. The external surface is charged with a network of veins like a window.

11. When Vāyu subsides after exciting the navel and the entrails and producing disorders, pain is felt in the chest, hips, navel, anus and the thigh joints.

12. The Vāyu comes out with a loud report (breaking

the wind) the patient passes a little urine. He is not eager for anything; the mouth is devoid of taste.

13. In the Vātodara there is intermescence in hands, feet, face and stomach and pain in the sides of the stomach, abdomen, hips and the back. The joints seem to break.

14. Dry cough, pain in the limbs, heaviness of the nether regions of the body, suppression of stool, blackness or reddish colour in the skin etc. and varied tastes in the mouth—these are the symptoms of Vātaja types of Ascites.

15. A breaking piercing pain is experienced in the abdomen. The surface is covered with a network of blue or black veins. The abdomen becomes distended and wonderful sounds are heard from within.

16. It is the Vāyu that makes the sound and produces the pain as it courses all about. In the Pittaja type of Ascites, fever, epileptic fits, burning sensation and bitter taste in the mouth are the symptoms.

17. (Other symptoms are) Vertigo, dysentery, yellow colour in the skin etc., greenish hue in the abdomen, having yellow or copper coloured network of veins on the surface of the abdomen, profuse perspiration and burning sensation.

18. The person feels that fumes escape from his stomach that is soft for the touch. He complains of pain as digestion takes place quickly. In the ailment of Ascites due to kapha excessive lassitude, perspiration, oedematous swelling of limbs and heaviness are experienced.

19. Moreover somnolence or painful sleep, nonrelish for food, dyspnea, cough, white colour in the skin etc. are also observed. The stomach is glossy and covered with net work of veins black and white in colour.

20. If the serous fluid increases the abdomen becomes hard, cool to the touch, firm and heavy. If the cause is the combined action of all the humours all the symptoms are present.

21-22. Defiled by all humours (doṣas) the waste matter with the contaminated blood comes to the abdomen and begins to putrefy. It produces an ailment of Ascites which is rapid in suppurating and very terrible. It produces emaciation epileptic fits and vertigo : During cold and windy days the ailment exhibits signs of aggravation.

23-26. Due to excessive intake of food, agitation, excessive travelling or drinking, injudicious use of beverages, misuse of emetics etc. the spleen which is on the left side gets dislodged and becomes enlarged. Or its enlargement may be caused by the obstruction of blood through fatty substances. This Asthita (seedlike growth) is very hard and raised like the back of a tortoise. While growing gradually it spreads all over the abdominal cavity and is attended with dyspnea, cough, thirst, dryness of the mouth, distension of the abdomen, fever, yellowness of skin, epileptic fits, vomiting, burning sensation and fainting.

27-28. The network of veins is crimson, blue or yellow colour or it may have various colours. Tympanites with suppression of stools, fainting, burning sensation in the chest and fever may supervene. Heaviness (of other organs), taking of food without appetite or hardness (of itself) may cause the dislodgement of the Yakṛt (Liver) from the right side of the body as in the case of spleen.

29. When the liver suppurates and when the faecal matter accumulates in the rectum the patient will be afflicted by piles, tympanites and other sorts of disorders.

30-31. The aggravated Vāyu obstructs faecal matter, pitta and kapha. When Apāna is also similarly obstructed by it there is pain and fever. Moreover, cough, dyspnea, severe pain in the thigh pain in the head, limbs, umbilical region and sides, non-evacuation of bowels, nonrelish for food, vomiting and permeation of the abdominal cavity by defiled wind are observed.

32. A permanent network of blue or red veins covers the outer surface of the stomach. Above the navel, generally, it takes the shape of a coin's tail.

33. When wounded by bones or weapons in the stomach the liver begins to suppurate emitting much pus through the wound.

34. Only the unripe ones having mucous come through the anus which is little by little. Although it has a fetid smell it is lubricious and yellowish red in colour.

35. What remains fills the abdominal cavity and begins to work disorders. It increases beneath the umbilical region and assumes the form of serous fluid.

36. When the doṣas get aggravated and all the symptoms such as dyspnea, thirst and vertigo appear the ailment is called Chidrodara by some and Parisrāvyudara by others.

37. This happens in an emaciated person of impaired digestion by drinking too much of water, or drinking with great deal of joy.

38. The Vāyu and Kapha become aggravated through such injudicious conduct and obstruct the path of acid secretions of the stomach and it increases to the extent of water taken in even if it be a drop.

39. Due to its aggravation the Udara roga is accompanied by thiıst and pain in the anus and the ears. There is cough, dyspnea and nonrelish for food. The surface is covered with a network of veins of various colours.

40. Because the abdomen is full of water, it is soft to the touch. There is agitation and shivering in the Dakodara. The abdomen is firm and glossy. It covers the nerves.

41. If neglected, all types of Ascites lead to further liquefactions of the serous accumulations and even the outlets of the ducts and joints.

42. If perspiration is obstructed the internal contents grow further. That serous fluid filling the stomach causes Kṣatodara ailment.

43. The dropsy becomes firm, heavy and spherical and does not produce any sound when pressed. The patient gets weaker every day. When the nerve is touched it moves.

44-45. The disappearance of the veins is an indication of Sannipātaja type. All the different types of Udara exhibit the symptoms of serous fluid within a fortnight and are incurable from their very inception.

CHAPTER ONE HUNDRED AND SIXTYTWO

Diseases

Dhanvantari said :—

1. O Suśruta, I shall tell you the pathology of Pāṇḍu (Chlorosis and Jaundice) and that of Śotha (Oedema and Anasarca). All the morbid humours with Pitta as their leader become aggravated due to various exciting factors mentioned before.

2. The more powerful of the doṣas lead them on and toss them about all over the body. Finally when they come to rest they permeate all the ten Dhamanīs (Nerves).

3. The kapha, skin, blood and the flesh are defiled. Different colours are given to the skin.

4. Among the colours the colour of yellow-like turmeric is predominant. Hence the ailment is called Pāṇḍu. A sort of heaviness of the body is caused by Vāyu.

5. In the Āmaja type (where much matter is present) the main constituents, Dhātus of the body, lose their consistency and become lighter. The patient becomes deficient in blood (Anaemic). The quantity of fat is diminished. The bones are not substantial. The sense organs do not function properly.

6. The limbs get thinner and thinner; clammy sweats exude in the cardiac region. Pain in the eyes, rigidity in the face and salivation are observed.

7. The patient does not feel much thirst. He abhors chillness . With his dishevelled hair fluttering in the air he patiently suffers from fever of equal intensity. He coughs, has pain in the ears and has vertigo.

8-10. The ailment is of five types, four of them being caused by the doṣas severally and in combination and the fifth by eating earth. The premonitory signs are perspiration in the region of the heart, dryness of the skin, nonrelish for food, scanty yellow urine and absence of perspiration. The Vāyu causes a stupor, excruciating pain, wetness all over the body, a sort of black or vermillion colour and dryness in the veins, nails, eyes, faeces and urine, intumescence dryness of mouth and nostrils, scantum of faeces and numbness in the sides.

11. The Pitta causes greenish or yellow colour in the vein, etc., fever, vanish of vision of light (darkness), thirst, emaciation of the body, swooning, foul smell, fondness for cold things and bitter taste in the mouth.

12. The Kapha causes diarrhoea, acid erectations, burning sensation, clamminess of the cardiac region, lethargy, saline taste in the mouth, horripilation and aphonia.

13. Cough and Vomiting the symptoms of a combination are very unbearable. The mucous expectorated is either bitter or sweet due to the prevalent Vāyu or Pitta.

14. The defiled kapha vitiates the fat and other vital constituents of the body and generating a condition of parchedness causes even haemorrhage. As said before, it may obstruct the various ducts and vessels of the body resulting in general debility.

15. In Jaundice the navel, feet, face and the penis become thinner and thinner; the faeces are infested with germs, loose and mixed with blood and mucous matter.

16. A patient affected by jaundice continuing to eat pitta-generating foodstuffs is afflicted by Kāmalā (chlorois). The pitta, coming of its seat in the abdominal cavity scorches up the blood and the flesh.

17. The colour of the urine, faeces, eyes, mouth and the face becomes yellow; the patient feels a burning sensation; indigestion sets in and the patient lies like a bloated toad weak in all his limbs and organs of sense.

18. The unabsorbed pitta of a jaundice patient gives rise to a kind of swelling and when these swellings are neglected, the dreadful ailment of Kumbha Kāmalā sets in.

19. The unassimilated Pitta produces greenness of complexion. The Vāyu and Pitta in combination produce vertigo, thirst, desire for the company of women and slight rise in temperature.

20. Moreover, there may be somnolence and impaired digestion. Sages call it Halīmaka. A great lassitude is also observed. All these are the premonitory symptoms of this disease.

21-22. Śotha (oedema) has already been mentioned as a grave ailment. Hence, it is being explained. The defiled

Vāyu takes the contaminated blood, pitta and kapha to the external vessels and gets obstructed in its path generating a raised and compact swelling in the local flesh and skin. This is called Śotha.

23-24. This ailment is divided into nine according to the causes—the three doṣas separately, in combination of twos, all combined, due to attack and due to poison. It is divided into three in accordance with their shapes (1) large, (2) raised and pointed, (3) knotty. They may be congenital or acquired. If they spread all over the body they are necessarily generated by overlustfulness.

25. A common cause for all types of Śothas is the deranged morbid humour. They are found in persons emaciated due to sickness, overwork, fasting, etc. rapidly growing.

26. In the case of others the intake of foodstuffs in large quantities especially such as are heavy, too cold, saline, acid or alkaline, green vegetables and water or excessive sleep or wakefulness may cause Śotha.

27-28. The voluntary suppression of natural urges, eating dried flesh, indigestion, exhaustion, sexual intercourse, travelling by foot or in a jolting vehicle—all these aggravate these diseases:—dyspnea, cough, dysentery, piles, ascites, leucorrhoea, fever, tympanites, flatulence, vomiting, hiccough, erysipelas and jaundice.

29. The morbid humours lodged in the upper, middle or lower parts of the body generate Śotha (oedematous swelling) in their seat or in the urinary bladder.

30. Its premonitory symptoms are burning pain in the nerves and heaviness of limbs. In the Vātaja type of swellings, they are found to be shifting in their character, rough, blackish or reddish in colour and have rough hair round their base.

31. The patient complains of breaking pain in the temples, bladder, entrails, etc. Due to the pain he is unable to sleep. The swelling grows rapidly and the whole body is painful.

32. The swelling is small during nights and grows large during the day. It is glossy. By pressure it may subside. If mustard is applied over the swelling a tingling sensation is experienced.

33. The pittaja type of swelling is black, red or yellow in colour; it produces Śoṣa (emaciation); it does not subside quickly. Before the advent and in the middle, it gives a burning sensation all o\ er the body.

34. Fever with thirst, burning sensation and perspiration, vertigo, pain, stupor, yearning for things, loose motion, foul smell and softness to the touch are characteristic symptoms.

35. In the kaphaja type the swelling gives an itching sensation, has yellow and gray hairs, is hardskinned, cold, firm, glossy, smooth and painful; it produces sleep, vomiting, sensation and indigestion.

36-37. A blow, a cut from any weapon or any hard thing, exposure to chill winds or sea breezes or the juice of Bhallātaka[1] or Kapikacchu[2] fruits may produce a swelling with erysipelas. It is marked by extreme heat and exhibits symptoms common to Pittaja type. It is red in colour.

38. Swelling due to poison is caused by poisonous insects and reptiles when they pass over the body or urinate there. Even when nonpoisonous insects and animals bite or scratch swelling may occur.

39-40. When one comes into contact with a cloth contaminated by faeces, urine, or semen or when one comes into contact with breeze coming from poisonous trees or when one grinds a poisonous medicine, a swelling may occur that is soft shifting, hanging loose and extremely painful and burning. A fresh swelling without disorders can be cured but not a chronic one.

1. Somecarpus anacardium.
2. Perhaps the same as Svayaṁguptā=Mucuna pruriens.

CHAPTER ONE HUNDRED AND SIXTYTHREE

Diseases

Dhanvantari said:

1. O Suśruta, I shall explain the pathology of Visarpa (Erysipelas—dry spreading itch), please listen. Visarpa may be caused by defiled morbid humours in the same way as swellings (Śotha). The humours are defiled either by the obstruction of the vessels or prevention of the outlet of excreta.

2-4. This is an external ailment. It may be caused by fright or overwork. These ailments are more and more difficult of cure in the order of enumeration. When the doṣas are aggravated by the usual exciting factors especially those parchifying foodstuffs they come out from within due to excessive thirst, or irregular functions of the excretory system or the impairment of the digestive system or physical strength. This brings on an attack of dry spreading itch.

5. In the Vātaja type the pain and disorders are the same as in Vātaja fever. A throbbing sensation is experienced, an aching piercing pain and misery of utter exhaustion is felt. It is attended with horripilation too.

6. In the pittaja type it spreads very rapidly; it is bright, red in colour and exhibits all symptoms of a Pittajvara (fever). In the kaphaja type of dry itch, it is very irritating, glossy and exhibits the symptoms of kaphaja fever and its pain.

7. Erysipelas of the Sannipātaja type exhibit all the symptoms. When neglected it flourishes with all sorts of eruptions.

8. Due to the combined action of Vāyu and Pitta, there is fever vomiting, fainting, diarrhoea, thirst, vertigo, breaking pain in the joints, the gastric fire becomes defunct, nonrelish for food and tamaka Śvāsa—all these manifest themselves.

9. All the body appears to be covered with burning charcoal. Wherever the itch spreads it gives the burning sensation.

10. The place from where the itch has shifted appears black or blue like the burnt cinders or becomes red and grows with eruptions as in the case of a burn. It is very rapid.

11. Hence, it invades the vital principles since the Vāyu is very powerful and produces pain all over the body, removes sensibility and sleep and makes him gasp for breath.

12. The patient has hiccough and does not get any permanent relief on the ground or bed or in seat, since he becomes insatiable.

13. Turning over sides he endures a lot of pain, experiences stupor and delusion mentally and physically and enters a sleep from which it becomes difficult to wake him up. This is called Agnivisarpa.

14-16. Vāyu obstructed by Kapha, shatters it into pieces. It then vitiates the blood in the vessels in the skin, sinews and flesh of a sanguinous person. A knotty garland (series) of a number of erysipelatic eruptions elongated or round in shape is produced by it. This exudes blood and gives excruciating pain. Dyspnea, cough, dysentery, parchedness of the mouth, hiccough, vomiting, vertigo, fainting, pallor, epileptic fits, breaking pain in the limbs and impaired digestive function—all these accompany it. This is called Granthivisarpa caused by the derangement of Kapha and Vāyu.

17-21. The derangement of Kapha and Pitta produce these—fever, numbness, somnolence, lassitude, headache, weakness and jerky movements of the limbs, delirium, repugnance for food, vertigo, epileptic fits, impaired gastric fire, breaking pain in the bones, thirst, dullness of the sense organs, undigested excreta and smearing of the ducts with slimy mucous. The itch usually starts from any part of the stomach and spreads. It does not pain much. It is surrounded by pustules deep, yellow, red or gray in colour. The main itch is glossy, black or blue in colour, dirty, heavy and has a swelling with hot grave suppurations. When it breaks, the fleshy portion is severed up making the sinews and nerves clearly visible. It emits the foul smell of a dead body. This is called Kardama Visarpa (Miry Visarpa).

22-23. When a blow or cut affects the body the Vāyu becomes aggravated and vitiates the blood and the Pitta. It then produces itches and eruptions resembling the pulse

Kulattha[1] (Horse gram). There is swelling, fever, pain and burning sensation. The blood is blackish-red in colour. The erysipelas caused by the doṣas severally can be cured. That caused by the doṣas in twos can be cured if disorders are not many.

24. Those itches caused by all the humours in combination, those affecting the vulnerable joints, those in which the sinews, nerves and flesh are shattered and those with pus emitting the foul smell of dead bodies are incurable.

CHAPTER ONE HUNDRED AND SIXTYFOUR

Diseases

Dhanvantari said:

1-3. Injudicious diet and conduct, sinful actions, ridiculing or killing good people, sinful fights, abductions, accumulated evils of the previous births—all these in combination aggravate the morbid principles Vāyu, Pitta and Kapha. They permeate the various ducts and vessels of the body and contaminate the skin, the fat, the blood and the flesh. After drying them up when the doṣas come out they discolour the entire skin. Authorities call this Kuṣṭha (cutaneous affections, leprosy etc.).

4. When neglected at the outset these Kuṣṭhas spread all over the body and vitiate the fundamental principles and constituents of the organism external and internal.

5. The affected part gets contracted or covered with perspiration and clammy discharges. Minute terrible germs infest the region. The hair, the skin, the sinews, and the vessels of various secretions are infested by them.

6. The body of the patient appears to be covered with ashes. Kuṣṭhas are of seven types being caused by the doṣas severally and in twos or all combined together.

1. Dolichos biftonus.

7-10. Although all the doṣas are present in every case the prevalent doṣa is to be considered as the main cause. The Kuṣṭha Kāpāla is due to Vāyu. Audumbara is due to Pitta and Maṇḍala is due to Kapha. Vicarcī and Ṛṣyajihva are due to Vāta and Pitta. Carmaikakuṣṭha (Prurigo) and Kiṭima (Keloid tumour), Sidhma, Alasa and Vipādikā are due to Vāyu and Kapha: Dadru (Ring worm) and Śatārus are due to Pitta and Kapha. Puṇḍarīka, Visphoṭa, Pāmā, Carmadala and Kākaṇa are due to the combined action of all the three doṣas. The first three (i.e. Kāpāla, Audumbara andMaṇ ḍala), Dadru, Kākaṇa, Puṇḍarīka and Ṛṣyajihva are the seven Mahākuṣṭhas.

11-14. Some of the affected patches are soft and some are rough; in some cases there is perspiration, in some cases there is no perspiration; Pallor, burning and itching sensations, somnolence (loss of feeling), pricking pain, affection of the optic nerves, darkness of vision, excessive pain in the limbs, rapid appearance and permanent stay of the patches, roughness to the touch, aggravation when the slightest cause is present, horripilation and dark black colour of the blood—all these are the preliminary symptoms of Kuṣṭha. The patches in the Kāpāla type of Kuṣṭha resemble a black and reddish skull, are attended with excruciating pain. They are dry and rough, of irregular formation and are covered over with dirty hair. This Kuṣṭha is highly dreadful.

15-17. The patch in the Audumbara type of Kuṣṭha has the colour of the Udumbara fruit (ficus Indica); it is circular in shape; it exudes copious discharge of pus; it is attended with excessive pain and a burning sensation. The patches are not contiguous nor do they burst. Many germs are found in them. In the Maṇḍalakuṣṭha (Erythema) the patches are firm, thick, glossy, exuding white and red discharge, congested and overlapping one another, raised, excessively irritating, of copious discharge and infested with parasites. They are of glossy yellow colour.

18. The Vicarcikā type of Kuṣṭha is irritating, black in colour and covered with exuding postules. Rough to the touch they are red in the extremities and black within and slightly raised.

19. The Kuṣṭha known as Ṛṣyajihva is infested with a number of germs. It resembles the tongue of the deer Ṛṣya. In the Carmākhya Kuṣṭha the patch is rough to the touch like the skin of an elephant.

20. In the Kiṭima type of Kuṣṭha the patch is dry and resembles the scales of a fish. It is hard and shining and has the colour of fire. It irritates.

21-22. A kind of patch rough within and glossy outside by rubbing which dust is scattered is smooth to the touch. There is no perspiration. It resembles a flower without dew-drops. It is usually formed in thin layers at its upper ends. It is characterised by itching sensation and red marks. This is called Vipādikā and usually affects hands and feet.

23-24. In the type of Kuṣṭha called Dadru (ring worm) the ulcer gives excruciating pain and itching sensation. The eruptions are red. They spread like the Dūrva grass tinged with a colour like that of an Atasī flower (linseed). It has an elevated ring-like groove. It produces itching sensation. Its roots are thick. It is characterised by burning sensation. It emits blood and is full of wounds.

25-26. It gives a burning sensation and is generally caused by all the humours in combination. The surrounding zone is red or tawny coloured. It gives an itching sensation and excruciating pain. The pustules are white or red and the patch appears like leaves of lotus covered with drops of water. This Kuṣṭha is called Puṇḍarīka.

27. In the type of Kuṣṭha called Pāmā the ulcers exude discharges and give itching sensation and excruciating pain. They have a dusky or reddish hue and are very rough. Generally they appear in elbows and buttocks.

28. An excruciating pain and burning sensation characterise the Kuṣṭhas Carmadala and Kākaṇa where the eruptions can be touched but emit blood when scratched.

29. The Kākaṇa type is at first red but turns into black, resembling the washings of Triphalā. All ulcers in all types of kuṣṭha become black due to their own respective reasons.

30. The different types of kuṣṭha must be understood through their symptoms and actions. That which is caused by all the doṣas shall be abandoned (as incurable).

31. The Kuṣṭha that affects the bones, marrows and semen is incurable, that which affects the fat Yāpya (treated by palliatives) and that which affects our bones or flesh can be cured.

32. The Kuṣṭha produced by Kapha and Vāyu in combination is not very difficult to cure. So also is the case of a kuṣṭha that has affected only the skin and does not secrete any discharge. When the kuṣṭha has affected only the skin, discoloration and roughness in the skin is observed.

33-34. Perspiration, heat and swelling, eruptions in hands and feet and in the joints, extreme pressure as if the fat is being crushed on account of the doṣas—all these symptoms characterise the kuṣṭha attacking the blood and flesh. The ability of the patient to feel sensations is impaired slightly. Voice becomes sunk and hollow, eyesight is affected, fat and marrow in the bones are destroyed.

35. When the germs affect the semen the patient transmits the disease to his wife and children. All these ailments with the characteristic symptoms affect even animals.

36. Śvitra (Leucoderma) and the dreadful disease Kilāsa have the same exciting factors as Kuṣṭha. They are not of the bleeding type. All the three dhātus are affected by them. All the doṣas cause them.

37-38. Śvitra caused by Vāyu is rough and red, that of pittaja type is copper-coloured and shaped like lotus leaves. It gives a burning sensation and the hair in the affected part fall off. The kaphaja type of Śvitra is thick and white and gives an itching sensation. It gradually affects the blood, flesh and fat. Both these are incurable.

39. Aśvitra with plenty of hair not turned white, not contiguous and of recent origin, can be cured, if it is not caused by scalds or burns. Other types are to be abandoned as incurable.

40. A Kilāsa (Psoriasis) in the private parts, lips or on the palms, even of recent origin has to be avoided as incurable by persons wishing for success.

41. All diseases are transmitted from person to person by touching, taking food together, sexual intercourse, sharing the same bed or seat or by using the same clothes, garlands, unguents, etc.

CHAPTER ONE HUNDRED AND SIXTYFIVE

Diseases

Dhanvantari said :

1. Kṛmis (bodily germs) are of two types: the external and the internal. The external ones are of four types being caused by 1) faecal matter 2) mucous matter 3) blood and 4) other discharges of waste matter.

2. The external parasites born of the waste matter are enumerated as twenty in number. They are of the shape and colour of gingelly seeds and take refuge in hair or garments.

3. Though they are very minute they have many feet. Two principal classes of these named Yūkās (lice) and Likṣās (nits or ticks) bring about Koṭha (Urticaria) and Kaṇḍugaṇḍa (itches in the neck).

4-6. The internal parasites cause kuṣṭha. The external ones are caused by deranged kapha by the intake of sweet rice, jaggery, milk, curds, fish and newly harvested grains. From the abdomen they spread all over the body. Some are potshaped and some are like earthworms. Some are like the germinating seeds of grains, some slender and long, some are like specks, some are white and some are copper coloured. They are seven with seven names.

7-8. They are Antrādas (gnawers of entrails), Udarāveṣṭas (permeating the abdomen) Hṛdayādas (eating the heart), Mahāgudas (rectal mousters) Cyurus (falling off), Darbhakusumas (like darbha flowers) and Sugandhas (sweet smelling). They cause disquietude, water discharge from mouth, indigestion, nonrelish for food, epilepsy, vomiting, fever, tympanites, emaciation, sneezing and Catarrh.

9. There are some parasites in the blood and the blood vessels. They have no feet. They are copper coloured and circular in shape. Some of them are so minute that they can not be seen by the naked eye.

10. They are Keśādas (eating the hair) Romavidhvaṁsas (destroyers of hair) Romadvīpas (hair-islanded), Udumbaras, Aurasas and Mātṛs and these produce Kuṣṭha quickly.

11-12. Some parasites grow in the abdomen originating from faeces. They take a downward course. But when they are fully grown they proceed towards the abdomen. Then they produce a foul faecal smell in the mouth, breath and eructations. They are like big circles, some small, some stout, tawny, yellow, white or black in colour.

13-14. They are five in number named Kakeruka, Makeruka, Sausurada, Saśūla, and Leliha. They produce loose motions, acute pain, obstruction to excretion, emaciation, pallor, horripilation, impaired digestion and itching sensation in the anus by travelling in wrong directions.

CHAPTER ONE HUNDRED AND SIXTYSIX

Diseases

Dhanvantari said :

1-3. O Suśruta, I shall explain the pathology of Vātavyādhi (disease of the nervous system). If we are to speak of disorders the reason thereof is an obstruction to the natural flow (of the wind). The Vāyu element in the body is actually the Viśvakarmā (the architect of the universe), Viśvātmā (the soul of the universe) Viśvarūpa (having all forms), Prajāpati (lord of the created beings) Sraṣṭṛ (creator) Dhātṛ (the originator) Vibhu (all pervading) Viṣṇu, Saṁhartṛ (Annihilator) Mṛtyu (Death) Antaka (Finisher). Hence one should endeavour to preserve it in equilibrium.

4. A correct knowledge of Prākṛta (physiological) and Vaikṛta (pathological) aspects with the diverse actions of the morbid principles in combination and severally must be had.

5. The vaikrta actions are of five types. They are being mentioned along with their pathology and characteristic signs.

6. Vāyu is aggravated by the defiling factors of the seven fundamental elements of the system. Such things shall not be used by the patient too much. The Vāyu obstructs the fourfold passages (ducts or vessels).

7-8. When these vessels are filled with the aggravated doṣas the vitiated Vāyu produces acute pain, tympanites, rumbling sound in the intestines, suppression of the stools, loss of voice, impaired sight, grip in the buttocks and the back and other similar grave disorders.

9. The Vātavyādhi originating from the abdomen gives rise to vomiting, dyspnea, cough, cholera, itching sensation and other ailments above the navel whose main characteristics will be some sort of obstruction.

10. The Vāyu located in the ducts produces ill functioning of the sense organs, roughness of the skin, eruptions, acute pain, dyspnea and symptoms of poisoning with discoloration.

11. The Vāyu located inside the entrails produces obstruction to evacuation, nonrelish for food leanness and vertigo knotty eruptions in the flesh and fat and roughness of the skin too are caused.

12. The body appears to be heavy and pains as if hit with the fist or a baton. The Vāyu located in the bone produces severe pain in the thighs and bones.

13. The Vāyu located in the marrow produces loss of firmness in the bones, loss of sleep and severe pain. A rapid emission of the semen and other disorders too are produced.

14. If the Vāyu is located in the semen or in the womb (in women) involuntary emission of semen or miscarriage is produced. The Vāyu located in the head produces scantness of faeces. The Vāyu located in any place produces intumescence when aggravated, which cannot be cured.

15. If the Vāyu is located in the joints the abdomen to the touch feels like a leatherbag full of water and located atrophy is

generated. If it is located in different limbs a piercing pain, a breaking ache, throbbing, etc. in the limbs are felt.

16. Numbness, convulsive jerky movements, somnolence, breaking and shaking of joints are observed. When the excited Vāyu permeates the nerves it produces constant convulsive movements of the limbs. The ailment is called Ākṣepaṇa (convulsion).

17. The enraged Vāyu when obstructed from below courses upwards and presses against the heart. It then generates pain in the head and the temples.

18. It may toss up the whole body and bend down his cheek bone. The victim then breathes hard closing both the eyes.

19-20. He may coo like a dove without any attachment to anything (unconscious). This ailment is called Apatantraka. When the enraged Vāyu moves on to the heart and the left nostril he may feel some slight relief and there may be relapse immediately. This and similar ailment caused by a violent flow cannot be cured easily.

21. When the body is severed by the wind the patient perspires and his body becomes rigid. When the body is stretched again the wind pervades the whole body.

22-23. The Vāyu lodged inside the vital constituents of the body produces the obstruction to the locomotion of the eyes, yawning, loss of energy and pain in the teeth: excruciating pain in the sides, grips in the cheek, back and the head, external curvature of the body at the back and a sense of heaviness in the heart and the head.

24. The chest is thrown up or the shoulders droop down. There is discoloration in the teeth and face. There is no perspiration in the limbs.

25-26. The external curvature and rigidity of the cheekbone indicate that the man is a victim of Vātavyādhi. The morbid principles after permeating the faeces urine and blood and being incited by the Vāyu bend the whole body from head to foot. The victim standing with the pale body finds the wound and curvature increased.

27-28. In its impetuosity the patient does not get any relief due to the ailment of Ākṣepaṇa (convolusion). Scraping the tongue, intake of hot food, and opening the mouth beyond measure enrages the Vāyu located at the root of the cheek-bone which makes the mandible rigid thus causing the mouth to be permanently gaping or firmly closed.

29. The above ailment is called Hanustambha (rigidity of the mandible). Due to this the victim will find it very difficult to chaw or speak. The nerve carrying the faculty or force of speech becomes rigid and Vāyu benumbs the tongue.

30-31. This is called Jihvāstambha (Rigidity of the tongue). Due to this the patient becomes incompetent to eat, drink or speak. Carrying heavy loads on the head, boisterous laughter and loud talks, resting the head on uneven or rough pillows and chewing hard foodstuffs aggravates the Vāyu lodged in the upper regions of the body.

32-34. Loud laughter and sudden glancing to the sides makes the face permanently distorted. Then the power of speech becomes lower and the eyes become numbed and motionless. Gnashing of the teeth, aphonia, impaired hearing, blurring of vision, loss of the power of smell, loss of memory, fright, dyspnea, Niṣṭhīva (Ptyalism—frequent spitting) pricking pain in the sides, permanent closure of an eye, severe pain above the clavicle and hemiplegia are the disorders in the wake of Vātavyādhi.

35. This ailment is called Ardita (Facial Paralysis) by some and Ekāṅga (Hemiplegia) by others. The blood flowing in the Vessels, especially those that traverse the head are affected.

36-37. The nerves become rough and black and produce severe pain and a sort of hemicrania which is incurable. The Vāyu affects a part of the body with all the nerves there. It is called Pakṣāghāta (Partial paralysis). One half of the entire body becomes inoperative and insensible.

38. Some call this Ekāṅgaroga by the name Kakṣaruk. If the Vāyu affects the entire body there is obstruction and rigidity in all the limbs.

39. The Pakṣa ailment caused by deranged Vāyu alone is curable though difficult. In conjunction with other morbid principles it is incurable as it is aggravated and hence causes debility.

40. The Vāyu in combination with Kapha with its path obstructed by mucous secretions rigidifies the limbs causing the ailment Daṇḍā Patānaka which is incurable.

41. The Vāyu located at the root of the shoulder blades contracts all the veins in the locality and prevents the circulation of blood there. The Ailment of Avabāhuka is caused.

42. The Vāyu located in the fingers and palms affecting the sinews in the back arm renders the arms inoperative. This ailment is called Viśvācī.

43. When the Vāyu located in the hips draws up the sinews in the thighs, the victim becomes lame due to the paralysis of both the thighs. The ailment is called Khañja vāta.

44. The victim begins to totter when he starts walking and goes like a lame man. The joints seem to be very loose. The ailment is called Kalāyakhañja.

45-48. When one takes too hot or too cold watery or dry heavy and emulsive foodstuffs injudiciously, when one indulges in extremely fatiguing physical labour immediately after the meal or after digestion or keeps awake till very late in the night, the fat with deranged Kapha gets accumulated and attacks the other principles too. The Kapha gets stuffed about the thigh bones and numbs the locality. The bones of the thighs become loose. The complexion assumes a dull tawny colour; Fever, somnolence, non relish for food and lassitude are the disorders that arise. This is called Urustambha which some call Bāhya vāta.

49. A swelling in the middle of the knee caused by Vāyu in combination with contaminated blood is called Kroṣṭukaśīrṣa since it is like the head of a jackal. It is big and produces acute pain.

50. The Vāyu located in the heels causes an ailment called Vātakaṇṭaka. After exhaustion when one takes a false step severe pain is felt in that locality.

51. Vāyu located in the heels, toes, umbilicus and throat violently tosses the locality and grips at them. This ailment is called Gṛdhrasī (Sciatica).

52-53. When the foot becomes insensible and horri pilation is present, the ailment is called Pādaharṣa. It is caused by the deranged Vāyu and Kapha. Vāyu in combination with Pitta and contaminated blood causes burning sensation especially when one walks. It is called Pādadāha.

CHAPTER ONE HUNDRED AND SIXTYSEVEN

Diseases

Dhanvantari said:

1-2. O Suśruta, I shall tell you about the pathology of Vātarakta. Incompatible articles of fare, injudicious eating, anger, sleeping during the day, keeping awake at night, etc. cause the derangement of Vāyu and blood, generally in persons of easy going temperament and delicate body and those who are extremely obese and indulge in injudicious eating and conduct.

3. When the blood in the body is contaminated by a blow or due to the impurities injected by cool things or Vāyu generating stuffs the aggravated Vāyu proceeds along a deviating path.

4. When obstructed by the blood of such a nature the Vāyu of the first variety (Prāṇa) vitiates the same blood and then produces foul wind through the anus or coos like a cuckoo and generates Vātarakta.

5. When piles grow due to the vitiated blood the Vāyu courses through the body and generates vomiting and other symptoms slowly.

6-7. An affection like Kuṣṭha or Arbuda (carbuncle, swelling) shall then rise. There may be itching sensation, throbbing, excruciating pain, breaking pain, heaviness and insensibility in knees, calves, thighs, hips, shoulders, hands, feet and the joints of limbs: The symptoms occur and vanish, recur again sometimes.

8. Sometimes it starts from the root of the feet and sometimes from the hands and getting aggravated courses through the whole body like the poison of a mouse.

9. The Vāyu (and the vitiated blood) located in the skin and the flesh rises up and after some time becomes grave and acute and attacks all the fundamental constituents of the body (Dhātus).

10. The Vāyu located at the bones and marrow produces intumescence, knotty eruptions and suppurations. The Vāyu located in the narrow constricted places like hips produces copper coloured or tawny or red colour in the skin.

11. Sometimes the Vāyu courses in the body as if piercing everything within. Sometimes it courses like a whirlwind in circuits and makes the body lame or limping.

12. When Vāyu is prevalent the pricking pain, throbbing and breaking pain is very much. The swelling is hard and rough and black in colour or tawny. Sometimes it increases. Sometimes it subsides.

13. Constriction of the nerves and junctions of the fingers, gripping pain tn the limbs, excruciating pain; abhorrence of chillness, non contiguity; rigidity, shivering and insensibility (in limbs).

14. The Vāyu located with blood produces tumour giving great pain and a piercing achu. It is copper coloured. It gives a very peculiar irritating sensation. Whether glossy or rough it never subsides. It is as it were like a bowl full of mucous substance.

15. When Pitta too is aggravated the following symptoms are observed:—A burning sensation, swooning, perspiration, epileptic fits, inebriety, thirst, not yielding to the touch, painful discharge, drying up, suppuration and excessive heat.

16. When Kapha is aggravated the following symptoms are observed:—rigidity, heaviness, insensibility, glossiness, (numbness), chillness, itchness and slight pain: When two or more doṣas combine the symptoms of either occur.

17. Ailments caused by a single morbid principle can be cured; those caused by two doṣas can be alleviated by medication though not cured completely A Rakta pitta caused by three doṣas is terrible and should be avoided.

18. The Vāyu located in the extremities and joints attacks the blood and both permeating each other generate excruciating pain and take away the life.

19-20. Vāyu is of five types. Prāṇa (one of them) is hard and rough. Hence, when it gets aggravated by injudicious conduct (of the patient), fasting, excessive eating, hurt from a blow, suppression or rapid egress of the natural urges, it produces affliction to the eyes, etc, and catarrh, burning sensation, thirst, cough, dyspnea etc. follow.

21. Prāṇa located on the top of the clavicle produces constriction of the throat, loose motions, vomiting, nonrelish for food, flowing of the nose and such diseases as goitre (Galagaṇḍa), etc.

22. Vyāna (second type of Vāyu) becomes vitiated and aggravated by too much of walking, bathing, playing, sexual exercises, coarse and incompatible (foodstuffs) fright, delight, sorrow, etc.

23. It then impairs manliness, enthusiasm and strength, grief, confusion in the mind, fever, piercing pain all over the body, horripilation, insensibility (somnolence), etc.

24. (Vyāna produces) Kuṣṭha, Erysipelas, exhaustion of the whole body and other disorders. Samāna (Third type of Vāyu) is defiled by incompatible and undigested foodstuffs that are too cold and of assorted nature.

25. It is defiled by untimely sleeping and waking up and produces pain, enlargement of the spleen, diarrhoea and diseases of liver and lungs.

26-27. Apāna (fourth type of Vāyu) is aggravated by the intake of coarse and heavy cooked rice, forcible blow, suppression of natural urges, too much of travelling, getting up and going round, etc. and produces disorders int he digestive organs and their seats, defects in urine and semen, piles, prolapse in the rectum and other places.

28 29. Due to lassitude, rigidity and heaviness, the Sāma (undigested mucous matter) pervades all the limbs. Due to its glossiness the disorders are lethargy, chillness, swelling and impaired digestion. The itching sensation is due to the loss of roughness and similar palliative measures. The Nirāma (free from mucous) shall be known by the opposites of Tandrā (lassitude), etc.

30. They mention many enveloping factors for the Vāyu. If it is enveloped by pitta and its symptoms, the disorders

are:—Burning sensation, thirst, pain, vertigo, darkness of vision and desire for pungent, hot, acid, saline, parchifying food and cool things.

31. If it is enveloped by Kapha too much of yearning and craving is evinced for fasting, labour, hard and coarse things and hotness. Chillness and heaviness are felt. Pain is experienced. Butter and milk are desired much. Pungent things are liked.

32. If Vāyu is enveloped by Kapha, the disorders are pressure felt on limbs, disquietude, heaviness and non relish for food. If Vāyu is enveloped by blood acute pain and burning sensation in the skin and flesh is experienced.

33. A red intumescence is found to occur with ringlike grooves all round. The swelling is hard with flesh. Disquietude and eruptions are also observed.

34. If the Vāyu is enveloped by fat it is called Āḍhyavāta. The swelling produced by it is incurable. It is either shifting or fixed; soft to the touch and pleasing to the eyes.

35. If it is covered it feels hot to the touch; it is cool to the touch when not covered. If the Vāyu is enveloped by Majjā (marrow) the swelling grows irregularly with surrounding eruptions. The patient feels pleasure in rubbing it with the hand otherwise it is painful.

36. When the Vāyu is enveloped by Semen, there is no rapidity or force in the swelling. When what is taken in is digested there is surely some relief.

37. If the Vāyu is enveloped by urine, urination takes place with the distension of the urinary bladder. If the Vāyu is enveloped by pores there is constriction and it splits the place of its seat.

38. The patient falls down with an attack of fever and the food taken is assimilated. The defiled semen further afflicted by food is discharged slowly.

39. If the Vāyu is enveloped by all the dhātus (seven fundamental constituents of the body) there is pain in the buttocks, thigh joints and the back. When the Vāyu courses in the opposite direction the heart is afflicted.

40. When the Prāṇa is enveloped by Pitta the disorders are vertigo, fainting pain and burning sensation. When Vyāna

is enveloped all round by Pitta the disorders are pain, lassitude aphome and burning sensation.

41. When Samāna is enveloped by Pitta the disorders are exhaustion, obstruction to the activities of the limbs, distress of mind with pain, loss of heat, perspiration, disinclination (towards everything) and thirst.

42. When Apāna is enveloped by Pitta the disorders are burning sensation, yellow colour in the faecal matter, increase of Rajas (quality of passion, etc.), heat, and urination with distension.

43. When Prāṇa is enveloped by Kapha the disorders are (rumbling) sound, obstruction to the ducts, ptyalism (excessive salivation), perspiration and difficulty in inhaling and exhaling.

44. When Udāna is enveloped by Kapha the disorders are heaviness of limbs, non-relish for food, aphasia (loss of speech) and aphonia (loss of Voice). When Vyāna is enveloped by Kapha the disorders are loss of strength and colour and constriction of bones in the joints.

45. When Samāna is enveloped by Kapha the disorders are heaviness of limbs, obesity, loss of awareness of many functions, non perspiration and impaired digestion.

46. If Apāna is enveloped by Kapha the disorders are mucous discharges along with urine and faeces. Thus Vātarakta ailments are of twenty two types.

47. Each of the five types of Vāyu can be enveloped by the other four. Thus twenty different enveloping factors are obtained.

48. When Apāna is enveloped by Prāṇa the disorders are disquietude, dyspnea, cold, headache, palpitation of the heart and dryness of the mouth.

49. When Prāṇa is enveloped by Udāna, debility is the result. All the other Āvaraṇas (enveloping factors) must be carefully observed by the physician and understood.

50. The increase and decrease of the activities of the Vāyus are based on their seats. Pitta can be the enveloping factor of all the five (Prāṇa, etc).

51. When Pitta and other doṣas are in combination,

their seat is along with the Prāṇa and others in combination. There are many such combinations of Pitta etc.

52. (The physician) shall observe them attentively from the symptoms shown. Their buying together is gradual. Even the firm ones recur again and again.

53. Life and longevity depend on the Prāṇa and strength depends on Udāna. If the two are afflicted there is loss of life and strength.

54. If the Vāyus with their enveloping factors, or their dislodgement from their seats are understood then even incurable ailments can with effort be made harmless.

55. By neglecting the Vāyus when enveloped these disorders occur:—Abscesses, enlarged spleen, palpitation of the heart, tumours, impaired digestion, etc.

56. O Suśruta, the pathology of the different ailments as narrated by the sage Ātreya has been explained by me to distinguish the different ailments and to know the means of increasing the longevity of men.

57. Thus diagnosing the different ailments one should proceed ahead with the treatment.

Triphalā[1] (Three kinds of myrobalan) is the panacea for all ailments when used in conjunction with honey, ghee and jaggery.

58. Triphalā used in conjunction with Vyoṣa,[2] Śatāvarī[3] Guḍūcī[4], Agniviḍaṅga[5] removes all sickness.

59-60. Śatāvarī, Guḍucī, Agni[6] Śuṇṭhī[7], Mūṣalikā[8],

1. Three fruits, viz., Terminalia Chebula. T. Bellerika and Emblica Officinalis.

2. Combination of Zingiber officinale, Piper longum, P. nigrum.

3. Asparagus racemosus.

4. Cocculus cordifolius.

5. Identity not clear.

6. Perhaps citraka=plumbago zeylanica or P. rosea. (*GVDB*, pp. 4, 156).

7. Zingiber officinale.

8. A species of chlorophytum or curcicligo orchioides (*GVDB*, pp. 312, 178).

Balā[1], Pūnarnava[2], Bṛhatī[3] Nirguṇḍī[4] Nimbapatra[5] Bhṛṅgarāja[6], Āmalaka[7], and Vāsaka[8] shall be soaked in Vāsaka juice along with Triphalā and purified seven times or once.

61. The above medicine can be used in powder form, or in pills or in the form of Vaṭikās (tablets) or prepared in ghee or squeezed into oil or in decoction. The same removes every illness especially emaciation. The dosage is one pala, or half a pala, one Karṣa or half a Karṣa.

CHAPTER ONE HUNDRED AND SIXTYEIGHT*

Diseases

Dhanvantari said:

1. O Suśruta, I shall succinctly explain the recipes of medicinal compounds removing all ailments for the sake of longevity of all living beings.

2-3. By the intake of astringent, pungent, bitter, acid or parchifying foodstuffs, anxiety, inordinate sexual intercourse, physical fatigue, fright, grief, keeping awake at night, loud talking, carrying heavy loads, undue exertions and pulling hard, Vāyu gets aggravated during the rainy season, when the food is digested or at the close of the day.

4-5. By the intake of hot acid, saline, alkaline and pungent foodstuffs, by taking food before perfect digestion,

1. Crataeva Rexburghii.
2. Boerhavia Procumbens
3. Solanum indicum.
4. Vitex negundo.
5. Leaf of Azadirachota Indica.
6. Eclipta prostrata or E. Erecta.
7. Emblica officianalis.
8. Lippia Nodiflora.

*The chapter describes the three humours, their disruption as the cause of diseases, the seven ingredients of the body, the three humours with their characteristics.

exposure to sunshine, warmth of fire, drinking of spirituous liquors and anger, Pitta gets aggravated. When the food is in the process of digestion, in the midday, after the rainy season, in summer and at midnight.

6-7. By the intake of sweet, acid, saline, fatty, heavy and very cold articles of food, by taking in newly harvested rice, flesh of animals living in marshy places and lubricious stuffs, want of sufficient exercise, sleep during the day, and luxurious easy going habits, Kapha gets aggravated immediately after food, or at dusk or in the spring season.

8-9. The symptoms of aggravation of Vāyu are these:—Roughness of the body, contraction of limbs, aching pain, obstruction to the passage of waste matter, insensibility, horripilation, rigidity, emaciation, a dark brown complexion, looseness of limbs, increase in exertion, etc. Hence ailments in which these symptoms are seen are those produced by Vāyu aggravation.

10. Burning sensation, heat, wetness of feet, anger without reason, lustfulness, exhaustion, pungent and acid (eructation), foul smell in the sweat like that of a dead body, fainting, excessive thirst, vertig, yellow and green colour—these are the symptoms of Pitta affliction in men.

11-12. Glossiness of the body, sweet taste in the mouth, delayed execution of things, obstruction, paralysed numbness, satiation, amassedness, anasarca, chillness, heaviness, itching sensation, and overwhelming attack of sleep are the symptoms of Kapha aggravation. Ailments caused by two doṣas in combination must be known by the combination of symptoms.

13. A Sannipātaja ailment exhibits all the symptoms as it is caused by all the doṣas in combination. The body is the receptacle and base for all the doṣas, dhātus (fundamental constituents of the body) and waste matter.

14. Equilibrium of doṣas indicates normal health; if any of them increases or decreases it indicates sickness. Fat, blood, flesh, suet, bones, marrow and semen are the seven Dhātus.

15. Vāyu, Pitta, and Kapha are the three doṣas. Faeces, urine etc. are called Malas (Waste matter). Vāyu is cool, light, subtle, cause of loss of voice, strong and unsteady.

16. Pitta is acid, pungent, hot; unripeness, undigested-

ness is the cause of sickness. Kapha is sweet, saline, glossy, heavy and lubricious.

17. Vāyu is seated in rectum and buttocks; Pitta is located in the digestive cavity; Kapha is located in the abdomen, throat and joints of the cranium.

18. Things of pungent, bitter and stringent taste aggravate Vāyu; things pungent, acid and saline in taste aggravate Pitta; Things sweet, hot and saline aggravate Kapha.

19. These are administered in reverse order to quell the aggravated doṣas. Doṣas coming back to their normal seats quell the ailment and bring relief.

20. Sweet taste improves the power of vision and increases lymph secretions and the Dhātus. An acid taste at the end is relishing, appetising and digestant.

21. A bitter taste is appetising, curative of fever, remover of thirst, laxative and cause of emaciation. An astringent taste excites pitta, is scraping, rigidifier and absorbant.

22. A drug is good if it is the receptacle of tastes, potency and relieving after-effects. A drug consistent in taste and after-effects has all properties.

23. The poteney of a drug is twofold: Śīta (cooling) Uṣṇa (Heating). The Pāka or digestive transformation of the tastes is twofold sweet and pungent.

24. Physician, Medicine, Patient and plenty of nurses—these four are the important constituents in the process of treatment. Any deficiency in them renders the process unfruitful.

25. A physician shall start his work after thoroughly understanding the habitation, season, age (of the patient), digestive power, physical temperament, nature of his constitution, drug, physical strength and the ailment.

26. That country is called Sādhāraṇa (common or ordinary) which has both the characteristics [of Jāṅgala (hilly forest) and Anūpa (marshy lands)]. A patient is a Bāla (child) till the sixteenth year, till the seventieth year Madhya (middle aged) and Vṛddha (old) thereafter.

27. Kapha, Pitta and Vāyu respectively predominate in the three stages of life. All modes of treatment except those involving alkaline, surgical and fire operations are to be followed in a debilitated or aged person.

28. A lean person must be given Bṛṁhaṇa (treatment making one stout) and to a corpulent man the treatment is Karṣaṇam (reducing bulk). A body of medium structure should be maintained as it is. Thus three kinds of bodies shall be known.

29. The strength of a patient should be understood from his steadiness, exercises, and gaiety of mind. An enthusiastic adventuresome man does not show signs of decline or decay.

30. Drink and diet though opposed to his temperament yet giving him relief and pleasure are termed his Sātmya or second nature.

31. If the pregnant woman takes Kapha-generating foodstuffs the child will be Kapha prakṛti (Kapha-temperamented). The same is the case with Vāyu generating and Pitta generating foodstuffs. If a balanced diet is maintained the child shall be Samadhātu (having all fundamental constituents in proper proportion).

32. A Vāta temperamented person is lean, harsh and volatile. He has few hair and he prattles in dream.

33. A pitta-temperamented person is irritable, scholarly and perspiring too much. His hair turn prematurely grey. He dreams of fiery blazing things.

34. A Kapha temperamented person is of steady mind, subtle in speech and of gay disposition. He has glossy hair. In dreams he sees water and rocks.

35. If a person exhibits the traits peculiar to two or three doṣas he must be considered mixed-temperamented. The predominant traits will be those of the predominant doṣa.

36. The digestive power is sluggish, sharp, irregular or normal if Kapha or Pitta or Vāyu predominates or remains in equilibrium.

37. The normal one should be preserved; the irregular one is to be remedied by curbing Vāyu; the sharp one by antidotes to Pitta and the sluggish one by eliminating Kapha.

38. The root cause of all ailments is indigestion resulting in the annihilation of the gastric fire; Indigestion is of four types—Āma, Amla, Rasa and Viṣṭambha.

39. The Āma sort of indigestion causes cholera, sluggishness of the heart, etc. The antidote for this is the administration of an emetic with the washings of the drug Vacā[1] with salt.

40. Due to Amla (acidity) the disorders, non secretion of semen, vertigo, fainting fits and excessive thirst are observed. The remedy there, is drinking of unboiled cold water and inhaling chill air.

41. In the Rasa type of indigestion (affecting lymph secretion) the symptoms are breaking pain in the limbs, sluggishness of the head and repugnance for food. The remedy in this case is complete abstention from food and drink and sleep during the day.

42. The two symptoms of acute pain and enlarged spleen indicate the Viṣṭambha form of indigestion marked by suppression of faeces and urine. Diaphoretic measures and salt water for drinking are the antidote in this case.

43-44. The types of indigestion Āma, Amla, and Viṣṭambha are respectively caused by Kapha, Pitta and Vāyu. A sensible man (suffering from any of these) shall plaster his stomach with a paste of Hiṅgu,[2] Tryūṣaṇa[3] and Salt and take a nap in the day time. All sorts of indigestion will be dispelled. Hosts of illness result from unwholesome articles and hence one should forsake all unwholesome articles.

45. Hot water taken after honey is a good digestant. Milk is incompatible with bamboo shoots, curd and fish.

46. The big five root drugs (Mahat Pañcamūla) are Bilva,[4] Śoṇa[5], Gambhārī[6], Pāṭalā[7], and Gaṇikārikā[8]. They are appetising and they dispel excess of Kapha and Vāyu.

1. Acorus calamus.
2. Asfoetida.
3. Also called Trikaṭu. It is a combination of Black Pepper, long Pepper and dry Ginger.
4. Aegle Marmelos.
5. Bignonia indica.
6. Gmelina arborea.
7. Bignonia suaveolenffs
8. Premna spinosa.

47. The small Pañcamūla drugs are Śālaparṇī[1], Pṛśniparṇī[2], two types of Bṛhatī[3], and Gokṣura[4] and they dispel excess of Vāyu and Pitta. They are aphrodisiac in character.

48. Both these two groups together are called Daśamūla[5] drugs. They cure all fevers of Sannipātaja type. They are very good in cough, asthma, somnolence and pain in the sides.

49-50. Madicinal oils, ghees and pastes prepared with these are very good in Alakā ailments (Sannipātaja). Drugs with four times water shall be boiled and reduced to one-fourth. Add four times of butter or oil to this with equal quantity of milk. The Kalka or residue will be one fourth of the oil or butter. This medicated butter of good pāka (proper cooking) is a good clyster in troubles with urinary bladder. The hard kalka can be applied over the body and the soft dust can be used as an errhine.

51. The gross body and the sense organs must be well thought of. If they are in their proper function that is called normalcy of health. A person destined for longevity must be properly attended to.

52. A person whose activities of the sense organs are perverted hasten towards death's door. A person who hates the physician friends and elders and he who loves enemies too follows suit.

53. He whose heel bones, knees, forehead, jaw bones, cheek bones suffer from prolapsus, dies ere long.

54. Left eye sinking in the socket; dark tongue, deranged nose, black lips dislodged from their seats, and a face turned black—all these indicate death and hence those patients must be given up.

1. Desmodium Gangeticum or Hedysarum G.
2. Flemionitis cordifolia.
3. Solanum Indicum.
4. Tribulus Lanuginosus.
5. Ten roots.

CHAPTER ONE HUNDRED AND SIXTYNINE

Diseases

Dhanvantari said:

1. In order to distinguish between what is wholesome and what is not, I shall tell you the rules of proper food and drink. The red species of Śālī (paddy) dispels the excess of all the three doṣas. It removes thirst and fat.

2. Mahāśālī is a good aphrodisiac. Kalama dispels both Kapha and Pitta. The Gauraṣaṣṭika generally dispels the three doṣas and is heavy. It is Śīta in potency (cooling).

3. Śyāmāka is absorbant, parchifying and productive of Vāyu principle. It dispels Kapha and Pitta. Similar properties are observed in Priyaṅgu, Nīvāra and Koradūṣa species of food grains.

4. Yava (barley) taken frequently generates Vāyu, Śīta in potency and dispels Kapha and pitta. Godhūma (wheat) is an aphrodisiac and cooling in potency. It dispels Vāyu. It is sweet and heavy.

5. Mudga[1] pulse dispels excess of Kapha, Pitta and blood. It is astringent, sweet and light. Māṣa[2] (Black gram) is strengthening, aphrodisiac and heavy. It dispels Pitta and Kapha.

6. The Rājamāṣa[3] is not an aphrodisiac. It dispels excess of Kapha and Pitta and removes disorders due to Vāyu. Kulattha (Horse gram), dispels Kapha and Vāyu and removes the disorders of dyspnea, hiccough and enlarged spleen.

7. Makuṣṭhaka[4] dispels the fever due to Raktapitta, it is cooling in potency and astringent. Caṇaka (gram) generates Vāyu, dispels Kapha and Pitta, destroys manly virility. It is styptic.

8. Masūra[5] (lentil) is sweet, cooling in potency, astrin-

1. Phaseolus mungo.
2. Phaseolus radiatus.
3. Dolichos catjang.
4. Phaseolus Acoritifolius ?
5. A variety of Lense.

gent and it dispels Kapha and Pitta. Kalāya[1] too has all these properties. It generates Vāyu excessively.

9. Āḍhakī[2] dispels Kapha and Pitta and is conducive to the generation of semen. Atasī[3] is Pitta Producing and Siddhārtha[4] dispels Kapha and Vāyu.

10. Tila[5] (gingelly seed) is alkaline, sweet, oily, strengthening, heat producing and pitta generating. The different minor seeds destroy strength, parchify and are cooling in potency.

11-12. Citraka[6], Iṅgudi[7], Nālīka[8], Pippali[9], Madhu[10], Śigru[11], Cavyā[12], Caraṇa[13], Nirguṇḍi[14], Tarkārī[15], Kāśamardaka[16], and Bilva destroy Kapha and Pitta; remove germs and are light and appetising. Varṣābhū[17] and Mārkara[18] destroy Vāyu and Kapha and remove all defects and disorders.

13. Eraṇḍa[19] is bitter in taste. Kākamācī[20] destroys excess of the three doṣas. Cāṅgerī[21] removes Kapha and Vāta. Sarṣapa[22] (mustard) generates all doṣas.

14. Kausumbha[23] is similar to Sarṣapa; Rājikā[24] generates

1. Pisum arvense.
2. Cajanus indicus.
3. Linum alsitatissimum.
4. Perhaps white veriety of Brassica campestris. (*GVDB*, pp. 433, 426-7).
5. Sesamum indicum.
6. Plumbago Zeylamica or p. rosea.
7. Terminalia catappa.
8. Perhaps a species of Ipomoca (*GVDB*, pp. 223-4).
9. Piper longum.
10. Honey.
11. Moringu Pterygosperma
12. Perhaps Piper chaba (*GVDB*, p. 155).
13. Identity not clear.
14. Vitex negundo.
15. Sesbania aegyptiaca.
16. Identity not clear.
17. Boerhavia Procumbens.
18. Identity not clear. The name Mārkava is used for Bhṛṅgarāja.
19. Ricinus communis.
20. Solanum nigrum (*GVDB*, p. 86.)
21. Oxalis corniculata.
22. Brassica campestris.
23. Identity not clear.
24. Brassica juncea or B. nigra.

Vāyu and Pitta. Nāḍīca[1] destroys Kapha and Pitta. Cucu is sweet and cooling in potency.

15. Padmapatra (Lotus leaf) destroys doṣas. Tripuṭa[2] is extremely Vāyu-generating. Kakṣāra[3] destroys all doṣas. Vāstuka[4] is highly appealing.

16. Taṇḍulīya[5], Pālaṅkya[6] and others are anti-toxic. Raw Mūlaka[7] (radish) generates doṣas, but cooked in steam dispels Vāyu and Kapha.

17. Karkoṭaka[8], Vārtāka[9], Paṭolaka[10], and Kāravellaka[11] when cooked and eaten destroy all doṣas and are good for heart and throat.

18. Kūṣmāṇḍa[12] is diuretic, relishing and destroys all doṣas. It is highly efficacious in Kuṣṭha, urinary diseases, fever, dyspnea and asthma as well as the disorders due to the derangement of Pitta and Kapha.

19. Kaliṅga[13] and Alābu[14] destroy Pitta and produce Vāyu. Trapuṣa[15] and Irvāruka[16] generate Vāta and Kapha and ward off Pitta.

20. Vṛkṣāmla[17] destroys Kapha and Vāyu; Jambīra destroys Kapha and Vāyu, Dāḍima[18] (Pomegranate) is astringent and destroys Vāyu. Nāgaraṅgaphala[19] (orange) is heavy.

1. Identity not clear.
2. Perhaps Pisum arvense or Ladhyrus sativus (*GVDB* p. 194).
3. Identity not clear.
4. Chenopodium alloum.
5. Amaranthus spinosus.
6. Spinacia oleracca.
7. Raphanus sativus.
8. Momordica dioica.
9. Solanum melongena.
10. Trichosanthes dioica.
11. Momordica charantia.
12. Cucurbita pepo.
13. Flolarrhena antidysenterica (*GVDB*, p. 84).
14. Lagenaria siceraria.
15. Cucumis sativus.
16. Identity not clear. The name *Urvāruka* is used for cucumis melo.
17. Garcinia indica.
18. Punica granatum.
19. Citrus reticulata.

21. Kesara and Mātuluṅga[1] are appetising and destroy Kapha and Vāyu. Māṣa removes Vāyu and Pitta and destroys the glossiness of the skin, heat and disorders of Vāyu.

22. All varieties of Āmalaka are sweet, relishing and aphrodisia but produce Amla type of indigestion. Harītakī induces taste for food, is holy and nectarlike.

23. Lakuca[2] is sweet and generates all Doṣas; Vakula[3] destroys Kapha and Vāyu; Bījapūraka[4] is efficacious in enlarged spleen, dyspnea and asthma and removes the disorders due to Vāyu and Kapha.

24. Haritaki is a laxative; destroys Kapha and Vāyu as well as three doṣas. The fruit of Tintiḍī[5] is laxative, acid, and removes Vāyu and Kapha.

25. Kapittha (horse apple) is astringent and dispels doṣas; when ripe it is heavy and antitoxic; when unripe it produces Kapha and Pitta but ripe it increases Pitta.

26. Ripe Āmra (mango) generates Vāyu and produces flesh, semen and strength and heightens colour (of the skin). Jambū fruit destroys Vāyu, Kapha and Pitta and produces Viṣṭambha form of indigestion as it is astringent.

27. Tinduka[6] fruit destroys Kapha and Vāyu; Badara destroys Vāyu and Pitta. Bilva generates Vāyu and causes Viṣṭambha. Priyāla[7] dispels Vāyu.

28. Rājādana[8] fruit, banana, jack fruit and coconut generate semen and flesh. They are sweet, emolient and heavy.

29. Drākṣā (grapes) Madhuka and Kharjūra (dates) and Kumkuma[9] dispel disorders in blood and Vāyu. The ripe Māgadhī[10] is sweet and destroys Pitta and disorders due to dyspnea.

1. Citrus medica.
2. Artocarpus lakoocha.
3. Identity not clear.
4. See fn. 1.
5. Rhus parviflora.
6. Dispyros tomentosa.
7. Buchanania lanzan.
8. Perhaps Mimusops bexandra (*GVDB*, p. 336).
9. Crocus sativus
10. A synonym of *pippali*, *GVDB*, p. 305.

30-32. Ārdraka[1] is relishing, appetising aphrodisiac and Kapha-Vāyu-destroying. So also Śuṇṭhī, Marica, and Pippalī. Physicians say that pepper is non aphrodisiac. Hiṅga (Asafoetida) dispels enlarged spleen, pain and constipation and disorders of Vāyu and Kapha. Yavānī[2], Coriander and Cummin seeds destroy Vāyu and Kapha. Rock salt improves eyesight and destroys all doṣas. It is an aphrodisiac.

33. Sauvarcala (Sechal) salt is purgative, heating in potency and it dispels acute pain in the cardiac region. The Viḍa Salt is heating in potency, removes pain, dispels Vāyu and is sharp.

34. Romaka salt generates Vāyu, is sweet, heavy, liquefacient and relishing. Yavakṣāra (Nitrate of potash) is an appetiser and is efficacious in all disorders of the heart, throat and jaundice.

35. Sarjikṣāra (Barilla) is caustic, appetiser, sharp and tearing (used to make abscess burst). Nābhasa (Rainwater) dispels all doṣas and poison. It is light and relishing.

36. Nādeya (River water) is parchifying and generates Vāyu; The Sārasa water (of the lake) is sweet and light; the water of Vāpī (natural tank) dispels Vāyu and Kapha and that of Taḍāga (artificial tank) generates Vāyu.

37. The Nairjhara (fountain) water is relishing, sharp, light and dispels Kapha. It induces digestion. The well water is appetising and generates Pitta. The Audbhida (Artesian well) water dispels Pitta.

38. The water where sun's rays fall during the day and the moon's beams at night is free from all defects and is equal to rain water (sky-water).

39. Hot water dispels fever, bronchitis, corpulence, Vāyu and Kapha. Boiled and cooled water dispels three doṣas but kept overnight increases doṣas.

40. Cow's milk dispels Vāyu and Pitta and is emulsive, heavy and rejuvinating. Buffalo's milk is heavier than cow's milk, emulsive and impairs digestive fire.

41. The milk of a goat dispels blood dysentery, asthma,

1. Ginger.
2. The same as *yavāni*=Trachyspermum ammi. *GVDB*, p. 328.

dyspnea and Kapha. Women's (breast) milk improves eyesight, cures Rakta Pitta and is saline.

42. Curd generates Pitta and Kapha and dispels Vāyu and is an aphrodisiac. Churned sour cream dispels all doṣas and cleanses all vessels of the system.

43. Fresh butter dispels diarrhoea, piles, etc; Products of milk turned sour like Kilāṭa (the solid residue of sour milk) are heavy and cause Kuṣṭha.

44. Butter milk, according to the former writers, dispels the three doṣas and is very efficacious in diarrhoea, tumour, piles, jaundice, dysentery and enlarged spleen.

45. Ghī is an aphrodisiac and sweet. It dispels Vāyu, Pitta and Kapha. Cow's ghī improves intellect, eyesight and after medication and purification dispels doṣas. (Vāyu, Pitta and Kapha).

46. Medicated and purified ghī dispels loss of memory, epileptic fits, insanity, fainting and other disorders. The ghee prepared from the milk of goat and other animals has the same good properties as cow's milk. Goat's urine dispels Kapha and Vāyu, germs and poison.

47. Gingelly oil is extremely efficacious in jaundice, dropsy, cutaneous afflictions, piles, tumour, enlarged spleen and diabetes. It destroys Vāyu and Kapha and is conducive to the growth of hair and strengthening of the body.

48. Mustard oil dispels worms and jaundice, Vāyu and Kapha and disorders due to corpulence. The linseed oil affects the eyes but dispels Pitta and Vāyu.

49. The oil extracted from Akṣa (the seed of the bead of rosaries) dispels Kapha and Pitta. It is conducive to the growth of hair. It soothes the skin and blood vessels. Honey is exalted as the remover of the excess of the three doṣas as well as generator of Vāyu.

50. (Honey) dispels hiccough, dyspnea, worms, vomiting urinary disorders, poison and thirst. Sugarcane dispels Raktapitta. It is conducive to strength, growth of Kapha and is an aphrodisiac.

51. Molasses produce Pitta and are sharp. The spirituous extract of jaggery and unrefined sugar is light. Candy is an

aphrodisiac, emolient, sweet and is efficacious in disorders of blood, Pitta and Vāyu.

52. Jaggery dispels Vāyu and Pitta, and produces Kapha. Old treacle is very wholesome and is a purifier of blood.

53. Treacle sugar along with ghee is an aphrodisiac and dispels Rakta Pitta. All kinds of wine produce Pitta due to their acidity and dispel Kapha and Vāyu.

54. Sauvīraja wine is sharp and generates Rakta Pitta. Maṇḍa (gruel) made of fried rice is appetising and digestive. It is wholesome.

55-56. Peyā (gruel with plenty of water) is light diuretic and restores deranged Vāyu. Peyā with butter milk, pomegranate, Vyoṣā, jaggery, honey and Pippalī dispels cough, bronchitis and diarrhoea. Pāyasa (Milk pudding) produces Kapha and is conducive to strength. Kṛśara (rice, gingelly seeds and black gram cooked together) destroys Vāyu.

57-58. A soup of watery nature is an emolient. Taken lukewarm it is relishing and light. Soup with bulbous roots, radish and fruits well cooked with ghī or oil is heavy and rejuvinating. In lukewarm state it is light. Vegetables cooked in steam and well seasoned after squeezing out water are wholesome.

59. A Yūṣa (soup without salt) made of Dāḍima and Āmalaka generates gastric fire and dispels Vāyu and Pitta. A yūṣa prepared with redish dispels cough, breathing disorders, cold and Kapha.

60. A Yūṣa made with Yava, Kola and Kulattha dispels Vāyu and is beneficial to the voice. That prepared with Mudga and Āmalaka is astringent and des roys Kapha and Pitta.

61. Curd with jaggery dispels Vāyu. Saktu (flour of fried grain) is sharp and generates Vāyu. Śaṣkulī (Coiled fried Jalebī) fried in ghī is an aphrodisiac and generates gastric fire.

62. Foodstuffs with cooked meat are rejuvinating; cakes are heavy; things fried in oil impair eyesight; those cooked in water or steam are difficult to be digested.

63. Hot maṇḍakas (gruel) are wholesome, cooling in

potency and heavy. After food, water is to be taken. It is destructive of thirst and exhaustion.

64-65. A person careful about Anupāna shall be free from poison and illness. Poison resembling the neck of a peacock brings about discoloration. Even the smell, touch or taste of poison brings great anguish to those who swallow it. If it is smelt an ailment of the eyes which cannot be cured even by great physicians results. The characteristic symptoms of poisoning are shivering, yawning, etc.

CHAPTER ONE HUNDRED AND SEVENTY

Diseases

Dhanvantari said:

1. Fever is of eight types inasmuch as it is produced by the doṣas severally or in twos or in combination or by external casual factors. Water boiled with these drugs:—Musta[1], Parpaṭaka[2], Uśīra[3], Candana[4], Udīcya[5] and Nāgara[6] and then cooled should be given to the patient to quench his thirst and rise in temperature.

2. A decoction made of Nāgara, Devakāṣṭa[7], Dhanyāka[8] and the two Bṛhatīs should be given to a fever patient. It is digestive and dispels fever.

3. A Kaṣāya or astrigent decoction made of Āragvadha[9] Abhayā[10], Mustā, Riktā[11] and Granthika[12] is digestive and

1. Cyperus rotindus or C. scariosus.
2. Perhaps the Fumaria species. (*GVDB*, p. 239-40.
3. Vetiveria zizanioides.
4. Santalum alloum.
5. Identity not clear.
6. A synonym of *ārdraka*.
7. A synonym of *devadāru*=Cedrus deodara.
8. Coriandrum sativum.
9. Cassia fistula.
10. A synonym of *harītakī*.
11. Identity not clear.
12. A synonym of *pippalimūla*.

very efficacious in an Āmajvara (fever with mucous secretions) attended with colic.

4. Madhūkasāra, Sindhūttha[1], Vacā, Ūṣaṇa[2] and Kaṇa[3] must be taken in equal parts and ground into fine powder. This, mixed with water, is a good medicine to restore a person from an unconscious state.

5. A decoction made of Trvrt[4], Viśālā[5], Triphalā, Kaṭuka and Āragvadha along with Kṣāra (Alkali) is a good purgative. When drunk it dispels fever of all varieties.

6. A decoction made of Mahauṣadha[6], Amṛtā[7], Mustā, Candana, Uśīra and Dhānyaka taken with sugar and honey dispels Tṛtīyaka (Tertian) fever.

7. Strips of Apāmārga, Jaṭā tied round the waist with seven red threads on a Sunday cure the Tṛtīyaka fever.

8. If one performs Tarpaṇa with gingelly seeds to a sonless ascetic who has passed away in the nothern bank of the river Gaṅgā he will be cured of Aikāhika (intermittent) fever.

9. A decoction of Guḍūcī, Triphalā, Vāsaka, Ṛjvīkā[8] and Balā along with its rudiment cooked with ghee removes fever.

10. A decoction of Dhātrī[9], Śivā[10], Kaṇā and Vahni[11] dispels all sorts of fevers.

I shall now explain the various remedial measures for dysentery attended with fever.

11. A decoction prepared with Pṛśniparṇi[12], Balā, Bilva, Nāgara, Utpala, Dhanyāka, Pāṭhā[13], indrayava, Bhūnimba,

1. Identity not clear.
2. Any one of the *pañcakola* group of drugs. (*GVDB*, p. 55).
3. Identity not clear.
4. Operculina turpethum.
5. Trichosanthes bracteata.
6. A synonym of *śuṇṭhī*.
7. Either *guḍūcī* or *harītaki*.
8. Identity not clear.
9. A synonym of *āmalakī*.
10. Perhaps *harītakī* (*GVDB*, p. 400)
11. A synonym of *citraka*.
12. Uraria picta.
13. Cissampelos paricra.

Mustā, Parpaṭaka and Mahauṣadha cures dysentery with fever and mucous discharge.

12. A decoction with Nāgara, Ativiṣā[1], Mustā, Bhūnimba, Amṛta and Vatsaka[2] cures all kinds of fever and all sorts of dysentery.

13-14. Water boiled with Mustā, Parpaṭaka, Udīcya and Śṛṅgavera[3] can be given to an Atīsāra (dysentery) patient. Along with his food he must take Śālaparṇī[4], Pṛśniparṇī, Bṛhatī, Kaṇṭakārikā, Balā, Śvadaṁṣṭrā[5], Viśvādi[6], Pāṭhā, Nāgara and Dhānyaka. It is efficacious.

15. A decoction made of Viśva and the seed of mango fruit taken with unrefined sugar and honey is a cure for Atīsāra. Similarly, Kuṭaja bark with Kaṇā is also efficacious.

16. A decoction of Vatsaka, Ativiṣā, Tiśva, Kaṇā and Kanda is very efficacious in Atīsāra with blood, colic and mucous discharge.

17. Now the treatment of Grahaṇī (diarrhoea) is explained. Grahaṇī is the result of impaired digestion. Ghī with the decoction and residue of Citraka dispels diarrhoea. It is appetising and efficacious in disorders of enlarged spleen, tumour, Ascites, colic and piles.

18-19. Five kinds of salt viz. Sauvarcala, Saindhava, Viḍaṅga, Audbhida and Sāmudra (of sea water) shall be used here. Three ways of the treatment of piles are : surgical operations, cauterisation and alkaline remedies. Buttermilk freshly made is also efficacious in piles.

20. Guḍūcī with Pippalī, Abhayā fried in ghee or Tṛvṛt with Amlaloṇikā[7] can be taken for destroying piles.

21. A mixture of gingelly seeds with sugarcane juice dispels piles and Kuṣṭha. Pañcakola (five spices), Marica and Tryūṣaṇa improve digestion.

1. Aconitum heterophyllum.
2. A synonym of *kuṭaja*.
3. A synonym of *ārdraka*.
4. Desmodium gageticum.
5. A synonym of *Gokṣura*.
6. A synonym of Śuṇḍhī.
7. Identity not clear.

22. Harītakī taken frequently with Nāgara, jaggery or rocksalt is an appetiser.

23. A decoction of Triphalā, Amṛtā, Vāsā, Tiktā, Bhūnimba and Nimba taken in with honey quells jaundice and chlorosis.

24. A confection made of Tṛvṛt, Triphalā, Śyāmā and Pippalī with honey and sugar is very efficacious in Sannipātaja fevers and Haemoptysis.

25. As long as Vāsā is available and there is hope to live why should patients of Haemoptysis, Pthysis and cough despair.

26. A decoction of Āṭarūṣaka[1], Mṛdvīkā and pathyā taken with sugar and honey quells cough, bronchitis and haemoptysis.

27. The juice of Vāsā with candy and honey when drunk arrests bleeding. Milk drunk with the juice of Sallakī, Badarī, Jambū, Priyāla, Āmra, Arjuna[2] or Dhava[3] has styptic power.

28. A patient prostrated by chronic consumption becomes free from all ailments and shines like a Deva if he drinks ghī medicated and purified with the juice of Nirguṇḍi roots, fruits and leaves.

29. A confection made of Harītakī, Kaṇā, Śuṇṭhī and Marica with jaggery destroys cough and quells thirst and repugnance for food.

30. Ghī, a Prastha by volume cooked with thirty palas (weight) of each of the juices of Kaṇṭakāri and Guḍūcī quells cough and improves digestion.

31. A decoction of Kṛṣṇā[4], Dhātrī, Śitā and Śuṇṭhī taken with honey destroys hiccough. A patient of Asthma shall drink the juice of Bhārgī[5] and Viśvā with hot water.

32. A person suffering from hoarse voice shall keep in his mouth catechu soaked in oil or Pathyā with Pippalī or Pathyā with Nāgara.

1. A synonym of *vāsaka*,
2. Terminalis *arjjuna*.
3. Anogeissus talifolia.
4. A synonym of *pippali*.
5. Clerodondum serratum.

33. Powdered Viḍaṅga[1] and Triphalā powder taken with honey removes vomiting. A decoction of Āmra and Jambū can also be taken with Mākṣika (honey).

34. Triphalā is a cure for vertigo and epileptic fits when drunk with honey. It removes all sorts of vomiting and quenches thirst.

35. Pañcagavya drunk quells hysteria and disorders due to adverse planets. Kūṣmāṇḍaka juice with Yaṣṭika[2] also serves the same purpose.

36. Old ghī cooked with Brāhmī juice, Vacā, Kuṣṭha[3] and Śaṅkhapuṣpī[4] shall be taken in for quelling insanity and Grahāpsmāra.

37. Medicated Ghī cooked with Aśvagandhā[5] decoction and residue in milk four times as much is an aphrodisiac. It increases flesh and quells sterility.

38. A decoction of cchinnā with the powder of Nīlī[6] and Muṇḍīrikā with honey and ghee when drunk, quells Vātarakta of the worst type.

39. Five Harītakīs taken with jaggery quell Kuṣṭha, piles and disorders due to Vāyu. The juice of Guḍūcī, its powder, decoction or its residue too has the same power.

40. Ghī cooked with milk and the decoction of Kālā and Guḍūcī and their residue quell Vātarakta, Kuṣṭha and Vraṇas (Abrasions).

41. Triphalā taken with Guggulu removes Vātarakta and epileptic fits. Guggulu taken with cow's urine removes Urustambha (paralysis of the thighs).

42-43. A decoction of Śuṇṭhī and Gokṣuraka removes disorders and pains due to Sāma Vāta. A decoction of Daśamūla, Amṛtā, Eraṇḍa, Rāsnā[7], Nāgara and Dāru[8] taken with Marica (pepper) and jaggery removes great tumours. A con-

1. Embelia ribes.
2. A synonym of *madhuka*.
3. Saussurea lappa.
4. Convolvulus pluricaulis.
5. Withania somnifera.
6. Indigofera tinctoria.
7. Pluchea lanceolata.
8. A synonym of *devadāru*

fection made of them removes cough and quells thirst and repugnance for food.

44. Take thirty palas of the juice of each of Kaṇṭakāri and Guḍūcī and cook it with a prastha of ghī. It removes cough and pain in the heart. It is an appetiser.

45. The decoction of Kṛṣṇā, Dhātrī, Sitā and Śuṇṭhī with Marica and rock salt taken with castor oil removes even acute Sāma Vāta.

46. A decoction of Balā, Punarnavā, Eraṇḍa, two types of Bṛhatī and Gokṣura drunk with salt and asafoetida destroys Vāta Śūla (flatulent colic).

47. The boiled decoction of Triphalā, Nimba, Yaṣṭika, Kaṭuka and Āragvadha drunk with honey removes burning sensation and colic.

48. Triphalā water with Yaṣṭīka quells Pariṇāmārti (a variety of colic). Dross (Maṇḍūra) purified in cow's urine mixed with Triphalā powder and licked with honey and ghee removes colic arising from the three doṣas.

49. Two parts of Trivṛt, four parts of Kṛṣṇā and five parts of Harītakī mixed with equal quantity of jaggery and made into pills remove constipation in the bowels.

50. Powdered Harītakī, Yavakṣāra, Pippalī and Trivṛt taken with ghī remove Udāvrata (tympanites with constipation).

51. Trivṛt, Harītakī and Śyāmā soaked and purified in Snuhī[1] juice must be dried (in the sun) and formed into Vaṭikā (tablets). These Vaṭikās taken with cow's urine destroy Ānāha (constipation).

52. Tryūṣaṇa, Triphalā, Dhanya, Viḍaṅga, Cavya and Citraka boiled and made into Kalka (residue) shall be purified with ghi. Taken in, this quells all disorders of Vāyu and enlarged spleen.

53. Roots of Nāgara taken with milk or Sauvarcala with Śivāghṛta (ghī from the milk of she-jackal, half its quantity drunk) quell palpitation of the heart.

54. Powdered Kaṇā, Pāṣāṇabheda[2], Elā and Śilājatuka

1. A species of Euphorbia. (*GVDB*, p. 459).
2. Bergenia ligulata.

drunk with the washings of rice and jaggery gives hope of life to a patient of strangury.

55. A decoction of Amṛtā, Nāgarī, Dhātrī, Vājigandhā and Trikaṇṭaka shall be drunk in all ailments of Vāyu, colic and strangury.

56. Yavakṣāra (carbonate of potash) with an equal quantity of sugar removes all kinds of strangury. Nidigdhika[1] juice with honey quells difficulty in passing urine.

57. Salt with Triphalā kalka (residue or paste) gives relief in suppression of urine. Powdered Karcūra also can be inserted into the urethra of the penis (to induce flow of urine).

58. A decoction of the root of Śigru drunk lukewarm quells heat (white urinating). Juice of Dhātrī and Niśā with honey removes all sorts of urinary ailments. The decoction of Triphalā, Dāru, Dārvī and Abja taken with honey removes urinary troubles.

59. A person wishing to be stout shall avoid keeping awake, sexual intercourse, physical exercise and worries. Obesity should be gradual.

60. A person accustomed to eat Yava and Śyāmāka and to drink sweet water will become stout. Hot boiled rice with maṇḍa (gruel) makes one lean.

61. Fried barley powder with honey, or a compound of Cavya, Jīraka, Vyoṣā, Hiṅgu, Sauvarcala and Amala is appetising and destructive of fat.

62. A prastha of ghī with equal quantity of milk shall be cooked with Kalka of Citraka and Utpala twice in quantity soaked in four times water and twice (cow's) urine. This is an antidote for all types of Ascites.

63-64. Starting with ten pieces of pippali and increasing it by ten every day the administration shall be continued for ten days. Then it shall be reduced by ten every day. Milk shall be taken along with it. The diet on these days shall be milk and Yaṣṭika. The same can be practised with Kṛṣṇa or Mudga. If a thousand pieces of Kṛṣṇa or other drugs are thus taken in all one shall be stout, live long and be free from dropsy and Ascites.

1. A synonym of *kaṇṭakaṃ*.

65. Ghī cooked and purified in the residue (Kalka) of the decoction of Punarnavā is a remedy for Anasarca. A patient of Anasarca, tumour, etc. shall take pippalī with milk in cow's urine or jaggery with equal quantity of Abhayā or Viśvā.

66. Castor oil taken in with a decoction of Balā with milk is a sure remedy for distension, hernia, colic, etc.

67. Pathyā residue mixed with Kṛṣṇā and Saindhava and the oil extracted from roasted castor seeds is a sure remedy of Hydrocela.

68. Scrofula is cured by the administration of the root of Nirguṇḍī as an errhine. Fomentations with the decoction of Snuhī and Gaṇḍīrikā[1] remove tumours.

69-70. Goitre can be cured by plastering with the paste of Hastikarṇa[2] and Palāśa. Plastering with the paste of Dhattūra, Eraṇḍa, Nirguṇḍī, Varṣābhu, Śigru and Sarṣapa dispels terrible long standing elephantiasis. Plastering with Śobhāñjanāka, Sindhūttha and Hiṅgu makes abscess subside.

71. Plastering with Śarapuṅkha[3] with honey heals all sorts of ulcers. Smearing with the paste of Nimba leaves makes ulcers non-septic.

72-73. A paste of Triphalā, Khadira, Dārvī and Nyagrodha cleanses ulcers and wounds. A physician shall wash and clean a fresh wound giving much pain with warm ghee with Yaṣṭi-Madhūka. An intelligent physician shall cure fresh wounds by casual factors by means of plastering.

74-76. The physician shall resort to cooling processes for subduing Pitta and the heat of the blood. A decoction of Bamboo bark, Eraṇḍa bark and Śvadaṁṣṭra bark drunk with honey, Hiṅgu and rock salt will let out the dislodged blood inside the viscera. For the sake of maintaining normal health rice shall be taken or Yavāgu (gruel) drunk with rock salt and along with the juice of Yava, Kola and Kulattha. The juice of Karañjariṣṭa and Nirguṇḍī destroys worms in the ulcers.

1. Perhaps Albizzia julibrissin or Dalbergia sericea (*GVD B*, p. 133).
2. Leea macrophylla (*GVDB*, p. 469).
3. Tephrosia purpurea.

77. Guggulu with Triphalā powder made into Vaṭakas (tablets) relieves pain, dispels constipation and purifies ulcers. They become non-septic.

78. A medicated oil cooked with the juice of Dūrvā, and Kampilla with the kalka of the bark of Dārvī is an important remedy in cases of ulcers.

CHAPTER ONE HUNDRED AND SEVENTYONE

Diseases

Dhanvantari said:

1. O Suśruta, please listen. I shall explain the remedial measures for fistula sinus and other disorders. A sinus should first be surgically operated and treatment proceeded with as in other wounds.

2. A fistula, sinus, colic etc. can be cured by the medicated ghee with equal quantities of Guggulu, Triphalā and Vyoṣa.

3. The oil extracted from the juice of Nirguṇḍī is a cure for sinuses and malignant ulcers. By drinking, smearing or administering as errhine this oil is efficacious in Pāmā Scabies.

4. Pills made of Guggulu, Triphalā and Kṛṣṇā in the proportion of 3:5:1 are wholesome for those who suffer from oldema, enlarged spleen, piles and fistula in ano.

5. In the cutting of veins in the middle of the penis the purity of the locality and in syphilis avoidance of suppuration should be maintained carefully—otherwise the penis may slough off.

6. A decoction of Paṭola, Nimba, Bhūnimba and Guḍūcī drunk with Guggulu and Khadira dispels syphilis.

7. Charred ashes of Triphalā burnt in an ironpan made into a paste with honey must be smeared on the sores in syphilis. The sores will heal instantaneously.

8. A medicated ghee cooked with decoction and residue of Triphalā, Nimba, Bhūnimba, Karañja, Khadira, etc. is highly efficacious in syphilis.

9-10. On locating the fracture of a bone it shall be first washed with cold water. Then it must be plastered with clay and bound with Darbha grass. The diet of the patient must be black gram meat, ghee, milk and a soup of gingelly seeds. Restorative and constructive diet and drink should be given to him.

11. Let the patient be on a diet of garlic, honey, fried grain water and sugar residue. Broken, cut or dislodged bones will be set right instantaneously.

12. Equal parts of Aśvattha, Triphalā and Vyoṣā should be added to Guggulu of the same quantity in the aggregate. Application of this heals fractures of bones and joints.

13-14. Emetics, purgatives and bleeding are to be employed in all forms of Kuṣṭha. A decoction of Vacā, Vāsā, Paṭolā and the barks of Nimba and Phali[1] should be drunk with honey as it is constructive and dispels Vāyu. The purgative is by means of Trivṛt, Dantī and Triphalā.

15. Oil medicated with Manaḥśilā and Marica dispels Kuṣṭha. In all forms of Kuṣṭha the above oil should be applied. The patient must take five kinds of myrobalans and rice with treacle.

16. Plastering with Karañja and Tagara soaked in cow's urine as well as rubbing with Karavīra after applying oil dispels Kuṣṭha.

17. A paste of Haridrā, Malaya, Rāsnā, Guḍūcī, Tagara Āragvadha and Karañja applied over the body removes all kinds of Kuṣṭhas.

18. A paste of Manaḥśila, Viḍaṅga, Vāgujī, Sarṣapa and Karañjī soaked in cow's urine removes Kuṣṭha and the body shines like the sun.

19. Plastering with Viḍaṅga, Aiḍavacā[2], Kuṣṭha, Niśā, Sindhūttha and Sarṣapa soaked in water and cow's urine removes ring worm and other cutaneous affections.

1. A synonym of *p.iyaṅgu*.
2. Perhaps *Airāvati*, said to be a synonym of *nāgabalā* (*GVDB*) p. 60).

20. Prapunnāṭaka[1] seeds, Dhātrī, Sarjarasa[2], and Snuhī soaked in Sauvīra urine can be applied as an unguent in ring worm.

21. Āragvadha leaves are to be ground into paste with Āranāla. This removes ring worm, Kiṭṭima, Kuṣṭha and Psoriasis.

22. Vāgujī taken hot with milk dispels Kuṣṭha. Gingelly seeds, ghī, Triphalā, honey, Vyoṣā, Bhallāta and sugar taken in equal parts act as aphrodisiac. They are conducive to increase brain power and dispel Kuṣṭha of persons who err due to lust.

23. Powdered Viḍaṅga, Triphalā and Kṛṣṇā with honey will be a good leha (lambative) in these ailments:—Kuṣṭha, worms, Diabetes, sinuses and fistula in ano.

24. He who eats for a month Niśā and Āmalaka with Abhayāriṣṭa will conquer Kuṣṭha thereafter. There is no doubt.

25. Ashes of Mango and Khadira sprouts burnt in a pot and pasted with Akṣa juice, Dhātrī juice, and honey is rejuvinating and dispels Kuṣṭha.

26. By drinking the decoction of Dhātrī and Khadira along with Vāgujī one can remove quickly leucoderma as white as conch and the moon. There is no doubt.

27. The patient will conquer leprosy by drinking the oil extracted from Bhallātaka within a month. Khadira water taken with other beverages conquers Kuṣṭha.

28-30. The medicated ghī cooked with Vāsā, Guḍūcī, Triphalā, Paṭola, Karañjaka, Nimba, Aśana[3] and Kṛṣṇa—Vetra decoction and residue dispels Kuṣṭha like Vajra the thunderbolt of Indra. The patient lives for a hundred years.

31. Juice of Dūrvā grass is to be cooked with four times of oil. Taking bath after smearing with this oil removes all skin diseases such as itches, Pāmā, Vicarcikā and Kacchū.

32. Oil duly cooked with the drugs, bark of Druma, Arka, Kuṣṭha, Lavaṇa, Citraka and Gaṇḍīrikā with cow's urine removes Kuṣṭha and all sorts of ulcers.

1. Perhaps *prapunnāṭa*, a synonym of *Cakramarda*.
2. A synonym of *devadhūpa*.
3. Identity not clear.

33. Dhātrī, Nimbaphala and Citraka soaked in cow's urine removes itches. A decoction of Vāsā, Amṛtā, Parpaṭikā, Nimba, Bhūnimba, Mārkara, Triphalā and Kulattha taken with honey cure Amlapitta (Acidity).

34. Triphalā, Paṭola and Tikta cooked into a decoction and drunk with sugar and Yaṣṭīmadhu is a sure remedy for fever, vomiting and acidity.

35. Ghī cooked duly with any of the drugs: Vāsā, Tikta, or Pippalī or Guḍa-kūṣmāṇḍa can be used to remove acidity.

36. Pippalī with honey dispels acidity. A confection made of Pathyā, Pippalī and jaggery dispels disorders of Kapha and impaired digestion.

37. Grind together Ajājī[1] and Dhanyākā and cook them well in a prastha of ghī. Duly taken, this removes disorders of Kapha and Pitta, non relish for food, impaired digestion and vomiting.

38. A decoction made of Pippalī, Amṛta, Bhūnimba, Vāsakāriṣṭa, Parpaṭa, and Khadirāriṣṭa removes fever with acute pain and carbuncle.

39. Ghī cooked with Triphalā juice and Trivṛtā shall be administered as a purgative to quell fever with erysipelas.

40. A decoction known as Aṣṭaka-kvātha (Eight drugged) is prepared with the eight drugs : Khadira the three myrobalans, Ariṣṭa, Paṭola, Amṛta and Vāsaka, and it conquers Romāntika (Measles) and Masūrikā (small pox).

41. The above decoction dispels Kuṣṭha, Visarpa (Erysipelas), Visphoṭa (carbuncle) and scratching sensation. Dusting the powder of Lasūna cures the skin disease called Maśaka.

42. In case Carmakīla begins to fade and decay and in Maśaka and Tilakālaka (dark spots and sabaceous growths) first scarify them with the surgical knife and cauterise with fire or alkalis without leaving even a bit.

43. A paste of Paṭola and Nīlī dispels the ailment Jalagardabha. Oil cooked with Guñjā fruits and juice of Bhṛṅgarāja removes itches and Kāpālakuṣṭha.

1. A synonym of *jīraka*.

44. The pulp of the seed of mango fruits cooked with Triphalā, Nīla, Bhṛṅgarājaka, Lauhacūrṇa and Kāñjika turns the hair deep black.

45. Take two prasthas of kṣīrī, Īśa and Arka leaves well squeezed into juice with a pala of Madhuka. Cook all well in a Kuḍava of oil. This is efficacious in preventing hair from turning grey due to old age.

46-47. In stomatitis, gargling with Triphalā is very effective. Chamber soot nitrate of potash, Pāṭhā, Vyoṣā and Rasāñjana too can be used for such gargles. Well powdered Lodhra, Triphalā and Citrak should be held in the mouth with honey for dispelling ailments of throat and teeth.

48. An astringent decoction named Pañcapallavaka is very efficacious in diseases of the mouth. They are the sprouts of Paṭola, Nimba, Jambīra, Āmra and Mālatī.

49. The juice of Laśuna, Ārdraka, Śigru, Pārulī, Mūlaka and Kadalī made lukewarm forms a good eardrop in ear troubles.

50. In Otorrhoea with acute pain and a humming sound, powdered rock salt dissolved in the juice of the leaves of Snuhi and made slightly warm is very effective.

51. In acute otitis, oil cooked in the juice of the leaves of Jātī is efficacious. In ear-ache Śuṇṭhī oil or mustard oil, slightly warm, shall be poured into the ears.

52. Milk cooked in Pañcamūlī juice, Citraka, Harītakī, Ghī and jaggery. This soup called Saḍaṅga (Six ingredients) Yūṣa quells catarrh.

53. Diseases of the eyes, diseases of the stomach, cold (catarrh), ulcers, and fever—these five ailments subside in five days by fasting.

54. The juice of Dhātrī poured into the eyes cures the inflammation in the area. A paste of Śigru, Dārvī, Rasāñjana and rocksālt in honey when applied over the eyes also serves the purpose.

55. Powdered Haridrā, Dāru, Sindhūttha, Rasāñjana and Gairika applied round the eyes removes eye troubles.

56. Abhayā fried in ghī and Triphalā soaked in water when applied around the eyes removes eye troubles. Śuṇṭhī, Nimbadala powdered with very little rock salt can be applied

to the eyes to remove small eruptions, itching sensations and pain.

57. One part of Abhayā with two parts of Akṣa and four parts of Amṛta well boiled can be used as decoction or pasted with honey and ghee can be used as a lambative (Avaleha) to cure eye pains.

58. Sticks or wicks made of Candana, Triphalā, Pūga[1] Palāśa and Tarumūlaka dissolved in water cure all types of Timira.

59. Marica ground to paste in curd, forms a good collyrium to cure night blindness. Ghī with milk well cooked with Triphalā decoction and residue when drunk at night fall will cure Timira quickly.

60-61. Pippalī, Triphalā, Kṣāra, Irondust, rocksalt and juice of Bhṛṅgarāja is called Guḍikāñjana. It removes piles, Timira, koṭha and eye ailments.

62-63. Vaṭikās or tablets made of Trikaṭu, Triphalā, Saindhava, Manaḥśila, Ketaka, Śaṅkhanābhi, Jātī flowers, Nimbaka, Rasāñjana, Bhṛṅgarāja, ghee, honey and milk well pasted together cure all sorts of eye ailments.

64. Burnt roots of Eraṇḍaka or the flower of Mucukundaka[2] ground with Kāñjika applied over the forehead cure headache.

65. Oil cooked with one pala each of Śatamūlī, Eraṇḍamūla, Cakrā and Vyāghrī can be used as errhine in curing disorders of Vāyu and Kapha as well as Timira and diseases of super clavicular regions.

66. Lavaṇa, Viśva and jaggery or Pippalī with rock salt is very effective in Bhujastambha (paralysis of the arms) and in all super clavicular afflictions.

67. In the migraine called Sūryāvarta the treatment is the application of errhines. Astringent decoction of Daśamūla drugs with ghee and rock salt can be used as an errhine also. It cures aching pain of the limbs as well as Sūryāvarta and headache.

68. A compound of Suvarcalā, Ajājī, Madhūka and

1. Areca catechu.
2. Pterospermum ocerifolium.

Nīlotpala stirred in curd and drunk with honey shall save a woman afflicted with leucorrhea of the Vātaja variety.

69-70. In the Pittaja type of leucorrhea the juice of Vāsaka, or that of Guḍūcī should be administered with Āmalakī bīja soaked in water and sweetened with honey and sugar. For the alleviation of Pāṇḍu type (jaundice) of leucorrhea a woman should take the juice of Āmalakī and honey or the juice of the root of Kārpāsa with the water with which rice has been washed.

71. A paste of Taṇḍulīyaka roots and Rasāñjana taken through the medium of water with which rice has been washed and honey cure all forms of leucorrhea. Roots of Kuśa grass pasted with water with which rice has been washed and drunk will cure all sorts of leucorrhea.

CHAPTER ONE HUNDRED AND SEVENTYTWO

Diseases

Dhanvantari said:

1. O Suśruta, I shall explain the mode of treatment for the peculiar disorders of women, please listen. In all Yoni-vyāpat (Vaginitis, etc.) types of disorders, measures to quell Vāyu are recommended.

2-3. Vacā, Upakuñcika[1], Jāti, Vāsaka, Rocksalt, Ajājī, Yavākṣāra, and Citraka shall be fried in ghī and then dissolved in water. Sugar shall be added. If this is taken the pain around the vagina, palpitation of the heart, piles and enlarged spleen get subdued.

4. By applying the paste of the leaves of Badarī the rupture of the Vagina can be cured. An application of the paste of Lodhra and Tumbīphala gives firmness to the muscles round the vagina.

1. Nigella salivā.

5. Ghī medicated with Pañcapallavas (five sprouts), Yaṣṭi, Arka and Mālatī flowers and cooked in sunshine is a sure remedy in leucorrhea. It removes foul smell from the vaginal passage.

6-7. Japā flowers with Kāñjika and a prastha of Jyotiṣmatīdala[1] pasted with Dūrvā shall be taken. Citraka with sugar and powdered Dhātrī, Añjana and Abhayā shall be drunk with water. This arrests excess of menstrual flow. Errhines or potions of Lakṣmaṇā with milk taken in enables conception.

8. Aśvagandhā taken with ghee and half an Āḍhaka of milk enables conception. Even a sterile woman taking ghee medicated with Vyoṣa and Kesara is sure to conceive.

9. Milk well boiled with the roots of Kuśa, Kāśa, Urubuka and Gokṣuraka taken with sugar by a pregnant woman removes her pain in the womb, uterus, etc.

10. Application of the pastes of Pāṭhā, Lāṅgalī, Apāmārgā or kuṭaja separately to the navel, lower abdomen and vagina of a woman in her labour ensures easy delivery.

11. The pain that a woman experiences after delivery, in the heart, head, urinary bladder, etc. is called Arkanda. Then she must take sour cream with Yavakṣāra dissolved in lukewarm water.

12. A decoction of Daśamūla drugs taken with ghee quells all post-parturient pains. Powdered Śālī rice taken with milk will increase her breast milk.

13. The juice of Vidārī flowers and the root of Kārpāsa also has the same property. A soup of Mudga is rejuvinating. It purifies the breast milk of a wet nurse.

14. A lambative (Avaleha) made of Kuṣṭha, Vacā, Abhayā, Brāhmī, Madhūka honey and ghee shall be given to the infant as it heightens the colour of the complexion, splendour and longevity.

15. If the breasts of the mother are deficient in milk, the child can be fed on goar's milk or cow's milk of the same quality. The swelling on the navel of the child subsides by means of fomentation with heated clay.

1. Celastrus paniculatus.

16. If the child has vomiting, cough and fever, a compound of Lauha, Mustaka and Ativisā shall be taken. If the child has dysentery Musta, Śuṇṭhī, Viṣā, Aruṇa and kuṭaja shall be taken.

17. A compound of Vyoṣa, Honey and Mātuluṅga removes hiccough and vomiting. Kuṣṭha, Indrayava, Siddhārtha, Niśā, and Dūrvā remove Kuṣṭha.

18. Bathing (the infant) with a decoction of Mahāmuṇḍitika[1] and Udīcya wards off the malignant influences of planets. It may be smeared with a paste of Saptacchada, Abhayā, Niśā and candana.

19. Amulets with Śaṅkha, Abjabīja, Rudrākṣa, Vacā, Lauha, etc. shall be worn. *Oṁ kaṁ taṁ gaṁ gam obeisance to Vainaeya. Oṁ Hoṁ Hāṁ Haḥ.* With this mantra Śānti (ceremonies for peace) shall be made for the sake of children. Mārjana and Balidāna also for the same purpose.

Oṁ Hrīṁ take Ye Your Bali from the Bālagraha (the planet afflicting the child) *but spare the child—Svāhā.*

20. The root of Śirīṣa drunk with the water with which rice is washed removes poison. The root of white Varṣābhū drunk with rice washings cures snake bite.

21. Taṇḍulīya, chamber soot, Niśā rock salt, curd, ghee and honey pasted together and drunk remove poison.

22. A decoction of the root of Aṅkoṭa drunk with ghee removes poison. That which dispels old age and sickness is a rejuvinating medicine.

23. Abhayā should be taken (in the six seasons) beginning with the rainy season along with rock salt, sugar, Śuṇṭhī, Kaṇā, honey and jaggery respectively by a person wishing for the benefits of the rejuvinating medicines.

24. At the end of fever (convalescing after fever) one shall take a single Abhayā or two Vibhītakas or four Dhātrīs in honey and ghī, one shall recover soon and live for a hundred years.

25-28. Aśvagandhā decoction drunk with milk and ghee dispels all body ailments. Juice of Maṇḍūkaparṇī, the nectar-like juice of Vidārī, Tila, Dhātrī and Bhṛṅgarāja taken in

1. Identity not clear.

enables one to live for a hundred years. A compound of Trikaṭu, Triphalā, Vahni, Guḍūcī, Śatāvarī, Viḍaṅga and oxide of iron taken with honey quells a number of diseases. Triphalā, Kaṇā, Śuṇṭhī, Guḍūcī, Śatāvarī, Viḍaṅga, Bhṛṅgarāja etc purified and regularly taken dispel all illness. Powdered Vidārī taken with honey and ghee increases sexual virility enabling one to conquer ten women.

29. Ghī should be cooked with Śatāvarī residue with ten times milk and taken in with honey, sugar and Pippalī. It is a good digestant.

30. Massage, application oil, errhine, emetics and purgatives are mentioned as Pañcakarma (five activities).

31. There are six seasons in the year beginning with Māgha (Dec-Jan.) and each consists of two months. In them one shall rseort to warning oneself with fire, or take honey, milk or milk products (as ordained).

32-34. In Śiśira and vasanta the company of women is recommended. But one shall not sleep during the day. In the rainy season too day sleep must be avoided. Moon beams in Śarat, Śāli, Mudga, Rain-water, boiled water—all these are wholesome. Oil extracted from Nimba, Atasī, Kusumbha Śigru, Sarṣapa, Jyotiṣmatī, Mūlaka, etc dispels worms, Kuṣṭha, diabetes, and headache due to deranged Vāyu and Kapha.

35-38. The drugs Dāḍima, Āmalakī, Kola, Karamarda, Priyālaka, Jambīra, Nāgaraṅga, Āmrātaka and Kapitthaka generate Pitta, subdue Vāyu and bring about derangement of Kapha. Jala, Jīmūtaka, Ikṣvāku, Kuṭaja, Kṛtabandhana and Dhāmārgava shall be used in all sorts of emetics. In the morning Madana, Indrayava and Vacā can be used as an emetic. A person has loose bowels due to Pitta, constipation due to Vāyu and Kapha and normal state when all the doṣas are in equilibrium. When Pitta is deranged Trivṛt is a good purgative.

39. Nāgara, Trivṛt and rocksalt taken with sugar and honey is a purgative. Harītakī and Viḍaṅga with cow's urine is also a purgative.

40. Oil extracted from Eraṇḍa and decoction of Triphalā twice in quantity can be used as purgative. In disorders due

to excessive action of Vâyu the patient must be fed before applying emetics.

41. For the application of enemate hollow bamboo sticks six, eight or twelve aṅgulas in leṅgth with the cavity as large as a Karkandhu fruit shall be used. The patient lies in a supine position.

42. In Nirūha (enema without oil) also this is the process. The dosage of clysters in the small one is half a pala, that in the middle is three palas and that in the full one is six palas.

43. One part of Pathya, two parts of Akṣa and four parts of Dhātrī purified with the juice of Śatāvarī, Amṛtā, Bhṛṅga, Sindhuvāra, etc., cures all sorts of pains.

CHAPTER ONE HUNDRED AND SEVENTYTHREE

Diseases

Dhanvantari said:

1-4. I shall enumerate the drugs coming under the classes Madhurādi, etc., which dispel various ailments. The chief drugs in Madhura (sweet) class are:—Śāli, Ṣaṣṭika, Godhūma (wheat), milk, ghi, Rasa (juice), honey, Majjā, Sṛṅgāṭaka, Kaśeru, Irvaru, Gokṣura Gambhīrī, lotus seed, grapes, dates Balā, coconut, sugarcane, Ātmaguptā, Vidārī, Priyālaka, Madhūka, Tāla and Kūṣmāṇḍa. Each of these is curative of epileptic fits and burning sensation. It soothes the sense organs. If taken in excess it produces worms and disorders of Kapha.

5. Drugs of Madhura type produce dyspnea, cough, sweet taste in the mouth, Aphonia, tumours, goitre, elephantiasis, Guḍalepa, etc.

6-7. Dāḍima, Āmalaka, Āmra, Kapittha, Karamardaka, Mātuluṅga, Āmrātaka, Badara, Tintiḍī fruit, Curd, Buttermilk Kāñjika, Lakuca, Amlavetasa and Loṇa are Amla varieties (Acid) of drugs. These with Śuṇṭhī are great digestant and appetising medicines.

8. These Amla drugs generate Vāyu and mucous secretions. They have aphrodisiac properties. They give a burning sensation. They soothe the system. If they are taken in excess they may sour the teeth.

9. (Excessive intake of Amla) causes looseness of limbs, burning sensation and coarseness in the voice, throat, mouth and heart. Excited by the gastric fire it makes wounds and ulcers suppurate.

10. The salts are Yavakṣāra, Sarjika, etc. The saline group acts as a laxative, liquefacient, digestant and generator of mucous secretions. Its potency permeates the whole system rapidly.

11. Exclusive and excessive intake of saline articles tends to obstruct the ducts of the system and produces itching sensation in the limbs, Koṭha, tumours and discoloration of the skin. It aggravates Raktavāta, Pittarakta, loss of manliness and pain in the sense organs.

12-13. Vyoṣa, Śigru, Mūlaka, Devadāru, Kuṣṭhaka, Laśuna, Valgujīphala, Musta, Guggulu, Lāṅgalī. These drugs form the Pungent group. They are appetising, purifying and anti-Kapha. They subdue Kuṣṭha and itching sensation. They remove corpulency, lassitude and worm infections. They reduce secretion of semen and fat. Exclusively and excessively taken they produce vertigo, burning sensation, etc.

14-17. Kṛtamāla, Karīra, Haridrā, Indrayava, sweet Kaṇṭaka, sweet Vetra, the two varieties of Bṛhatī, Śaṅkhinī, Guḍūcī, Dravantī, Trivṛt, Maṇḍūkaparṇī, Kāravellaka, Vārtāku Karavīraka. Vāsaka, Rohiṇī, Śaṅkhapuṣpī, Karkoṭī, Jayantikā, Jātī, Varuṇaka, Nimba, Jyotiṣmatī and Punarnavā form the bitter group of drugs. They set the secretions of serum, lymph, etc flow. They are relishing and appetising. They purify the ducts, remove fever and thirst, prevent fainting and reduce itching sensation.

18. Excessive intake of bitter drugs dries up faeces, urine and mucous secretions. It removes paralysis of the mandible, wry neck, convulsive pain, headache and ulcers.

19-20. Triphalā, Śallakī, Jambū, Āmrātaka, Vaṭa and kindred drugs, Tinduka, Vakula, Śāla, Pālaṁka, Mudga and Cillaka form the astringent group of drugs. They are absorbant.

They produce granulation in ulcers. They arrest and dry up mucous secretions. Exclusively and excessively taken they give rise to pain in the chest and generate parchedness of the mouth, fever, distension of the abdomen and paralysis of the mandible (wry mouth).

21-22. Haridrā, Kuṣṭha, Lavaṇa, Meṣaśṛṅgī, the two types of Balā, Kacchurā, Śallakī, Punarnavā, Śatāvarī, Agnimantha, Brahmadaṇḍī, Śvadaṁṣṭrā, Eraṇḍakā, Yava, Kola, Kulattha, etc., Karṣāśī, Daśamūla (ten drugs) : these drugs severally and in combination remove excess of Vāyu, Pitta and Kapha.

23-25. Śatāvarī, Vidārī, Bālaka, Uśīra, Candana, Dūrvā, Vaṭa, Pippalī, Badarī, Śallakī, Kadalī, Utpala, Padma, Udumbara, Paṭolaka, Haridrā, Guḍa, Kuṣṭhaka, Śatapuṣpī, Jātī, Vyoṣa, Āragvadha and Lāṅgalī are called Kapha-subduing group of drugs. Among lardaceous substances, ghī, oil, fat and marrow are the most excellent.

26-29. Those who like to improve intelligence, memory, understanding power and digestive faculty must take ghee regularly. In a Pitta patient ghee alone should be administered. In a Vāta patient it is administered with salt. In a patient of excess of Kapha it shall be administered with Vyoṣa and alkalis. Similarly, in the case of patients of glandular tumour, sinus, worms, obesity and deranged Kapha and Vāyu also. Oil is administered to the patients of hardened bowels for the sake of lightness and firmness. So also in persons whose fundamental constituents have been weakened by exposure to gusts of wind, sunshine and rain, bearing of burden, excessive sexual indulgence and physical exercises. In persons who have coarseness of the skin, pain, debility, quick digestion and constriction of vessels due to Vāyu (oil can be administered). Now (I shall explain) Yonikarma in chronic headache. The vein is first cauterised before enemata is used.

30. A full dose of clyster is one pala, three Akṣas in the middle one, and half a pala in the small one, in the case of oil, decoction and medication.

31. In Sneha Karmas (administering oil or ghee) hot water is given along with ghee but separately in the case

of oil. A pitta patient undergoing Sneha treatment shall drink over hot water if he feels thirsty.

32. A person who has been made Dīptāgni (of good digestive power) and varcasnigdha (motion-oily) must be given such treatment as ensures pacifying the deranged Vāyu. Persons suffering from coarseness must be given Sneha treatment and those of extreme glossiness, parchifying treatment.

33. In the case of disorders due to Vāyu and Kapha in combination or separately diaphoratic measures are to be used with a compound of Śyāmāka, Koradoṣa, Anna, buttermilk, Piṇyāka and fried grain flour. These measures are not for excessively corpulent, coarse, weak or swooning persons.

CHAPTER ONE HUNDRED AND SEVENTYFOUR

Diseases

Dhanvantari said:

1-3. O Suśruta, I shall enumerate some medicated ghees and oils quelling ailments. A prastha of ghee must be cooked with an Akṣa of each of the drugs Śaṅkhapuṣpī, Vacā Brāhmī, Somā, Brahma, Suvarcalā, Abhayā, Guḍūcī, Āṭarūṣaka and Vāguji, a prastha of the juice of Kaṇṭakāri and a prastha of milk. This is called Brāhmī ghṛta. It heightens memory, power and intellect.

4. Ghī is to be cooked with the following drugs in full or as many as are available:—Triphalā, Citraka, Balā, Nirguṇḍī, Nimba, Vāsaka, Punarnavā, Guḍūcī, Bṛhatī and Śatāvarī. This medicated ghī quells all ailments.

5-7. Half an Āḍhaka of oil is to be cooked in the decoction of a hundred balās along with the residue of Madhūka, Mañjiṣṭhā, Candana, Utpala, Padmaka, Sūkṣmailā, Pippalī, Kuṣṭha, Tvagelā, Aguru, Kesara, Aśvagandhā, Jīvanīya drugs and an Āḍhaka of milk. After this is well cooked in low fire it must be kept in a silver vessel. This oil is called Balyā and is a favourite of kings. It removes all disorders of Vāyu and all Dhātu derangements.

8-13. A prastha of Śatāvarī juice, a prastha of milk, a karṣa each of the drugs Śatapuṣpa, Devadāru, Māṁsī[1], Śaileyaka, Balā, Candana, Tagara, Kuṣṭha, Manaḥśilā and Jyotiṣmatī and a prastha of ghī or oil must be cooked well. This is called Nārāyaṇa Ghṛta or Taila (as the case may be). Viṣṇu Himself has given this recipe. It is highly efficacius in hunchbacks, dwarfs, lame persons, deaf persons, persons of defective limbs, lepers, those affected by Vāyu, those who are unable to satisfy their partners in sexual intercourse, those whose limbs have been weakened by old age and debility. Diseases affecting the skin, veins, sinews, etc. are quelled by this medicated oil or Ghṛta.

14-16. (Oil or ghee can be used in the following medical preparations) (1) Śatāvarī and Guḍūcī, (2) Citraka, Vyoṣa, Nimbaka and Nirguṇḍī, (3) Juice of Prasāraṇī and Kaṇṭakārī, (4) Varṣābhū and Bālā, (5) Vāsaka, Triphalā Brāhmika, Eraṇḍaka, Bhṛṅgarāja, Yaṣṭi, Muṣalī, Daśamūla, Khadira and Vaṭa. Tablets, confections or powders of the above drugs too are efficacious in all sorts of ailments.

17. The powders, etc, can be taken with ghee, honey, water, candy, jaggery etc., salt or pungent things. They cure all ailments.

18-19. An intelligent man shall cook oil with Citraka, Arka, Trivṛt, Yavānī, Hayamāraka, Sudhā, Bālā, Gaṇikā, Saptaparṇā, Suvarcikā and Jyotiṣmatī. This is called Niṣyandana Taila and is very efficacious in fistula in ano.

20. This efficacious oil, consisting of drugs, Citraka, etc suppresses all ailments. It purifies, enables tissues to grow and gives good colour to the skin.

21-23. Cook mustard oil in combination with Ajamoda Sindūra, Haritāla, the two sorts of Niśā, two Kṣāras, Phena, Ārdraka, Sarala, Indravāruṇī, Apāmārga, Kadala, Syandana and goat's urine in low fire and add cow's milk. This Ajamodādika taila is very effective in goitre.

1. Nardostachys jaṭāmāṁsi.

24. A skilful physician shall cook to the correct point, shall purify the ripened suppurating sores, and shall use this Taila for the growth of the tissues and smoothness of skin.

CHAPTER ONE HUNDRED AND SEVENTYFIVE

Diseases

Rudra said:

1. Thus Dhanvantari who is Viṣṇu Himself, explained to Suśruta and others. Hari then said to Hara explaining different medical preparations quelling ailments.

Hari said:

2. O Śaṅkara, in all fevers the first process is to make the patient fast. Then he must be kept in a place where gusts of wind do not blow. Only boiled water should be given for drinking.

3. All fevers are subdued by dry fomentations, O Īśvara. The decoction of Guḍūcī and Mustaka removes Vātajvara.

4-6. Listen, the decoction of Durālabha[1] removes pittajvara. A decoction of Śuṇṭhī, Parpaṭa, Musta, Bālaka, Uśīra, Candana, Ghī and Durālabha removes the fever of Kaphaja type. A decoction of Bālaka, Śuṇṭhī and Parpaṭa cures all types of fever. A decoction of Tiktaka, Eraṇḍa, Guḍūci Śuṇṭhī and Mustaka removes Pitta jvara. Now hear other types of medical compounds.

7-8. A decoction of Bālaka, Uśīra, Pāṭhā, Kaṇṭakārī and Mustaka and Suradāru removes fevers if cooked with Dhanyāka, Nimba and Musta and taken with honey. A decoction of Triphalā, Paṭolapatra and Guḍūcī removes all kinds of fever. This increases appetite and dispels disorders due to Vāyu.

9-11. Harītakī, Pippalī, Āmalī and Citraka powdered together is a remedy for fever. The above boiled with Dhanyāka, Uśīra and Parpaṭa or Āmalakī, Guḍūcī, and Candana

1. Jagonia cretica.

and taken with honey cures fever of every type. Now listen to the compounds removing Sannipātaja fever.

12. An astringent decoction of Haridrā, Nimba, Triphalā Mustaka and Devadāru with Kaṭurohiṇī[1], leaves of Paṭolā when drunk removes fever arising from the three doṣas.

13. Nāgabalā powder taken with powdered Kaṇṭakārī, Nāgarā, Guḍūcī and Puṣkara removes cough, asthma, etc.

14-15. In fever due to Kapha and Vāyu the thirsty patient should be given hot water. Water boiled with Viśva, Parpaṭaka, Uśīra, Musta and Candana and cooled later can be given to quell thirst, vomiting, fever and burning sensation. In Vātaja fever, a decoction of Bilva and other drugs of Pañcamūla group is very effective.

16. The root of Pippalī is appetising. In Vātajvara a decoction of Guḍūcī and Viśva gives great relief. A decoction of Parpaṭa and Nimba taken with honey removes Pitta jvara.

17. Even after remedial measures if the patient does not regain consciousness, his legs or forehead must be cauterised with an ironrod.

18. A purgative decoction of Tiktā, Pāṭā, Paṭolā, Viśālā, Triphalā and Trivṛt taken with milk removes all kinds of fever.

CHAPTER ONE HUNDRED AND SEVENTYSIX

Diseases

Lord said:

1. Within seven nights even a bald man will grow his hair if a plaster of burnt ashes of elephant's tusk with Rasāñjana and goat's milk is applied.

2. Oil cooked with the juice of Bhṛṅgarāja one fourth in volume and mixed with Guñjā powder enables the growth of hair.

3. Rub the bald head with Elā, Māṁsī, Kuṣṭha and Mura and plaster it with Gunjāphala. This will cure Candralupta (baldness).

1. Picrorhiza kurroa.

4. By plastering with powdered stones of mango fruit hair become fine. Application of Karañja, Āmalaka, Elā and Lākṣā cures Aruṇa (redness).

5. Application of plaster of the powdered pulp or mango stones gives the hair a thickness and silky gloss. They grow with firm roots very long and glossy. They never fall off.

6. Anointment of the head with a medicinal oil cooked with Viḍaṅga, Gandhapāṣāṇa and Manaḥśilā with four times cow's urine destroys lice and dandruff.

7. O Vṛṣabhadhvaja, (Śiva whose banner has the emblem of a bull) if fresh burnt conch ashes mixed with filings of lead are applied as a paste, hair turns darkblack and glossy.

8-9. Equal parts of Bhṛṅgarāja, iron-filings, Triphalā, Bījapūraka, Nīlī and Karavīra cooked with an equal quantity of jaggery constitute a powerful hairdye that can turn white hair black.

10. Pulps of the seeds of mango fruits Triphalā, Nīlī, Bhṛṇgarāja, burnt Lohacūrṇa and Kāñjika constitute a good hair dye turning it black.

11. Seeds of Cakramardaka, Kuṣṭha, and roots of Eraṇḍa ground into a good paste in hot sour gruel (Kāñjika) and applied on the head or forehead cure every sort of headache.

12-13. Oil is to be cooked with rock salt, Vacā, Hiṅgu, Kuṣṭha, Nāgeśvara, Śatapuṣpā and Devadāru. In this medicated oil mix the watery portion squeezed out of cowdung, one fourth of it in volume. This compound is very effective as an eardrop for all sorts of earache.

14. O Śiva, rock salt dissolved in sheep's urine poured into the ears removes fetid smell, foul discharges and worms in the ears.

15. Pouring the juice of Mālatī flowers and leaves into the ears or pouring cow's urine alone into the ears arrests fetid discharges from the ears.

16-17. A paste prepared from Kuṣṭha, Māsa, Marīca, Tagara, Pippalī, Apāmārgā, Aśvagandhā, Bṛhatī, white mustard, Yava and Tila with honey and rock salt applied over the penis removes its numbness, over the arms their paralysis and over the ears makes them grow larger.

18. Mustard oil cooked well with Bhallātaka, Bṛhatī, Dāḍima and bark can be applied to the penis to make it longer.

CHAPTER ONE HUNDRED AND SEVENTYSEVEN

Hari said:

1. There is no doubt in this that the eye salve prepared from the juice of the leaves of Śobhāñjana with honey cures all ocular affections.

2-3. Eighty flowers of Tila and Jāti mixed with Upanimba, Amalā, Śuṇṭhī, Pippalī and Taṇḍulīyaka must be dried in shade and prepared in the form of Vaṭīs. These Vaṭīs can be pasted in rice washings and applied to the eyes like collyrium. It removes all Timira defects.

4. The pulp of the stones of Vibhītaka Śaṅkhanābhi, Manaḥśilā, leaves of Nimba, and Marīca must be ground into paste in goat's urine. As an eye salve this compound removes the troubles of the wall-eyed and the night-blinded. Timira and afflictions of the coat of the eyes are also quelled.

5-6. Four parts of Śaṅkha, two parts of Manaḥśilā (realgar) and one part of rock salt are to be ground into paste and dried in shade and formed into Vaṭikā. This can be applied like collyrium: It cures Timira and Paṭala and is very effective in Piñjaṭa (mucus excretion of the eyes).

7-8. Trikaṭu, Triphalā, fruits of Karañja, rock salt and the two kinds of Rajanī[1] are to be ground in the juice of Bhṛṅgarāja and applied as collyrium. It cures Timira, etc.

9. Roots of Āṭarūṣaka ground into paste in sour gruel and applied thickly over the eyes remove all sorts of pain in the eyes.

1. Haridrā and Dāru-haridrā.

10-12. A decoction of Śatadru and the root of Badarī taken in gives relief from aching sensation in the eyes. Mustard oil cooked with the root of Apāmārga and ground into paste with rock salt, milk and sour gruel in a copper vessel can be used as a collyrium. O Śaṅkara, Piñjaṭa (accumulation of mucus in the eyes) is removed by this while applying this collyrium one shall reapeat this mantra:—

Oṁ Dadru Sara Kroṁ Hriṁ Ṭhaḥ Ṭhaḥ Dadru Sara Hriṁ Hrim Oṁ Uṁ Uṁ Sara Kriṁ Kriṁ Ṭhaḥ Ṭhaḥ. The nine Durgas called Ādyās can be brought under one's control.

13. An eyesalve prepared with Bilvaka and roots of Nīlī quells Timira instantaneously.

14. A stick or a wick prepared with Pippalī, Tagara, Haridrā, Āmalaka, Vacā and Khadira ground well can be applied as collyrium in all eyesores.

15. A person who holds water in his mouth and washes his face and eyes regularly in the morning every day can keep himself free from eyesores perpetually.

16. Roots of white Eraṇḍa and its leaves cooked with goat's milk can be used for fomentation in Vātaja eyesores.

17. Candana, rocksalt, Vṛddhapalāśa, Harītakī, Paṭala flowers, Nīlī and Cakrikā made into a collyrium remove eyesores. Guñjā roots ground into a paste in goat's urine quell Timira.

18. The body of a jaundice patient must be rubbed with rods of silver, copper and gold and the above paste applied as a plaster. He will get relief, O Rudra.

19-20. Smelling or drinking the decoction of Ghoṣa fruit dispels chlorosis and jaundice. The juice of Dāḍimapuṣpa, Dūrvā, Alaktaka and Hārītaki used as an errhine removes haemorrhoid growths in the nose and Vātarakta.

21. O Vṛṣabhadhvaja, Nīlalohita, (both mean Śiva) Roots of Jiṅginī[1] ground into paste in its own juice can be used as an errhine in Nāsārśas (haemorrhoid growths in the nose).

22. Ghī from cow's milk, Sarjarasa, Dhanyāka, rocksalt, Dhattūraka and Gairika must be cooked well and ground into

1. Lannea grandis.

paste with cooked rice and oil. This can be applied if there is an ulcer in the lips or if they are split.

23. Jātī leaves must be chewed well and kept in the mouth for some time. This cures sores in the mouth. By chewing and eating seeds of kośa, teeth shaking in their roots become steady.

24. Chewing Muṣṭaka, Kuṣṭha, Elā Yaṣṭika, Bālaka and Dhanyāka with honey removes bad odour from the mouth, O Hara.

25-26. Daily intake of astringent, pungent and bitter vegetables fried in oil removes fetid smell from the mouth and all ulcers of the gum and teeth are removed by this.

27. Gargling with sour gruel mixed with oil removes the pain due to the burning of the mouth on account of lime while chewing betel, O Śiva.

28-29. Just as mucous secretions of Kapha are generated by chewing Śuṇṭhī so also the application of the lambative prepared with leaves of Mātuluṅga, Elā, Yaṣṭī, Madhu, Pippalī and the leaves of Jāti, cause the same. Chewing the sprouts of Śephālikā proves effective in curing goitre.

30-31. O Śaṅkara, by extracting the impure blood from the veins of the nostril Jihvikā is quelled. The juice of the seeds of Śirīṣa cooked with fourtimes that of Haridrā can be used as an errhine, O Bhūteśa, for removing headache. An instantaneous relief from sore throat also is possible.

32. By chewing the root of Guñjā all the worms in the teeth perish. An astringent decoction of Kākajaṅghā, Snuhī, and Nīlī mixed with honey, O Śiva, destroys worms originating in and affecting the teeth.

33. Rubbed with the ghī cooked in milk with Karkaṭa, feet as well as teeth do not produce a coarse sound in gnashing.

34-37. O Śiva, (in the above case) it is enough if teeth are rubbed with Karkaṭapāda alone. Fruits of Jyotiṣmatī must be soaked in water for twentyone days and ground into paste with the pulp of white Abhayā. If this compound is used for rubbing the teeth it removes dark spots and tartar in the teeth. A compound of powdered Lodhra, Kumkuma, Mañjiṣṭhā, Loha Kāleyaka, Yava, rice grain and Yaṣṭimadhu with water can be applied over the face by ladies for making it bright and shining.

38. A prastha of Taila (oil) is to be cooked with two parts of goat's milk and karṣaka each of Raktacandana Mañjiṣṭhā and Lākṣā or Yaṣṭīmadhu and Kuṁkuma. This gives bright lustre to the face in seven days.

39-41. Water boiled with Suṇṭhī, powdered Pippali, Gūḍucī and Kaṇṭakārikā when drunk improves digestion. O Śiva (Pramatheśvara—lord of spirits) it removes the ache due to the deranged Vāyu. A decoction of Karañja, Karkaṭa, Uśīra, Bṛhatī, Kaṭurohiṇī, and Gokṣura when drunk quells vertigo, burning sensation, Pittajvara, emaciation and fainting.

42. A decoction of powdered Pippalī with milk, honey and ghee when drunk quells palpitation of the heart, cough, and chronic intermittent fever.

43. The usual dosage for all drugs in decoction is half a Karṣa. O Vṛṣabhadhvaja, according to the age of the patient slight alteration is also recommended.

44. Watery portion squeezed out of cowdung mixed with the juice of Kākajaṅghā and drunk with milk quells Viṣmajvara (chronic intermittent fever).

45-46. Milk boiled with Śuṇṭhī also cures viṣama jvara. Yaṣṭīmadhu, Musta, rock salt, Bṛhatīphala used as errhine induces sleep. The above compound can be mixed with Marica and honey, O Śiva, to make them more soporific.

47-48. Bandaging the head with the roots of Kākajaṅghā induces sleep. Oil cooked with sour gruel and Sarjarasa and applied with cold water allays heat and burning sensation due to fever with contamination of blood.

49-50. A decoction of Śailī[1], Saivāla, Agnimantha, Śuṇṭhī, Pāṣāṇabhedaka Śobhāñjana or Gokṣura, Varuṇa[2], Channa[3], and the root of Śobhāñjana with Hiṅgu and Yavakṣāra removes Pitta and Vāyu.

51. Water boiled with Pippalī, root of Pippalī and Bhallātaka when drunk quells colic epileptic fits.

1. Identity not clear.
2. Crataeva nurvala.
3. Identity not clear.

52. Aśvagandhā, Mūlaka and the clay from anthill applied as a plaster, O Rudra, quells Urustambha (paralysis of the thighs).

53. The root of Bṛhatīka ground into paste with water and drunk quells Saṅghātavāta.

54. The root of Ārdraka and Tagara drunk with butter-milk dispels Jhiñjinīvāta like the thunderbolt felling a tree.

55. The drug Asthisaṁhāra taken with a single meal everyday, or drunk with gravy dispels deranged Vāyu and sets broken bones right.

56. Powdered fried grain mixed with goat's milk and ghee can be applied to the feet to relieve them of aching sensation. There is no doubt.

57. A compound of honey, ghee, rock salt, Siktha (cooked rice), jaggery, Gairika, Guggula and Sarjarasa when applied as plaster gives relief to affected lungs.

58. O Vṛṣabhadhvaja, clay-eaten soles of the feet smeared with mustard oil must be warmed over a smokeless fire for quick relief.

59. Ghī medicated with Sarjarasa, Jīraka, and Harītaki and pasted with cooked rice can be applied over scalds and burns for instantaneous relief.

60. Heated oil mixed with ashes of Yava frequently applied over scalds and blisters heals them.

61. Fried and powdered Tila mixed with butter from buffalo's milk and Bhallāta applied as an errhine removes cardiac colic, and applied as a plaster heals ulcers.

62. Karpūra and butter from cow's milk must be applied over a cut from any weapon and bandaged with a white cloth, O Śaṅkara. O Vṛṣabhadhvaja, it will cease to give pain and will not suppurate.

63. A sword cut heals when the juice of the root of Āmra is applied. When smeared with ghee it does not begin to turn into an ulcer.

64. Śarapuṅkhā, Lajjālukā, Pāṭhā and their roots ground into paste in water and applied to sword-cuts heal them.

65. Root of Kākajaṅghā applied to ulcerating wounds for three days removes their suppuration, pain and fetid odour.

66. Pain caused by a blow can be quelled by fomentation with the root of Apāmārga cooked in water and oil.

67. O Śaṅkara, Abhayā, rock salt and Śuṇṭhī ground into paste with water when taken in quells indigestion.

68. Roots of Nimba worn round the waist remove excruciating pain in the eyes. If the root of Śaṇa is eaten with Tāmbūla it removes the disorder of urination with semen discharge.

69. Haridrā cooked in steam with rice, root of white mustard and seeds of Mātuluṅga applied over the body for seven days give it a bright hue.

70. O Vṛṣabhadhvaja, the juice of the leaves of white Aparājitā and Nimba or the juice of Madhuka pith used as an errhine removes the evil influence of Dākinīs, manes and Brahmarākṣasas.

71. When moon enters the star Puṣya cull the roots of white Jayantī[1], white Aparājitā, Arka and Citraka, grind all these into paste and prepare Vaṭikās thereof. If a man marks his forehead in the form of a Tilaka with these Vaṭikās, women will be under his control.

72-73. O Rudra, Pippalī, iron filings, Śuṇṭhī, Āmalaka, rocksalt, honey and sugar taken in equal quantities must be ground into paste. A daily dose of this compound, of the size of an Udumbara fruit for seven days makes the man strong and longlived. He may live even up to two hundred years. The mantra, *Oṁ Ṭha Ṭha Ṭha* employed in all activities involving charms blesses one with everything one wishes for.

74-77. Take a crow's nest from the tree and burn it over the funeral pyre. If the ashes are cast on the head of the enemy, O Śaṅkara, the enemy will be driven from his place of rest. O Rudra, hear some more such black devices of high potency. If a man places the faeces of his enemy on the hide of a wild rat and ties it round his waist band the enemy will suffer from suppression of stools. O Hara, if the name of any man is written on a mango leaf with the blood of a black crow

1. A synonym of *agnimantha*.

and that leaf is cast among filthy substances he is sure to be eaten by crows. A woman also can be killed like this.

78. Sugar, honey, goat's milk and equal quantities of Tila and Gokṣuraka must be cast off (with the desire for the extinction of the enemy). It is sure to destroy him, O Hara.

79. Hundred twigs of Bilva dripping with the blood of an owl and a black crow must be put into the sacrificial fire by reciting the names of two enemies. These two persons are sure to be bitter enemies.

80. Oil cooked in the milk of a bear with the flesh of the fish Rohita if applied over the body cures all ailments. The washings of sandalwood used as an errhine facilitates the reappearance of fallen hair.

81. He who holds a Lāṅgalikā[1] bulb in his hand and rubs it over his body, removes the arrogance of Hydrocele (he will be cured of it).

82. O Īśvara, O Śiva, one can take away the life of blazing (poisonous) serpents even if they are in their holes, by means of the blood of a peacock.

83. If a serpent Ajagara (Boa constrictor) is burnt to ashes in a funeral pyre and the ashes are cast off in front of the enemies they will be struck down.

84. If they are cast off with the following mantra their destruction will be more terrible:—

Oṁ Ṭha Ṭha Ṭha Cāhīhi Cāhīhi Svāhā. Oṁ Udaraṁ Pāhīhi Pāhīhi Svāha.

85. When the moon enters the asterism Puṣya cull the root of Sudarśanā and keep it in the middle of the house; Serpents will avoid that house.

86. Roots of Arka plant soaked in the oil of Siddhārtha and dried in the sun and made into wicks remove the serpents on the way.

87-89. The flesh of a cat, its excreta and Haritāla well cooked in goat's milk should be smeared over the body of a rat. The rat thrown into a house will drive away other rats from the place. O Rudra, there is no doubt about it. Fumigating with the vapours of a compound consisting of Triphalā, Arjuna

1. Gloriosa superba.

flowers, Bhallātaka, Śirīṣaka, Lākṣā Sarjarasa, Viḍaṅga and Guggula destroys all flies and mosquitoes.

CHAPTER ONE HUNDRED AND SEVENTYEIGHT

Diseases

Hari said:

1-2. A woman shall repeat the mantra *Om Nārāyaṇyai Svāhā* and give the man she loves Tāmbūla medicated with a compound of Brahmadaṇḍī, Vacā, Kuṣṭha, Priyaṅgu and Nāgakesara. After giving the betel-leaf she must repeat the *Oṁ Hariḥ Hariḥ Svāhā*. The man to whom it is given will surely be under her control.

3. Cow's tooth, Haritāla, and crow's tongue powdered together and deposited on the head of a man will make him be under the control of the person who deposits it. But if the victim had kept a garland of white mustard flowers in his house this will not be effective.

4. There will be perpetual quarrel in the house at the threshold of which Vaibhītaka and Śākhoṭaka with the roots and leaves are deposited.

5. A woman shall grind the flesh of Khañjarīṭa bird with honey and apply the compound to her vaginal passage during the period of menstruation. Her husband will be her slave.

6. Fumigating one's body with a compound of Aguru, Guggulu, Nīlotpala and jaggery one shall be a great favourite in the Royal threshold.

7. A Tilaka (mark on the forehead) with the root of white Aparājitā ground with Rocanā will enable one to captivate anyone he sees in the royal palace.

8. Kākajaṅghā, Vacā, Kuṣṭha, leaves of Nimba, Kumkuma and one's own blood compounded together will enable any one to control others.

9. Take the blood of a wild cat and purify it by cooking it in the oil of Karañja. Smear a lotus leaf with this and

holding this above Rudrāgni (funeral pyre) take the root as well and make a collyrium of all together. If this is applied to the eyes one can be invisible.

10. The mantra to be recited is as follows:—*Oṁ namaḥ Khaḍgavajrapāṇaye Mahā-Yakṣasenāpataye Svāhā Oṁ Rudraṁ Hrāṁ Hriṁ Varaśaktātvaritāvıdyā. Oṁ Mātaraḥ Stambhayata Svāhā.* The root of Mahāsugandhikā kept round the hips arrests the rapid emission of semen.

11. Reciting the following mantra

Oṁ Namaḥ Sarvasattvebhyaḥ Namaḥ Siddhiṁ Kuru Kuru Svāhi

seven times, the man should whirl the flowers of Karavīra in front of women. He can bring under his control whomsoever he wishes.

12. Brahmadaṇḍī, Vacā and Patra should be ground into paste with honey and applied over the organ (of generation). The woman will never wish for another husband.

13. Clumps of Brahmadaṇḍī kept in the mouth at the time of sexual intercourse will arrest the rapid emission of semen. Roots of Jayantī kept in the mouth will give the man splendid victory in cohabitation.

14. Roots of Bhṛṅgarāja ground into paste with semen and applied to the eyes like collyrium will enable any woman to captivate her lover.

15. Handing over betel leaves with clumps of Aparājitā with Nīlotpala is an effective means of captivating others.

16-18. The regions where Candrakalās (erotic centres) are located in men and women are Big toes, feet, heels, knees, pelvis, navel, chest, abdomen, armpits, throat, cheeks, lips, eyes, forehead and head. In men they are in the right side and in women they are in the left side. By tickling these centres love can be aroused. Different centres from the head to the toe should be tickled in the bright half and from toe to head in the dark half. In the Kāmaśāstra (Science of Erotics) sixty four arts and measures of fascination have been fully explained by which man and wife can enamour mutually. Girls and women are charmed by close embraces.

19. Rocanā, fragrant flowers, Nimba flowers, Priyaṅgu, Kuṁkuma and Candana marking the forehead can keep the

whole world captivated. The mantra to be recited in this process of fascination is:—

20. *Oṁ Hrīṁ Gaurī Devi, Saubhāgyaṁ Puruṣavaśyādi Dehi Me.*

Oṁ Hrīṁ Lakṣmi Devi Saubhāgyaṁ Sarvaṁ Trailokya-Mohanam

[O Goddess Gauri, give unto me all fortunes and amiability of children. O goddess Lakṣmi, give unto me the fortune that charms the three worlds].

21. O Rudra, sweet scents, turmeric, saffron, etc. applied over the body, fumigations, flowers, incense, etc, are things that charm others.

22. By applying a plaster of Durālabhā, Vacā, Kuṣhaṭ Kuṁkuma and Śatāvarī ground into paste in oil, to the vaginal passage, a woman can charm her lover.

23. Fumigating her vaginal canal with the smoke of Nimba twigs a woman will become fortunate enslaving her husband.

24. Butter taken from buffalo's milk, Kuṣṭha, Madhuyaṣṭikā, etc applied to the vagina makes a woman fortunate in conjugal bliss and her husband her slave.

25. Cook Madhuyaṣṭi, Kaṇṭakārikā and cow's milk taken in equal quantities in water and reduce the entire thing to onefourth. This decoction drunk hot enables a woman to conceive quickly.

26. Seeds of Mātuluṅga should be purified and cooked in milk. Drinking this a woman will be able to conceive. There is no doubt in this.

27. A woman desiring to beget a male child must drink ghee medicated with seeds of Mātuluṅga and roots of Eraṇḍa.

28. Aśvagandhā cooked in milk and mixed with ghee is a good medicine enabling conception. Seeds of Palāśa ground into paste with honey when drunk by a woman in menses stop the menstrual flow as well as conception.

CHAPTER ONE HUNDRED AND SEVENTY NINE

Diseases

Hari said :

1-2. O Rudra, after cleaning the teeth with an astringent decoction of Harītakī apply a paste of Haritāla, Yavakṣāra, Patrāṅga, Raktachandana, Jātī, Hiṅgulaka and Lākṣā well cooked, over the teeth. O Rudra, by this means teeth will turn red. There is no doubt.

3. Cook Mūlaka in low fire by steaming and then squeeze out its juice. This is a good ear drop arresting the fetid discharge from the ears.

4. Take leaves of Arka and heat them in low fire. The juice squeezed out of these leaves is a good remedy for earache.

5. Oil cooked and medicated with Priyaṅgu, Madhukā, Yaṣṭi, Dhātakī, Utpala leaves, Mañjiṣṭhā, Lodhra, Lākṣā and the juice of Kapittha when applied to the vaginal passage removes fetid leucorrbic discharges.

6. A medicated compound of dry Mūlaka and Śuṇṭhī burnt to ashes, Hingu, Mahauṣadha, Śatapuṣpā, Vacā, Kuṣṭha Dāru and Śigru is a great rejuvinating elixir.

7-8. Oil medicated and cooked with Sauvarcala, Yavakṣāra, Sarjaka, Saindhava, Granthi, Viḍam, Musta, four lines of Madhu, juice of Mātuluṅga and juice of Kadalī, undoubtedly arrests all sorts of foul discharges.

9-10. Mustard oil poured into the ears destroys all worms.

O Hara, these seven drugs:—

Haridrā, Nimba leaves, Pippalī, Marica, Viḍaṅgabhadra, Musta and Viśvabheṣaja ground into paste with cow's urine and made into pills constitute a great medicine. Even a single pill dispels indigestion, two pills will cure cholera.

11. These pills mixed with honey remove Paṭala (coating in the eye) taken in with cow's urine remove tumours. Wicks thus made are called Śāṅkarī Varti and are called efficacious in all sorts of eyesores.

CHAPTER ONE HUNDRED AND EIGHTY

Diseases

Hari said :—

1. Equal parts of Vacā, Māṁsī, Bilva, Tagara, Padmakeśara, Nāgapuṣpa and Priyaṅgu powdered together and used for fumigating the body enables the man to become as handsome as Cupid himself.

2. A paste of Karpūra and Devadāru with honey applied over the penis enables a man to enamour any woman.

3. After sexual intercourse a man should take the discharged semen with his left hand and apply the same to the left hand of the woman whom he wants to keep under his power. She will never wish the company of any other man.

4. *Oṁ Raktacāmuṇḍe Amukaṁ Me Vaśaṁ Ānaya Ānaya Oṁ Hrīṁ Hruṁ Hraḥ Phaṭ*. Repeat this mantra ten thousand times and apply a tilaka mark on the forehead with your own blood and Gorocanā. You can keep everyone under your control, O Śaṅkara.

5-8. Saindhava, Kṛṣṇalavaṇa, Sauvīra, Matsyapitta, honey, ghī and sugar pasted together should be applied to the Vaginal passage. A man having sexual intercourse with that woman will never approach another woman. A compound of Śaṅkhapuṣpī, Vacā, Māṁsī, Somarājī and Phalguka[1] pasted with butter taken out of buffalo's milk must be formed into pills. Lotus with its stalk should be pasted with milk and ghee. The pills are to be purified with this juice and inserted into the vaginal passage of a woman. Even if she had given birth to ten children the local muscles will be so toned as to make her seem a virgin.

9-11. A compound of Sarṣapa, Vacā, fruits of Madana, Cat's faeces, Dhattūra and the hair of a woman when fumigated destroys cāturthaka fever (quotidian fever) and the fever due to the malignant influence of Ḍākinīs. A compound of flowers of Arjuna, Bhallātaka, Viḍaṅgaka, Bālā, Sarjaras,

1. Ficus hipida.

Sauvīra and Sarṣapa when fumigated drives out serpents, fleas, lice, flies and mosquitoes.

12. Powdered Bhūlatā inserted into the vaginal passage induces numbness of the local muscles.

CHAPTER ONE HUNDRED AND EIGHTYONE

Diseases

Hari said :

1. Tāmbūla pasted with ghī, honey, salt and milk in a copper vessel removes pain in the eyes.

2. A lambative made of Harītakī, Vacā, Kuṣṭha, Vyoṣa, Hiṅgu and Manaḥśilā taken with honey and ghī dispels cough, hiccough and Asthma.

3. Powdered Pippalī and Triphalā shall be licked with honey, Catarrh, cough and chronic acute dyspnea will be removed.

4. The aches of Citraka along with its roots and the powder of Pippalī shall be licked with honey. O Vṛṣadhvaja, dyspnea, cough and hiccough shall subside.

5. Equal quantities of Nīlotpala, Madhuka and Padmaka taken with sugar and washings of rice quell all disorders in the blood.

6. Powdered Śuṇṭhī mixed with sugar and honey and taken in makes the voice as sweet as that of a cuckoo.

7. A compound of Haritāla, Śaṅkha, and ashes of plantain leaves all pounded well and rubbed over the body is a great depilatory.

8. Lavaṇa, Haritāla, fruits of Tumbinī pasted with the juice of Lākṣā is also a fine depilatory.

9. Sudhā Haritāla, Ash of Śaṅkha, Manaḥsilā and Rock salt must be ground into paste with goat's urine. This removes all unwanted hair immediately after application.

10-11. Śaṅkha, Āmaḷaka Patra and flowers of Dhātakī ground into paste with milk and kept in the mouth for a week gives a shining glossy lustre to the teeth.

CHAPTER ONE HUNDRED AND EIGHTYTWO

Diseases

Hari said :

1. In the seasons of Vasanta (spring) Grīṣma (summer) and Śarad (Autumn) use of curd is not recommended. It is very good in Hemanta, Śiśira and the rainy season.

2. Sugar taken with butter makes the intellect keen. Daily intake of old jaggery, about a pala per dose, makes the man so strong that he can satisfy a thousand women, O Hara.

3. Kuṣṭha powdered well and ground into paste with ghī and honey must be taken at bed-time. It dispels wrinkles and greying hair.

4. O Śaṅkara, Atasī, Māṣā and Godhūma ground into paste with ghī and powdered Pippalī when applied over the body make it shine with lustre like that of Kandarpa (Cupid).

5. Yava, Tila, Aśvagandha, Muśalī and Saralā[1] ground into paste with jaggery and taken in regularly make the man young and strong.

6. A decoction of Hiṅgu, Sauvarcala, and Śuṇṭhī when drunk dispels Pariṇāma Śūla (a type of Gastralgia) and impaired digestion.

7. Dhātakī and Somarājī ground and cooked with milk and taken regularly, make the weakest man the stoutest. There is no doubt.

8. Sugar taken with honey and butter makes one strong. A consumptive patient taking to a diet of milk can nourish himself and become intelligent.

1. A synonym of trivṛt.

9-10. Powdered Kulīra[1] drunk with milk dispels tuberculosis Bhallātaka, Viḍaṅga, Yavakṣāra, Saindhava, Manaḥśilā and Śaṅkhacūrṇa powdered and cooked with oil is a great depilatory. There is no doubt about it.

11. Leech ground into paste with the juice of Mālūra and applied to the palm gives it the power to hold fire.

12. The juice of Śālmalī mixed with urine of a mule and thrown into fire extinguishes it immediately.

13. Take the abdomen of the she crow and paste it with the suet of a frog. Pills made of this compound cast into fire can extinguish fire immediately.

14. Muṇḍītvak, Vacā, Musta, Marica and Tagara chewed well give the power to lick even fire immediately.

15. Gorocanā and Bhṛṅgarāja powdered and pasted with ghī act as a protection against rain with this mantra *Oṁ Aganistambhanaṁ Kuru Kuru.*

16. *Oṁ Namo Bhagavate Jalaṁ Stambhaya Saṁ Saṁ Saṁ Keka Keka Cara Cara O Śiva.* This is the mantra to numbify water. It benumbs water.

17. If a person buries the bones of a vulture and a cow along with Pūjā garlands at the threshold of the enemy's house he is sure to die.

18-19. If a man or woman squeezes red flowers of five different species of plants and mixes the juice of the same with Kuṁkuma, his or her own blood and a pala of Rocanā and marks his forehead he or she can captivate any one.

20-21. Brahmadaṇḍī administered in food or drink on a day when moon enters the Puṣya star is a captivating charm. A pala of Yaṣṭimadhu cooked in water, O Maheśvara, and drunk dispels suppression of faeces and urine and cardiac colic. The mantra *Oṁ Hrūṁ Jaḥ* removes the poison of a scorpion, O Rudra.

22. Pippalī, Śṛṅgavera, Saindhava, Marica and Kuṣṭha ground into paste with butter and curd is an antitoxic remedy whether used as an errhine or a beverage.

23. O Śiva, Triphalā, Ārdraka, Kuṣṭha and Candana cooked with ghī and drunk or applied as a plaster removes poison.

1. A synonym of karkanasṛṅgī.

24. A compound of the eyes of dove, Haritāla and Manaḥśilā removes poison as Garuḍa kills serpents.

25. O Vṛṣabhadhvaja, Saindhava, Tryūṣaṇa powder, curdand ghī pasted together when applied over the body remove the poison of scorpion.

26. A decoction of Brahmadaṇḍī and Tila drunk with Traikaṭuka removes Gulmas, O Rudra, and obstructed blood.

27. Milk taken with honey prevents haemorrhage. The navel and the Vaginal canal must be smeared with the root of Āṭarūṣaka. A woman in labour easily delivers of her child.

28. O Vṛṣadhvaja, sugar, honey and rice washings drunk quells Raktātisāra (blood dysentery).

CHAPTER ONE HUNDRED AND EIGHTYTHREE

Diseases

Hari said :—

1. A decoction of Marica, Śṛṅgavera, Kuṭaja and Tvaca when drunk removes Grahaṇī (diarrhoea) O Śiva, with the crescent moon for crest.

2-3. Pippalī, Pippalīmūla, Marica, Tagara, Vacā, Devadāru juice, and Pāṭhā must be ground into paste with milk. When drunk, this removes dysentery. A collyrium made of Marīca and Tila flower removes chlorosis.

4. O Rudra, Equal quantity of Harītakī and jaggery taken with honey is a good laxative, there is no doubt about it.

5. Triphalā, Citraka, Citra, and Kaṭukarohiṇī constitute a good purgative and a remedy for Ūrustambha (paralysis of the thighs).

6. A decoction of Harītakī, Śṛṅgavera, Devadāru and Candana cooked with goat's milk and root of Apāmārga or Jayantī remove Ūrustambha in seven days.

7. Pills made of a compound of Anantā, Śṛṅgavera (finely powdered) and equal quantities of Guggula and jaggery

are very effective in all disorders of Vāyu, nerves and sinews and impaired digestion.

8. Cull the Śaṅkhapuṣpī plant with roots and leaves when Puṣya star is in conjunction with moon and cook it in goat's milk. It is a good remedy for hysteric fits.

9. A decoction of Aśvagandhā and Abhayā in equal quantities is a sure remedy for Raktapitta (Haemorrhage).

10. Take a mouthful of powdered Kuṣṭha and Harītakī and wash it down the throat with cold water. All sorts of vomiting vanish.

11-12. A decoction of Guḍūcī, Padmaka, Ariṣṭa, Dhanyāka and Raktacandana removes fevers due to Pitta and Kapha, vomiting, burning sensation, and thirst and improves digestion. With the mantra *Oṁ Huṁ Namaḥ* Śaṅkhapuṣpī is to be tied to the ears. Then recite the following mantra. All fevers will be dispelled — *Oṁ Jambhini Stambhini Mohaya Sarvavyādhīn Me Vajreṇa Ṭhaḥ ṭhaḥ Sarvavyādhīn Me Vajreṇa Phaṭ.*

13. Take the flower and recite the above mantra eight hundred times and hand it over to the patient and touch his nail. O Rudra, the Cāturthaka and other types of fever calm down immediately.

14. A compound of Jambūphala, Haridrā and the slough of a serpent fumigated removes all fevers and especially the quotidian.

15. Oil should be cooked with Karavīra, Bhṛṅgapatra, Lavaṇa, Kuṣṭha and Karkaṭa in four times cow's urine. This removes itches, Vicarcikā and Kuṣṭha. By anointing this all ulcers heal.

16. Pippalī and honey or sweet diet or the bulbous root Sūraṇa cure enlarged spleen.

17. Pippalī and Haridrā pasted with cow's urine must be inserted into the rectum. It removes piles.

18-19. An oral administering of Ārdraka with goat's milk is a cure for enlarged spleen. Saindhava, Viḍaṅga, Somarājī, Sarṣapa, the two types of Rajanī and Viṣa must be ground into paste with cow's urine and applied with leaves of Nimba, etc. This removes Kuṣṭha.

CHAPTER ONE HUNDRED AND EIGHTYFOUR

Diseases

Hari said :

1. Rajanī and the ashes of Kadalī when pasted remove blotches and scabs. A decoction of one part of Kuṣṭha and two parts of Pathyā if drunk removes all aches of the pelvic region.

2. Abhayā taken with butter, sugar and Pippalī removes piles; there is no doubt in this.

3. Cook powdered Āṭarūṣaka leaves in butter over a low fire. Plastering with this cures piles effectively.

4-5. A decoction of Guggulu and Triphalā removes fistula in ano. Cook Ajājī and Śṛṅgavera in curd and gruel. This taken with salt cures strangury. Yavakṣāra taken with sugar is also a remedy for strangury.

6. The excreta of Khañjarīṭa and the foam of a horse mixed with Śobhāñjana fumigated or applied to the eyes as a collyrium makes the man invisible even to the gods. O Śiva what then about mere mortals ?

7. Burn Yava and paste it with gingelly oil. An application of this is a sure remedy for burns and scalds. An application of the paste of Lajjālu and Śarapuṅkha with butter is also similarly effective.

8. This mantra is to be recited— "Oṁ Namo Bhagavate ṭha ṭha cchindhi cchindhi. Jvalanam Prajvalitaṁ Nāśaya Naśaya Huṁ Phaṭ".

9-10. Roots of Nirguṇḍī tied round the wrist cure all types of fever. Roots of white Guñjā must be cut into seven pieces and tied to the wrists remove piles. There is no doubt in this. Viṣṇukrāntā pasted with goats' urine and applied over the body affords a great protection from thieves and tigers.

11. Roots of Brahmadaṇḍī enable one to do many wonderful acts. Powdered Triphalā taken with butter removes Kuṣṭha.

12. Butter cooked and medicated with Punarnava, Bilva and Pippalī removes hiccough, cough, Asthma and bronchitis. Internally administered to women, it facilitates conception.

13-15. The drugs mentioned before are to be cooked with milk and butter and daily taken with honey and Sugar. They secrete semen profusely. Viḍaṅga, Madhuka, Pāṭhā, Māṁsī, Sarjapasa, Haridrā, Triphalā, Apāmārga, Manaḥśilā, Udumbara and Dhātakī must be ground to paste in gingelly oil. This applied over the penis and vaginal passage gives very great pleasure to the man and woman in their sexual embrace.

16. "Namaste Īśa Varadāya Ākarṣiṇi Vikarṣiṇi Mugdhe Svāhā." The man and woman must rub the vaginal passage and penis with the oil after repeating this mantra, O Śaṅkara.

17-18. Mercury must be mixed with the juice of Jātikā and the seeds of Punarnavā Amṛtā Dūrvā, Kanaka and Indravāruṇī[1]. This compound must be put in a crucible. This Rasa is a great death-giving agent. Milk taken with honey and butter removes wrinkles and greying it hair.

19. Copper burnt with the compound of honey, butter, jaggery, and juice of Kāravella becomes silver. Now hear me explain the process of converting it into gold.

20. A Pala of lead, yellow Dhattūra flower and a twig of Lāṅgalikā burnt together makes it converted into Gold.

21. A yogin seated in Samādhi posture with a lamp burning with the oil of Dhattūra, cannot be seen even by those who are in heaven.

22. A clay model of a bull grappling a frog shall be fumigated with the smoke of this Dhattūra oil lamp. The clay frog will bellow like a living bull, O Śaṅkara.

23. An oil lamp burns down the insect Khadyota. Both burning together produce a great conflagration.

24. O Rudra, burn the dead body of a rat. The ashes when rubbed over the body produce a severe burning sensation. When sandal wood is applied or drunk he will be free from the distress.

25. Apply the ichor of an elephant in rut to its own eyes, O Śiva. The elephant will be victorious in battles. The man also becomes a great hero.

26. Keep a piece of ivory in the mouth of water snake

1. Citrullus colocynthis.

and throw it in water. It will stay steady in water as on land.

27. A compound of the eyes, teeth, bones, blood and suet in oil must be smeared over the body. The man can stay under water for three days.

28. The eyes of crocodile, the heart of a tortoise, the suet and bones of a rat and the suet of a Śiśumāra (porpoise) pasted together and applied over the body enable a man to stay under water as in his own house.

29-30. Iron filings drunk with butter milk cure jaundice. Roots of Taṇḍulīyaka and Gokṣuraka drunk with milk remove chlorosis and all ailments of the mouth. The roots of Jātī and Kola drunk with buttermilk cure impaired digestion.

31. The roots of Kuśa or Bākucī taken with buttermilk cure indigestion. Roots of Bākucī taken with sour gruel dispel diseases of the teeth.

32. O Śiva, roots of Indra-Vāruṇī drunk with water remove poison of drinking. The roots of Surabhikā cure disorders due to the derangement of Vāyu.

33-35. Powdered Guñjā plastered on the head with sour gruel cures headache. Powdered Balā, Atibalā and Yaṣṭi mixed with honey and sugar taken by even a sterile woman enables her to conceive. There is no doubt. Roots of white Aparājitā, ground together with Pippalī and Śuṇṭhī and applied over the head remove acute headache. Drinking clusters of Nirguṇḍikā removes goitre.

36-37. Ashes of the leaves of Ketakī taken with jaggery or Śarapuṅkhā taken with butter milk cures enlarged spleen. Juice of Mātuluṅga taken with jaggery and butter remove disorders due to Vāyu and Pitta. Drinking Śuṇṭhi, Sauvarcala and Hiṅgu removes all heart pains.

CHAPTER ONE HUNDRED AND EIGHTYFIVE

Diseases

Hari Said :

1. Oṁ Namo Gaṇapataye (obeisance unto the Lord of Gaṇas). This is the mantra of Lord of Gaṇas that gives wealth and learning.

2. After reciting this eight thousand times a man shall tie his tuft and enter litigation. He is sure to win. By repeating this a hundred times he will be a favourite of all men.

3. O Rudra, Repeating this mantra a thousand and eight times the devotee shall offer a thousand and eight libations of black gingelly seeds soaked in butter. The king will be under his control in three days.

4. The devotee shall observe fast on the eighth and fourteenth days of the lunar fortnight and worship Vighnarāṭ (Gaṇeśa). Thereafter he shall offer a thousand and eight libations of gingelly seeds and raw rice grains. He shall be invincible in battle. All people are bound to serve him.

5. Having repeated this mantra for eight thousand times and then for eight hundred times the devotee shall tie his tuft and then enter the Royal court or the court of litigation. He is sure to win.

6. He who repeats this mantra after placing Hrīmkāra and Visarga (mystically) on the forehead of women is sure to keep them under his control.

7. With great concentration he shall place the Nyāsa mantras mystically in the organ of reproduction in the maidens and repeat the mantras. There is no doubt in this that he will be able to make the maidens swell with love.

8. Pure in body and mind he who offers ten thousand libations will be able to keep women under his control by merely looking at them.

9. He who puts on his forehead a Tilaka with pasted Gorocanā Patra, Manaḥśilā and Kuṅkuma keeps women under his control.

10. He who puts on his forehead a tilaka with pasted Sahadevī Bhṛṅgarāja, Śvetā Parājitā and Vacā keeps the three worlds under his control.

11. He who puts on his forehead a Tilaka by means of sticks made of Gorocanā and Mīnapitta (gall of fish) with the little finger of his left hand keeps the three worlds under his control. There is no doubt.

12. She who puts on her forehead Tilaka with Gorocanā treated with her own menstrual blood keeps under he control any man whom she sees. There is no doubt.

13-15. O Hara, O Īśvara, fumigating with a compound of Nāgeśvara, Śaileya, Tvak, Patra, Harītakī, Candana, Kuṣṭha, Sūkṣma Ailā and Raktaśāli is a great instrument of fascination through the arrows of Kāmadeva (Cupid) O Mahādeva. O Śaṅkara beloved of Pārvatī, he who after his sexual intercourse takes his semen with his left hand and smears the left leg of his beloved with it becomes her favourite lover.

16. Smearing the penis with Saindhava, excreta of a pigeon and honey, O Mahādeva, a man can satisfy any woman.

17. Take five red flowers of any species and equal quantity (by weight) of Priyaṅgu and grind them into a paste. He who smears his penis with this, gives thrilling pleasure to his partner whom he can enslave.

18 He who smears his penis with a compound of Aśvagandhā, Mañjiṣṭhā, flowers of Mālatī and white mustard is loved by women.

19. The root of Kākajaṅghā drunk with milk removes pulmonary consumption. They who regularly take a compound of Aśvagandhā, Nāga Balā, jaggery and Māṣa retain the same health and vivacity of young men.

20. O Rudra, powdered Triphalā alone or with Lohacūrṇa taken with honey removes Pariṇāmaśūla. (Gastralgra).

21. Drinking of boiled water with Śambūkakṣāraka too serves the same purpose. O Śiva, the horn of a deer burnt in fire taken with cow's butter removes cardiac and back pain.

22. Vṛṣadhvaja Hiṅgu, Sauvarcala and Śuṇṭhī boiled in water with Mahauṣadha and drunk removes all colics.

23. Root of Apāmārga taken with sea-salt removes impaired digestion and colic.

24. Sprouts of Vaṭa washed with water with which rice has been washed should be drunk O Rudra, with butter milk. O Śankara, it dispels dysentery.

25. O Bhūtapa, (Śiva) Half Karṣa of the roots of Aṅkoṭa[1] ground into paste with rice washings and drunk removes all sorts of dysentery and diarrhoea.

26. Marīca, Śuṇṭhi, powdered barks of Kuṭaja and jaggery taken in increased proportion of twice the former and drunk removes all sorts of diarrhoea.

27. O Śiva, pills made of a compound of the roots of white Aparājitā, Haridrā, cooked rice, Apāmārgā and Trikaṭuka pasted well undoubtedly remove the great sickness of cholera.

28. O Bhūteśa, Triphalā, Aguru, Śilājatu and Harītakī powdered separately and taken with honey, O Śaṅkara, destroys all sorts of urinary complaints.

29-30. A Pala each of Manaḥśilā, Marīca and Sindūra ground into powder and cooked in a copper vessel with exudations of Arka and gingelly oil and dried in sunshine and drunk with exudations of Snuhi and Saindhava removes colic.

31-33. Trikaṭu, Triphalā, Alakta gingelly oil, Manaḥśilā, leaves of Nimba, flowers of Jātī, Śaṅkhanābhi and Candana cooked well in goat's milk and urine and made into sticks should be used as collyrium for the eyes. Wall-eyes, eyecoatings, night-blindness etc. heal. Powdered Vibhītaka taken with honey removes dyspnea.

34. Pippalī, powdered Triphalā, honey and Saindhava cure all types of fever, cough, consumption, and catarrh.

35. Devadāru powder soaked and purified in goats' urine twentyone times and applied as collyrium to the eyes cures night blindness, eyecoatings and depilations of eyelashes.

36. O Rudra, a compound of Pippalī, Ketaka,[2] Haridrā, Āmalaka and Vacā cooked in milk and applied as a collyrium to the eyes cures all ocular afflictions.

37. O Śiva, O Hara, Roots of Kākajaṅghā and Śigru kept in the mouth and chewed well remove all germs in the teeth.

1. Alangium salvifolium.
2. Pandanus tectorius.

CHAPTER ONE HUNDRED AND EIGHTYSIX

Diseases

Hari said :

1-2. The essence of Guḍūcī taken with honey removes Prameha (diabetes and urinary complaints). Roots of Gohālikā mixed with gingelly seeds, curd and butter cooked well dispels strangury, O Śaṅkara. The same taken with sauvarcala removes hiccough.

3. O Rudra, powdered Gorakṣa and roots of Karkaṭī drunk with washings of Vāsya for three days dispel gravel and similar urinary complaints.

4. Roots of Mālatī collected in summer and cooked in goats' milk when drunk with sugar cure strangury gravel and jaundice.

5. Roots of Dvijayaṣṭi ground into paste in water with which rice has been washed when applied as a plaster cure serofula, hydrocele and goitre.

6. The above compound with the admixture of Rasāñjana and powdered Harītakī when applied to the penis cures loss of manhood and virility, there is no doubt.

7. By applying the paste of the roots of Karavīra or Pūgaphala to the genitals, loss of sexual vigour can be cured. O Rudra, I shall mention another medical compound.

8. By applying the paste of the roots of Dantī, Haridrā and Citraka, fistula in ano is cured. I shall mention another treatment. If the blood is sucked off by leeches, fistula in ano can be cured.

9. Washed with the water of Triphalā the locality should be smeared with the paste of cat's bone. Then bleeding ceases. There is no doubt in this.

10. Haridrā should be purified many times with the exudations of Snuhī and formed into Vaṭikās. O Vṛṣabhadhvaja, an application of this cures Piles. Ghoṣāphala and Saindhava ground into paste together is a sure remedy for Piles.

11. Butter made from the cow's milk cooked with Trikaṭuka and drunk with the washings of Palāśa and Kṣāra, three times in Volume cures Piles.

12. By eating Bilvaphala, or black gingelly seeds with butter, bleeding piles can be cured.

13. O Vṛṣabhadhvaja, equal quantities of Yavakṣāra, powdered Śuṇṭhī and jaggery early in the morning improves digestive power.

14-15. Water boiled with Śuṇṭhī and drunk improves digestion. O Rudra, powdered Harītakī, Saindhava, Citraka and Pippalī drunk with hot water increases appetite and hunger, Pig's flesh taken with butter increases appetite and hunger.

CHAPTER ONE HUNDRED AND EIGHTYSEVEN

Diseases

Hari said :

1. O Śaṅkara, pound the leaves of Hastikarṇapalāśa. O Śiva, a hundred Palas of this powder is a great cure for all ailments.

2. If the above powder is taken with milk O Vṛṣabhadhvaja, for seven days the man gains the power of memory, O Rudra, and becomes as powerful and valorous as a lion.

3. If the powder is taken with milk for sixteen days, O Rudra, the body begins to glow like a ruby, the shape and features become brilliant and he can live even for a thousand years.

4. Taken with honey and butter it is conducive to longevity. Taken with honey it enables one to live even for ten thousand years.

5. Taken daily with curd it builds up the body as strong as adamant and makes the man endowed with keen power of memory and a great favourite of young maidens.

6. Taken with sour gruel it enables a man to live even for a thousand years with thickly grown glossy hair.

7. Taken with Triphalā it enables the man to live for a hundred years with a divine body free from wrinkles and grey hair and without any defect in the eyes.

8-9. If the powder is taken with butter even a blind man begins to see. When applied over the head with buffalo's milk it turns grey hair black. O Vṛṣabhadhvaja, hair begin to grow even on a bald head. The powder used for massage with oil removes wrinkles and grey hair.

10. By using it as an unguent one is freed from all ailments. If it is applied as a collyrium with goat's milk for a month, the lost eyesight can be regained.

11-12. Seeds of Palāśa are to be gathered in the month of Śrāvaṇa and dehusked. Powder them well and take half a Karṣa of it daily with butter after due worship of Lord Hari. The diet is to be restricted to old rice of the Ṣaṣṭi variety. Water is to be abjured. The man can live for a thousand years free from wrinkles and grey hair.

13-14. Cull the roots of Bhṛṅgarāja when the moon is in Puṣya star. Powder them well. The powder is to be taken daily with Sauvīra for a month. The man becomes free from wrinkles and grey hair. He will be endowed with the strength of an elephant. He can live even for five hundred years with the power of hearing unimpaired. O Rudra, the course must be started on the day when the moon enters the asterism of Puṣya.

CHAPTER ONE HUNDRED AND EIGHTYEIGHT

Diseases

Hari said:

1. A cut from a sharp instrument, filled with butter immediately gets healed without inflammation and pus-formation. To stop excessive bleeding, roots of Apāmārga must be squeezed with hands and the juice must be poured into the wound.

2. O Rudra, if the tip of any weapon or any other foreign matter gets embedded in any wound, roots of Lāṅgalikā and Hijjala must be squeezed and poured over the wound. O

Śaṅkara, even if the foreign matter had been there for a long time it comes out instantaneously.

3. Roots of Balā or of Meṣaśṛṅgī ground into paste with water and applied over sinuses make them subside even if they be of long duration.

4. Powdered roots of Kaṅku applied over sinuses quell them. The diet of the patient must be restricted to cooked Kodrava rice with curd from buffalo's milk.

5. Brahmayaṣṭi fruits ground into paste with water and applied over the skin remove the disorder due to impurity in the blood. There is no doubt in this.

6-8. Ashes of Yava, Viḍaṅga, Gandhapāṣāṇa and Śuṇṭhī treated with chameleon's blood and applied cures carbuncles and tumours, O Śiva. Root of Śobhāñjana and burnt linseed mixed with white mustard and applied over knotty tumours with buttermilk not turned sour, cures it.

9. Root of white Aparājitā ground into paste in water with which rice has been washed can be used as an errhine to drive away malignant hosts of Bhūtas (evil ghosts).

10. An errhine prepared with the flower of Agastya with Marīca removes colic, O Śiva. A paste with the slough of a serpent, Hiṅgu, leaves of Nimba, Yava and white mustard removes malignant spin.

11. A collyrium prepared with Gorocanā, Marīca, Pippalī, Saindhava and honey wards off the evil influences of planets and Bhūtas, O Śiva.

12. Fumigating with Guggulu and the tail of the owl wards off the influence of evil planets. A patient of Cāturthaka fever shall be wrapped with a black cloth and fumigated thus. He will be cured.

CHAPTER ONE HUNDRED AND EIGHTYNINE

Diseases

Hari said :

1. Dropping the juice of the flower of white Aparājitā flowers in the eyes heals the coating of the eyes. There is no doubt in this.

2. O Nīlalohita, O Surāsuravimardana (Śiva the destroyer of Devas and Asuras), by chewing the roots of Gokṣura one is relieved of the pain due to germs in the teeth.

3. A woman patient of enlarged spleen must apply the paste of the root of white Arka in cow's milk to her vaginal passage, after fasting during the menstrual period. She will be freed of the pain due to the tumour.

4. The flower of the white Arka should be culled after duly reciting the mantras before. After the purificatory bath at the cessation of the flow of blood duringmenses she must tie it round her hips. This will facilitate her conception and delivery (in the natural course).

5. O Hara, the root of Palāśa or Apāmārga tied round the wrist dispels all sorts of fever and wards off the evil influence of Bhūtas and ghosts.

6. O Parameśvara, the root of Vṛścika drunk with water kept overnight, removes the burning sensation due to fever.

7. The same tied round the tuft removes intermittent fever. When drunk with the washings of Vāsya it quells all poisons.

8. A man is sure to be inimical with any one, man or woman, to whom he hands over the root of Lajjālukā soaked in his own semen.

9. He who drinks cow's butter medicated with the roots of Pāṭhā surely mitigates the baneful influences of all kinds of poisons. There is no doubt in this.

10. If the ears are filled with the juice of the root of Raktacitraka as well as Śirīṣa along with Vāsya water, jaundice and chlorosis are sure to be dispelled.

11. The root of white Kokilākṣa[1] cooked with goat's milk when drunk for three days cures Consumption.

12. The flower of coconut palm drunk with the goat's milk dispels the three types of Vātarakta.

13. Roots of Sudarśanā must be wreathed into a garland. Worn round the neck it dispels the fever "Tryāhika" (Tertian) and wards off adverse planets and ghosts.

14. The excellent root of white Guñjā must be gathered when the moon enters Puṣya star. This kept in the mouth removes several kinds of poison.

15. The same root along with stems tied round the wrist or the neck wards of evil planets. Culled and tied round the waist on the fourteenth day of the dark fortnight it removes the fear of lions and other beasts of prey, O Nīlalohita (Śiva).

16. O Bhūteśa the root of Viṣṇukrāntā tied round the ears with a silken cord removes the fear of crocodiles, O Īśa.

CHAPTER ONE HUNDRED AND NINETY

Diseases

Hari said :

1. The root of Aparājitā drunk with cow's urine removes goitre. There is no doubt in this.

2. A decoction of the root of Indra-vāruṇī taken duly or an errhine with the paste of the juice of Jinginī with Śūka-Śimbi grains and cold water removes many kinds of pain in arms or neck.

3. Aśvagandhā, Pippalī and the two drugs Vacā and Kuṣṭha ground into paste with butter from buffalo's milk when applied to the penis or chest alleviate the pain in the ducts of penis and the cardiac region.

1. Astercantha langifolia.

4. Powdered Kuṣṭha and Nāgabalā pasted with butter and applied over the breasts of young women give them a shapely beauty.

5. Indravāruṇikā must be uprooted and cast off far away shouting the name of the patient of splenic enlargement. He is relieved of the ailment.

6. Root of Punarnavā of the white variety drunk with rice washings removes abscesses. There is no doubt in this.

7. Ashes of burnt Kadalī leaves boiled in water and drunk quell all sorts of dropsy and Ascites.

8. Roots of Kadalī cooked well in butter and jaggery and swallowed destroy the worms in the abdomen.

9. Daily intake of powdered Nimba leaves and Āmalaka early in the morning quells Kuṣṭha and similar cutaneous afflictions.

10. A compound of Harītakī, Viḍaṅga, Haridrā, white mustard, Roots of Somarāja and Karañja, and Saindhava ground into paste in cow's urine removes Kuṣṭha.

11. One part of Triphalā and two parts of the seeds of Somarāja taken in along with the observation of strictness in diet cure ring worm, O Śiva.

12. Sour butter milk boiled with cow's urine with salt in a vessel of bell metel thickly applied removes Kuṣṭha.

13. A plaster of Haridrā, Haritāla, Dūrvā and rock salt pasted with cow's urine removes ring worm Pāmā and skin poisons.

14. Seeds of Somarāja pasted with butter and honey taken in remove white leprosy. O Rudra, butter milk must be taken as Anupāna (subsequent drink). There is no doubt in this.

15. Root of white Aparājitā purified recurrently in its own washings applied for a mouth, O Rudra, quells leucoderma.

16. Butter from buffalo's milk, Sindūra and Marīcaka applied over the affected part removes Pāmā (scabies) and Piles, O Vṛṣabha-Dhvaja (Śiva).

17. O Īśvara, Dry roots of Gambhārī cooked and taken with milk is a remedy for Śuklapitta.

18. Seeds of Mūlaka ground with the juice of Apāmārga and applied over the body, O Rudra, quell Silhikā.

19. Haridrā mixed with the ashes of Kadalī quells Silhikā. Ashes of Rambhā[1] and Apāmārga mixed with Eraṇḍa if applied over the body, O Mahādeva, remove scabs immediately.

20-21. Burnt ashes of Kūṣmāṇḍa creeper mixed with cow's urine and Haridrā pasted with water must be cooked in a crucible lutoed with buffalo dung over a low fire, O Vṛṣabhadhvaja. An unguent of this compound, O Īśvara produces shapeliness and beauty of limbs.

22. A compound of gingelly seeds, mustard, two sorts of Haridrā and Kuṣṭhaka applied over the body as an unguent turns body odour into a sweet fragrance.

23. Application of Dūrvā and Kākajaṅghā too similarly increases the beauty day by day. An application of the paste of flowers of Arjuna leaves of Jambū and Lodhra removes the bad odour of the body.

24. A person who smears his body with a solution of Lodhra water and powdered Kanaka is never affected by the rigours of summer.

25. Sprinkling profusely with milk relieves the body of the defects of heat. An unguent of Kākajaṅghā is a good cosmetic.

26. A decoction of Yaṣṭīmadhu and juice of Vāsaka drunk with sugar and honey is a curative for Raktapitta (Haemoptysis) chlorosis and Jaundice.

27. Mere juice of Vāsaka taken with honey quells Haemoptysis. Taking in cold water in the morning quells even acute catarrh.

28. O Maheśvara, powdered Vibhītaka, Pippalī and Saindhava taken with sour gruel cures the hoarseness of voice (Aphonia).

29-30. In cases of Asthma the patient takes a decoction of powdered Āmalaka, Manaḥśilā, root of Balā, leaves of Kola and Guggulu with cow's milk; and smokes a Varti in Badari fire, prepared with Jātīpatra, Kolapatra, and Manaḥśilā. Undoubtedly he will be cured.

1. A synonym of *kadalī*

31. Powdered Triphalā and Pippalī taken with honey before the meal relieve thirst and fever.

32. A decoction of Bilvamūla, and Guḍūcī drunk with honey removes three types of vomiting undoubtedly. Dūrvā ground into paste with rice washings removes vomiting.

CHAPTER ONE HUNDRED AND NINETYONE

Diseases

Hari said :

1. Roots of white Punarnavā must be taken out on a day when the moon enters the Puṣya star and should be drunk with water. No serpent will ever come near him nor infest his house.

2. O Vṛṣadhvaja, he who wears as an amulet the image of Garuḍa made of bear's teeth, will never be bitten by a serpent in his life.

3. O Rudra, Serpents will find their fangs ineffective in him who drinks a decoction of the root of Śālmalī in water.

4. If the root Lajjālukā is culled on a day when the moon enters the Puṣya star and tied round the wrist or its paste is smeared over the body he will undoubtedly be able to catch hold of a serpent with impurity.

5. If the root of white Arka culled under the auspices of the asterism Puṣya is drunk with cold water, the poison due to the bites of insects or the sepsis due to sword cut etc. is quelled.

6. Smearing with the paste of the root of Mahākāla in sour gruel quells the poison of Voḍras and Dundubhas (different kinds of water snakes).

7. Roots of Taṇḍulīyaka soaked in rice washings and pasted, taken with clarified butter remove all kinds of poisons.

8. Roots of either Nīlī or Lajjālukā but not both, pasted with rice washings, if drunk, remove the poison due to insect bite.

9. The expressed juice of Kūṣmāṇḍa taken with jaggery or sugar and milk is an antidote for the poison due to insect bite.

10-12. The expressed juice of Kodrava root taken similarly removes loss of sense. Yaṣṭīmadhu taken with sugar and milk removes the poison of a rat in three days. If the mouth is burnt due to excess of lime while chewing betel leaves, three mouthfuls of cold water drunk will stop salivation. Ghī taken with sugar arrests intoxication and inebriety.

13. O Maheśvara, boiled water drunk with the roots of black Aṅkoṭa destroys undigested poison within three days.

14. O Mahādeva, the cow's fresh butter mixed with Saindhava quells the pain due to scorpion bite.

15-16. O Śiva, swallowing the compound of Kusumbha, Kuṁkuma, Haritāla, Manaḥśilā, Karañja, and ground root of Arka removes human bite poison, O Śaṅkara. Applying the oil from an oil lamp the poison of insects and Kharjūraka (scorpion) is removed. There is no doubt in this.

17. The place of bite must be smeared with a paste of Śuṇṭhī and Tagarapādika. By smearing these the poison of the sting of a honey bee is quelled.

18-19. In the above case a paste of Śatapuṣpā, Saindhava and butter does great good. O Mahādeva, an application of a paste of the seed of Śirīṣa cooked in milk removes the poison of dog bite. Frog bite is to be treated by burning the site of bite and pouring water there.

20. O Śiva with moon for crest, rat poison is quelled by drinking the juice of Dhattūraka mixed with milk, butter and jaggery.

21. Gargling with water boiled with the barks of Vaṭa Nimba and Śamī removes the pain due to poison in mouth or teeth.

22. O Lord of Umā, application of a paste of Devadāru and Gairika or a compound of Nāgeśvara, the two varieties of Haridrā, and Majīṭhikā[1] quells the poison of spider.

23. There is no doubt in this that a compound of the seeds of Karañja, barks of Varuṇa, Tila and Sarṣapa quells poison.

1. Perhaps the same as Mañjiṣṭhikā = rubia cordifolia.

24. The itching sensation of the horse can be removed in ten days, O Hara, by applying the paste of Kumārī patra with butter and salt.

CHAPTER ONE HUNDRED AND NINETYTWO

Diseases

Hari said :

1-3. Take eight parts of Citraka, sixteen parts of Śūraṇa[1] four parts of Śuṇṭhī, two parts of Marica, three parts of Pippalīmūla, four parts of Viḍaṅga, eight parts af Muṣalikā, and four parts of Triphalā. Take jaggery double the quantity of these drugs and prepare a Modaka (sweet meat) of them. This is a sure remedy for impaired digestion, jaundice, chlorosis, dysentery, indigestion and enlarged spleen.

4-7. Take these drugs each weighing ten palas :—Bilva, Agnimantha, Śyonāka, Pāṭalā, Pāribhadraka, Prasāraṇī, Aśvagandhā, Bṛhatī, Kaṇṭakārikā, Balā, Atibalā, Rāsnā, Śvadaṁṣṭrā, Punarnavā, Eraṇḍa, Śāribā[2], Parṇī, Guḍūcī and Kapikacchukā. They are to be boiled in pure water. When reduced to one fourth pour the decoction into an oil vessel and cook again. Four times this quantity of cow's or goat's milk must be poured and Śatāvarī and Saindhava equal to the oil must be added.

8-9. I shall mention the names of the drugs the residence of which is to be added :—Śatapuṣpā, Devadāru, Balā, Parṇī, Vacā, Aguru, Kuṣṭhā Māṁsī, Saindhava and Punarnavā. Each of these must be a pala in weight. The oil thus prepared can be used for anointing or as an errhine or as a potion.

10. This oil is a cure for cardiac pain, pleurodynia, goitre, hysteria and Vātarakta. The man shall regain lost manhood.

1. Amorphophallus campanutatus.

2. Perhaps Sārivā=(1) Hemidesmus indicus (ii) Cryptelepis bachanami (*GVDB*, p. 429-30).

11. By taking in this oil even the she-mule can conceive without risk to life. O Hara, what then about woman ? Horses and elephants affected by deranged Vāyu can be cured with this. Man afflicted by deranged Vāyu should be given this oil.

12. Mustard oil cooked with Hiṅgu, Tumburu and Śuṇṭhī is an efficacious ear drop for pain in the ear (otalgia).

13-14. Oil cooked in a decoction of dry Mūlaka and Śuṇṭhī reduced to ashes, Hiṅgula and Nāgara with four times of butter milk is a sure remedy for deafness, otalgia, and fetid discharges from ears. By pouring this oil into the ears all germs can be killed.

15-17. Oil cooked with the following drugs is a sure remedy for all sorts of earache. The ashes of dry Mūlaka and Śuṇṭhī, Hiṅgula, Nāgara, Śatapuṣpā, Vacā, Kuṣṭha, Dāru, Śigru, Rasāñjana, Sauvarcala, Yavakṣāra, sea salt, Granthika, Viḍa Musta, Madhu (honey) and Śukta four times in quantity, juice of Mātuluṅga and Kadalī.

18. Deafness, rumbling sound in the ears, fetid discharges and germs in the ears can be cured by pouring this oil into the ears.

19. The germs are killed instantaneously, O Śiva, with the moon for crest. This taila or oil is called Kṣārataila and it removes all sorts of impurities in mouth and teeth.

20-22. The Candanādi oil :—Oil is cooked with these drugs :—Candana, Kuṅkuma, Māṁsī, Karpūra, Jātipatrikā, fruits of Jātī, Kakkola, Pūga and Lavaṅga, Aguru, Kuṣṭha, Kastūrī, Tagarapādigā, Gorocanā, Priyaṅgu, Balā, Nakhī, Sarala, Saptaparṇa, Lākṣā, Āmalakī and Padmaka.

23. It cures excessive perspiration, bad odour, itching sensation and skin diseases. Internally administered it gives the man the virility to have sexual intercourse with a hundred women, and the women the ability to conceive though discarded as a sterile woman before.

24-25. Citrakaghṛta :—Butter a prastha in volume with water eight prasthas in volume should be cooked with these drugs :—Citraka, Yamānī, Dhanya, Trayūṣaṇa, Jīraka, Sauvarcala, Viḍaṅga, Pippalīmūla and Rājika. This butter cures piles, enlarged spleen, tumour, etc. and improves digestive power.

26-29. A prastha of mustard oil should be cooked in eight prasthas of cow's urine in a mud pot or iron cauldron slowly in low fire, with the following drugs each weighing a Karṣa :—Marica, Trivṛt, Kuṣṭha, Haritāla Manaḥśilā, Devadāru, the two kinds of Haridrā, Māṁsī, Candana, Viśālā, Karavīra, milky exudations from the Arka plant, watery serum extracted from cowdung and half a pala of Viṣa. This oil externally applied cures Pāmā, Vicarcikā, ring worm, and all foul sores. It gives a smoothness to the skin.

30. Many kinds of skin diseases like Śvitra can be cured with this oil. Even a chronic leucoderma gets cured instantly.

31-34. Butter should be cooked with Paṭolapatra, Kaṭukā, Mañjiṣṭhā, Śāribā, Niśā, Jātī, Śamī, Nimbapatra and Madhuka. O Śiva, external application of this mitigates the pain of suppurating ulcers.

Brāhmī Ghṛta :—A prastha of butter, juice of Kaṇṭakārī and milk should be cooked with an Akṣa weight of these drugs :—Brāhmī, Śaṅkhapuṣpī, Vacā, Soma, Vṛkṣasuvarcalā, Abhayā, Guḍūcī, Āṭarūṣaka and Vāgujī. This is called Brāhmī ghṛta. It increases power of memory and intellect.

35. A compound of Agnimantha, Vacā, Vāsā and Pippalī taken with honey and Saindhava for seven days enables one to sing as sweetly as the Kinnaras.

36. A three-day course of the compound of Apāmārga, Guḍūcī, Kuṣṭha, Śatāvarī, Vacā, Śaṅkhapuṣpā, Abhayā and Viḍaṅga with butter enables a man to retain in his memory the contents of eight hundred books.

37. Vacā taken with mere water, milk or butter daily for a month makes a man so intelligent as to grasp anything as soon as it is heard.

38. A pala of Vacā drunk with milk during lunar or solar eclipse makes a man highly gifted with intelligence instantly.

39-41. Water boiled with Bhūnimba, Nimba, Triphalā, Parpaṭa, Paṭolī, Mustaka, and Vāsaka cures carbuncles and impure blood. There is no doubt about this. Sticks prepared from Ketaka fruit, Śaṅkha, Vacā, Saindhava, Tryūṣaṇa, Phena,

Rasāñjana, Viḍaṅga, Manaḥśilā and honey cure Kāca (opaque eyes), blindness, and coatings in the eyelids.

42-44. A droṇa of water boiled two prasthas of Māṣaka must be reduced to one fourth. Pour a prastha of oil and cook with an Āḍhaka of sour gruel. Then add the following drugs well ground :—Punarnavā, Gokṣuraka, Saindhava, Tryūṣaṇa, Vacā, Lavaṇa, Suradāru, Mañjiṣṭhā and Kaṇṭakārīka. Internally administered or used as an errhine this oil cures acute earache.

45-46. O Maheśvara, the preceding oil anointed over the body quells deafness and many other ailments. Cook a prastha of oil with two palas of Saindhava, five palas each of Śuṇṭhī and Citraka with five prasthas of Sauvīra. This is a sure remedy for leucorrhoea, Aphonia, enlarged spleen and all types of disorders due to deranged Vāyu.

47-48. Oil cooked in a decoction of Udumbara, Vaṭa, Plakṣa, the two varieties of Jambū, Arjuna, Pippala, Kadamba, Palāśa, Lodhra, Tinduka, Madhūka, Āmra, Sarja, Badara, Padmakeśara, Śirīṣabīja and Ketaka quells all sorts of sores and ulcers though long standing, by means of an external application.

CHAPTER ONE HUNDRED AND NINETYTHREE

Diseases

Hari said :

1-2. A compound consisting of Palāṇḍu, Jīraka, Kuṣṭha, Aśvagandhā, Ajamodaka, Vacā, Trikaṭuka and salt powdered together must be treated with the juice of Brāhmī. Taken with honey and butter for seven days, it makes a man's intellect pure and keen.

3-5. A compound of Siddhārthaka, Vacā, Hiṅgu, Karañja, Devadāru, Mañjiṣṭhā, Triphalā Viśva, Śirīṣa, the two varieties of Rajanī, Priyaṅgu, Nimba and Trikaṭu ground with cow's urine can be used as an errhine, a plaster or as an unguent. It cures hysteria, poisoning, insanity, emaciation, fever and discoloration of the skin. It removes the fear from evil spirits and affords honour in the royal palace.

6-7. Nimba, Kuṣṭha, two varieties of Haridrā, Śigru, Sarṣapaja, Devadāru, Paṭola and Dhanya must be pasted together with buttermilk. The patient must be anointed with oil and the above medicated compound must be applied as an unguent. All sorts of Pāmās (scabs), Kuṣṭhas and itches are certainly removed.

8-10. Equal quantities of sea salt, rock salt, Kṣāra, Rājikā, Viḍalavaṇa, Kaṭu, iron filings, Trivṛt and Suvarṇaka must be cooked over low fire with curd, cow's urine and milk. This is called Agnibalacūrṇa. It must be taken with hot water after food or after digestion. The patient can have as his diet Māṣa and butter. It cures all sorts of colic of the umbilicus, urinary tracts and those due to enlarged spleen.

11. A compound of Abhayā, Āmalaka, Drākṣā, Pippalī, Kaṇṭakārikā, Śṛṅgī, Punarnavā and Śuṇṭhī cures Asthma and cough.

12. Abhayā, Āmalaka, Drākṣā, Pāṭhā, Vibhītaka and sugar taken in equal quantities is a sure remedy for fever.

13. Triphalā, Badara, Drākṣā, and Pippalī is a good purgative. Harītakī taken in hot water with salt is a good purgative.

14-15. Fumigating with the excreta, blood, hair or flesh of tortoise, fish, horse, buffalo, cow, jackal, monkey, cat, peacock, crow, boar, owl, fouls and swan is useful for the alleviation of the pain and disorder of the patients of fever and insanity.

16. O Bhaveśvara, all these medicines quell the ailments like the thunderbolt of Indra felling down trees.

17. When a medicine is being administered Lord Viṣṇu should necessarily be remembered. Thought of, worshipped or praised, He quells all ailments. There is no doubt in this.

CHAPTER ONE HUNDRED AND NINETYFOUR

Vaiṣṇava-Kavaca

Hari Said :

1. O Śambhu (Śiva), I shall explain the Vaiṣṇava Kavaca (the mystical Coat of mail of Viṣṇu) by means of which protection is afforded and which removes all ailments.

2-3. Having bowed to the divine Lord, the unborn, the eternal, the unsick lord of all the all pervading, omnipresent Janārdana I am tying this (Kavacam) which will never be in vain, which is incomparable and which wards off all miseries.

4. May Viṣṇu protect me in the front. May Kṛṣṇa protect me from behind. May Hari protect my head and Janārdana my heart.

5. May Hṛṣīkeśa protect my mind. May Keśava protect my tongue. May Vāsudeva protect my eyes. May the all pervading Saṅkarṣaṇa protect my ears.

6. May Pradyumna protect my nose. May Aniruddha protect my skin. May Vanamālī protect my inner throat. May Śrīvatsa protect the lower portion.

7. May the divine Discus, the destroyer of demons, protect my left side. May the divine Gadā (club) the destroyer of all demons protect my right side.

8. May the divine threshing rod protect my stomach; may the divine ploughshare protect my back. May the divine Śārṅga (bow) protect the upper part of my body. May the divine Nandaka (sword) protect my calves.

9. May the divine Śaṅkha (conch) protect my heel. May the divine Padma (lotus) protect my feet. May Garuḍa protect me for the fulfilment of all my activities.

10. May the divine Boar protect me in the waters. May Vāmana protect me in all difficult situations. May the Narasiṁha protect me in the forest. May Keśava protect me from all sides.

11. May Lord Hiraṇyagarbha grant me gold. May Kapila the propounder of the Sāṅkhya system cause the equilibrium of all my vital constituents.

12. May Aja (the unborn) the resident of Śveta Dvīpa (the white continent) lead me to Śvetadvīpa. May the slayer of Madhu and Kaiṭabha destroy all enemies.

13. May Viṣṇu extract for ever the sin from my body. May the divine Swan, Fish and Tortoise protect me on all sides.

14. May lord Trivikrama curb all my sins. May lord Nārāyaṇa guard my intellect.

15. May Śeṣa make my wisdom perfect and destroy ignorance. May Lord with the submarine fire for his mouth destroy whatever sin I may have committed.

16. May Lord Vāmana place on my head all bliss by means of his feet. May Dattātreya endow me with sons, cattle and kinsmen.

17. May Paraśurāma destroy all my enemies with his divine axe. May Rāma, the son of Daśaratha the powerful slayer of Rākṣasas protect me.

18. May Balarāma, the scion of Yādava family destroy my enemies by means of his divine ploughshare. May the infancy of Lord Kṛṣṇa marked by the annihilation of Pralamba, Keśi, Cāṇūra, Pūtanā and Kaṁsa, grant me all I desire.

19. I see a Being more terrible than pitch darkness, dark and tawny resembling the God of death with the noose in his hands and am terrified.

20. Hence, I sought refuge in Acyuta the lotus-eyed. I am fortunate and fearless in having for ever the lord Hari (at my side).

21. Contemplating on the Lord Nārāyaṇa, the destroyer of all harassments I have tied this Kavaca and am roaming over the Earth.

22. I am invincible to all living beings, for verily I identify myself with all devas inasmuch as I remember the lord of lords Viṣṇu of unlimited splendour.

23. May success befall me for ever as indicated in the Mantra. He who sees me with wicked eyes, whom I see (with contempt) in the eyes, let him be bound and hit in the eyes, the sinner and the vicious that he is.

24. Let the spokes of the divine discus of Vāsudeva chop off my sins, let them hit those who perpetrate violence on me.

25-27. This above mantra is to be recited when Rākṣasas and Piśācas attack, while one is in the wild woods and forests, when there is an argument, in the high ways, at the gaining table, during quarrels, while crossing a river, when a danger faces one, when there is a conflagration, when thieves attack in a body, when all the planets (or any of them) are adverse, when lightning strikes, when the fury of the poison of serpents spreads, in sickness, when there is distress due to obstacles, in fact whenever there is something to fear from.

28. This is Lord's own mantra, the most sacred of all mantras. This famous Kavaca is an esoteric secret. It destroys all sins. It has created and destroyed everything by means of the Māyā that originates from it. It is the Great. It is inscrutable.

29. Oṁ Padmanābha, the beginningless, the endless, the seed of the Universe, obeisance unto thee. Oṁ Svāhā to Time. Oṁ Svāhā to the personified Being of Time. Oṁ Svāhā to Kṛṣṇa(the black). Oṁ Svāhā to Kṛṣṇarūpa (black in form). Oṁ Svāhā to Caṇḍa (the fierce). Oṁ Svāhā to Caṇḍarūpa (the fierce in form). Oṁ Svāhā to Pracaṇḍa. Oṁ Svāhā to Pracaṇḍarūpa. Oṁ Svāhā to Sarva. Oṁ Svāhā to Sarvarūpa. Oṁ obeisance to the lord of the universe, to the creator of the three worlds. Here, Viṭi Siviṭi Siviṭi Svāhā. Oṁ obeisance to Ayokheti to the divinity called "Ye ye".

This body of mine is subject to the attacks of undeserving persons, Daityas, Dānavas, Yakṣas, Rākṣasas, Bhūtas, Piśācas and Kūṣmāṇḍas and such vile ailments as hysteria, vomiting, the unbearable fevers as the intermittent, diurnal, tertian, quotidian, nocturnal, dusk fevers etc and the injection of poison from spiders, insects, thorns, Pūtanā spirits, and serpents. Poisoning agents may be mobile or immobile. Let it be kept sound. Tumburu Sphuṭa Sphuṭa Prakoṭa Laphaṭa. May Vikaṭadaṁṣṭra, (of crooked teeth) protect me from the East. Oṁ Hai Hai Hai Hai Hai. O you the deity endowed with ten thousand suns and Kāla be victorious and protect me from the west. Oṁ Nivi Nivi O Mahākapila, resplendent like the flame of the glowing fire protect me from the north. Oṁ Vili Vili Mili Mili Gaṛuḍi Garuḍi. May Gaurī and Gāndhārī delude with the upsetting swoons of poison Svāhā; protect me from the south.

Turn your glance towards me; save, save me from the harassment of the terrific onslaught of all living beings. Be victorious; be victorious. Let the enemy dwindle by that. Let the rays as multitudinous as the turns of Yugas afford protection and fearlessness. Let them enter the abdomen as they set. May the different manifestations of Lord Hari—Vāsudeva, Saṅkarṣaṇa, Pradyumna and Aniruddha, Viṣṇu and Nārāyaṇa destroy all my fevers.

CHAPTER ONE HUNDRED AND NINETYFIVE

A Lore for fulfilling a desire in seven nights

Hari said :

1-2. Listen to that Lore which fulfils all desires in seven nights—"Obeisance unto Lord Vāsudeva whom we meditate upon. Obeisance unto Pradyumna and Aniruddha. Obeisance unto Saṅkarṣaṇa. Obeisance unto the giver of wisdom, the embodied form of perfect Bliss.

3. Obeisance to Thee that resteth in the soul, the quiet, free from dualistic vision. Thou art all the forms. Obeisance unto thee.

4 Obeisance unto Thee the great Hṛṣīkeśa, of endless manifestation, in whom all these visible creations stay and from whom other forms of creation emerge.

5. Thou bearest this terrestrial sphere. Obeisance unto Thee the Brahman, whom the mind, the intellect, the sense organs and the vital airs touch not nor know. Thou movest both within and without like the expansive firmament. I bow unto Thee .

6. Oṁ obeisance to the Lord the great Puruṣa, the lord of the great Bhūtas, having two lotus like feet in the form of all Sāttvika qualities manifested in arts and Dhārmika activities.

O Parameṣṭhin obeisance unto Thee. Citraketu attained the status of a Vidyādhara by means of this Vidyā (Esoteric mystic knowledge).

CHAPTER ONE HUNDRED AND NINETYSIX

Viṣṇu-dharma

Hari said :

1. Indra was reinstated in his position by reciting the Viṣṇu Dharmavidyā after defeating his enemies. O Maheśvara, I shall mention it.

2. The syllables Om etc. must be psychically located in the feet, knees, thighs, belly, heart, chest, mouth and th head in order.

3. (The eight syllabled mantra). "Oṁ Namo Nārāyaṇāya" can be located in the inverse order as well. Then Karanyāsa can be made with the twelve syllabled mantra : Oṁ Namo Bhagavate Vāsudevāya).

4. Beginning with Praṇava and ending with 'ya' they are to be located in the knots of the fingers including the thumbs and the Oṅkāra in the chest (heart) and the entire mantra on the head.

5. The Oṅkāra of the mantra 'Oṁ Viṣṇave' is to be located between the eyebrows and the other syllables in the tuft, eyes and head. This is called Mantranyāsa.

6. The devotee should then meditate on the great Ātman with whose power Śeṣa is endowed. May Hari protect me. May the fish manifestation protect me in waters.

7. May Trivikrama protect me in the sky. May Vāmana protect me on land. May Narasiṁha protect me in the forest. May Rāma protect me on the mountain.

8. May the Boar manifestation protect me on the Earth. May Nārāyaṇa protect me in the firmament. May Kapila save me from the bondage of Karma. May Datta guard my Yogas.

9. May Hayagrīva, Kumāra (Lord Kārttikeya) the protector of deities and Makaradhvaja save me. May Nārada distract me from the worship of another deity. May Lord Kūrma protect me in the south-west always.

10. May Dhanvantari save me from incompatible diet. May Nāga save me from the clutches of anger. May Yajña save me from all ailments. May Vyāsa protect me from the pitfalls of ignorance.

11. May Buddha save me from the heretic multitude. May Kalki save me from sins. May Viṣṇu protect me at midday. May Nārāyaṇa protect me in the morning.

12. May the slayer of Madhu save me in the afternoon. May Mādhava save me in the evening. May Hṛṣīkeśa protect me at dusk. May Janārdana protect me at dawn.

13. May Śrīdhara protect me at midnight. May Padmanābha protect me in the small hours of the night. May the divine discus, Kaumodakī (the club) and the arrows destroy my enemies and Rākṣasas.

14-15. May the Śaṅkha and Padma protect me from the enemies. May Śārṅga (the bow) and Garuḍa protect my intellect, sense organs, mind and vital airs. May the side ornaments of the lord and the remaining form of the lord protect me everywhere and at all times. May Narasiṁha protect me in the quarters and the interstices always.

16. Whomsoever the wearer of this divine mantra sees with his eyes, shall be under his control, free from sins and ailments.

CHAPTER ONE HUNDRED AND NINETYSEVEN

Gāruḍamantra

Dhanvantari said:

1. I shall explain the Gāruḍa mantra first mentioned to Kaśyapa by his great friend Garuḍa whereby this great Gāruḍī vidyā dispels poison.

2-3. The five elements of Earth, Water Fire, Wind and Ether are presided over by the deities. They are the presiding deities of the mystical diagrams. They are attained by the devotees of Viṣṇu. The letters other than long vowels represent them. The deities are other than the Napuṁsakas.

4. The six parts of the body include two calves, two arms, the navel and the head. The Kavaca covers the heart, head and the tuft with the eyes. The Astra mantra is used for Nyāsa which is the location in their respective seats.

5. At the end of the realisation of every thing the Kāla Vahni (Death fire) and Vāyu (wind) are represented beneath. The sixth vowel in conjunction with the crescent moon (Ū and Anusvāra) is the mystic great syllable.

6. The Parā and the Aparā are said to be above and below. In all the Aṅgas the Nyāsa is to be made duly with Repha (the letter 'RA').

7. The Nyāsa is made in the heart, palms, body, ears and the eyes. By means of the Japa all success can be achieved. The Maṇḍala (mystical diagram) has four faces.

8. The Earth must be meditated upon as a spacious square yellow in colour and presided over by Indra. The zone of Varuṇa is in the middle.

9-11. At its centre is the lotus with the semicircular moon with sapphire splendour. This is gentle. Or an Āgneya-maṇḍala (a fiery zone) triangular in shape can be contemplated upon. A flaming fire with Svastika shall then be meditated over. Beyond that, a circle decorated with the central Bindu (point) and resembling a cut block of antimony is to be contemplated upon. Beyond this, the Vyomāmṛta maṇḍala is to be thought of. It resembles waves of milk and has the splendour of pure crystal. It sweeps the entire universe.

12. Vāsuki and Śaṅkhapāla are stationed in the maṇḍala of the Earth. Karkoṭa and Padmanābha are stationed in the Varuṇa maṇḍala.

13-14. Kulika is stationed in the Āgneya maṇḍala. Takṣaka and Mahābjaka are stationed in Vāyumaṇḍala. The five elements are to be located in the fingers beginning with thumb and ending with the little finger; in the usual order and in the inverse order. In the joints of fingers Jayā and Vijayā are to be located.

15. The Śivaṣaḍaṅga mantra is to be located in the mouth, etc. The Hṛd-mantra is to be located in the arms or in the fingers or in the tuft.

16-17. The Vyāpaka mantra is to be located before that in the knotty joints of the fingers. The Bhūtanyāsa and other rites should be performed as well as Śivāṅga mantras located with Praṇava in the beginning and Namaḥ in the end. Thus the rule for establishing and worshipping has been explained.

18. The mantra of the eight varieties of serpents consists of the first letters of their respective names, by invoking which they can be drawn to one's vicinity.

19. The Pañcabhūta mantras duly preceded by Oṁ Svāhā when recited will draw Tārkṣya to one's presence fulfilling all activities.

20-22. After performing the Karanyāsa with the vowels, Śarīra Nyāsa must be performed again. He must think of Prāṇa as blazing and purifying the Ātman. The Bīja mantra is to be contemplated in the act of showering nectarine downpour. Thus invigorating oneself and contemplating on the head the earth is to be located at the feet—the earth shining like molten gold, surrounded by the entire universe and guarded by the Lokapālas.

23. The intelligent scholar shall locate this divine earth in his body. Beyond that the region is twice that of the Earth and is dark blue in colour.

24-25. Ravi's maṇḍala is triangular in shape and is to be located between the navel and the neck. The entire Brahmāṇḍa is illuminated by clusters of flames. Beyond that is the fierce maṇḍala of Vāyu that should be contemplated having the colour of a block of antimony and ensconced in the image of Self.

26. The Vyoma (Ether) maṇḍala is to be contemplated as situated over the tuft. It is of pure crystal splendour, unlimited, all pervasive and nectarine.

27-28. After performing the Bhūta Nyāsa and that of the Nāgas with the mantras ending with the letter 'La' and coupled with the Bindu (Nasal sound 'M'), Śiva Bīja must be given and the maṇḍala must be contemplated. The clever devotee must strictly follow the order in the case of the Maṇḍalas and the colour should be meditated upon at the time of the rite.

29-30. In the cases of poisoning due to stationary and mobile factors (animals and vegetables) Tārkṣya should be contemplated as ornamented with black serpents in the feet, wings and beak. In the case of the malignant attack of evil planets, Bhūtas, Piśācas, Ḍākinīs, Yakṣas and Rākṣasas, Śiva should be located in the body after making him encircled by serpents.

31. Thus the twofold Nyāsas have been explained for the serpents and the five elements. After contemplating thus the practice of the charm should be commenced in due order.

32. After giving the Tritattva, the Śivatattva must be given above it. The Nyāsa is the same in Deva and joints of fingers as in the body.

33-34. After performing Deha-Nyāsa first in the usual and inverse orders, the Kanda, Nāla, Padma, Dharma and Jñāna should be worshipped with the final letters of the different Vargas (gutturals etc.) appended with the second vowel. The mantra Kṣaum should be located in the pericarp with Repha appended on the head.

35. The Vargas are—A-, Ka,- Ca-, Ṭa-, Ta-, Pa-, Ya-, and Śa- They are to be placed in the east, west, etc. Two letters each should be placed in leaves and petals.

36. The vowels are to be located in the petals where sixteen principles ending with Īśa are to be worshipped : The Śaktis are Vāmā and others. The three Tattvas are to be located therein.

37. The auspicious limb (Śivam Aṅgam) should be invoked on the head. Thereafter the Deva shall be located in the pericarp with all attendants and followers.

38. The Pṛthivī principle shall be worshipped in the western leaf; the Āpaḥ (water) principles are located in the northern leaf; Tejas principle is to be worshipped in the southern leaf and Vāyu principle is to be worshipped in the eastern leaf.

39. The respective Bīja as mentioned before shall be duly assigned in the Mūrtirūpa (in the form of idol). 'Yam' is the

Mūla (root) of Vāyu and should be placed in south west. The Bīja 'Ra' is located in the south east.

40. The bīja 'Vam' is located in the north east and worshipped always. Oṁ should be worshipped located in the heart. The Tanmātrās (material principles) and Bhūtamātrās (gross matter) are to be worshipped outside the occult diagram.

41. The Śivāṅgas are to be contemplated thereafter and worshipped. The heart is to be worshipped in the south east and the head in north east.

42. The tuft is to be located in the south west. The Kavaca is to be located in the north west. The Astra is to be given outside the diagram. The Netra (eye) is located in the north.

43-45. The devotee shall worship the Bījas at the tip of the petals and the pericarp. The eight Nāgas beginning with Ananta and ending with Kulīra are located from the east to the north east in order. The devotee repeating the mantras shall worship using the procedure separately either in the heart-lotus or in the diagram drawn on the slate, etc. This procedure is to be adopted in all Nitya and Naimittika rites [Rites enjoined as daily duty are Nityas and special rites for special occasions are Naimittikas].

46. The devotee shall constantly think of the Ātaman as Kāmarūpa (able to assume any form he wishes), pleasing to the mind and sweeping the entire universe which it creates and annihilates.

47-48. He must remember Bhairava who illuminates the entire cosmos beginning with Brahman and ending with the world, by means of clusters of flames, who has ten arms, four faces, tawny eyes, three eyes and the moon for his crest, who wields the trident and who is terrific on account of the curved teeth for the purpose of achievement. He must remember Garuḍa too in all activities.

49-54. For the destruction of snakes and serpents Garuḍa the terrible is to be remembered. His feet are placed on the leaves. His wings rest in the quarters. The seven heavens touch his chest. The cosmos comes upto his throat. All the Rudras ending with Īśa are to be contemplated as stationed in his head. The three Śaktis located in the matted hair of Sadāśiva identified with Garuḍa must be thought of. Tarkṣya is the great

Śiva himself greater than the greatest and lord of the universe : He has therefore three eyes. He is terrific in appearance. He destroys poisonous serpents. His mouth devours everything. Garuḍa's body is constituted with mantras. He is as blazing as the Kālāgni (Death fire) In every activity he must be remembered. After performing this Nyāsa duly whatever the devotee thinks in his mind becomes possible for achievement. The devotee becomes Garuḍa himself. Ghosts, Bhūtas, Yakṣas, Nāgas, Gandharvas, Rākṣasas, etc. die at his very sight. Cāturthika and other fevers get quelled.

Dhanvantari said :

55. Lord Śiva himself told thus to Garuḍa and Garuḍa narrated this to Kaśyapa. Now listen to the Vidyā which Maheśvara explained to Gaurī.

CHAPTER ONE HUNDRED AND NINETYEIGHT

Eulogy of Tripurā

Bhairava said :

1. I shall explain the Tripurā Vidyā, (otherwise known as) Nityaklinnā, that accords worldy enjoyment as well as salvation.

Oṁ Hrīm come thou, O Goddess. Aiṁ Hrīṁ Hrīṁ Rekhākāraṇam (the delineation) Oṁ Hrīṁ Kledinī Bhaṁ obeisance; so also with the exciter of lust. Aiṁ Yaṁ Yaṁ Krīṁ Vā Gaṇarekhayā Hrīṁ Madanāntare Ca (in the midst of cupid's activity) Aiṁ Hrīṁ Hrīṁ Ca Nirañjanā Vāgati Madanāntarekhe Khanetrāvalīti Ca. Vegavati Mahā Pretāsanā is to be worshipped. Oṁ Hrīṁ Kraiṁ Naiṁ Kraiṁ Nityaṁ Madadrave Krīṁ obeisance. Aiṁ Hrīṁ obeisance to Tripurā. Oṁ Hrīṁ Krīṁ Paścimavaktram (Western face). Oṁ Aiṁ Hrīṁ Hrīṁ Ca Tathottaram (the northern) Aiṁ Hrīṁ Dakṣiṇam (southern) Cordhvam Vaktram Tu Paścimam. Oṁ Hrīṁ Pāśāya (to the noose), krīṁ Aṅkuśāya (to the goad), Aiṁ Kapālāya Namaḥ (obeisance to the skull). Ādyam Bhayam Aiṁ Hrīṁ Hrīṁ Ca Tathā Śiraḥ Tathā Śikhāyai Kavace Aiṁ Hrīṁ Krīṁ Astrāya Phaṭ (These are the Nyāsa mantras).

2. In the east obeisance to Kāmarūpa Asitāṅga Bhairava. Obeisance to Brahmāṇī. In the south obeisance to Kanda. Invocation to Rurubhairava and Māheśvarī.

3. Similarly, in the west obeisance to Caṇḍa, to Kaumārī. In the north obeisance to Ulka and Krodha (anger), obeisance to Vaiṣṇavī.

4. In the south east obeisance to Aghora, to Unmatta-bhairava, to Vārāhī. In the south west obeisance to Sāra, to Kapālin, to Bhairava, to Māhendrī.

5. In the north west obeisance to Jālandhara, to Bhīṣaṇa, ṭo Bhairava to Cāmuṇḍā. In the north-east obeisance to Vaṭuka. Saṁhāra and Caṇḍikā are to be worshipped.

6. Rati, Prīti and Kāmadeva i.e. Pañcabāṇa should be worshipped then. Devī is propitiated by contemplation, worship, recitation and sacrificial offerings.

7. The eternal Tripurā worshipped in the Jvālāmukhī order removes all ailments. I shall explain the Jvālāmukhī order. She is to be worshipped at the centre. She is auspicious.

8-10. These are to be worshipped outside the diagram:— Nityā, Aruṇa, Madanātura, Mahā Mohā, Prakṛti, Kalanā, Śrī, Bhāratī, Ākarṣaṇī, Mahendrāṇī, Brahmāṇī, Māheśī, Kaumārī, Vaiṣṇavı, Vārāhī, Māhendrī, Cāmuṇḍā, Aparājitā, Vijayā, Ajitā, Mohinī, Tvaritā, Stambhinī, Jṛmbhiṇī and Kālikā are to be worshipped outside the mystical Padma. By worshipping in the Jvālāmukhī order poisons will be removed.

CHAPTER ONE HUNDRED AND NINETYNINE

Cūḍāmaṇi

Bhairava said :

1. I shall explain the process of Cūḍāmaṇi for the discrimination of good and bad omens. The soothsayer shall

write after remembering Sun, goddess, Gaṇanātha[1] and Somadeva (Śiva).

2. As soon as he hears the Praśna Vākya (the question put by the consultant) he shall draw three lines horizontally, vertically in the form of an idol or eight separate chambers in the eight quarters wherein he shall indicate the symbols banner, etc.

3. He shall write these in Nāmamantra form (the initial letters) :— (1) banner (2) smoke (3) lion (4) dog (5) bull (6) mule (7) elephant and (8) crow.

4. Seeing banner in the chamber of the banner prognosticates anxiety over kingdom, wealth etc. Smoke situated in the chamber of the banner presages anxious thought about metals and gain.

5. If lion is stationed in the chamber of the banner acquisition of wealth, etc. is the result. Dog stationed in the chamber of the banner indicates worries over maid-servants, pleasure, etc.

6. Bull seen in the chamber of the banner indicates worries over position and gain. Seeing a mule in the chamber of the banner indicates misery, pain, etc.

7. An elephant seen in the chamber of the banner presages worry over position, victory, etc. A crow stationed in the chamber of the banner indicates worries over pain and loss of wealth.

8. Seeing a banner in the chamber of smoke indicates misery first and then wealth. Seeing smoke in the chamber of the smoke presages quarrels and miseries.

9. If lion is stationed in the chamber of the smoke it indicates mental worries and acquisition of wealth. Dog stationed in the chamber of smoke prognosticates victory and gain.

10. Seeing a bull in the chamber of smoke presages acquisition of women, cows, horses, wealth etc. Seeing a mule in the chamber of smoke indicatessickness and loss of wealth.

1. Gaṇeśa, Lord of Gaṇas, the younger son of Lord Śiva. He is represented in iconography with the head of an elephant possessed of a single tusk.

11. If elephant is seen in the chamber of smoke it indicates acquisition of kingdom, victory etc. If crow is stationed in the chamber of smoke it presages destruction of wealth and kingdom.

12 Seeing banner in the chamber of the lion one can prognosticate acquisition of kingdom, etc. If smoke is stationed in the chamber of the lion it indicates acquisition of virgin's wealth.

13. If lion is stationed in the chamber of lion it indicates victory and meeting with friends. Dog stationed in the chamber of the lion indicates worries about women and acquisition of village.

14. Seeing a bull in the chamber of the lion indicates acquisition of house, field and gain. Seeing elephant in the chamber of the lion indicates ownership of a village.

15. Seeing an elephant in the chamber of the lion indicates health, longevity, happiness, etc. If crow is stationed in the chamber of the lion it indicates acquisition of virgin's grains, good qualities.

16. Seeing a banner in the chamber of a dog indicates worries of the position, pleasure, etc. Smoke stationed in the chamber of the dog indicates quarrels and failure in business.

17. If lion is stationed in the chamber of the dog it inditates successful achievement in business. If dog is stationed in the chamber of the dog it will result in loss of wealth.

18. Seeing a bull in the chamber of the dog the patient will be free from sickness. Seeing a mule in the chamber of the dog there is fear of quarrel.

19. Seeing an elephant in the chamber of the dog indicates a re-union with sons and wife. If a crow is stationed in the chamber of the dog it indicates affliction and ruin of the family.

20. Seeing a banner in the chamber of the bull indicates honour in the royal court, pleasure etc. If smoke is stationed in the chamber of the bull it indicates royal favour and happiness.

21. If the lion is stationed in the chamber of the bull it indicates all round fortune, wealth, etc. If dog is stationed in the chamber of the bull it augurs strength, splendour and love.

22. Seeing a bull in the chamber of the bull indicates fame, satisfaction, pleasure, etc. Seeing a mule in the chamber of the bull indicates great gain, etc.

23. Seeing an elephant in the chamber of the bull indicates acquisition of women and elephants. If a crow is stationed in the chamber of the bull it indicates gain of good position and honour.

24. Seeing banner in the chamber of the mule indicates illness, sorrow, etc. If smoke is stationed in the chamber of the mule it indicates fear from thieves.

25. If lion is stationed in the chamber of the mule it indicates honour, fame, victory, etc. If dog is stationed in the chamber of the mule, it indicates torment and loss of wealth.

26. Seeing a bull in the chamber of the mule indicates pleasure and reunion with the beloved. Seeing a mule in the chamber of the misery, affliction can be prognosticated.

27. Seeing an elephant in the chamber of the mule indicates pleasure, acquisition of sons, etc. If crow is stationed in the chamber of the mule it indicates quarrel and sickness.

28. Seeing a banner in the chamber of the elephant indicates acquisition of women, victory, splendour, happiness, etc. If smoke is stationed in the chamber of the elephant it indicates acquisition of wealth and grain.

29. If lion is stationed in the chamber of the elephant it indicates victory and achievement of success. If dog is stationed in the chamber of the elephant it indicates health, happiness and prosperity.

30. Seeing a bull in the chamber of the elephant indicates royal honour, wealth, etc. Seeing a mule in the chamber of the elephant indicates misery first and pleasure afterwards.

31. Seeing elephant in the chamber of the elephant indicates fields, grains, happiness etc. If crow is stationed in the chamber of the elephant it indicates acquisition of wealth and grains.

32. Seeing banner in the chamber of the crow indicates failure in ventures. If smoke is stationed in the chamber of the crow it indicates involvement in quarrels and misery.

33. If lion is stationed in the chamber of the crow it indicates quarrels and misery. If dog is stationed in the chamber of the crow it indicates great fear and split in the house.

34. Seeing a bull in the chamber of the crow indicates fall from position, terror, etc. Seeing a mule in the chamber of the crow indicates loss of wealth and defeat.

35. Seeing an elephant in the chamber of the crow. indicates wealth, fame, etc. If a crow is stationed in the chamber of the crow it indicates a visit to a foreign land.

CHAPTER TWO HUNDRED

Diseases

Bhairava said :

1. O Goddess ! I shall explain the subjugation of Vāyu. This will indicate success or failure as the case may be. Vāyu, Agni, Jala and Śakra[1] are the four auspicious things.

2. Vāyu stationed in the right and left sides flows in various directions. If it takes an upward course it is designated Agni. If it takes a downward course it is designated Varuṇa (or Jala).

3. Mahendra (or Śakra) is the stationary Vāyu taking the middle course. In the bright half of the lunar month it is stationed in the left side. In the dark half it is stationed in the right side. Once it rises it follows the same course for three days and changes thereafter.

4-5. At the beginning of a fortnight it flows upwards and then comes down. If its rise is along the sun's path and its setting is along the moon's, all the good qualities increase, otherwise there is obstruction. There are sixteen periods of transit in the course of a day and night, O bright-faced lady !

1. Indra, lord of the gods but here it means wind.

6. At the close of a period of an hour and a half when the Vāyu changes its course there is a likelihood of a man losing his normal health.

7-9. If the course of the Vāyu is in the right side that period is good for taking food or indulging in sexual intercourse Wielding a sword, going to the battle out of one's own will, etc. are to be undertaken when Vāyu is taking its leftward course. When Vāyu is stationary or the course is favourable asking questions (study, seeking knowledge, etc.) is good. When the Vāyu is in the Māhendra state, no evil befalls him. In the atmosphere if the Vāyu takes a right hand course there is drought. If it takes a leftward course there will be rain.

CHAPTER TWO HUNDRED AND ONE

Medical treatment of horses and elephants

Dhanvantari said :

1-4. I shall explain the Āyurveda of horses wherein all things connected with them and their treatment are mentioned in detail. There are many types of horses fit only to be set aside They are :—Kākatuṇḍī (crow-lipped), Kṛṣṇajihva (black-tongued), Ṛkṣāsya (bear-faced), Uṣṇatāluka (hot-palated), Karāla (fierce looking) Hīnadanta (Deficient or lacking in teeth), Śṛṅgī, (horned), Viraladantaka (few-toothed), Ekāṇḍa (single -testicled), Jātāṇḍakañcuka (Born with Scrotal tumour), Dvikhurī-cleft hoofed), Stanī (Teated), Mārjārapāda (cat-footed), Vyāghrābha (resembling tigers), Kuṣṭhavidradhisannibha appearing as if affected by Kuṣṭha and tumours), Yamaja (Twin-born), Vāmana (diminutive in size), Mārjāraloana (cat-eyed) and Kapilocana (monkey-eyed). The first clcass horse is the Turkish (Turuṣkaja). The middling is five hastas tall and the lowest, three hastas tall.

5. Those horses whose limbs are not short, whose ears are short and whose hue is of a mixture of many colours lightly shaded live long and are not afflicted.

6-7. Ways of guarding against evil are the worship of Revanta, sacrificial offerings and feeding of brahmins. A compound of Sarala, leaves of Nimba, Guggulu, Sarṣapa, Tila, Vacā, and Hiṅgu with butter should be tied round the neck of a horse. Ulcers affecting horses are of two types (1) due to extraneous causes (2) due to derangement of humours.

8. Vātaja type of ulcers is marked by delayed suppuration, the Kaphaja ulcers suppurate quickly, the pittaja type of ulcers gives a burning sensation at the throat and ulcers due to impure blood do not pain much.

9-10. What we call due to extraneous causes is the wound caused by weapons, etc. In order to wash off the impurities in the wounds and ulcers the following compound is used: Roots of Eraṇḍa, two shoots of Haridrā, Citraka, Viśvabheṣaja[1] and Rasona[2] or Saindhava well ground with butter milk and sour gruel. Tila, fried grain flour pasted with curd and salt or a paste of Nimba leaves and ball of rice applied over a wound purifies and heals it.

11-13. A compound of powdered Paṭola, Nimba leaves, Vacā, Citraka, Pippalī Śṛṅgavera given to the horse with water for a drink destroys worms, mucous discharges, intoxication and deranged Vāyu. If there is cutaneous affection the horse must be bled and a decoction of Nimba leaves, Paṭola, Triphalā and Khadira must be given to the horse.

14. Application of mustard oil is effective in Kuṣṭhas with ulcers. A decoction of Laśuna, etc. administered as a drink alleviates it.

15-17. In certain afflictions when errhines become necessary either the juice of Mātuluṅga or that of Māṁsī should be used for that purpose. The first day's dosage is two Palam weight. Every day it has to be increased by a Pala. The maximum for a first class horse is eighteen Palas. In the middling it is fourteen and for the lowest class of horse it is eight Pala weight. Errhines are not to be administered in Autumn or summer.

1. Zingiber officinale.
2. Allium sativum.

18. In a Vātaja type of disease the medium is oil in combination with sugar, butter and milk. In a Kaphaja type Vyoṣa with mustard oil must be the medium. In a pittaja ailment with water Triphalā can be used as the medium.

19. A horse regularly fed on Ṣaṣṭika Śāli grains and milk will never come to a state of being condemned. A golden coloured horse or one of the complexion of ripe Jambū fruit is never to be condemned.

20. A horse slightly injured should be given Guggulu and fed on milk pudding. It will be immediately relieved and be normal.

21. In a Vātaja ailment the diet of a horse is Śāli grains and milk. In a Pittaja ailment a Karṣa of gravy with Mudga soup, honey and butter shall be given.

22. In Kaphaja diseases mudga or Kulattha can be given. If the horse is affected with deafness and deranged kapha it should be fed with pungent and bitter articles of diet. If the ailment is of Tridoṣa origin Guggulu is to be administered along with its mouthfuls (of grass, etc).

23-24. In all ailments Dūrvā should be given along with other grasses. On the first day a Pala weight of it is to be given. Increasing it by a Karṣa every day, up to five Palas per day can be given. In drinks or diet eight Palas should be the maximum limit, in the middling it is sixty and in the lowest type it is forty.

25-26. If the horse is affected by Kuṣṭha, ulcers, or lameness it shall be administered with the decoction of Triphalā; if it is affected by impaired digestion or tumour it shall be administered with cow's urine. If it is affected by Vātapitta or ulcers it is administered with cow's milk and butter; for lean horses the diet shall be supplemented by meat.

27. In the mornings during Autumn and summer horses should be given five Palas of well powdered Guḍūcī with butter.

28. This quells ailment, nourishes, increases strength and splendour. It can be given alone or in combination with some Alkali.

29. Along with the administration of Guḍūcī, four palas (in the case of the middling) and three palas (in the case of lowest type of horse) of Śatāvarī and Aśvagandhā also must be given.

30. When suddenly the horses assume uniformity in colour and features or die together it must be immediately considered as an epidemic.

31. Sacrificing Horses, giving oblations or feeding of Brahmins may cause their suppression. Or Harītakīkalpa can be resorted to.

32. Harītakī is soaked in cow's urine and Taila (oil) and salt is added. On the first day, five such Harītakīs are given. Every day the dosage is increased by five Harītakīs till the maximum of hundred in the case of the best horse, eighty in middling and sixty in the least one is reached.

33. I shall now explain Gajāyurveda (treatment etc. of elephants). The medical decoctions etc. mentioned before are efficacious in elephants too. The dosage is four times of that of a horse. All ailments can thus be cured.

34. In an epidemic among elephants the alleviation is by means of a pacifying rite (Śānti Karma)[1] by the worship of gods and brahmins and the gift of a Kapilā (pale-brown or tawny) cow.

35. The physician must observe fast and tie a consecrated garland round the tusks of the elephant along with Vacā and Siddārthaka drugs equally consecrated.

36. The worship of Sun, Śiva, Durgā, Śrī and Viṣṇu protects the elephant. Oblations must be given to Bhūtas. The elephant must be bathed with four pitcherfuls of water.

37. The diet of the elephant must be consecrated with mantras. The elephant must be smeared with holy ashes. The pure auspicious propitiation of the Bhūtas will protect the elephant.

38-39. A pungent decoction of Triphalā, Pañcakola, Daśamūla, Viḍaṅgaka, Śatāvarī, Guḍūcī, Nimba, Vāsaka, and Kiṁśuka[2] is very efficacious in quelling all ailments of an elephant. Thus I have summarised what is mentioned in the two Āyurveda treatises (that of horses and that of elephants).

1. Observances or ceremonies calculated to remove calamities.
2. Butea monosperma.

CHAPTER TWO HUNDRED AND TWO

Diseases

Hari said:

1. O Śiva, a single fresh root of punarnavā or apāmārga, when inserted into the vagina of a woman, is capable of removing the local pain. It can also alleviate the young mother's pain experienced during delivery.

2. The roots of Bhūmi-Kūṣmāṇḍa alongwith the powder of Śāli[1], if taken with milk for a week, increase the milk in women's breasts.

3. O Śiva, the paste of roots of Indra-vāruṇi[2] removes the pain in female-breasts. It may be cooked in butter and a bread be prepared out of it which, when eaten, will remove the vaginal pains, O Siva.

4. If the vagina has come out, then apply to it the paste of Kāravella[3] roots; it will attain its natural position, there is no doubt about it.

5. The roots of Nīlī[4] and Poṭola[5] when pasted into a solution of tila and butter and applied to (the patient), remove the Jvālā-gardabha[6] disease.

6. O Rudra, the roots of Pāṭhā,[7] when ground in the scum of boiled rice and drunk, remove pāpa-roga.[8] Kuṣṭha roots taken in the same way also act likewise.

7. The solution of Vāsya, when drunk with honey, relieves the internal itching pain experienced during the pāpa-roga, O Śiva.

8. Equal quantity of butter and lākṣā, when drunk with milk, cure pradara,[9] there is no doubt in this.

1. Variant *śāli-taṇḍula-vārinā*.
2. Citrullus colocynthis.
3. Momordica charantia.
4. Indigo.
5. Trichosanthes Diecca.
6. A skin disease.
7. Clypea Hernamdifolia.
8. Perhaps small-pox (*SSED* p. 331)
9. Leucorrhoea.

9-10. O Śiva, the powder of Dvijayaṣṭi and Trikaṭuka when drunk with the decoction of sesame, removes women's Raktagulma; and is a good emanagogue for young ladies, O Śiva.

11. The bulbs of Red Lotus, when drunk with sugar and sesame, cure abortion in women. The flow of blood can be stopped with the help of cold water.

12-13. O Rudra, a decoction of Kāñjikā, Śarapuṅkha, Hiṅgu and rock-salt hastens the delivery in women. If the roots of Mātuluṅga are tied to the waist, they quicken the delivery.

14. If, after pronouncing the name of the pregnant woman, the roots of Apāmārga are taken out fully, then a son will be born. If broken, a daughter will be born.

15. If the roots of Apāmārga are placed on the head of the pregnant woman; the pain in her embryo will disappear, there is no doubt about it.

16. O Śiva, if the vagina is filled with Karpūra, Madanaphala and Madhuka, it will be good even for that of an old woman, what to speak of the young ladies.

17. If a tilaka of Gorocana is applied on the forehead of a child and he is made to drink kuṣṭha with sugar, he will be free from the fear of poison, ghosts, planets and diseases, O Śiva.

18. Constant wearing of Śaṅkhanābhi, Vacā, Kuṣṭha and iron by children, protects them against children's ailments, O Śiva.

19-20. If a man drinks the powders of Palāśa, Viḍaṅga and Āmalaka with honey and cow's butter, he will instantly become highly intelligent and if he drinks the same continuously for a month, he may even win old age and death, O Mahādeva.

21. O Rudra, if one takes the seeds of Palāśa alongwith butter, sesame and honey for one full week, then old age disappears.

22. If a man takes the powder of Āmalaka alongwith honey, oil and butter continuously for one month, he will become young and master of speech, O Rudra.

23. O Śiva, if the powders of Śiva and Āmalaka are

1. Perhaps *harītakī* (*GVDB*, p. 400).

taken alongwith honey or water every morning, they give strength to the nasal parts.

24. If a man takes every morning the powder of Kuṣṭha alongwith butter and honey, he will possess virtually a fragrant body and may live for one thousand years.

25-26. When the seeds of Māṣa, split and without husk, are soaked dry in butter and boiled in milk, and are taken by a man alongwith honey, butter and milk, he will be able to satisfy hundred women from that very moment, O Mahīdeva, there is no doubt about it.

27. Mercury is made suitable with the help of sulphur and castor oil. This mercury gives strength when taken.

28. When milk, in which the seeds of huskless Māṣa and Śimbī have been cooked, is drunk alongwith the oil of Apāmārga, it makes one capable of satisfying a hundred women.

CHAPTER TWO HUNDRED AND THREE

Diseases

Hari said :

1. To a cow, who is not fond of her calf, her own milk should be given mixed with salt; the calf will be loved by her.

2. If a dog's bone is tied to the neck of a cow or a buffalo; the germs from their bodies will be shed off, there is no doubt about it.

3. By making the cattle eat the roots of Guñjā, their horns are cast off.

4. The juice of Varuṇa-phala.[1] pressed with hands and applied to the biped or the quadruped makes their germs shed off, O Śiva.

5. O Rudra, if the powder of Jayā is filled in the wounds, they are healed up. If the urine of elephant is drunk by cows or buffaloes, their ailments are cured.

1. Crataeva nurvala.

6. If the oxen drink the powders of Masūra and Śāli pounded in whey and mixed in the milk of a cow or a buffalo, it will be beneficent to them.

7. If the leaves of Śarapuṅkha are administered with salt, they cure the disease called Vāri-sphoṭa in the manes of horses.

8. O Hara, when the leaves of Ghṛta-kumārī are administered alongwith salt, they cure the itches in the manes of horses.

CHAPTER TWO HUNDRED AND FOUR

Medicinal drugs

Sūta said:

1. Thus Dhanvantari explained to Suśruta the science of Āyurveda (medicine). I shall now mention the different names of drugs in brief.

2. Sthirā, Vidārigandhā, Śālaparṇī and Aṁśumati are the names of Desmodium Gangeticism. Lāṅgalī, Kalasī, Kroṣṭupucchā and Guhā (Mucuna Pruriens).

3. Varṣābhū and Punarnavā—(Spreading hogweed—Boerhnaria Diffusa) Kaṭhilyā and Kāruṇā (Hairy mordica Momardica Charantea)

Eraṇḍa, Urubūka, Āmarda, Vardhamānaka) Castor seed Riconus comamnis.

4. Jhaṣā, Nāgabalā — Sida Spinosa.

Śvadaṁṣṭrā, Gokṣura — Tygo phylleae Tribulus terestris.

Śatāvarī, Varā, Bhīru Pīvarī, Indīvarī, Varī) As paragus Racemosus.

5. Vyāghrī, Bṛhatī, Kṛṣṇā, Haṁsapadī, Madhuśravā Dhamanī, Kaṇṭakārī, Siṁhī Kṣudrā, Nidigdhikā) Solanum Janthocarpum

6. Vṛścikā, Tryamṛtā, Kālī Viṣaghnī, Sarpadaṁṣṭrikā, Markaṭī, Ātmaguptā, Ārṣeyī, Kapikacchukā	)	Mucuna Pruriens.
7. Mudgaparṇī, Kṣudrasahā	—	Phaseolus Trilobus.
Māṣaparṇī, Mahāsahā	—	Ternamuns Labialis.
Nyagrodha, Vaṭa	—	Banyan Tree.
Aśvattha, Kapila	—	Ficus Religiosa.
8. Plakṣa, Gardabhāṇḍa Parkaṭī, Kapītana	)	Thaspesia Pahulnea.
Pārtha, Kakubha, Dhanvī Arjuna and all Arjuna's names	)	Farminalia Arjuna.
9. Nandīvṛkṣa, Prarohī, Puṣṭi-	—	a species of Fig.
karī Vañjula, Vetasa	—	Calamus rotong.
Bhallātaka, Aruṣkara	—	Semecarpus Anacardium.
10. Lodhra, Sāravaka, Dhṛṣṭa, Tirīṭa	)	Symplocas Racemosa.
Mahājambū, Bṛhatphalā Bālaphalā (Second Variety)	)	Euginea Jambolana.
11. Nādeyī, Jalajambū (Third Variety)	)	Wild Jamboline.
Kaṇā, Kṛṣṇopakuñcī Śauṇḍī, Māgadhikā,	)	Piper Longum.
12. Pippalī Pippalīmūla,	—	Piper officinarums.
Granthika Ūṣaṇa, Marica	—	Piper Nigrum.
Śuṇṭhī, Viśva, Mahauṣadha	—	dry ginger.
13. Vyoṣa, Kaṭutraya,	—	(The three above together).
Tryūṣaṇa Lāṅgalī, Halinī, Śreyasī, Gajapippalī	)	Pothes officinalis.
14. Trāyantī, Trāyamāṇā Utsā, Suvahā	)	Thalictrum Faliolosum a variety of the above.
Citraka, Śikhi, Vahni all names of fire	)	Plumbago Zeylanica.
15 Ṣaḍgranthā, Ugrā, Vacā Śvetā, Haimavatī	)	Sweet flag.
Kuṭaja, Vṛkṣaka, Śakra Vatsaka, Girimallikā	)	Wrightia Anti-dysenterica

16. Kaliṅga, Indrayava, Ariṣṭa	seeds of the above.
Mustaka, Kauntī, Hareṇukā and all names of cloud	Mariscus Cyprus.
17. Elā, Bahulā	— Cardamom
Sūkṣmailā, Truṭi	— Smaller Cardamom.
Padmā, Bhārṅgī, Kāñjī, Brāhmaṇayaṣṭikā	Clerodendron, Siphonanthus.
18. Mūrvā, Madhurasā, Tejanī, Tiktavallikā	Sanseveria Zeylanica.
Mahānimba, Bṛhannimba Dīpyaka, Yamānikā	Ptychotis.
19. Viḍaṅga, Krimiśatru, Rāmaṭha, Hiṅgu	Embelia Ribus.
Ajājī, Jīraka	— Cummin Seeds.
Kāravī, Upakuñcikā	— Nigella Sativa
20. Kaṭukā, Tiktā, Kaṭuka	— Black Hellibore.
rohiṇī Tagara, Nata, Vakra, Coca, Tvaca, Varāṅgaka	Cinnamon bark.
21. Udīcya, Bālaka, Hrībera and all names of water	Pavonia Odorata.
Patraka and names of leaves Coraka and names of thieves	Lourus Cassia.
22. Hemābha, Nāgakesara and all names of elephants	Mesua Ferrea.
Asṛk, Kuṁkuma, Kāśmīra, Vāhlika	Saffron.
23. Ayaḥ, Loha	— Iron filings.
Pura, Kuṭanaṭa, Mahiṣākṣa, Palaṅkaṣā	Kutannat.
24. Kāśmarī, Kaṭphalā, Śrī-	— Myrica Sapida.
parṇī Śallakī, Gajabhakṣyā, Patrī, Surabhi, Śrávas	Bos Wellia Serrata.
25. Dhātrī, Āmalakī	— Emblic Myrobalans.
Akṣa, Vibhītaka	— Terminalia Belirica.
Pathyā, Abhayā, Pūtanā Harītakī	Indian Myrobalans.
26. Triphalā, Phalatrika	— The three above together.

Udakīrya, Dīrghvṛnta) Karañji.
Karañja) Liquorice root.
27. Yaṣṭī, Yaṣṭyāhvaya,)
Madhuka, Madhuyaṣṭikā) Woodfordia floribondia.
Dhātakī, Tāmraparṇī,)
Samaṅgā, Kuñjarā) White Sandalwood.
28. Sita, Malayaja, Śīta)
Gośīrṣa, Sitacandana) Red Sandal wood.
Raktacandana)
29. Kākolī, Vīrā, Vayasyā)
Arkapuṣpikā) Rhus Succedania.
Śṛṅgī, Karkaṭaśṛṅgī, Mahā-)
ghoṣā) Manna of Bamboo.
30. Tugākṣīrī, Śubhā, Vāṁśī)
Vaṁśalocanā) Vitis Vinifera (grapes)
Mṛdvīkā, Drākṣā, Gostanikā —
31. Uśīra, Mṛṇāla, Sevya,) Juncus odoratus.
Līmajjaka)
Sāra, Gopavallī, Gopī, Bhadrā — Hemidesmus Indicus.
32. Dantī, Kaṭaṅkaṭerī — Cascinium Fenestratum.
Dāruniśā Haridrā, Rajanī,) Turmeric.
Pītikā and all names of night)
33. Vṛkṣādanī, Chinnaruhā,) Tinaspora Cordifolia.
Nīlavallī, Rasāmṛtā)
Vasukoṭa, Vāśira, Kāmpillā — Polanisia Icosundra.
34. Pāṣāṇabhedaka, Ariṣṭa) Coleus Amboinicus.
Aśmabhit, Kuṭṭabhedaka)
Ghaṇṭāka, Śuṣkaka, Vaca,) Pentaptera tomentosa.
Sūcaka)
35. Surasa, Bījaka, Pītaśāla — Indian Kinotree.
Vajravṛkṣa, Mahāvṛkṣa) Uphorbia Neraīfolia.
Snuhī, Sruk, Sudhā, Guḍā)
36. Tulasī, Surasā, Upasthā — Holy basil
Kuṭheraka, Arjunaka, Parṇī,) Assinium Bajilicum
Saugandhiparṇika)
37. Nīla, Sindhuvāra, Nir-) Vitex trifolium.
guṇḍī Sugandhkiā, Sugan-)
dhiparṇī Vāsantī, Kulaja)
38. Kālīyaka, Pītakāṣṭha Kataka— Yellow Sandalwood.

Gāyatrī, Khadira, Kandara	— Acacia Catechu.
39. Indīvara, Kuvalaya Padma, Nīlotpala, Saugandhika, Śatadala, Abja, Kamala	Lotus.
40. Ajavarṇa, Ūrja	— Shoria Robusta.
Vājikarṇa, Aśvakarṇa	— Indian Sal tree.
Śleṣmātaka, Śelu, Bahuvāra	Cordya Myxa with narrow leaves.
41. Sunandaka, Kakud, Bhadra Chatrākī, Chatrasaṁjñaka, all names of umbrella	Andropogon citratus.
Kabarī, Kumbhaka, Dhṛṣṭa, Kṣudvidha, Dhanakṛt,	
42. Kṛṣṇārjaka Karāla, Kāmamāna	
Prācī, Balā, Nadīkrāntā Kākajaṅghā, Vāyasī	Leea Hvita.
43. Mūṣikaparṇī, Bhramantī, Ākhuparṇikā	Croton Polyandrum.
Viṣamuṣṭi, Drāvaṇam, Keśamuṣṭi	Melia Azendarach.
44. Kiṁlihī, Kaṭukī	— Black hellebore,
Dantaka, Amlavetasa	— Sorrel-Acido Zeyfolia.
Aśvatthā, Bahupatrā Bhū-Āmalakī	Phyllanthus hiruri.
45. Arūṣaka, Patraśūka, Kṣīrī, Rājādana	Minronsopia Hexenbra.
Mahāpātra, Dāḍima, Karaka	— Pomegranate.
46. Masūrī, Vidalī, Śaṣpā Kaṇṭakākhyā, Mahāśyāmā Vṛkṣapādī	Ipomea Tarpethum.
47. Vidyā, Kumbhī, Nikumbhā, Tribhaṅgī, Tripuṭī Trivṛt.	
Saptalā, Yavatiktā, Carmā, Carmakasā	Origaum Vulgaris.
48. Śaṅkhinī, Sukumārī, Tiktākṣī Akṣipīluka	Kalmegh.

Gavākṣī, Amṛtā, Śvetā Girikarṇī, Gavādanī	Colocynth.
49. Kāmpillaka, Raktāṅga, Guṇḍā, Rocanikā	Melloctus Phillipinesis.
Hemakṣīrī	Yellow variety Phillipinesis.
Gaurī, Kāladugdhikā	Black Phillipinesis.
50-51. Gāṅgerukī, Nāgabalā	Side Spinosa.
Viśālā, Indravāruṇī	Colocynth.
Tārkṣya Śaila, Añjana Rasāñjana	Extract of Indian Barbary.
Mocarasa, Śālmalīniryāsa	Bonabax Malabaricum.
Pratyak - puṣpī, Kharī, Apāmārga, Mayūraka	Achyranthus Aspera.
52. Siṁhāsya, Vṛṣa, Vāsāk Aṭarūṣaka	Adhatoda Vasaca.
Jīvaka, Jīvaśāka, Śaṭī Karbura	Curcoma Gedoaria.
53. Kaṭphala, Somavṛkṣa, Agnigandhā, Sugandhikā	Myrica Sapida.
Śatāṅga, Śatapuṣpā, Misi Madhurikā	Dill seed Aurthum graveyleus.
54. Puṣkara, Puṣkaramūla	Alpotaxis auriculata.
Yāsa, Dhanvayāsa, Duḥsparśa, Durālabhā	Alhagimaurorun Fogonia Arabica.
55. Vākucī, Somarājī Somavallī	Serratula Anthelmintica.
Markara, Keśarāja Bhṛṅgarāja	Wedelia Calendulacea.
56-57. Eḍagaja, Cakramarda	Cassiatora.
Suraṅgī, Tagara, Snāyu Kalanāśā, Vāyasī, Mahākāla, Vela, Taṇḍulīya, Ghanastana	Leeia Hista (?)
Ikṣvāku, Tiktatumbī Tiktālābu	Bottle gourd.
58-59. Dhāmārgava, Koṣātakī, Yāminī	Laffu Aegyptiaca.
Vidyut, Kṛtabhedana, Jīmūtaka, Khuḍḍāka, Devatāḍaka	A variety of the above.

Gṛdhrādanā, Gṛdhranakhī	)	Caparis Sepiaria.
Hiṅgukākādanī	)	
60. Aśvāri, Aśvamāraka	)	Sweet Scented Oleander
Karavīra	)	Nerrium Odorum.
Sindhu, Saindhava, Sindhūt-	)	Rock Salt.
tha, Maṇimantha	)	
61-62. Kṣāra, Yavāgraja	—	Carbonate of Potash Barilla.
Yavakṣāra	)	
Sarjikā, Sarjikākṣāra, Kāśīśa,	)	Green Sulphate of iron.
Puṣpakāśīśa Netrabheṣaja	)	
Dhātukāśī, Īsakāśī	)	
63. Saurāṣṭrīmṛttikākṣāra,	)	Iron pyrites.
Kākṣī, Paṅkaparpaṭī,	)	
Samākṣi kādhātu, Tāpya,	)	
Tāpyutthasambhava	)	
64. Śilā, Manaḥśilā, Naipālī	)	Red sulphate of Arsenic.
kulaṭī	)	
Ālam, Manastālaka, Haritāla	—	Tri-sulphide of Arsenic.
65. Gandhaka, Gandhapāṣāṇa,	)	Sulpher.
Rasa, Pārada	)	
Tāmra, Audumbara, Śulva	)	Mercury Copper.
Mlecchamukha	)	
66-67. Adrisāra, Ayas, Tīkṣṇa	)	Iron, steel.
Lohaka	)	
Mākṣika, Madhu, Kṣaudra	)	Honey.
Puṣparasa	)	
Jyeṣṭha	—	Watery gruel.
Kāñjika, Sauvīraka Sitā,	—	Sour gruel.
Sitopalā, Matsyaṇḍī, Śar-	)	Sugar.
karā	)	
68. Trisugandhi, Trijātaka	)	Cinnamon, Cardamom and
	)	Cassia (equal parts).
Caturjātaka	)	The above with Mesua
	)	Ferrea.
69. Pañcakola	)	Five drugs Pippalī, Pippalī-
	)	mūla, Cavya, Citraka
	)	and Nāgara.
70. Priyaṅgu, Kaṅgukā	—	Panicum Stalicum.
Koradūṣa, Kodrava	—	Paspalum Scroliculatum.

Tripuṭa, Puṭa, Kalāpa Laṅgaka)	Lathyrus Sativus.
71-72. Satīna, Vartula, Veṇu	— Pisum Sativium.
Picuka, Pittala, Akṣa Viḍālapādaka, Karṣa Suvarṇa, Kavalagraha)	A weight of sixteen Māśas.
Palārdha, Śukti	— Half a Pala.
73. Pala, Bilva, Muṣṭi	— One Pala.
Prasṛti)	Two Palas.
Añjali, Kuḍava	— Four Palas.
74. Aṣṭamāna, Māna	— Eight Palas.
Prastha)	Four Kuḍavas.
Āḍhaka)	Four Prasthas.
75. Kāṁsyapātra, Droṇa)	Four Āḍhakas.
Tulā)	Hundred Palas.
Bhāra	— Twenty Palas.

76. The measurements and weights thus mentioned are for solid matters. In liquids these measures should be taken as double.

77. Bhadradāru, Devakāṣṭha Dāru, Devadāruka)	Pinus Deodara.
Kuṣṭha, Āmaya	— Drug Kuṣṭha.
Māṁsī, Naladaṁśana	—
78. Śaṅkha, Śuktinakha, Śaṅkhī	— Couch.
Vyāghrī, Vyāghranakha	— Tiger's claw.
Pura, Palaṅkaṣa, Mahīṣākṣa, Guggulu)	Bdellium.
79. Rasa, Gandharasa, Vola	— Myrrh.
Sarja, Sarjarasa	— Resin.
Priyaṅgu, Phalinī Śyāmā, Gaurīkānta)	See ante.
80. Karañja, Naktamāla, Pūtika, Cirabilvaka)	Pongamia glabra.
Śigru, Śobhāñjana Jñānamāna)	Horse-radish.
81. Jayā, Jayantī, Śaraṇī Nirguṇḍī, Sindhuvāraka)	See before.
Moraṭā, Pīluparṇī	— See before.
Tuṇḍī, Tuṇḍikerikā	— See before.

82. Madana, Gālava, Bodha,) Randia Denmetorum.
Ghoṭā, Ghoṭī)
Caturaṅgula, Sampāka Vyā-) Kamila.
dhighāta)
83. Āragvadha, Rājavṛkṣa — Cassia Fistula
Raivata Daṣṭakā, Atitiktā,) Flacourtia Romontchi.
Kaṇṭakī Vikaṅkaṭa)
84-85. Nimba, Ariṣṭa — Melio Azadirachta.
Paṭola, Kolaka —
Vayasthā, Viśvā, Chinnā) Tinaspora Cordifolia.
Chinnaruhā, Amṛtā)
Vatsādanī, Guḍūcī)
Kirātatiktaka, Bhūnimba) Agrathotes Chirayta.
Kāṇḍatiktaka).

Sūta said :

86. O Hari, these are the names of drugs obtained in the forest. O Śaunaka, now I shall mention Grammar as narrated by Kumāra Kārttikeya.

CHAPTER TWO HUNDRED AND FIVE

Grammar

Kumāra said :

1. O Kātyāyana, I shall explain grammar in brief for a proper understanding of the formation of words (from bases) and to help children to learn the derivatives.

2. Words are either Subantas or Tiṅantas. (Substantives or verbs). 'Sups' are the seven case endings. Su, Au, Jas are the terminations in the nominative and vocative. The base is called Prātipadika.

3. A Prātipadika must be a meaningful word devoid of Dhātu and Pratyaya (root and termination).

4. Am, Au, Śas are the terminations in the Accusative case. What is done is Karma (object). In the object

Accusative case is to be used. So also when the words Antarā and Antareṇa are used.

5. Tā, Bhyām, Bhis are the terminations in the Instrumental case. They are to be added to the instrument or agent. That through which something is done is called Karaṇa, Kartā is he who does it.

6. Ṅe, Bhyām, Bhyas are the terminations in the Dative case. They are to be used to Sampradāna Kāraka. Sampradāna is he to whom something is desired to be given, something is owed or something is appealing.

7. Ṅasi, Bhyām, Bhyas are the terminations in the Ablative case. They are to be used with Apādāna Kāraka. That from which something moves away, or is taken off, or drawn, something is feared is called Apādāna.

8. Ṅas, Os, Ām are the terminations in the Genitive case. They are to be added to the chief in the relationship of possession. Ṅi, Os, Sup are the terminations in the locative case. They are to be added to the Adhikaraṇa (the base).

9. Ādhāra (support) is Adhikaraṇa. When verbs implying protection are used, Ablative is used. What is desired and what is disliked are also called Apādānaka (i.e. Ablative is used).

10. Ablative is to be used when Pari, Apā and Āṅ, Itara and Ṛte are used so also with the words denoting quarters. When Ena is used Accusative terminations are to be added to 'Karmapravacanīyas'[1]

11. In Vīpsā[2] and Itthambhāva[3] the symbol used in Abhi; in severance the symbols are Pari and Prati. Anu is used in these senses and also in the sense of Saha (with). In Hīnārtha (without) Anu and Upa are used.

12, When going or attempt at it is implied Accusative or dative can be used. In the case of inanimate object of the root 'Man' when disrespect is implied both the cases are used.

13. In combination with Namaḥ (obeisance), Svasti (Hail), Svadhā, Svāhā, Vaṣaṭ (sacrificial offerings), Alam

1. A term for certain prepositions, particles or adverbs when they are not connected with verbs and govern a noun in some case.
2. Repetition of words to imply continuous or successive action.
3. Being in a certain state.

(competant) and Tādarthya (for that purpose) Tumarthāt (in order to) dative case is used.

14. Instrumental case is used with 'Saha' (accompanied by), in an attribute and a defective limb. While denoting time and abstract notions both Locative and Genitive are used.

15. Both of these are used in denoting ownership, lordship, chieftaincy, kinship, "born of" and "Nirdhāraṇa" (specificating one from many). Only Genitive in 'Hetuprayoga' (for that reason).

16. In the objects of verbs implying memory, doing, exertions for, violence to, and in subjects of derivative verbs.

17. In the use of Past Participles 'Niṣṭhā' Genitive is not used. There are two kinds of bases substantives and roots.

18-19. Bhū, Vā and other roots take Tiṅ terminations. La means Lakāra i.e. tenses and moods which are ten in number Tip, Tas, Anti are the terminations in the third person. Sip, Thas, Tha are the terminations in the second person. Mip, Vas, Mas are the terminations in the first person. These above terminations are in the Parasmaipada. In the Ātmanepada, Te, Āte, Ante are the terminatious in the third person and Se, Āthe, Dhve are the terminations in the second person.

20. E, Vahe, Mahe are the terminations in the first person. Even if the names are used the terminations of the third persons are appended.

21. In denoting 'You', second person and in denoting 'I', first person is used. Bhū etc. are the roots. Similarly Sannantas etc. are also called roots.

22-23. When the present tense or past tense with the use of 'Sma' is to be implied Laṭ is to be used. In denoting the past, not of the same day, Laṅ or Luṅ can be used. In denoting benediction, injunction, permission, etc. Loṭ is to be used. It can be used in advice, invitation, enquiring after health, prayer and blessings.

24. Liṭ is to be used for all past not observed personally by the speaker. Luṭ signifies futurity. In denoting conditional, Lṛṅ is used. Sometimes Loṭ is used in the sense of Liṭ.

25-26. Kṛt suffixes can be used in Impersonal Passive and Active voices. They are Tṛṇ, Tavya, Anīya, Śatṛ etc.

CHAPTER TWO HUNDRED AND SIX

Grammar

Sūta said—

1-10. Now I shall give the ready made examples in accordance with the Saṁhitās—

Vipra+Agram	= Viprāgram
Sā+Āgatā	= Sāgatā
Vi+Idam	= Vīdam
Su+Uttamam	= Sūttamam
Pitṛ+Ṛṣabha	= Pitṛṛṣabha
Lāṅgala+Īṣā	= Lāṅgalīṣā
Manas+Īṣā	= Manīṣā
Gaṅgā+Udakam	= Gaṅgodakam
Tava+Lakāra	= Tavalkāra
Ṛṇa+Ṛṇa	= Ṛṇārṇa
Pra+Ṛṇa	= Prārṇa
Śīta+Ārta	= Śītārta
Sa+Aindrī	= Saindrī
Sa+Ukāra	= Sokāra
Vadhū+Āsana	= Vadhvāsana
Pitṛ+Artha	= Pitrartha
L+Anubandha	= Lānubandha
Ne+E	= Naye
Je+Et	= Jayet
Nai+Aka	= Nāyaka
Lo+Aṇa	= Lavaṇa
Gau+Aḥ	= Gāvaḥ
Te+Ete	= Ta Ete
Te+Īśvarāḥ	= Ta Īśvarāḥ
Devī+Gṛha	= Devīgṛha
Atho+Atra	= Atho Atra
A+Avehi	= A Avehi
Paṭū+Imau	= Paṭū Imau
Amī+Aśvaḥ	= Amī Aśvāḥ
Ṣaṭ+Asya	= Ṣaḍasya
Tat+Na	= Tanna
Vāc+S	= Vāk

Ṣaṭ+Dalāni	=	Ṣaḍdalāni
Tat+Caret	=	Taccaret
Tat+Lunāti	=	Tallunāti
Tat+Jalam	=	Tajjalam
Tat+Śmaśānaka	=	Tacchmaśānaka
Sugaṇ+Atra	=	Sugaṇṇatra
Pacan+Atra	=	Pacannatra
Bhavān+Chādayati	=	Bhavāṁscchādayati
Bhavān+Jhanatkara	=	Bhavāñjhanatkara
Bhavān+Tarati	=	Bhavāṁstarati
Sam+Smṛtam	=	Saṁsmṛtam
Bhavān+Likhati	=	Bhavāllikhati
Tām+Cakre	=	Tāñcakre
Bhavān+Śete	=	Bhavāñśete
Api+Amī	=	Apyamī
Amī+Īdṛśam	=	Amīdṛśam
Bhavān+Ḍīnam	=	Bhavāñḍīnam
Tvam+Tarasi	=	Tvantarasi
Tvam+Karoṣi	=	Tvankaroṣi
Sat+Arcanam	=	Sadarcanam
Kaḥ+Caret	=	Kaścaret
Kaḥ+Takāreṇa	=	Kaṣṭakāreṇa
Kaḥ+Kuryāt	=	Kaḥkuryāt
Kaḥ+Phale sthitaḥ	=	Kaḥphalesthitaḥ
Kaḥ+Śete	=	Kaśśete
Kaḥ+Ṣaṇḍaḥ	=	Kaṣṣaṇḍaḥ
Kaḥ+Arthaḥ	=	Korthaḥ
Kaḥ+Yāti gauravam	=	Koyātigauravam
Kaḥ+Iha+Atra	=	Ka Ihātra
Kaḥ+Eva	=	Ka Eva
Āhuḥ+Devāḥ	=	Āhurdevāḥ
Devāḥ+Āhuḥ	=	Devā Āhuḥ
Āhuḥ+Ca	=	Āhuśca
Bhos+Vraja	=	Bho Vraja
Svapūḥ+Viṣṇuḥ+ vrajati	=	Svapūrviṣṇurvrajati
Goḥ+Pati	=	Goṣpati
Dhūṣ+pati	=	Dhūṣpati
Eṣaḥ+Vrajet	=	Eṣa Vrajet

Saḥ+Syāt	=	Sa Syāt
Saḥ+Ca	=	Sa Ca
Kuṭī+Chāyā	=	Kuṭīcchāyā
Tathā+Chāyā	=	Tathācchāyā

Other Sandhis are to be understood similarly.

11-26. Compounds are six in number.

Saddvija = A good brahmin (Karmadhāraya)

Trivedi = A group of three platforms (Dvigu)

Tatkṛta, Tadartham)	
Vrkabhīti; Jñānadakṣa)	Tatpuruṣa
Tātvajñe)	
Yaśodhana	Bahuvrīhi
Adhistri, Yathoktam	Avyayībhāva
Devarṣimānavāḥ	Dvandva

Pāṇḍava, Śaiva, Brāhmyam, Brahmatā. These are examples of Taddhitas. Deva, Agni, Sakhi, Pati, Aṁśu, Kroṣṭṛ, (Kroṣṭu), Svayambhū, Pitṛ, Nṛ, Praśāstṛ—All these are Masculine. The Halantas (Consonant ending) Asṛk, Kṣmābhṛt, Kravyāt, Mṛgāvidh, Rājan, yuvan, Pathin, Pūṣan, Bramhahan, Ahan, Vid, Vedhas, Uśanas, Anaḍvah, Madhuliṭ Kāṣṭhatakṣ are also masculine. Vana, Vāri, Asthi, Vastu, Jagat, Sāman, Ahan, Karman, Sarpis and Tejas are neuter.

Jāyā, Nadī, Lakṣmī, Śrī, Strī, Bhū, Vadhū, Bhrū, Punarbhū, Dhenu, Svasṛ, Māṭṛ, Camū—These are feminine. Similarly Vāk, Srak, Dik, Krudh, Yuvati, Kakup, Dyau, Upāvṛt, Sumanaḥ, Uṣṇik are also faminine. Qualities can be used in any gender according to the substantives Śukla, Kīlāla, Śuciḥ Grāmaṇī, Sudhīḥ.

Bāhu, Kamalabhūḥ, Kartṛ, Svamātṛ Svanauḥ, Satya—all these are Masculine. Dīrghapāt—mesculine.

The Sarvanāmans (Pronouns) are Sarva, Viśva, Ubhaya, Ubha, Anya Anyatara (suffixes Ḍatara, Ḍatama), Pūrva, Apara, Adhara, Yāvat, Kim, Yuṣmat, Asmat—These are Aliṅgas and used in all genders. Śṛṇoti, Juhoti, Jahāti, Dadhāti, Dīpyati, Stūyati, Putrīyati, Dhanāyati, Truṭyati, Mriyate, Cicīṣati, Ninīṣati. These are examples of verbs.

The special declensional forms of Sarva are Sarve, Sarvasmai, Sarvasmāt, Sarvataḥ Sarveṣām, Sarvasmin. Similarly

Viśva is to be declined. In Pūrva, alternative forms Pūrvasmāt, Pūrvāt; Purve, Pūrvāḥ; Pūrvasmin, Pūrve are to be noted.

27. The readymade examples of subantas and tiṅantas are simply noted only in a few cases. Kātyāyana has mentioned everything in detail after hearing the same from Kumāra.

CHAPTER TWO HUNDRED AND SEVEN

Prosody

Sūta said :

I. With an obeisance to Vāsudeva, the preceptor Gaṇeśa,[1] Śiva and Sarasvatī I shall tell the ignorant about the metres which are classified according to mātrās[2] or varṇas.[3]

2. According to the position of Guru[4] or Laghu[5] in the beginning, in the middle or in the end; there are eight Gaṇas[6] namely, Ma-gaṇa[7] Nagaṇa[8], Bha-gaṇa[9], Ya-gaṇa[10], Ja-gaṇa[11], Ra-gaṇa[12], Sa-gaṇa[13], and Ta-gaṇa[14].

3. A vowel is Guru when it is followed by a consonant, Visarga, or a ccnjunct. A Dīrgha[15] vowel is always Guru. A

1. *Gaṇa*=*Gaṇeśa* (*SSED*, p. 178).
2. Syllabic instants.
3. Syllables.
4. Long syllable (—).
5. Short syllable (◡).
6. Syllabic feet each consisting of three syllables are distinguished from one another according to the position of long and short syllables (in the beginning, in the middle, in the end).
7. — — —
8. ◡ ◡ ◡
9. — ◡ ◡
10. ◡ — —
11. ◡ — ◡
12. — ◡ —
13. ◡ ◡ —
14. — — ◡
15. *ā, ī, ū, ṝ, e, ai, o, au.*

vowel which is followed by Anusvāra or which comes in the end is also Guru. It is of two Mātrās.

4. When the order of Laghu and Guru varies, it is called Śloka. When there is pause, it is called Yati.

5. A quarter is called a Pāda. When the quarters are equal, it is called Sama. When the quarters are un-equal, it is called Viṣama. Hence the metres are of three types—Sama[1], Ardha-sama[2], and Viṣama[3].

CHAPTER TWO HUNDRED AND EIGHT

Prosody

Sūta said :

1. Āryā is of eight Gaṇas out of which the odds should not have Ja-gaṇa. The sixth one may be Ja-gaṇa or Na-gaṇa with Laghu, and the foot should end with it (the sixth Gaṇa), after the second Laghu.

2. The seventh Gaṇa from the beginning consists of Laghu. In the second half of Āryā, the foot ends with the fifth Gaṇa. When the foot ends with the first three Gaṇas in each half, it is called Pathyā. When the foot ends after the first three Gaṇas in each half, it is called Vipulā.

3. When the second and the fourth ones are Ja-gaṇas flanked by two Gurus, it is called Capalā. When the first half is like Capalā and the second half like Āryā or Pathyā or Vipulā, it is called Mukha-Capalā. When the first half is like Āryā and the second half like Capalā, it is called Sajaghanā.

4. When the first half and the second half both are like the first half of Āryā, it is called Gīti. When the first half and the second half both are like the second half of Āryā, it is called Upagīti. When the first half is like the second half of Āryā and the second half is like the first half of Āryā, it is called Udgīti.

1. Equal.
2. Half-equal.
3. Unequal.

5. When one more Guru is added after the first half of Āryā it is called Āryāgīti. When there are six Mātrās in the odds and eight Mātrās in the even feet and after each feet there is Ragaṇa, Laghu and Guru, it is called Vaitālīya.

6. When after each feet of Vaitālīya, there is Ragaṇa and Yagaṇa, it is called Aupachandasika.

7. When Bha-gaṇa is followed by two Gurus, it is called Āpātalikā. When the second Mātrā is dependent and there is Laghu in all the feet, it is called Dakṣiṇāntikā.

8. When the second is dependent in the odd feet, it is called Udīcyavṛtti. When the fourth and the fifth Mātrās are dependent in the even feet, it is called Prācyavṛtti. When both the characteristics are these, it is called Pravṛttaka.

9. When all the feet are even like the even feet of Pravṛttaka it is called Ekapādikā. When all the feet are like the odd feet of Pravṛttaka, it is called Cāruhāsinī. The aforesaid metres come under the category of Vaitālīya.

10. When N-gaṇa and Sa-gaṇa do not come after the first syllable, and Ya-gaṇa comes after the fourth syllable, it is called Vaktra. When there is Ja-gaṇa after the fourth syllable in the even feet, it is called, Pathyā-vaktra. If it is so in the odd feet, it is called Viparīta-pathyā-vaktra.

11. When there is Na-gaṇa after the fourth syllable in the odd feet, it is called Capalā-vaktra. When the seventh syllable is Laghu in the odd feet, it is called Vipulā. In the opinion of Saitava, it is so in all the feet. If there is Ma-gaṇa after the fourth syllable it is called Ma-vipulā; if Ra-gaṇa, Ra-vipulā; if Na-gaṇa, Na-vipulā and if Ta-gaṇa, Ta-vipulā.

12-13. When these are sixteen Laghus in each feet, it is called Acala-dhṛti. When the ninth syllable is Laghu and the last one Guru, it is called Mātrā-sama. If there is Ja-gaṇa or Na-gaṇa with Laghu after the fourth Mātrā, it is called Vilśoka, When these are four Laghus in feet, it is called Vānavāsikā.

14. When the fifth, the eighth and the ninth Mātrā in each foot is Laghu, it is called Citrā of sixteen Mātrās. A mixture of the metres of even Mātrās is called Pādākulaka.

15. When the number of Varṇas is deducted from the total number of Mātrās in the metre we get the number of Gurus. When the number of Gurus is deducted from total

number of Mātrās in the metre, we get the number of Laghus. When the number of the Laghus is deducted from the total number of Mātrās in the metre and the resultant is divided by two, we get the number of Gurus.

16. When there are twenty eight Laghus in the first half and thirty Laghus in the second half, it is called Śikhā. The reverse of this is Khañjā.

17. When there are sixteen Gurus in the first half and thirty-two Laghus in the second half, it is called Anaṅga-krīḍa. When there are twenty-seven Laghus in both the halves, it is called Rucirā.

18. Thus I have told about the metres based on Mātrās. Now I shall tell you about those based on Varṇas.

CHAPTER TWO HUNDRED AND NINE

Prosody

Sūta said :

1. When there is one Guru in each foot, it is Śrī Ukthā. When there are two Gurus in each foot, it is called Strī-Atyukthā. The metre which has Mā-gaṇa in each foot is called Nārī; which has Ra-gaṇa likewise is Mṛgī—Maghyī. When Ma-gaṇa is followed by a Guru, it is called Kanyā-Pratiṣṭhā.

2. When the same is followed by two Gurus, it is called Paṅkti-Supratiṣṭhā. When there is one Ta-gaṇa and one Ya-gaṇa in each foot, it is called Tanu-madhyā. When there is one Na-gaṇa and one Ya-gaṇa, it is called Bāla-lalitā—Gāyatrī.

3. In Madalekhā, there is Ma-gaṇa and Sa-gaṇa followed by Guru—Uṣṇik. In Citrapadā two Bha-gaṇas are followed by two Gurus. In Vidyunmālā, two Ma-gaṇas are followed by two Gurus.

4. In Māṇavaka, there are Bha-gaṇa, Ta-gaṇa, Laghu and Guru. In Haṁsaruta, there are Ma-gaṇa, Na-gaṇa and two Gurus. In Samānīkā, there are Ra-gaṇa, Ja-gaṇa, Guru and Laghu. In Pramāṇika. there are Ja-gaṇa, Ra-gaṇa, Laghu

and Guru. Vitāna is dissimilar to these two. So these are the Anuṣṭup-metres.

5. Halamukhī has Ra-gaṇa. Na-gaṇa and Sa-gaṇa. Śiśubhṛtā has two Na-gaṇas and one Ma-gaṇa—Bṛhatī. Virājita has Sa-gaṇa, Ma-gaṇa, Ja-gaṇa and Guru.

6. Paṇava has Ma-na-ya-gaṇas and one Guru. Mayūrasāriṇī has ra-ja-ra-gaṇas and one guru. Rukmavatī has Bha-ma-sa-gaṇas and one Guru.

7. Mattā has Ma-bha-sa-gaṇas and Guru. Manoramā has na-ra-ja-gaṇas and Guru. Upasthita has Ja-gaṇa, Sa-gaṇa and Ta-gaṇa followed by a Guru. Paṅkti has been told.

8. Indravajrā has two Ta-gaṇas, Ja-gaṇa, and two Gurus. Upendravajrā has Ja-ta-ja-gaṇas and two Gurus.

9. Upajāti begins or ends with any one of the above two metres (i.e. it is a mixture of Indravajrā and Upendravajrā). Sumukhī has Na-ja-ja-gaṇas and Laghu and Guru. Dodhaka has three Bha-gaṇas and two Gurus. Śālinī has Ma-ja-ta gaṇas and two Gurus.

10. Vātormi has ma-bha-ta-gaṇas and two Gurus and Yati is after the fourth and the seventh syllables. Śrī has bha-ta-na-gaṇas and two Gurus with yati on the fifth and the sixth syllables.

11. Bhramara-vilasita has ma-bha-na-gaṇas and Laghuguru. Rathoddhatā has ra-na-ra-gaṇas and Laghu-guru. Svāgatā has ra-na-bha-gaṇas and five Gurus.

12 Vṛttā has na-na-sa-gaṇas and two Gurus. Smadrikā (Bhadrikā) has na-na-ra-gaṇas and Laghu-guru. Śyenikā has ra-ja-ra-gaṇas and Laghu-guru. Śikhaṇḍita has ja-sa-ta-gaṇas and two Gurus. Thus Triṣṭup-metre has been stated by Mahātmā Piṅgala.

13-14. Candravartma has ra-na-bha-sa-gaṇas. Vaṁśastha has ja-ta-ja-ra-gaṇas. Indravaṃśa has ta-ta-ja-ra-gaṇas. Toṭaka has four Sa-gaṇas. Drutavilambita has na-bha-bha-ra-gaṇas. Puṭa has na-na-ma-ya-gaṇas with Yati after the eighth and fourth syllables. Mudita Vadanā has na-na-ra-ra-gaṇas. Kusuma-vicitrā has na-ya-na-ya-gaṇas.

15. Jaloddhatagati has ja-sa-ja-sa-gaṇas (with Yati after every six syllable). Sragviṇi has four ra-gaṇas.

16. Bhujaṅgaprayāta has four ya-gaṇas. Priyaṁvadā has na-bha-ja-ra-gaṇas. Maṇimālā ta-ya-ta-ya-gaṇas.

17. Lalitā has ta-bha-ja-gaṇas. Pramitākṣarā has sa-ja-sa-sa-gaṇas. Ujjvalā has na-na-bha-ragaṇas.

18. Vaiśvadevī has ma-ma-ya-ya-gaṇas with yati on fifth and seventh varṇas. Jaladharamālā has ma-bha-sa-ma-gaṇas with Yati on the fourth and eighth varṇas.

19. Kṣamā has na-na-ta-ta-gaṇas and Guru with Yati on the seventh and sixth varṇas. Praharṣiṇī has ma-na-ja-ra-gaṇas and guru with yati on the third and tenth varṇas.

20. Rucirā has ja-bha-sa-ja-gaṇas and guru with yati on the fourth and ninth varṇas. Mattamayūra has ma-ta-ya-sa-gaṇas and Guru with Yati on the fourth and ninth varṇas.

21. Mañjubhāṣiṇī has sa-ja-sa-sa-gaṇas and Guru. Sunandinī has sa-ja-sa-ma-gaṇas and Guru. Candrikā has na-na-ta-ta-gaṇas and Guru with Yati on the seventh and sixth varṇas.

22. Asambādhā has ma-ta-na-sa gaṇas and two gurus with yati on the fifth and ninth varṇas. Aparājitā has na-na-ra-sa-gaṇas and Laghu-guru.

23. Praharaṇa-kalikā has na-na-bha-na-gaṇas and laghu-guru. Vasanta-tilakā (Siṁhonnatā) has ta-bha-ja-ja-gaṇas and two Gurus.

24. Indu-vadanā has bha-ja-sa-na-gaṇas and two Gurus. Sukeśara has na-ra-na-ra-gaṇas and Laghu-guru. Thus Śarkarī-(Śakvarī ?) has been described.

25. Śaśikalā has fourteen Laghus and one Guru. If Yati is on sixth and ninth varṇas, it is called Srak. If Yati is on the eighth and seventh varṇas, it is called Maṇi-guṇa-nikara.

26. Mālinī has na-na-ma-ya-ya-gaṇas with Yati on the eighth and seventh Varṇas. Prabhadraka has na-ja-bha-ja-ra-gaṇas.

27. Elā has sa-ja-na-na-ya-gaṇas. Chitralekhā has ma-ra-ma-ya-ya-gaṇas with Yati on the seventh and eighth Varṇas. Thus Atiśarkarī has been described.

28. Vṛṣabha-gaja-jṛmbhita has bha-ra-na-na-na-gaṇas and Guru with Yati on the seventh and ninth varṇas. Vāṇinī has na-ja-bha-ja-ra-gaṇas and Guru. Thus Aṣṭi has been defined by Piṅgala.

29. Śikhariṇī has Ya-ma-na-sa-bha-gaṇas and Laghu-Guru with Yati on the sixth and eleventh varṇas. Pṛthvī has Ja-sa-ja-sa-ya-gaṇas and Laghu-Guru with Yati on the eighth and ninth varṇas.

30. Vaṁśa-patra-patita has Bha-ra-na-bha-na-gaṇas and Laghu-Guru with Yati on the tenth and seventh Varṇas. Hariṇī has Na-sa-ma-ra-sa-gaṇas and Laghu-Guru with Yati on the sixth, fourth and seventh Varṇas.

31. Mandākrāntā has Ma-bha-na-ta-ta-gaṇas and two Gurus with Yati on, the fourth, sixth and seventh varṇas. Narttaṭaka has Na-ja-bha-ja-ja-gaṇas and Laghu-Guru with Yati on the seventh and the tenth Varṇas.

32. If the Yati is on the seventh, sixth and fourth Varṇas, it is called Kokilaka. So for Atyaṣṭi. Kusumitalatā has Ma-ta-na-ya-ya-ya-gaṇas with Yati on the fifth, sixth and seventh Varṇas. So for Dhṛti.

33. Meghavisphūrjitā has Ya-ma-na-sa-ra-ra-gaṇas and Guru with Yati on the sixth and seventh Varṇas. Śārdūlavikrīḍita has Ma-ja-ja-sa-ta-ta-gaṇas and Guru with Yati on the twelfth and seventh Varṇas.

34. So far Atidhṛti metre has been told. Now will come Kṛti. Suvadanā has Ma-ra-bha-na-ya-bha-gaṇas and Laghu-Guru with Yati on seventh, seventh and sixth Varṇas.

35. Vṛtta has Ra-ja-ra-ja-ra-ja-gaṇas and Guru-Laghu. So far Kṛti. Sragdharā has Ma-ra-bha-na-ya-ya-ya-gaṇas with Yati on the seventh, seventh and seventh Varṇas. So far Prakṛti.

36. Bhadraka, has Bha-ra-na-ra-na-ra-na-gaṇas and Guru with Yati on the tenth and twelfth Varṇas. So far Ākṛti. Aśvalalita has Na-ja-bha-ja-bha-ja-bha-gaṇas and Laghu-Guru with Yati on eleventh and twelfth Varṇas.

37. Mattākrīḍa has Ma-ma-ta-na-na-na-na-gaṇas and Laghu Guru with Yati on the eighth and fifteenth Varṇas. So for Vikṛti. Now Saṅkṛti is told.

38. Tanvī has Bha-ta-na-sa-bha-bha-na-ya-gaṇas with Yati on the fifth and seventh Varṇas. Krauñcapadā has Bha-ma-sa-bha-na-na-na-na-gaṇas and Guru with Yati on the fifth, fifth, eighth and eighth Varṇas.

39. So far Atikṛti metre has been told. Now Utkṛti is being told. Bhujaṅgavijṛmbhita has Ma-ma-ta-na-na-na-ra-sa-

gaṇas and Laghu-Guru with Yati on the eighth, eleventh and seventh Varṇas.

40. Apavāha has Ma-na-na-na-na-na-na-sa-gaṇas and two Gurus with Yati on 9, 6, 6, 5 Varṇas.

41. Caṇḍavṛttiprapāta has Na-na-ra-ra-ra-ra-ra-ra-gaṇas. Many varieties of this Daṇḍaka-metre are formed by the addition of one Ra-gaṇa in each of them.

CHAPTER TWO HUNDRED AND TEN

Prosody

Sūta said :

1-2. Upacitraka has Sa-sa-sa-gaṇas and Laghu-Guru in odd feet, and Bha-bha-bha-gaṇas and Guru-Guru in even feet. Drutamadhyā has bha-bha-bha-gaṇas and two Gurus in odd feet and Na-ja-ja-ya-gaṇas in even feet.

3-4. Vegavatī has Sa-sa-sa-gaṇas and Guru in odd feet and Bha-bha-bha-gaṇas and two Gurus in even feet. Bhadravirāṭ has Ta-ja-ra-gaṇas and Guru in odd feet and Ma-sa-ja-gaṇas and two Gurus in even feet. Ketumatī has Sa-ja-sa-gaṇas and Guru in odd feet and Bha-ra-na-gaṇas and two Gurus in even feet. Ākhyānakī has Ta-ta-ja-gaṇas and two Gurus in odd feet and Ja-ta-ja-gaṇas and two Gurus in even feet.

5. The opposite to the same is Viparītākhyānaka as illustrated by Piṅgala.

6. Puṣpitāgrā has Na-na-ra-ya-gaṇas in odd feet and Na-ja-ja-ra-gaṇas and Guru in even feet. Aparavaktra is called Vaitālīya and Puṣpitāgrā is called Aupacchandasika.

7. Vāṅmatī has Ra-ja-ra-ya-gaṇas in odd feet and Ja-ra-ja-ra-gaṇas and Gurus in even feet.

CHAPTER ONE HUNDRED AND ELEVEN

Prosody

Sūta said :

1. Pādacaturūrdhva has 8 Varṇas in the first foot, 12 in the second, 16 in the third and 20 in the fourth.

2. When in a Pādacaturūrdhva all the Varṇas are Laghu except the last two which are Guru, it is called Āpīḍa.

3. Kalikā has 12, 8, 16 and 20 Varṇas in each foot respectively. Lavalī has 12, 16, 8 and 20 Varṇas in respective feet. Amṛtadhārā has 12, 16, 20 and 8 Varṇas in its feet.

4. Udgatā has Sa-ja-sa-gaṇas and Laghu in the first foot, Na-sa-ja-gaṇas and Guru in the second, Bha-na-ja-gaṇas and Laghu-Guru in the third and Sa-ja-sa-ja-gaṇas and Guru in the fourth.

5. Saurabhaka has Ra-na-bha-gaṇas and Guru in the third feet and other feet are like those of Udgatā. Similarly. Lalita has Na-na-sa-gaṇas in the third feet, the rest being like Udgatā.

6. Upasthitapracupita has Ma-sa-ja-bha-gaṇas and two Gurus in the first foot, Sa-na-ja-ra-gaṇas and Guru in the second, Na-na-sa-gaṇas in the third and Na-na-na-ja-ya-gaṇas in the fourth.

7. Viśeṣa has Na-na-sa-na-na-sa in the third foot, the rest being like Upasthitapracupita.

8. Similarly, Śuddhavirāḍ, Ārṣabha has Ta-ja-ra-gaṇas in the third foot and the rest like Upasthitapracupita.

9. If there are odd syllables or odd feet like five or six in a metre, it is known as Gāthā like 'Daśadharmam' (Mbh 5. 33. 82).

CHAPTER TWO HUNDRED AND TWELVE

Prosody

Sūta said :

1. In Prastāra first all Gurus should be noted down. Then Laghu should be noted down below the first Guru and the rest should be done as before. In Naṣṭa Laghu should be written for even numbers and Guru should be written for odd numbers. The same holds good about the half of numbers.

2. In Uddiṣṭaka upon each Varṇa numbers beginning from one should be written respectively multiplied by two. The numbers of Laghu should be added and then one should again be added.

3-5. [Being not clear are left untranslated]

CHAPTER TWO HUNDRED AND THIRTEEN

Dharma-Śāstra

Sūta said :

1. The conduct of Brahmins and others which Brahmā heard from Hari and explained to Vyāsa, I shall explain to you, O Śaunaka.

2. After knowing fully the Vedic Texts and Smṛti Texts one shall perform what is enjoined in the Vedas. If that is not possible one shall do what is mentioned in the Smṛti texts.

3. If he is unable to perform even that an intelligent man shall perform acts of good conduct. Śruti and Smṛti are the two eyes of Brahmins for the proper understanding of duties.

4. What is mentioned in the Śruti is the greatest virtue; the next one is what is mentioned in the Smṛti texts. Activities of the virtuous are the next ones. All the three are eternal virtues.

5. Truthfulness, gifts, sympathy, noncovetousness, learning, sacrifice, worship and restraint are the eight holy characteristics of the virtuous.

6. The brilliant sense organs of the virtuous and their physical bodies never get tainted with sin like the lotus with water.

7. For all castes virtuous actions are very important; truthfulness, sacrifice, austerities and gifts are the symbols of Dharma.

8-9. Not taking back what is given, gifts, study of Vedas, austerities, learning wealth, penance, valour, nobility of birth, health, annihilation of worldly bondage, happiness, knowledge —all these result from Dharma. One gets salvation due to knowledge.

10. Sacrifices, study of Vedas and gifts in accordance with the instructions in the Śāstras constitute the common virtue of Brāhmaṇas, Kṣatriyas and Vaiśyas.

11. Sages say that presiding over others' sacrifices, teaching of Vedas and acceptance of Pratigraha (money gifts etc.) constitute the extra activity of the highest class.

12. The duty of the kings is to live with weapons and protect all living beings. Rearing of cattle, agriculture, trading and business are the ways of sustenance for Vaiśyas.

13. The duty of the Śūdra is to serve all other twice-born people. The duty of a student is residence in the preceptor's house, maintenance of the sacrificial fire and self-study of Vedas.

14. The student must have three ablutions every day, taking alms, and living in the house of the Guru till his death. While yet a student he must wear mekhalas (girdles of Kuśa grass) matted hair or shave off the hair entirely.

15-16. The duties of a householder are the maintenance of Agnihotra, practice of hereditary duties, indulgence in sexual inter-course with only his wife avoiding the Parva days, the worship of Gods, manes and guests and the grasping of the import of Śrutis and Smṛtis.

17-18. The duties of a Vanavāsin (in the stage of Retirement) are : conquest of senses, maintenance of Agnihotra, wearing of deer-skin lying on the bare ground, residence in a secluded spot, living on milk, bulbous roots, fruits and Nīvāra grains, avoidance of prohibited activities, thrice ablutions, continuance of rites and worship of gods and guests.

19-21. The duties of a Parivrāṭ (complete renouncer) Avoidance of all worldly enterprises, begging of alms, residence at the roots of trees, non-acceptance of any gift whatsoever, non injury to others, equality of vision towards all living beings, bearing of both pleasant and unpleasant, viewing of happiness and sorrow equally, purity internally and externally, restraint on speech, contemplation, curbing of all sense organs, perpetual grasping of the fundamental principle of life and a pure volition.

22. The common characteristics of all walks and stages of life are non-violence, truthful and pleasing words, truthfulness and purity, forgiveness and mercy.

23. Those who strictly adhere to these injunctions attain the greatest goal. I shall now explain the duties of a householder from getting up in the morning to going to bed at night.

24. He must get up in the Brāhma Muhūrta (An hour and a half before dawn) Think about his Dharma and Artha. By the end of the night be must finish answering calls of nature and purify himself in mind and body.

25. He must clean his teeth, take his bath and perform Sandhyā prayers.

26. Evacuation of the bowels and urination during the day must be done sitting facing the north. During the nights by sitting facing the south. At dusk and dawn he must do as during the day.

27. In shade, darkness, during night or day, if there is any commotion endangering life, a brahmin can sit facing any quarter convenient, while passing urine or stools.

28. Neither faeces nor urine shall be passed on cowdung, burning charcoal, anthill, a ploughed field, pure water, and under way side trees.

29. Earth for purificatory purposes, shall not be taken from under water, temples, anthills, rat holes, faeces of others, or from burning ghāṭas.

30. The penis must be cleaned once with earth. The left hand must be cleaned twice with earth and both the feet

twice with the earth. This is the purificatory wash after passing urine.

31. After passing stools, the penis must be cleaned with earth once, the anus three times, the left palm ten times and the feet ten times (each foot five times). Both the hands must be cleaned with the earth then seven times.

32. The first application of the earth must be half a handful. The second and third ones half of the previous.

33. He who is unable to urinate or evacuate in a sitting posture need do only half of this purificatory process.

34. The purificatory process during the night is either half or one-fourth of the foregoing. This elaborate process is for the hale and hearty. The sick man can do as suits his strength.

35. The twelve types of dirt from human body are—Fat, semen, blood, marrow, saliva, faeces, urine, ear wax, phlegm, tears, grit in the eyes and sweat.

36. Purificatory process is to be continued till full purity is achieved. There is no limit to the number of times of the cleansing process.

37. Purification is twofold—the external and the internal. The external purification is with earth and water. Purity of feelings and volition is the internal cleansing.

38. He shall perform Ācamana three times, then he must wipe his face twice. After rubbing with the root of the thumb the mouth shall be touched thrice.

39. The nostril shall be rubbed with the thumb and the index finger. Eyes and ears must be touched frequently with the ring finger and the thumb.

40. The navel shall be rubbed with the little finger and the thumb and the chest with the palm. The head must be touched with all the fingers. The arms shall be rubbed with the tips.

41. By taking the Ācamanas the brahmin propitiates Ṛks, Yajus and Sāmans. By wiping off twice he pleases Atharvāṅgiras and Ṣaṇmukha.

42. He propitiates Itihāsas, Purāṇas and the six Vedāṅgas. By touching the mouth he propitiates the Ether, nostrils —the Vāyu, eyes—the sun, and the ears—the quarters.

43. By touching the navel he propitiates the Prāṇagranthis and touching the heart he propitiates the Brahman; the head—Rudra and the tuft—the sages.

44-45. By touching the arms Yama, Indra, Varuṇa, Kubera, Vasudhā and Anala are propitiated. By washing his feet he pleases Viṣṇu and by washing hands he pleases Indra and Viṣṇu; by touching the joints of fingers he pleases Agni, Vāyu, Sūrya, Indu and the mountains. The lines in the palms represent the rivers, Gaṅgā, etc.

46. Early in the morning after duly performing Śauca he must clean his teeth and take his bath.

47. A man becomes impure if the mouth is not washed after the night. Hence, a man must cleanse his teeth carefully.

48-49. Twigs of Kadamba, Bilva, Khadira, Karavīra, Vaṭa, Arjuna, Yūthī, Bṛhatī,[1] Jātī, Karañja, Arka, Atimuktaka, Jambū, Madhūka, Apāmārga, Śirīṣa, Udumbara and Asana are good tooth brushes. Trees exuding milk juices, and thorny trees are very good for cleansing teeth.

50. Pungent, bitter and astringent twigs increase wealth, health and happiness. After cleansing the teeth, the twig must be cast off in a pure place. He must then perform Ācamana.

51. On new moon days, the sixth day and the ninth day and the first day of the lunar fortnight, twigs must be avoided. On Sundays too they shall be avoided.

52. If the twigs are not used the cleansing can be done by gargling with water twelve times.

53. By taking bath early in the morning he achieves visible and invisible merits. A person who regularly bathes in the morning and purifies himself deserves the performance of Japa, etc.

54. A man with many pores all over his body exudes dirt always by day and by night. He is extremely dirty. The morning bath purifies him.

55. Like a dip in the holy Ganges the morning ablutions give pleasures to the mind, increase beauty and fortune and remove sorrow and misery.

1. Jasminum aurialetum.

56-58. While taking bath he shall recite this Mantra—"I am taking my bath as it were in the Ganges to remove ten sins of mine *viz.*—(1) Sin of not giving a gift on days when moon enters Hasta star, on the tenth day in the bright half of the month of Jyeṣṭha and ten other auspicious occasions, (2) doing forbidden things, (3) violence, (4) committing adultery, (5) speaking harsh words, (6) uttering falsehood, (7) scandalising words, (8) nonsensical words, (9) coveting another man's wealth (10) wishing evil of others."

59. Thus I have explained briefly the process of ablution of a householder and a Vānaprastha (a man who retires from life).

60. A Yati (or an ascetic) takes three baths during the day, but a student (Brahmacārin) only once. Whenever one takes bath, one shall invoke holy rivers after performing Ācamana and meditating on eternal Hari.

61. There are three and half crores of demons named Mandehas. These wicked spirits desire to swallow the rising sun.

62. These demons can be burnt by means of the water sanctified by Mantras which act as fire. Hence, he who does not perform Sandhyā prayers actually commits the murder of the sun.

63. The junction of night and day is called Sandhyā. Its duration is for two Nāḍikās till the appearance of the sun or the stars.

64. At the end of the Sandhyā prayers sacrificial offerings of butter must be made personally. What is acquired by performing Homa, by him, cannot be acquired by performing it through others.

65. A Homa done through a Ṛtvik, Preceptor, one's own son, brother, nephew or the Viṭpati (the king or the leader of society) is as good as a Homa performed by oneself.

66. The Gārhapatya fire is Brahmā, the Dakṣiṇa fire is Śiva and the Āhavanīya fire is Viṣṇu; Kumāra (Lord Kārttikeya) is truth personified.

67. After the timely performance of Homa the brahmin shall recite the Mantras pertaining to the sun. Then with his

mind fully concentrated he must repeat the Sāvitrī[1] and Praṇava Mantras.

68. There is absolutely no danger for the person who perpetually repeats the Praṇava, the seven Vyāhṛtis and the Sāvitrī Mantra consisting of three metrical feet.

69. If a man repeats the Gāyatrī[1] every day after getting up early in the morning he will never be tainted by sin like the leaf of the lotus by drops of water.

70. The auspicious goddess Gāyatrī is described white complexioned, wearing silk garments and having the rosary garland of Akṣasūtra. She is seated in a lotus.

71-72. The Devas desirous of seeing the goddess seated in the midst of solar zone in the Brahmaloka invoked Her with the Yajus Mantras 'Tejosi'[2] etc. [Thou art the light]. The brahmin too shall invoke Her with the same Mantra and after bowing to Her he shall discharge Her (mystically).

73. The worship of all deities must be performed in the forenoon itself. There is no deity greater than Viṣṇu and hence, He must be worshipped always.

74-75. An intelligent devotee shall not differentiate among Brahmā, Viṣṇu and Śiva. There are eight very auspicious things in this world :—brahmins, cow, fire, gold, butter, the sun, water and eighth the king. Hence, everyone shall view, worship and go round these always.

76. The practice of Vedas is in five ways : Reading them, understanding them, transcribing them, deliberating over their import and teaching them to disciples.

77. Those who write the meanings of vedic passages, the Yajñaśāstras and the Dharmaśāstras for remuneration for the sake of others will obtain the fruits of vedic practice.

78. He who gives to others manuscripts of Itihāsas and Purāṇas is twice blessed with the merit of making a gift of Vedas.

79-80. In the third part of the day one shall be engaged in earning the wherewithals for the sake of maintaining the dependants. The dependants are :—mother, father, preceptor, brother, poor people who seek refuge, casual visitors

1. Gāyatrī ṚV. 3.62.10; VS. 3.35.
2. VS. 1.31; TS. 1.1.10.3

and specially invited guests. The sacrificial fire must be included among them as worthy of being nourished and nurtured.

81. It is the duty of everyone to sustain the dependants by every means. His is the true life who looks after many.

82. Other persons who fill their own bellies are as good as dead, though they live. Even a dog fills its belly.

83. It is from the accumulated and flourishing wealth that all activities (sacred or profane) emerge even as rivers originate from mountains.

84. The earth, the mine of all precious gems, grains, cattle, womenfolk all these can be termed wealth inasmuch as they serve the purpose of wealth.

85. When there is no danger threatening, a brahmin must maintain himself by choosing such a profession as does not entangle him in injury or harm to any living being; if that is not possible, the least form of injury is to be perpetrated.

86. The wealth of a brahmin is of three types the white, the black and the variegated, each again classified into seven sub-divisions.

87. The wealth of others irrespective of their caste is of three types: the inherited, the wealth given out of love and the wealth acquired through the wife (as dowry, etc).

88. The special wealth of a brahmin is of three types that earned as fees for officiating in sacrifices, the fees received for teaching and the gift received from good people.

89. The special wealth of a Kṣatriya is mentiond to be of three types :—the pure wealth acquired by way of revenue, the fines realised and all that which is seized after victory in battle.

90. The special wealth of a Vaiśya is also of three types:— that acquired through agricultural activities, that received from cattle and cattle products and that from trading activities. That of a Śūdra is the wealth he acquires due to the favour of the other people.

91. Usury, agriculture and trading activities can be pursued by a brahmin. Doing these himself in times of danger (i.e.

when no other source is available) a brahmin is not tainted by sin.

92. Many means of livelihood have been enumerated by sages. Among them all usury yields the most profit.

93. In the pursuit of agriculture there are dangers due to drought, due to king's tyrannical activities and due to rodents. But in usury none of these causes any risk.

94. Prosperity does not subside even in bright half or dark half, night or day, summer, rains or winter.

95. The prosperity achieved by those who thrive on merchandise by going to different countries can be realised by a man practising usury staying at home.

96. Gaining much (in usury) he must propitiate the manes, the gods and the Brahmins. Propitiated thus, they quell the evil effects (of usury) undoubtedly.

97-99. A usurer who donates cloth, cow, gold, etc, and brahmin practising as a husbandman gets absolved from the incidental sin by making gifts of drink and food, vehicles, beds or seats and handing over twenty heads of cattle or a hundred pieces of gold to the king. One fourth, he should keep as reserve; by half, he should sustain himself and by one fourth he should increase the capital.

100. (Thus in brief) there are ten main ways of sustenance, *viz*:—learning, arts and crafts, salaried profession, service rendered to rich people, cattle breeding, trading activities, agriculture, brokerage and liaison activities, begging alms and usury.

101. Wealth accumulated by brahmins by accepting gifts, by Kṣatriyas acquired through weapons, by Vaiśyas earned through lawful means and by Śūdras by serving others—that wealth is (honourable).

102. The commendable possessions of a brahmin:—a river with plenty of water, vegetables and leaves, sacrificial twigs and Kuśa grass, the sacrificial fire and the reverberating sounds of Vedic mantras.

103. There is no harm in accepting an unsolicited gift. Gods consider it on par with the nectar. Hence, it should not be refused.

104. A man desiring to worship gods and guests may even forcibly take wealth from his preceptor. Hence, one shall accept from anywhere anything that makes them (gods and guests) contented.

105. A meritorious brahmin with few blemishes can accept gifts from good or bad people. A man who is utterly devoid of good qualities sinks in sin if he accepts gifts.

106. Thus (in the third part of the day) a brahmin may pursue any of the above mentioned activities for the sake of sustenance. But immediately thereafter he must perform expiatory rites.

107. In the fourth part of the day he must keep ready clods of earth for the ablution as well as gingelly seeds, Kuśa grass and flowers. The bath must be taken in natural water.

108. Baths are of eight types: (1) the daily bath, (2) bath on special occasion, (3) bath for the realisation of desires, (4) bath as an ancillary for a sacred rite, (5) bath for removal of dirt, (6) rubbing and scrabbing, (7) Ācamana and (8) plunging into a river.

109. A man who has not taken his bath is unfit for performing Japas, sacrificial offerings, etc. The morning bath is for that purpose. It is called the Nitya Snāna (the daily bath).

110. The Naimittika Snāna (or the bath on special occasions) is the bath taken to wipe off the impurity on account of touching a Cāṇḍāla, corpse, faeces, etc. or a woman in her menses.

111. The Kāmya Snāna (bath for the realisation of desires) is the bath taken in holy rivers, etc., when the moon enters Puṣya star and on similar occasions in accordance with the instructions of an astrologer. A man free from such desires need not take this bath.

112. The Kriyāṅga Snāna (bath as an ancillary rite in the course of a religious ceremony) is the bath taken by a man on the occasion of worships of gods and guests for the recital of special Mantras.

113. Malāpakarṣaṇa Snāna is the bath taken for the removal of bodily impurities and not for any other purpose. It can be taken in ordinary tanks, natural puddles, holy tanks, rivers, etc.

114. This bath is only a natural activity of a man. The waters make the body clean and if it is taken in waters special merits also do accrue.

115. Mārjana or rubbing and wiping the body with water repeating Mārjana mantra removes sin quickly. The Nitya, Naimittika, Kriyāṅga and Malāpakarṣaṇa baths are to be performed in hot or cold water in case there is no holy tank or river nearby.

116. Water taken out (from well) is better than surface water; still better is the water from springs and fountains; still better is the lake water and still better is the river water.

117. The water in a holy place is still better and the Ganges water is the holiest of all. The Gaṅgā water removes all sins committed till death.

118. The Ganges water is better than the water in Gayā or Kurukṣetra. It is the holiest.

119. Baths in the night are recommended on the occasions of birth of a son, the special conjunctions of planets and stars, the transit of the sun from one zodiacal sign to another and at the sight of Rāhu (i.e. during lunar eclipse) and not otherwise.

120. The bath early in the morning, at dawn or immediately after sunrise removes even Mahāpātakas (deadly sins) since it is on a par with the Prājāpatya rite.

121. A person who takes early morning bath regularly for a year with great faith acquires the merit accruing from the performance of Prājāpatya for twelve years.

122. He who wishes for worldly enjoyment as expansive as the moon and the sun shall regularly take the early morning bath for the two months Māgha and Phālguna (Mid-Jan. to Mid-March).

123. He who takes the early morning bath and takes only Haviṣya food in the month of Māgha quells all cruel sins within a month.

124. If the devotee takes the bath recalling any one, his mother, father, brother, friend or preceptor he shall receive a twelfth of his merit.

125. Āmalaka (Emlylic Myrobalam) fruits appeal to Lord

Viṣṇu especially on the eleventh day of the lunar fortnight. A person desiring prosperity shall always take bath with the Āmalaka fruits.

126. Distress, fame, shortage of life, wealth, death, health and achievement of all desires are the effects of taking oil bath on the seven days from Sunday to Saturday respectively.

127. A person who observes fast, a person observing rites and a person who has got his hair cropped by a barber shall not take oil bath. He will be blessed by the Goddess of Fortune if he does not touch oil.

128. After performing the bath (in the manner mentioned before), the devotee shall perform Tarpaṇa to the manes, gods and human beings. Standing in water navel-deep he shall raise his head up and contemplate on the manes, etc.

129. "May my manes come and accept my handful water libation." Saying this he shall offer three handfuls each of libation towards the sky and towards his right side.

130. After wearing dry clothes and sitting on a dry place where Kuśa grass has been spread, the devotee conscious of the rules shall perform Tarpaṇa and never in a vessel.

131-133. 'Whatever is cruel and impure in this water that has not subsided so far shall be removed by this', reciting this Mantra he shall take water in his left hand and sprinkle it towards the south west. This will ward off the malignant demons.

134-136. 'May Indra, Varuṇa, Bṛhaspati, Savitṛ, Bhaga, and the sages Sanaka and others sanctify me and quell the sins committed by me by words, mind, body or acting and the sins due to taking prohibited food, and acceptance of gifts from sinners and let everything in the world from Brahmā to a blade of grass be pleased', saying this he shall sprinkle three handfuls of water. This is Saṁkṣepatarpaṇa (Tarpaṇa in brief).

137. He shall then worship gods without having any distinction among Brahmā and others with the Mantras pertaining to Brahmā, Viṣṇu, Rudra, Savitṛ and Mitrā-Varuṇa.

138. He shall bow to all Devas with their respective Mantras and place flower offerings separately for them saying 'Namaḥ'.

139-140. He shall worship Viṣṇu who incorporates in Himself all the deities and also Bhāskara (the sun). He who offers flowers or water reciting the Puruṣa Sūkta Mantra has actually worshipped the whole world, the movable as well as the immovable. The devotee shall worship Janārdana with other Tāntrika Mantras too.

141. Arghya offering must be made at first. The application of unguents, offerings of flowers, incenses and the fruits as Naivedya must be performed in due order.

142. The Mārjana and Ācamana types of Snāna is only with water inside the house. The water is invoked with Mantras and holy waters are psychically invoked with the Aghamarṣaṇa Sūkta. Everyday this must be done thrice.

143. The procedure of bath has been laid down thus by great men. While taking bath Brahmins, Kṣatriyas and Vaiśyas have to repeat Mantras. A Śudra has to observe silence during bath and perform Namaskāra also silently.

144. Teaching of Vedas is called Brahmayajña; Tarpaṇa is called Pitṛyajña; performance of Homa is Devayajña; offering of oblations is Bhūtayajña and the hospitality to guests is Nryajña.

145-146. If these religious rites are performed in a cowshed, tenfold merits accrue; if performed in the chamber of sacrificial fire hundredfold merits accrue; if performed in the abode and presence of enlightened persons thousandfold merits accrue; if performed in holy places hundred thousandfold merits accrue; if performed in temples crorefold merits accrue and if performed in the presence of Viṣṇu endless merits accrue.

147. In the fifth part of the day man must distribute foodstuffs among the Pitṛs, gods, human beings and insects.

148. He who first gives excellent food to a brahmin and then shares his food with friends attains Svarga (Heaven). Hence, one must make gifts of food.

149. One should take sweet things first. Savouries and cooked rice must be taken in the middle. Pungent, bitter and astringent things must be taken in the end with water and milk.

150. During nights, green vegetables must be completely or to a great degree abjured. Never should a man take a food stuff exclusively of one taste.

151. The sumptuous food rice, etc of a brahmin is on a par with nectar; that of a Kṣatriya is like milk; that of a Vaiśya is real food and that of a Śūdra is like blood.

152. Goddess of Fortune and wealth resides in the place where people observe fast on new moon day for at least a year.

153. The Gārhapatya fire is located in the belly; the Dakṣiṇa fire is located in the back; the Āhavanīya fire is located in the mouth and the Satya fire along with all others is located in the head.

154. He who understands the five types of fires is called Āhitāgni. The body, the water, the Soma all these are different types of food.

155-156. The Prāṇa, the fire, and the Sun—these three are the selfsame enjoyers. Reciting the Mantra, "Let food be for my strength. Let there be happiness to the earth, to the waters, to the fire, to the wind and to me also after the food has been digested fully." Having rubbed belly with the hand the betel leaf should be chewed.

157-159. The sixth and seventh parts of the day shall be spent listening to Itihāsas, Purāṇas etc. attentively. Then after taking bath the evening prayers should be offered. Thus I have mentioned the daily rites, O brahmin. He who reads this or hears it will attain heaven. Keśava is the author of all these rules of conduct.

CHAPTER TWO HUNDRED AND FOURTEEN

Dharmaśāstra

Brahmā said:

1-2. Now, I shall explain the rules and rites regarding bath since all other rites are based on bath. The person who wishes to take bath shall bring earth, cowdung, gingelly seeds, Kuśa grass and fragrant flowers at the time of bath. He must place all of them on the bank in a secluded place along with the scented water.

3-8. The earth and the cowdung should be divided into three parts. With water and earth he should wash his hands and feet. With the sacred thread worn as usual (Upavītī) and the tuft tied he should perform Ācamana silently with the mantra "Om uruṁ hi rājā Varuṇo[1] Varuṇāya namaḥ" he must propitiate the water and circumambulate. With the Ṛk mantra "Om ye te śatam[2].... svarkāḥ svāhā" he must whirl the water all round. With the Ṛk "Oṁ sumitriyā na[3].... yañca vayaṁ dviṣmaḥ" he shall take two handfuls of water and scatter it to the north and he shall then wash his feet, calves and hips three times.

9-11. He shall wash his hands and perform Ācamana and then bow to the water. With the seven Vyāhṛti mantras he shall perform Ācamana again. He shall then rub his limbs with earth repeating the mantra "Idaṁ Viṣṇuḥ[4]....pāṁsure." Then he shall face the sun and take his dip repeating the mantra —"Om āpo asmān mātaraḥ[5].... śucirā pūtaemi".

12-13. Then he shall clean the vessels, dip and dip again himself slowly. Repeating the mantra "Oṁ mā nastoke[6].... sadasi tvā havāmahe" he shall rub cowdung over the limbs.

14-16. Then he shall dip himself into the water repeating the various Varuṇa mantras such as "Imaṁ me[7].... satyāmṛtayaḥ" "Tattvā yāmi.... pramoṣīḥ", etc.

17. After plunging again and standing up he shall drink the water from Kuśa grass.

18-19. The nine Ṛks, viz—"Āpo hi ṣṭhā and the two following ones, "Devīrāpa"[8] and the next, "Āpo devā"; the Ṛk "Drupadādiva"[9], the Ṛk "Śanno devī"[10] the Ṛk "Āpo devī" the Ṛks called "Pāvamānyaḥ"—all these nine Ṛks must be repeated.

20-21. Repeating the mantra 'Citpatirmā'[11] he shall slowly plunge again. He shall then repeat the other mantras of Varuṇa according to his ability.

1. ṚV. 1.24.8.
2. KŚ. 25.1.11.
3. VS. 6. 22.
4. ṚV. 1.22.17.
5. *Ibid.* 10.17.10.
6. *Ibid.* 1.114.8.
7. *Ibid.* 1.25.19.
8. MS. 1.1.11.
9. AV. 6.115.3.
10. ṚV. 10.9.4.
11. VS. 4.4.

22. The first dip and the last dip should be accompanied by the repetition of Praṇava, the seven Vyāhṛtis and the Gāyatrī.

23. The Mārjana should be done inside water. The Aghamarṣaṇa[1] mantra should be repeated thrice.

24. Other Mantras that he remembers correctly can be repeated with great devotion and concentration.

25. He can repeat Praṇava and Gāyatrī as many times as possible. Or he can remember Viṣṇu the imperishable.

26. Āpaḥ (waters) constitute the residence of Viṣṇu. He is called Appati, hence Lord Viṣṇu and the waters should be remembered. [For Mantras see Text]

27-29. With the Mantra 'Tad Viṣṇoḥ'[2] he should take as many plunges as possible. Gāyatrī is the Mantra for the remembrance of Viṣṇu. Various mantras should be repeated in the course of the bath.

30. After the bath is over he should wear clean dry cloth. He should wash his hands and feet with earth.

31. He must perform Ācamana repeatedly. Bath and Meal are to be taken with mantras repeated. Drupada[3] mantra should be repeated three times. Aghamarṣaṇa Mantra[4] is also to be repeated.

32. After Ācamana he should repeat the Asu mantra. Then he should worship the sun with flower offerings above the head.

33-34. After scattering water he should repeat the mantra Udu tyam[5], Citram[6] etc. Then he should look at the sun and repeat the mantras "Taccakṣuḥ"[7] etc. and "Haṁsaḥ Śucisad"[8] etc. and worship the sun with Gāyatri.

35-36. The Anuvāka "Vibhrāṭ" etc. and Puruṣa Sūkta, Śiva Saṅkalpa and Maṇḍala Brāhmaṇa should be repeated and Japayajña performed duly.

37-39. Adhyātmavidyā should be practised for the fulfilment of Japa. Śrī, Medhā, Dhṛti, Kṣiti, Vāk, Vāgīśvara, Puṣṭi,

1. ṚV. 10.190.
2. *Ibid*. 1.22.20.
3. AV. 6.115.3.
4. ṚV. 10.190.
5. *Ibid*. 1.50.1.
6. *Ibid*. 1. 115.1.
7. *Ibid*. 7.66.16.
8. *Ibid*. 4.40.5.

Tuṣṭi, Umā, Arundhatī, Śacī, the Mātṛs (mothers) Jayā, Vijayā, Sāvitrī, Śānti, Svāhā, Svadhā, Dhṛti and Aditi shall be duly worshipped.

40. The wives of sages, the Virgins and the Kāmyadevatās should be propitiated. He who wishes for everything auspicious should propitiate the goddess Sarvamaṅgalā.

41. "May the whole universe beginning with Brahmā and ending with a blade of grass be propitiated," saying thus three handfuls of water should be sprinkled. Tarpaṇa is thus duly performed.

CHAPTER TWO HUNDRED AND FIFTEEN

Dharmaśāstra

Brahmā said :

1-2. I shall explain Tarpaṇa which propitiates the gods and the manes. Om, may the spirits Modās be propitiated. Om, may Pramodās be propitiated. Om, may Sumukhās be propitiated. Om, may Durmukhās be propitiated. Om, may Vighnas be propitiated. Om, may Vighnakartāraḥ (those who hinder) be propitiated. Om, may the metres be propitiated. Om, may the Vedas be propitiated. Om, may the medicinal herbs be propitiated. Om, may the Sanātana (the Eternal) be propitiated. Om, may the other Ācāryas be propitiated. Om, may the parts of the year be propitiated. Om, may the gods be propitiated. Om, may the celestial damsels be propitiated. Om, may the Devāndhakas be propitiated. Om, may the oceans be propitiated. Om, may the serpents be propitiated. Om, may the mountains be propitiated. Om, may the rivers, men and Yakṣas be propitiated. Om, may the malignant spirits be propitiated. Om, may the Piśācas (the ghosts) be propitiated. Om, may the Suparṇas be propitiated. Om, may the Bhūta be propitiated. Om, may the four kinds of living beings be propitiated. Om, may Dakṣa be propitiated. Om, may Pracetas be propitiated.

Om, may Marīci be propitiated. Om, may Atri be propitiated. Om, may Aṅgiras be propitiated. Om, may Pulastya be propitiated. Om, may Pulaha be propitiated. Om, may Kratu be propitiated. Om, may Nārada be propitiated. Om, may Bhṛgu be propitiated. Om, may Viśvāmitra be propitiated. Om, may Kaśyapa be propitiated. Om, may Jamadagni be propitiated. Om, may Vasiṣṭha be propitiated. Om, may Svāyambhuva be propitiated. Om, may Svārociṣa be propitiated. Om, may Tāmasa be propitiated. Om, may Raivata be propitiated. Om, may Cakṣus be propitiated. Om, may Mahātejas be propitiated. Om, may Vaivasvata be propitiated. Om, may Dhruva be propitiated. Om, may Dhava be propitiated. Om, may Anila be propitiated. Om, may Prabhāsa be propitiated.

3. Wearing the sacred thread in the form of a garland (Nivītī)—Om, may Sanaka be propitiated. Om, may Sanandana be propitiated. Om, may Sanātana be propitiated. Om, may Kapila be propitiated. Om, may Āsuri be propitiated. Om, may Voḍhu be propitiated. Om, may the Kavyavāṭs of men be propitiated. Om, may Soma be propitiated. Om, may Yama be propitiated. Om, may Aryamā be propitiated.

4. Wearing the sacred thread over the right shoulder and under the left arm (Prācīnāvītī).

Om, may the manes Agniṣvāttas be propitiated. Om, may the manes Somasthas (Saumyāsaḥ) be propitiated. Om, may the manes Barhiṣads be propitiated. Obeisance to Yama. Obeisance to Dharmarāja. Obeisance to Mṛtyu. Obeisance to Antaka. Obeisance to Vaivasvata. Obeisance to Kāla. Obeisance to the slayer of all living beings. Obeisance to Audumbara. Obeisance to Dadhna. Obeisance to Nīla. Obeisance to Parameṣṭhin. Obeisance to Vṛkodara (Brahman). Obeisance to Citra. Obeisance to Citragupta.

5. May the universe from Brahmā to a blade of grass be propitiated. Obeisance and Svadhā to the manes, Obeisance and Svadhā to the grandfathers. May our Pitṛs of gentle face, the Agniṣvāttas come unto this sacrifice through the paths of gods, elated with Svadhā; let them protect us and speak within me.

6. Om, repeating the mantra Ūrjaṁ vahantīḥ[1] etc. may the Pitṛs be propitiated. Obeisance to Pitṛs and Svadhā. Obeis-

1. VS .2.31

ance to Pitāmahas (grandfathers) and Svadhā. Obeisance to Mātāmahas (maternal grandfathers) and Svadhā. Obeisance to Pramātāmahas (maternal great grandfathers) and Svadhā. Obeisance to Vṛddhapramātāmahas (maternal great-great-grandfathers) and Svadhā. Let the imperishable Pitṛs of Pitāmahas be propitiated. These Pitṛs within me be propitiated. Then repeat the mantras "Pitaraḥ Svadhadhvam" etc. and "Madhu vātā ṛtāyate",[1] etc.

7. Then Añjali (joined palms) be offered to great grandfather. Obeisance unto ye, O Pitṛs. Obeisance to Rasa. Obeisance to ye, O Pitṛs. Obeisance to Śoṣa. Obeisance to ye O Pitṛs. Obeisance to Jīva. Obeisance to ye O Pitṛs. Obeisance to Svadhā. Obeisance to ye O Pitṛs. Obeisance to Manyu. Obeisance to ye O Pitṛs. Our homes are your residence, O ye Pitṛs. Three Añjalis are offered to maternal grandfathers. Then to mothers and others.

8. Those who are born in our family, those who died issueless, let those be propitiated. I have offered water by squeezing this cloth.

CHAPTER TWO HUNDRED AND SIXTEEN

Dharmaśāstra

Brahmā said :

1. I shall explain the characteristics of the Homa called Vaiśvadeva. First repeat the mantra "Kravyādam Agnim,"[2] etc after kindling the fire and performing Paryukṣaṇa (Sprinkling of water) Om, O Pāvaka (fire god) Vaiśvānara, here is a seat unto you sanctified by Araṇīgarbha.

O Mahā Brahman ! I am wakening up Vaiśvānara. Then repeat the mantra "Om Vaiśvānareṇa"[3] etc.

2. Oṁ Svāhā to Prajāpati. Oṁ Svāhā to Soma. Oṁ Svāhā to Bṛhaspati. Oṁ Svāhā to Agni and Soma. Oṁ Svāhā to Indra and Agni. Oṁ Svāhā to Earth and Heaven. Oṁ Svāhā to Indra, Oṁ Svāhā to all Devas. Oṁ Svāhā to Brahman. Oṁ Svāhā to waters, to herbs and plants, to the planets, to the

1. RV. 1.90.6
2. *Ibid.*, 10.16.9
3. AV. 7.108.2

deities, to Indra, to Indra's officers, to Yama, to the officer of Yama, to all beings roaming the firmament, to Vasudhā Pitṛs. I offer oblation to those beings which, in their woe, roam in the mid-world and desire all round nourishment. May Puṣṭipati grant me nourishment. May he grant everything even to Cāṇḍālas and crows.

CHAPTER TWO HUNDRED AND SEVENTEEN

Dharmaśāstra

Brahmā said :

1. I shall mention, in brief, the process of Sandhyā for the twice-born. Whether he is pure or impure, whether he is in any plight or not, whoever remembers the lotus-eyed Lord Viṣṇu is pure internally and externally.

2-6. Om, the metre is Gāyatrī. The sage is Viśvāmitra. It has three feet. The ocean is its belly. The moon and the sun are its eyes. The fire is its mouth, Viṣṇu is its heart, Brahmā is its head. Rudra is its tuft. Its use is in the investiture of sacred thread. Oṁ Bhūḥ Nyāsa on the foot, Bhuvaḥ on the knees, Svaḥ on the chest, Mahaḥ on the head, Janaḥ on the tuft, Tapaḥ on the throat, Satyam on the forehead. Oṁ obeisance to the heart. Oṁ Bhūḥ Svāhā to the head. Oṁ Bhuvaḥ Vauṣaṭ to the tuft. Oṁ Svaḥ Hum to the Kavaca. Oṁ Bhūrbhuvaḥ Svaḥ Phaṭ to the Astra. Oṁ Bhūḥ Oṁ Bhuvaḥ Oṁ Svaḥ Oṁ Mahaḥ Oṁ Janaḥ Oṁ Tapaḥ Oṁ Satyam. Then the three-footed Gāyatrī Mantra "Āpo Jyotīraso 'mṛtam Brahma Bhūrbhuvasvar Om."[1] Then the Mantras "Sūryaśca[2]" in the morning "Āpaḥ punantu[3]" etc. in the midday and "Agniśca[4]" etc. in the evening.

7. O you, the grantress of Boons, you are of white hue in the forenoon. You the great goddess of Gāyatrī wearing white cloth, You are seated on the shoulders of a bull. You hold the excellent trident.

1. TA. 10.15.1.
2. *Ibid.* 10.25.1.
3. *Ibid.* 10.23.1.
4. *Ibid.* 10.24.1.

8. May the goddess of Gāyatrī of dark hue come at midday, like the flower of Atasī, Viṣṇu's deity seated on Garuḍa, wearing yellow cloth and holding Śaṅkha, Cakra, Gadā and Padma.

9. She is of white hue, seated in the solar sphere on a white lotus. She is decorated with white flowers. May Sarasvatī the form of Gāyatrī in the evening, the goddess granting boons come hither.

10-11. The various mantras—"Oṁ Āpo hi ṣṭhā"[1] etc. "Oṁ Tasmā araṅga mām avo"[2] etc. "Oṁ sumitriyā na" etc. "Oṁ Drupadādiva"[3] etc "Oṁ ṛtañca satyañca"[4] etc are to be repeated duly.

12. The Mantras to be repeated thereafter—Oṁ, the sage of Gāyatrī is Viśvāmitra; the metre is Gāyatrī. Savitṛ is the deity. Its use is in Japa "Om udu tyam." etc, "Om citraṁ devānām"[5] etc. "Oṁ taccakṣuḥ"[6] etc. "Oṁ Viśvatascakṣuḥ"[7] etc. are to be repeated.

13. Born of the excellent summit, residing on the mountain on the surface of the Earth and permitted by Brahmā O Goddess ! be pleased to depart according to convenience.

CHAPTER TWO HUNDRED AND EIGHTEEN

Dharmaśāstra

Brahmā said :

1. O Vyāsa, I shall explain the procedure of Śrāddha which yields worldly enjoyments and salvation to men. The performer of Śrāddha shall invite Brahmins particularly Brahmacārins (unmarried students).

2. For the worship of devas, the sacred thread should be in the normal way and for the worship of Pitṛs, the sacred thread should be in the Prācīnāvīta form (on the right shoulder and under the left arm), when the worship of feet is to be performed 'Saṁyoga' mantra is to be used.

1. RV. 10.9.1
2. *Ibid.* 10.9.3
3. AV. 6.115.3
4. RV. 10.190
5. *Ibid.* 1.115.1
6. *Ibid.* 7.66.16
7. *Ibid.* 10.81.3

3. The householder asks—Om, you all have come ?" When they reply—"Om, well. Well, we have come" the householder says—"Om, To Viśvedevas (to all Devas), here is the water offering and Arghya—Svāhā" and offers the sacred deity water through the bent Kuśa grass on the feet of the brahmin intended to be (the representative of) Viśvedevas.

4. The householder faces the south. He wears the sacred thread in the opposite way and repeats the names and Gotra of the person to whom he performs Śrāddha and says "here is the offering of water to the feet and Arghya, Svadhā." He takes the sacred Pitṛ water and pours it through the bent Kuśa grass alongwith flowers over the feet of the brahmin intended to represent the Pitṛs.

5. Similarly, for maternal grandfather and others. 'Here is the Ācamanīya water, Svāhā, Svadhā', Saying so it is poured into the hand of the brahmin. 'Here is Arghya,' saying so, the flower is handed to the brahmin.

6-7. The householder then says that in such and such a place, in such and such a month, in such and such transit of the sun, in such and such Tithi (day of the lunar fortnight he is preparing to perform the Vaiśvadeva Śrāddha of his father, grandfather and great grandfather of such and such gotra and named such and such.

He asks the brahmins 'Is the seat ready ?' When they say 'Yes, it is ready' he begins Oṁ Bhūḥ, Oṁ Bhuvaḥ, Oṁ Svaḥ, Oṁ Mahaḥ, Oṁ Janaḥ, Oṁ Tapaḥ, Oṁ Satyam—These are the seven Vyāhṛtis. With these he makes the brahmin representing gods sit facing the east. Then he makes the other brahmin representing the Pitṛs sit facing the north. Then he goes round them saying—"Obeisance, obeisance, always obeisance to the deities, to the Pitṛs of great Yogic power, obeisance to Svadhā and Svaha" He repeats this thrice.

Again, he takes the Saṅkalpa as mentioned in the first paragraph of this section. Om Svāhā unto the Viśve Devas. I shall invoke the Viśve Devas. When they give permission saying 'Yes Invoke', he repeats the Mantra 'Oṁ Viśve devāḥ śṛṇutemam' etc. upto 'Rājānam pārayāmasi' and invokes 'May the powerful Viśve Devas of noble dignity come. Those who are engaged in this Śrāddha shall be cautious. Om, may the platform be free from Asuras and Rākṣasas. After this, he scatters barley grains thrice.

8. The householder then says:' Oṁ, I shall prepare the Pātra (the vessel) when they permit saying 'Yes do' he takes the blades of Kuśa grass and twists them in the form of Trivṛt Pavitra repeating the Mantras 'Pavitre stho vaiṣṇavyau' and 'Oṁ Viṣṇurmanasā pūte sthaḥ' and places the Pavitra inside the vessel.

9. Repeating the mantra 'Oṁ śanno devīḥ' he pours water in the vessel. Repeating the mantra 'Oṁ yavosi' etc. he puts the yava grains. Repeating the mantra 'Gandha Dvārām etc' he offers the scents. Repeating the mantra 'Oṁ yā divyā āpaḥ' etc. he offers water to the brahmin and places the Saṁśrava and Pavitra near the brahmin. Then pouring the Saṁśrava water in the former vessel he places it over the Kuśa grass upright and places a blade of Kuśa over it also.

10. Here are these scents, flowers, incense, lamp, a pair of garments and Sacred Thread to the Viśve Devas. Obeisance. Let this offer of scents, etc., be unimpaired. The brahmins say 'Be it so'.

11. Then he seeks permission saying 'Shall I perform the Śrāddha of Pitṛs, grandfather, great grandfather, maternal grandfather, maternal great grandfather and maternal great great grandfather ?" When the brahmins say 'Yes, do', he repeats 'Oṁ Devatābhyaḥ' etc thrice.

12. Here is the seat and Svadhā unto our father, grandfather, etc. of such and such names accompanied by their wives. Saying so, he places the seat towards the left of the brahmin. Om, I invoke the Pitṛs. The brahmin says 'yes invoke'. He repeats the mantra 'Om āyantu naḥ pitaraḥ', etc. Thus the invocation. Then 'Oṁ may the Asuras and Rākṣasas clear away from the platform.' He scatters Tila grains. Repeating the mantra 'Tilosi Somadaivatyo' etc and hands over Tila seeds to the brahmin.

13. After giving scents and flowers to the brahmin he takes the Pitṛpātra and repeats 'Yā divyā' etc 'Om. My father of such and such gotra and such and such a name accompanied by thy wife, here is Arghya and Svadhā unto thee. The vessel

1. ṚV. 10.9.4

with Pavitra is then placed on the left side of the brahmin over the Kuśa grass. Repeating the Mantra 'Oṁ Pitṛbhyaḥ sthā namasi' he places the vessel face down.

14. 'Om, may the worlds occupied by the Pitṛs be sanctified. Thou art the seat of the Pitṛs,' he touches the vessel face down. Thou art the ball of rice soaked in ghī. He asks the Pitṛbrahmin 'Shall I place it on fire ? then he says, 'Yes do' Oṁ Svāhā unto Agni the bearer of Kavya and sprinkles two drops of ghī in the hands of Deva brahmin and gives a portion of the ball of rice in his hand. A portion of the rice is kept for the ball of rice (piṇḍa)and the remaining is put in the vessel of Pitṛs and that of maternal grandfather.

15. He covers the vessel with Kuśa grass and lifts it with both the hands kept prone. Repeats the mantra 'Om Pṛthivi te pātram' etc and invokes the vessel. Repeating the mantra 'Idam Viṣṇuḥ' etc, the thumb of the brahmin is placed in the middle of the rice.

16. Repeating the mantra 'Apa hata' he scatters Yava grains thrice. Reaping the mantra 'Oṁ Nihanmi' etc. he scatters the sum of money intended.

17. Oṁ Svāhā, here is the rice with ghī, pickles and drinking water to the gods named 'Madhuvilocana' and with water and Kuśa the same is contemplated as such. Om, may this rice be unimpaired. Om, may the contemplated be realised.

18. Then wearing the sacred thread in the opposite direction be places all foodstuffs, side-dishes, ghī, etc in a vessel in front of the Pitṛbrahmin and places a blade of grass half covering the vessel and half over the ground. Then be lifts the vessel with his palms supine repeating the mantra 'Oṁ Pṛthivī' etc. Repeating the mantra 'Idaṁ Viṣṇoḥ' he places the thumb of the brahmin in supine position over the foodstuff. Then he repeats the Mantra 'Apahata' etc and scatters gingelly seeds. He then kneels with his left knee touching the ground. Here is the foodstuff with side dishes, drinking water and ghī, devoid of forbidden food, and Svadhā unto my Pitṛs, Pitāmaha, etc. accompanied by their wives and named such and such belonging to such and such Gotra. The Saṅkalpa (contemplation) for the food is the mantra 'Om Ūrjam Vahantīḥ' etc. He then pours a few drops of water facing the South.

19. Oṁ, may this Śrāddha be unimpaired. Oṁ, may the contemplated be realised. Oṁ Bhū Bhuvaḥ Svaḥ, and after that he recites the mantra 'Om Madhu Vātāḥ', etc.

20-21. He shall then say—'Ye be pleased to take food conveniently and refraining from speech.' He shall then repeat the Pitṛ Stotra beginning with 'Sapta Vyādhāḥ' 'Seven hunters are in the Daśārṇa lands. The deer are in the mountain Kālañjara. The Cakravāka birds are in the Śaradvīpa and the Swans are in the Mānasa lake. Those brahmins of noble family and the extensive knowledge of the Vedas are in Kurukṣetra. You have started on a long journey and are likely to be tired out by them."

22. Then he shall say 'Be satiated.' With the sacred thread worn left-ways and facing south, the mantra 'Om Agnidagdhāḥ' etc shall be repeated. "May the Pitṛs who were duly cremated and those who were not, in our family be pleased with what I offer on the Earth and becoming satiated may they attain the highest goal." Saying so he shall place the rice soaked in ghī on the Kuśa grass on the ground pouring water over it.

23. Then water is to be offered to the brahmins in order as the last mouthful. He then repeats Gāyatrī with the Vyāhṛtis and the mantra 'Madhuvātā' etc. He then asks the Deva brahmin 'The food appealed to you, I hope'. When he says 'Yes very much', he asks—'Om, what shall I do with the remaining food ?' The brahmin replies 'Let it be partaken by you along with your near and dear'. Then he asks the Pitṛ brahmin wearing the sacred thread left ways. 'Om I hope you are satiated?' He replies 'Om we are satiated'. Thereafter the ground is sprinkled with water, a circle and a square are drawn and gingelly seeds are scattered.

24. O my father ! of this name, of this gotra, accompanied by thy wife, here is the seat for the Piṇḍa unto thee and Svadhā. Similarly, for grandfather too in the middle of the line. Then Gāyatrī with Vyāhṛtis is repeated and the Mantra 'Madhu Vātā' etc is repeated thrice. The ball of rice soaked in ghī is placed on the blade of Kuśa grass invoking father and grandfather with respective names Gotra, etc, saying 'Here is the Piṇḍa unto Thee and Svadhā. Then with the Mantras as

before, the piṇḍa is scattered. Near the piṇḍa 'Om may the Lepabhuks (those who take lambatives) be pleased.' Then he wipes his hand on the Kuśa grass. With the water washing the piṇḍa he repeats the mantra and says 'O my father (name Gotra, etc.) accompanied by thy wife, I am making this water libation unto thee and to those that are after thee. Svadhā unto thee." Thus the Pitṛpiṇḍa is sprinkled. Then he places the Piṇḍapātra face down. With hands joined together he repeats the Mantra—'Oṁ Pitar Mādayadhvam' etc. Touching water he turns about on the left and faces the north. He then takes Prāṇāyāma thrice and says obeisance unto the six seasons.

25. Turning again to the left a flower is handed over. May this rite be unimpaired and unbothered. May merit accrue. Facing the south he repeats the Mantra 'Amī madanta Pitaraḥ' etc. Untying the upper cloth, and joining palms he says 'Obeisance unto ye, obeisance unto ye. O Pitṛs, rice of the house is given." Saying this he looks at the house (all round). "Here is your cloth, O Pitṛs of this Gotra and Svadhā." Then the thread is given. He lifts the water pitcher with the left hand. Repeating the Mantra 'Ūrjaṁ vahantīḥ' the water is poured over the piṇḍa.

26. From the water pitcher placed before, the remaining water is taken and the piṇḍas are sprinkled. Invoking the piṇḍa, scents etc are given. Kuśa grass and a leaf is placed over the piṇḍa. Then he repeats the Mantra—"Akṣaṇṇamī"—etc, three times.

27. Similarly, everything is performed for the brahmins representing maternal grandfather and others—Ācamana "Om, may the sprinkling be excellent." He sprinkles the water. 'Om, Gods are stationed in the middle water. Everything is founded in the water. May the water placed in the hand of the brahmin be holy into us all.' Then he hands over the water to the brahmin, "Lakṣmī is stationed in the lotus. Lakṣmī stays in the cowshed always. Let there be good will of thine for ever.' He repeats the Mantra 'Somasya' etc. 'Whatever is progressive and conducive to the welfare in the world shall be mine forever. Om, may this be unimpaired and unbothered.' Then Yava grains are given.

28. 'May the food and drink offered to my father, grandfather and great grandfather with their wives, belonging to such and such gotra, be everlasting.' He then hands over the gingelly seeds. The brahmin says 'Be it so' 'May the benediction of maternal grandfather and others be unending. Om, may the Pitṛs be non cruel. May our gotra flourish. May our donors flourish. May Vedas and progeny flourish. May not our faith recede. May there be much for us to give. May our foodstuffs increase. May we get guests. May there be mendicants flocking to us. Let us not beg of anyone. May these blessings be given.

29. May there be good will.' When the brahmin says—'Be it so' in the place where piṇḍa is given he drops the Pavitra for the sake of Arghya. He then takes up the Pavitra and Kuśa and with it he touches the brahmin.

He asks—'Shall I recite the Svadhā'. He replies "Oṁ, let it be recited'. 'Oṁ, let the Svadhā be announced to father, grandfather and greatgrandfather of such and such names along with their wives.' When the brahmin says—'Let the Svadhā be presented' he shall repeat the Mantra 'Ūrjaṁ Vahantīḥ" and pour water.

30. 'Om. May Viśvedevas be pleased in this Yajña' saying thus he places Yava grains in the hand of the brahmin. When he says 'Om, let them be pleased' he shall repeat 'Oṁ devatābhyaḥ' etc. three times.

31. Looking down he moves the Piṇḍa Pātras to and fro and performs Ācamana. He wears the sacred thread in the normal way and faces the east 'Oṁ, I offer unto thee of such and such gotra, named so and so, of brahmanical clan and accompanied by thy wife, this silver piece as Dakṣiṇā for the fulfilment of this Śrāddha.' Saying so the Dakṣiṇā is handed over. Similarly, the Dakṣiṇā is given to the Devabrāhmaṇa also.

32. Then facing the Pitṛ Brahmin the question is put 'Are the Piṇḍas ready'. He replies 'Yes very well.' He pours the milk over the Piṇḍa. Then the Piṇḍa is moved to and fro. The guest brahmin keeps the Piṇḍa Pātra in supine position. The Mantra 'Oṁ Vāje vāje' etc is repeated and Piṇḍa is cast. Then the mantra 'Āmāvājasya' etc is repeated and the Devas are bid farewell to.

With the Mantra 'Om, Abhiramyatām' the Pitṛ brahmin is bid farewell to. The householder returns without the brahmins following. The Piṇḍas are then given to cows, etc.

33-34. This is the rule of procedure in a Śrāddha. If this is read it quells sins. Wherever Śrāddha is performed according to these rules the ancestors are ever lastingly propitiated. The performer is sure to attain heaven. Thus I have explained the Pārvaṇa Śrāddha which helps the manes attain Brahmaloka.

CHAPTER TWO HUNDRED AND NINETEEN

Dharmaśāstra

Brahmā said:

1. I shall explain the Nityaśrāddha (the daily Śrāddha). As the previous one, this too has a special variety.

Om, I shall perform the Śrāddha of my father, grandfather and great grandfather of such and such names, such and such Gotra and accompanied by their wives by means of cooked rice offered to you.

The procedure of seating, etc has to be followed (as before) except that of Viśve devas.

2. I shall explain Vṛddhiśrāddha (i.e. Śrāddha on special joyous occasions). As before everything is followed and its special variety too. On the joyous occasions of seeing the new born son's face, etc, Vṛddhi Śrāddha has to be performed. The brahmins face the east while sitting. The householder wears the sacred thread in the normal way. Yava seeds and Badara fruits are used with Kuśa grass. Devatīrtha (holy water consecrated), Namaskāra and the offering of Dakṣiṇā everything as usual.

3. The householder touches his right knee and says 'Oṁ, today on this joyous occasion, when the Śrāddha of our grandmother and mother of such and such Gotra and of such

and such name has to be performed. 'I have first to perform the Śrāddha of Viśvedevas named Vasus and Satyas by means of cooked rice offered to you.' Saying this he invites the Deva brahmin. When he says 'Oṁ you shall perform it' he proceeds to invite the other brahmin.

4. Thereafter is the procedure of Nāndī Mukha Śrāddha of the greatgrandmother mentioning the name, Gotra etc. followed by the invitation of the brahmin representing great grandmother, his formal permission, etc. Thereafter the same procedure for maternal great grandmother and the brahmin representing her.

5. The items of seating the brahmins representing the principal deity, Pitṛs and all Devas and the other usual ancillary rites are performed duly. He then repeats the Mantra 'Oṁ Viśve Devāḥ śṛṇutemām' etc. This is the invocation of Viśvedevas. Scents etc. are given. Statements about the Śrāddha being unimpaired.

6. Similar items concerning activities and statements with regard to great grandmother, grandmother, mother, great grandfather great great maternal grandfather etc. Then food is placed and offered to the Devas named Vasus and Satyas along with the side dishes, Badara fruit, curd and devoid of forbidden foodstuffs. "Om, O Nāndīmukhi, of such and such Gotra, my grandmother, named so and so here is the food unto you alongwith Badara fruit and curd. Obeisance." Similarly for maternal grandfather and great grandfather.

7. Ekoddiṣṭa (The Śrāddha for a single mane) is also performed as before. I shall explain its special variety, listen. First the invitation. Then washing of the feet, seating. 'Today I shall perform the Ekoddiṣṭa Śrāddha, the annually recurring one, of my father of such and such a name and of such and such a Gotra, by means of cooked rice offered through you. Permission is formally sought and given. Seat, scents etc. are given. The food is placed and contemplated. Japas are performed with the sacred thread worn in the opposite direction. Facing the north he performs the Atithi Śrāddha.

8. He then enquires about their being satiated. He faces the south with the sacred thread worn in the opposite

direction. He stands near the place where they had taken food and repeats the Mantra 'Agnidagdha' (duly cremated with fire). Then the piṇḍānna is scattered. 'O my father ! of such and such a name, of such and such a Gotra, I offer this water libation to thee as well as to those that follow thee. Svadhā unto thee. Water is poured over the line. All other things as before.

CHAPTER TWO HUNDRED AND TWENTY

Dharmaśāstra

Brahmā said:

1. I shall mention the rite of Sapiṇḍīkaraṇa (Joining the piṇḍa of the recently dead father with that of the other ancestors) which, if performed on the day of the first anniversary of the death, duly enables the dead father to attain the Pitṛloka (the region of the manes).

2. The Sapiṇḍīkaraṇa has to be performed in the afternoon. The other rites are the same as before. The brahmins representing grandfather, etc, are invited. Om, obeisance, here is the seat unto the deities named Purūrava and Ādrava. The seat is offered on the left side. Then the invocation is done. Permission is formally sought for the performance of the Śrāddha of grandfather and great grandfather accompanied by their wives. Three separate vessels are placed. Kuśa grass is placed over the vessels. They are covered with other vessels. All the items are duly performed till the request for the Śrāddha being unimpaired. Then all these items for the recently dead father and mother mentioning names, etc, till the request for its being unimpaired.

3. After concluding that, the covering vessels are taken off. The three vessels representing grandfather, great grandfather and great great grandfather are slightly shaken in the due order. 'Om, those that are similar and similar-minded,

the Pitṛs in the region of Yama,—to them we offer Svadhā and obeisance. Let this Yajña be of the same efficacy as in the case of the Devas.'

'Om, May the splendour of those living beings who are mine, similar to me and similar-minded among other living beings, be efficacious to me for a hundred years.' Repeating the above two Mantras, he pours the water from the vessel of grandfather into that of great grandfather and the water from both these vessels as well as Pavitra is kept in the vessel representing the recently dead father. The vessel of great great grand-father is left off.

4. The Pavitra in the vessel is handed over to the brahmin representing Pitṛ (father). With the flower in the vessel, his head, hands and feet are worshipped. Water from another vessel is slightly poured into the hand of the Pitṛ brahmin. The vessel is then held in both the hands and the Mantra 'Yā divyāḥ' etc is repeated. Then he invokes the grandfather along with his wife mentioning their name and gotra and says 'here is Svadhā and Arghya unto you.' He then pours water from Pitṛ vessel for Arghya into the hand of the brahmin representing grandfather. Some water is taken for sprinkling the Piṇḍa. On the left side, the vessel is placed prone on a Kuśa grass the tip of which is turned towards the South. He says 'Thou art the seat of the Pitṛs.'

5. Scents are offered to grandfather, great grandfather and great great grandfather. Then Agnikaraṇa (offerings in the fire) is performed. The remaining cooked rice is put in the vessel of grandfather. All other rites upto invoking the Mantra of the vessel of grandfather are concluded. Then the vessel of Pitṛ (father) and the brahmin representing him are touched. The thumb is placed over the food. Gingelly seeds are scattered. 'Om, here is thy food with ghī, drinking water and side-dishes devoid of forbidden foodstuff. The same unto those that follow thee. Svadhā unto thee.'

6. Then food and water are offered to Deva brahmin. If there is a guest as well, his Śrāddha too is performed. But no grain is scattered on this occasion. The householder then asks Pitṛ brahmin 'Om, is it tasted by your holiness?' Piṇḍa is then offered with necessary ancillary questions and split into

two. The two Mantras 'Ye samānāḥ samanasaḥ' are repeated. The piṇḍa is put in the vessels of great great grandfather and grand-father. Scents are offered to piṇḍas. Piṇḍa is slightly stirred. The Atithi Brahmin is asked 'Is it tasted by your holiness?' The brahmins are given Ācamana water and betel leaf in due order. May the sprinkling be in order. May the waters be holy and beneficent. Water is handed to the brahmin representing great great grandfather and others in due order. May the gotra enjoy unending bliss. Water with gingelly seeds is given to the Pitṛ brahmin saying, 'may this stay by.'

7. 'May the manes be non-fierce'. When the brahmin says 'be it so', he says 'Shall I repeat Svadhā?' When the grandfather brahmin replies 'Om, let it be repeated'. This is frequently asked and permission is given.

8. The mantra 'Ūrjaṁ vahantīḥ' is repeated. The householder faces south and pours water. 'Om may Viśve Devas be satiated with this Yajña' Barley and water is given to the Deva brahmin. The Mantra 'Devatābhyaḥ', etc is repeated thrice.

9. Piṇḍa pātras are stirred. Ācamana is performed. Dakṣiṇā is offered to the grandfather brahmin. The Pitṛ brahmin is requested for blessings. Then he blesses the householder repeating the mantra 'Dātāro nobhivardhantām' etc. The vessel is then placed supine. The brahmins are bid adieu with 'Vāje Vāje' Mantra. The Pitṛ brahmin is bid farewell to by saying 'may you rejoice.'

10. O Vyāsa I have thus explained to you the 'Sapiṇḍīkaraṇaśrāddha.' The Śrāddha, the performer of Śrāddha and the fruit thereof is Hari Himself.

CHAPTER TWO HUNDRED AND TWENTYONE

Dharmasāra

Brahmā said:

1. I shall briefly mention the essence of Dharma (Virtue and Righteousness), please listen, O Śaṅkara. It is subtle. It quells all sins. It yields worldly enjoyment and salvation.

2. It is grief that destroys learning, righteousness, strength, courage, happiness and zeal of every man. Hence, grief must be eschewed.

3. One gets a wife according to one's actions. One finds one's surroundings according to one's actions. His kinsmen and relatives behave in accordance with his actions. It is the action of a man that prompts him to activities generating happiness and misery.

4. Giving of gifts is the greatest virtue. Everything good is secured by making gifts. It is charity that enables one to attain heavenly kingdom. Hence, a man must make liberal gifts.

5. Making of gifts with excellent and entire money gifts (dakṣiṇā) is on par with the saving of life of a terrified being.

6. Dharma is acquired by means of austerities, practising celibacy, sacrifices and holy ablutions. Those who destroy the same go to hell.

7. Persons desirous of performing Homas, Japas, holy ablutions and worship of deities and those who possess truthfulness, forgiveness and mercy attain heaven.

8. There is no one making a gift of happiness or misery and there is no one who removes the same. Men experience happiness or misery brought about by his own actions.

9. He who dedicates his life for the sake of virtue crosses all difficulties. If there is contentment, who is he who cannot sustain himself by means of fruits and roots?

10. Every one sinks into misery due to association and intimacies. The same is caused by greed which cannot be warded off.

11. Greed generates anger, malice results from greed; greed begets delusion, illusion, false prestige and rivalry.

12. He who is free from lust, hatred, falsehood, anger, greed, delusion and haughtiness becomes calm and tranquil and he attains the highest region divested of sins.

13. O Hara, the deities, the sages, the serpents, the Gandharvas and the Guhyakas honour a virtuous man and not a rich or lustful man.

14. By means of unlimited valour, intelligence or manliness a man secures even things difficult to get. Hence, there is nothing to grieve over.

15. This is the highest achievement that a man is merciful to all living beings, is able to curb all sense organs and has the notion that everything is transitory.

16. If a man does not perform meritorious actions although he sees Death staring at him face to face, his life is as worthless as the teatlike sebaceous growth under the chin of a goat.

17. The slayer of a child in the womb, the murderer of a brahmin, he who kills a cow or his own father and the wretch who defiles his own preceptor's bed can get rid of the sin by making a gift of a land possessing all good features.

18. In my view, there is no other gift surpassing the gift of a cow. A cow acquired by lawful means, if handed over as a gift, makes the entire family cross all difficulties.

19. O Vṛṣadhvaja, there is no gift better than the gift of food. It is food that sustains the world of mobile and immobile beings.

20-21. The gift of a virgin, the gift of a bull, pilgrimage, high erudition, the gift of an elephant, horse and chariot or that of gems, jewels and lands—none of these is equal to even a sixteenth part of the gift of food. Vital airs, strength, splendour, valour, fortitude and power of memory take their origin from food.

22. If a person digs wells, tanks and lakes or lays parks for the sake of the public, he raises the members of his family even to the twentyfirst remove and himself revels in the region of Viṣṇu.

23. Even the very sight of good men purifies one. It is better than the holy places of pilgrimage. The benefit from a holy place is derived later but that from the contact of good men is immediately effective.

24. Truthfulness, restraint, penance, purity, contentment, forgiveness, straightforwardness, wisdom, tranquillity, mercy and charity—these are eternal virtues.

CHAPTER TWO HUNDRED AND TWENTY-TWO

Expiation

Brahmā said :

1. I shall explain the rites of atonement quelling sins conducive to being confined in hell. Flies, sprays of water, woman, water on the surface of the earth, fire, cat and mungoose are always pure.

2. If inadvertently a brahmin takes food defiled by the Ucchiṣṭa (residual of food partaken) of a Śūdra he should fast for a day and night and drink Pañcagavya. He shall be purified.

3. If a brahmin and another brahmin are mutually defiled by their Ucchiṣṭa, the expiatory rite is taking a bath and Japa. They shall take food only at the end of the day.

4-5. If anyone takes food containing flies or bits of hair he shall immediately vomit it out for purity. He who takes foodstuffs keeping them in the palms, or licks the finger or eats food placed on the arms shall be purified after the expiry of a day and night. Or he shall drink water poured out to him. Water drunk with the left hand, or water drunk by others partially is like toddy and so shall not be drunk or if drunk one incurs the sin of drinking toddy.

6-7. Water taken in a leather bag is impure. If a low caste person resides in the house of any one of other castes, without declaring that he is of low caste, the expiatory rite for the twice-born is Cāndrāyaṇa or Parāka. That for a Śūdra is the Prājāpatya rite. If the person resides knowingly, other types of expiatory rites are to be performed.

8. He who takes cooked food there shall perform half of a Kṛcchra penance. Those who take the food of these people shall perform a fourth of the Kṛcchra penance.

9. The brahmin who takes food of a washerman, an actor, a bamboo worker or a cobbler has to perform Cāndrāyaṇa penance.

10. If inadvertently he drinks water from a well or waterpot belonging to a Cāṇḍāla he shall perform the Sāntapana penance. A Vaiśya shall perform half of that.

11. A Śūdra in the circumstances shall perform a quarter of that. For inadvertently taking food in the house of a lowcaste, the atonement is three Kṛcchras. For approaching an Antyajā (low caste) woman, the expiatory rite is a Parāka.

12. A brāhmaṇa taking the Ucchiṣṭa of a low caste man becomes pure by performing Cāndrāyaṇa. If inadvertently he takes a Cāṇḍāla's food he should perform Aindhana (a variety of Sāntapana) form of an expiatory rite.

13. A Kṣatriya shall perform Sāntapana and the others shall perform Japa Yajña for a night. If a brahmin eats the fruit from the same tree as a Cāṇḍāla inadvertently he becomes pure after the lapse of a day and a night.

14. By eating Ucchiṣṭa impurity is incurred which shall be removed by vomitting it off. If he touches a Cāṇḍāla he shall repeat Gāyatrī eight thousand times or Drupadā Mantra a hundred times.

15. The atonement for taking the food of a Cāṇḍāla or a Śvapaca (those who cook dogs) or taking food after evacuating the bowels or urination (without the customary washing) is fasting for three nights. The expiation for approaching an Antyajā woman is Parāka penance.

16. Expiation for indulging in sexual intercourse with an unwilling woman is Parāka. There is no expiation for a low caste man in a similar context.

17. If a brahmin drinks water in a vessel that had contained wine and hence had been defiled, he is purified by a quarter of Kṛcchra penance and by undergoing all the Saṁskāras (investiture with sacred thread and other rites) all over again.

18-19. Brahmins who had once renounced the world but are desirous of starting the life of a householder again, after gathering food and drink, shall perform three Kṛcchras and three Cāndrāyaṇas. The Sage Vasiṣṭha has laid down all the Saṁskāras beginning with post-natal rites.

20-21. A defiled woman shall become pure again by Prājāpatya and other rites or by feeding two brahmins. A brahmin defiled by the touch of a dog or a Śūdra defiled by Ucchiṣṭa shall fast for a night and drink Pañcagavya. He shall become pure. Touched by an outcaste he shall fast for five nights.

22. A continuous stream of water is never defiled; dust blown out by wind is pure; women, children and old men are never polluted.

23. The mouth of women is always pure; the fruit struck down by birds is pure; a calf at the coming out of its mother animal's womb is pure; a dog in the act of seizing a beast of game is pure.

24. Aquatic animals while in water and surface and non-aquatic animals in the ground are pure. A person standing in water and performing Ācamana shall attain purity.

25. A vessel of bell metal not defiled by wine becomes pure by the application of ashes. If defiled by wine, it becomes pure by cow's urine or by heating.

26. Bell-metal vessels smelt by cows, or containing the Ucchiṣṭa of a Śūdra or struck by crow or a dog become pure by rubbing them with ash ten times.

27-29. A brahmin taking food in the vessel of a Śūdra should fast and then take Pañcagavya. A brahmin who has not rinsed his mouth after taking food becomes impure when touched by a dog or a Śūdra or others of a higher caste. He shall fast for regaining purity. Defiled by the touch of a woman in her menses he shall take Pañcagavya for purity. If a person evacuates his bowels or urinates in a dry place or in a road infested by thieves and tigers he is not defiled if he holds some coins in his hand. While taking Śauca he shall place the coins on the ground.

30. Gruel; curd, milk, buttermilk and Kṛśara (mixture of jaggery, rice and gingelly seeds) can be taken even from a

Śūdra. These together with pulse and honey can be taken from a low caste person.

31. If a brahmin or other castes drink Gauḍī, Paiṣṭī or Mādhvika type of wine they shall expiate by drinking red-hot wine.

32. Defiled by taking food or drinking water in a house defiled by the impurity of death or birth of a child, a brahmin should repeat Gāyatrī five hundred times. A Kṣatriya and a Vaiśya in similar circumstances shall repeat Gāyatrī a hundred times.

33. When someone dies in the family, a brahmin remains impure for ten days and a Kṣatriya for twelve days. A Vaiśya becomes pure after fifteen days and a Śūdra in a month.

34. If a king dies in battle, or while performing a sacrifice or during a sojourn in a foreign land, if a child less than a month old dies, the purity is instantaneous (there is no impurity).

35-36. An unmarried girl, a brahmin boy not yet invested with the sacred thread, a boy who has cut his first tooth, and a three year old girl, if these die the impurity is for three days. If there is abortion the impurity is for as many days as the number of months of conception. A woman in her menses becomes pure on the fourth day.

37-38. In times of famine, civil commotion, etc., during the days of initiation, in the practice of a religious rite, marriage preparation, invitation to a brahmin for a Śrāddha, etc. impurities due to birth or death do not act as obstacles. Nor can the regular charity, etc. be disturbed.

39-40. A brahmin becomes impure by touching his wife in confinement. There is no impurity due to birth where sacrificial fires are daily nurtured, Vedas are regularly recited, or Vaiśva Deva Śrāddha is constantly performed. If a brahmin takes food in a house where the impurities are present he becomes pure after three days.

41-42. Women of four castes in their menses become impure again due to mutual touch. The brahmin woman becomes pure after three days, the Kṣatriya woman after two days, the Vaiśya woman after fasting for a day and the Śūdra woman after taking a bath. Things measured in Droṇas are not to be cast off as defiled by them.

43. Cooked food touched by dogs or crows becomes defiled. The upper layer of such food should be thrown away. For the purification of the remaining food, it should be sprinkled with water from a vessel in which a piece of gold is kept and heated over fire for a short while.

44. If any one happens to drink water from a well where the dead body of a dog, jackal or a monkey has fallen, the expiation for a brahmin is fasting for three days, for a Kṣatriya two days and for a Vaiśya a single day.

45. If bones, hides, faeces or the dead body of a mouse fall into a well, the water shall be drained off and the well should be sprinkled with Pañcagavya. It becomes pure again.

46. If a tank or a lake is defiled as above, holy ashes should be sprayed over it and six potfuls of water should bet aken out. If Pañcagavya is poured thereafter it becomes pure again.

47-48. The menstrual blood flowing into a tank contaminates it. Thirty potfuls of water should be taken out of the tank for purification. If any one indulges in sexual intercourse with a forbidden woman, drinks wine or eats beef he becomes impure. The atonement for a brahmin then is Cāndrāyaṇa penance, for a king it is Prājāpatya penance, for a Vaiśya it is Sāntapana and for a Śūdra it is fasting for five days.

49. After performing the expiatory rite they should make gifts of cows and feed brahmins. During sports wearing of blue cloth is not forbidden. Nor is it forbidden as a bedsheet. An indigo dyed cloth should not be touched otherwise. Persons regularly using blue cloth will fall into hell.

50-53. The slayer of a brahmin, the wine addict, the thief, the defiler of a preceptor's bed and those who associate with such sinners become pure after seeing the 'Great Bear'. Then he should make a gift of a hundred cows and feed brahmins. The slayer of a brahmin must stay in a cottage in a forest for twelve years. The wine-addict should fall into fire. The thief should hand over everything he possesses to a brahmin. The defiler of a preceptor's bed shall make the gift of a bull or a thousand cows.

54. Binding the two legs of a cow, tying it illegally, and

allowing it to die in conflagration or in a forest makes one a sinner and he should perform the complete Kṛcchra penance.

55-56. If a cow dies due to the defect in tying the bell round its neck, if one breaks its bones or horns, if one strips its skin, if one cuts its tail or wounds its nose, one shall expiate by taking over barley water for a fortnight. Injuring elephants or horses by means of weapons is also sinful and should be atoned for by performing the complete Kṛcchra penance.

57. Inadvertently taking in faeces or urine or touching wine the twice-born becomes sinful and should undergo all the Saṁskāras all over again.

58. While undergoing the Saṁskāras all over again, the items of tonsure, wearing of Kuśa girdle, holding of the staff, and the rites of begging alms can be omitted.

59. Raw flesh, ghī, honey and oil kept for a long time when taken out of the vessel of an Antyaja become automatically pure.

60-61. The onefourth Kṛcchra consists of taking a single food for the first day, a single night food for the second day, and unsolicited food for the third day. The same with a fast for the fourth day is half a Kṛcchra. Twice that is Prājāpatya which atones for all sins. A Kṛcchra with seven days' fast is called Mahāsāntapana.

62. Taking hot water alone for three days, then taking hot milk alone for three days and then taking hot ghī alone for three days, is called a Taptakṛcchra. It quells all sins.

63. A Parāka penance that quells all sins consists of fasting for twelve days. In the expiatory rites morsels of food must be increased by one each in the bright half and decreased by one each in the dark half.

64-66. The constituents of Pañcagavya are as follows:—Milk taken from a gold-coloured cow; the cow dung of a white cow; urine of a copper coloured cow; clarified butter of the milk of a blue cow and the curd of the milk of a black cow. Water added should be consecrated by Kuśa grass. Eight Māśas of cow's urine, four Māśas of dung, twelve Māśas of milk, ten Māśas of curd and five māśas of ghī form the correct proportion. This Pañcagavya removes all impurities.

CHAPTER TWO HUNDRED AND TWENTYTHREE

Yuga-dharma

Brahmā said:

1. O Vyāsa, I have narrated with devotion the various acts of piety practised by the sages. Through them Viṣṇu can be propitiated. They are conducive to happiness.

2-3. Lord Viṣṇu who dispenses virtue, love, wealth and salvation can be attained by Tarpaṇa, Homa and Sandhyā prayers. Virtue is Lord Viṣṇu Himself; worship is Viṣṇu; performance of Tarpaṇa, Homa, Sandhyā prayers, contemplation, everything is Lord Hari Himself.

Sūta said:

4. I shall explain, O Śaunaka, the Pralaya (dissolution) of the universe. Please listen to everything. A thousand sets of the four Yugas constitute a Kalpa which is one day for Brahmā, the lotus born deity.

5. Know the characteristic features of the four Yugas viz Kṛta, Tretā, Dvāpara and Kali. In Kṛta age virtue rests on its four feet, viz. Truth, Gift, Penance and Mercy.

6. Hari protects Dharma then. All the wise men are contented. Men lived for four thousand years then.

7. At the end of Kṛta, brahmins were conquered by Kṣatriyas and Vaiśyas and Śūdras remained submissive to the twice-born. The powerful Viṣṇu, the valorous, killed the Rākṣasas.

8. In the Tretā age, virtue stands on three feet, viz. Truth, Gift and Mercy. Men are devoted to Yajñas (sacrifices) then. The universe takes its origin (sustenance) from Kṣatriyas.

9. Hari of the red hue is worshipped by men who live for a thousand years. Viṣṇu has a mighty chariot in this age. Kṣatriyas killed Rākṣasas. [Or Viṣṇu who incarnated as Bhīmaratha of the Kṣatriya caste killed the Rākṣasas].

10. In the Dvāpara age, when Viṣṇu takes the yellow hue, virtue stands on two legs. People live for four hundred years and take their origin and sustenance from brahmins and Kṣatriyas.

11. On seeing people deficient in intellect, Lord Viṣṇu incarnating as Vyāsa divided the Vedas into four books.

12-13. He taught the Vedas to his disciples. Please know the details. Disciple Paila was taught Ṛgveda; Jaimini was taught Sāmaveda; Sumantu was taught Atharvaveda and Mahāmuni was taught Yajurveda. Sūta in the company of Vaiśampāyana was taught the Purāṇas. He who knows the eighteen Purāṇas is Lord Hari himself.

14. The five topics dealt with in a Purāṇa are (1) creation (2) subsidiary creation (3) genealogy (4) Manvantaras and (5) the detailed description of the exploits of various kings.

15-16. The eighteen Purāṇas are—(1) Brāhma (2) Pādma (3) Vaiṣṇava (4) Śaiva[1] (5) Bhāgavata (6) Bhaviṣya (7) Nāradīya (8) Skānda (9) Liṅga (10) Varāha (11) Mārkaṇḍeya (12) Āgneya (13) Brahmavaivarta (14) Kaurma (15) Mātsya (16) Gāruḍa (17) Vāyavīya and (18) Brahmāṇḍa.

17. Many Upapurāṇas have been mentioned by sages. The first one is narrated by Sanatkumāra. The next one is that of Narasiṁha.

18. The third one is Skānda as narrated by Kumāra. The fourth one is Śivadharma as narrated by Nandīśvara.

19. The next one is the one of wonderful features narrated by Durvāsas. The next one is narrated by Nārada. Then come those narrated by Kapila, Vāmana and Uśanas.

20. The other ones are Brahmāṇḍa, Vāruṇa, Kālikā, Māheśvara, Sāmba, Sarvārthasañcaya, Parāśarokta, Mārīca and Bhārgava.

21. The eighteen Vidyās are :—(1) Purāṇas (2) Dharmaśāstras (3-6) the four Vedas (7-12) the six Vedāṅgas (13) Nyāya (14) Mīmāṁsā (15) Āyurveda (16) Arthaśāstra (17) the Gāndharva vidyā (Science of Music) and (18) Dhanurveda the Science of Archery, O Sage Śaunaka.

22. By the end of Dvāpara, Lord Hari had already removed the weighty burden of the earth. Then Lord Hari

1. Sometimes *Vāyu Purāṇa* is inserted in place of *Śiva Purāṇa* in the list of eighteen *Mahāpurāṇas*.

incarnated as Kṛṣṇa (the black) when virtue began to stand on a single foot.

23. Then (in the Kali age)men will become vicious, ruthless and evilminded. There are three qualities in a man viz. Sattva, Rajas and Tamas. Actuated by Kali (Kāla) these qualities undergo various changes in the Ātman.

24. When the Sattva quality is predominant in the mind, the intellect and the sense organs know that to be the Kṛta Yuga when people are devoted to knowledge and penance.

25. O Śaunaka, when the energy of people is turned towards the fulfilment of their desires and Rajas predominates, know that to be Tretā Yuga.

26. When Rajas and Tamas are equally powerful giving rise to greed, discontent, false prestige, haughtiness, rivalry and eager pursuit of desired objects, know that to be Dvāpara.

27. When Tamas alone is predominant, the people utter falsehood always, are lethargic, somnolent, seeking violent means and overwhelmed by grief, delusion, terror and wretchedness, know that to be Kali age.

28. Then people are lustful and harsh in speech. Country is overrun by thieves and robbers. Vedas are spoiled by Pāṣaṇdas (misinterpreters).

29. Kings will be begging of the subjects. People will be overpowered by their penises and bellies. [They will be carnal minded and gluttonous). The religious students will be divested of their rites and impure. Mendicants will turn householders.

30. Ascetics will begin to stay in villages. Depositors will be covetous of wealth. People will be short in stature but very gluttonous. Thieves and robbers will be considered holy.

31. Servants will leave their masters in the lurch; the ascetics will cast off their religious rite; Śūdras will begin to receive Dakṣiṇās and Vaiśyas will turn to austerities.

32-33. All people will be disgruntled appearing like Piśācas. They will be worshipping fire, deities and guests by means of unjustifiable means of feeding. When Kali age sets in, people will never offer water libations to their Pitṛs. They will be devoted to womenfolk and for all appearance they will not be different from Śūdras, O, Śaunaka.

34. Women will give birth to many children. Their good fortune will decline. If they are rebuked they will simply scratch their heads and defy all orders.

35. Overwhelmed by heretics people will cease to worship Viṣṇu. But, O Brahmins, though the Kali age is full of defects there is a great virtue in it.

36-37. In Kali, by singing songs in praise of Lord Kṛṣṇa one can free oneself from the great bondage. In Kṛta age people have to perform sacrifices and in the Tretā they have to recite Japas. In the Dvāpara age, by serving the lord they can attain salvation but in Kali that is possibe only by singing songs in praise of the Lord. Hence, Hari is to be contemplated upon for ever and worshipped, O Śaunaka.

CHAPTER TWO HUNDRED AND TWENTYFOUR

Dissolution

Sūta said :

1. At the end of a thousand sets of four Yugas there will be a causal dissolution of all created beings called Brāhma laya or Naimittika laya. At the end of a Kalpa there will be a drought extending over a hundred years.

2. Then seven fierce suns will blaze in the sky. Drying up every drop of water they will wither up the three worlds.

3. The earth, Bhuvaḥ, Svaḥ and Mahar Lokas with all their inmates mobile and immobile will be completely dried up. Lord Viṣṇu in the form of Rudra, will burn nether worlds as well.

4. First burning up the three worlds, Lord Viṣṇu will begin creating clouds from his mouth. These clouds of various delusive nature will shower water for a hundred years.

5. The whole world will appear like a vast ocean of water. All mobile and immobile beings will be destroyed.

Viṣṇu will then lie down on the back of the serpent Ananta assuming the form of the Supreme Brahman.

6. After sleeping for a thousand years he will begin creating the universe again. Now I shall explain the dissolution called Prākṛtika Pralaya (Natural dissolution), O Śaunaka, please listen.

7. When a hundred years (of Brahmā) are completed, Lord Hari with his yogic powers destroys the whole universe after absorbing within himself the deity Brahmā.

8. A long period of drought and blazing sun will be followed by the formation of clouds that will pour heavy showers for a hundred years and fill the cosmos with water.

9. With water within, the Aṇḍa (the Cosmic Egg) will burst when the life span of Brahmā is over and dissolve in water.

10. The whole Earth sustaining the world will dissolve in water. The waters will merge in fire and the fire will merge in wind.

11. The wind will merge in Ether and the Ether in Bhūtādi (the essential matter). This essential matter merges into Mahān (the Cosmic Intellect). The Mahān merges into Avyakta Prakṛti (the undifferentiated Nature) which loses itself into the Puruṣa (the eternal subjectivity).

12. Hari sleeps for a hundred years and then creates on the onset of day in the same order manifesting finally into the world.

CHAPTER TWO HUNDRED AND TWENTYFIVE

Results of good and bad acts

Sūta said :

1. After knowing the three types of misery such as the Ādhyātmika (physiological) etc. the wise man conscious of the Saṁsāra cakra (the wheel of worldly existence) will become possessed of wisdom and non-attachment (to things

mundane) and then merge into Ātyantika Laya (Psychic annihilation).

2. I shall mention the wheel of worldly Existence from the time of death without knowing which the individual self (Puruṣārtha) cannot become sub-merged in the supreme self (Paramātman).

3. After casting off the outer garment (i.e. the gross body) the man takes another body (the subtle one). In twelve days, he is led by the attendants of Yama.

4. The water libations with gingelly seeds offered by the kinsmen in the world as well as the ball of rice (piṇḍa) offered by them is partaken of by him in the region of Yama.

5. From there the meritorious man goes to heaven and the sinner to hell.

6. After experiencing the benefits or torture of heaven and hell, the individual enters the womb of women. First nucleus is formed in the umbilical region which splits into bifurcated seed.

7. The foetus is then evolved with frothy exudations. Blood and muscles are formed thereafter when the lump may weigh a Pala in weight. Then it is said to sprout.

8. Limbs begin to grow; fingers are developed; eyes, nose, nails, etc are formulated.

9. Hairs begin to grow on the body and the head; the child is placed in a topsyturvy position and is born in the tenth month.

10. Then the most delusive Māyā (Illusory Power) of Viṣṇu begins to envelop him as he proceeds from infancy to childhood, youth and old age.

11. Then he dies and reaps the fruit of his different activities of virtue or otherwise. Thus man is caught in the cogs of the wheel of worldly existence that continues to turn like the water wheel.

12. A life coming back from hell becomes born of sinful wombs. O wise scholar, a man accepting gifts from a fallen man takes birth in a lower stratum.

13. A beggar, on returning from hell is born as a worm. A brahmin defrauding his preceptor is born as a dog.

14. Mentally coveting his (preceptor's) wife or riches he undoubtedly is born as a dog. Alike dishonouring friends he is reborn as an ass.

15-16. A person harassing the parents is reborn as a tortoise. If a servant trusted by his master and partaking of his food deceives him out of delusion he is reborn as a monkey after death. A misappropriator of trust property after experiencing the hardships of hell is reborn as a worm.

17. A person always envio is of others goes to hell and is born again as a Rākṣasa. A man committing breach of trust is reborn as a fish.

18. A person hoarding barley grains is reborn as a mouse after death. A person committing rape on other men's wives is reborn as a vile wolf.

19. A person pursuing an affair with his brother's wife is reborn as a cuckoo. A man indulging in sexual intercourse with the wife of a preceptor or other elders is reborn as a pig.

20-21. If a person causes any impediment to a sacrifice, act of charity or performance of a marriage he shall be reborn as a worm. If a person takes food without first offering the same to deities, manes or brahmins he is reborn as a crow after undergoing the hardships of hell. A man insulting his elder brother is born again as a crane.

22. A Śūdra ravishing a brahmin women is born again as a worm. If he makes her pregnant as a result of his vile act he is reborn as a white ant eating away wood and trees.

23. An ungrateful wretch is born successively as bacteria worm, locust and scorpion. A person abducting an unarmed person is reborn as a mule.

24. A slayer of women and infants is reborn as a worm. A person stealing cooked food is born again as a fly.

25. A stealer of cooked rice is born as a cat, that of gingelly seeds a mouse, that of ghī a mungoose and a stealer of sheat-fish and flesh is born as a crow.

26. A man stealing honey is reborn as a gnat. A thief of fried pie is born as an ant. The sinner of illegal theft of (irrigation) water is reborn as a crow.

27. A stealer of timber is born as a Hārīta bird or a pigeon. The stealer of a gold vessel is reborn as a worm.

28. A stealer of cotton garments is born as a crane ; a fire-thief becomes a stork; a thief of paints and vegetables is born as a peacock.

29. If a person steals any red object he is born as a Jīvañjīvaka bird (a cakora). If a man steals auspicious scents he is born as a mole. A thief of rabbits is reborn as a rabbit.

30. A thief of kalāpa (peacock's plumes or a woman's girdle or any other ornament) is reborn as a eunuch. A stealer of wooden pieces is born again as a grass worm. If a person steals flowers he is born as a poor beggar. If a person steals lac-juice he is born again as a lame man.

31. A thief of greens is reborn as a Hārīta bird; a person stealing stored water is reborn as a Cātaka bird. A person illegally occupying another man's house undergoes hardships in fierce hells Raurava etc. and is born again.

32. A person stealing grasses, hedges, creepers and barks of these is born again as a tree. This is the same in the case of the stealers of cow, gold, etc.

33. A stealer of knowledge (a person who does not pay for instructions received) undergoes hardships in many hells and is born again as a dumb man. If a person casts ghī and other offerings in unkindled fire he is reborn as a man suffering from chronic impairment of digestion.

34-35. The characteristic features of those who had had their hardships in hell and are reborn are: scandalising others, ingratitude, outraging the limits of decency, ruthlessness, cruelty, attachment to other men's wives, stealing other men's property, blasphemy, harassing and deceiving others, and miserliness.

36-37. The characteristic features of those who had had a happy sojourn in heaven and are reborn are :—Sympathy towards all living beings, pleasant conversation, belief in a supreme region, helping in return, truthfulness, whole-some advice to others, belief in the authority of Vedas; devotion to preceptors. Devas, divine sages, enlightened sages, etc, association with good men, eagerness in performing noble deeds and friendship.

A man attains Ātyantika Laya (final emancipation of the soul) by a thorough comprehension of the Yogavidyā alongwith its eight subsidiary components.

CHAPTER TWO HUNDRED AND TWENTYSIX

Yoga and its Components

Sūta said :

1. I shall explain the great Yoga with its component parts, that yields worldly enjoyments and salvation. It quells all sins if read with devotion. Please listen to it.

2. The feeling of 'My-ness' is the root cause of all miseries which can be removed by a feeling of 'Not-mine'. The noble-minded Dattātreya mentioned the same to Alarka.

3-5. The tree of Ignorance sought by the worldly minded for the sake of happiness and peace has the great basin round it in the form of riches and foodgrains. Its root is Sin. The germinating sprout is the feeling of Egoism. The great main trunk is the feeling of 'My-ness'. Houses, fields etc. are its branches. Wives, sons, etc are the tender leaves. Those who imbibe the divine Brahmarasa free from dusts (of Rajoguṇa) and are thornless hew it down with the axe of learning and merge themselves in the Supreme God.

6-7. Intellectually efficient persons thus attain the highest bliss. O king (Alarka) the self in which the sense-organs get merged is neither your physical body nor mine. It is not what you see and feel as important. Nor is it the Tanmātrā (essential matter) nor the speech nor the mind (the internal sense organ).

8-9. The self identified with the body dies today and is born again tomorrow. It is due to the three Guṇas. Though the body and the soul seem to be one, there is actually the distinction between the two. A Yogin who knows this distinction attains salvation which is the identity with the supreme soul. O son, it is due to the Triguṇas that this identity is not realised.

10. That is called house where one stays; that is diet whereby one sustains oneself. Similarly, that is real knowledge which is conducive to salvation. Ignorance brings about adverse results.

11. Merits and demerits, O king, can be exhausted by duly experiencing the fruits thereof. The annihilation of the activities yet to be performed is possible by non-performance.

12. The Yamas or Niyamas (Restraints) are of five types, *viz* :—Non-violence, truthfulness, non-stealing, celibacy and non-acceptance of gifts. Śauca or purity is of two varieties (the internal and the external).

13. Dama (Suppression) is contentment, quiescence due to austerities and the worship of Vāsudeva. By Āsana we mean the different postures such as Padmaka, etc. Prāṇāyāma means full control of breath.

14-15. It is of three types—Pūraka,[1] Kumbhaka[2] and Recaka[3] each of which is again subdivided into three. The Laghu (of short duration) consists of ten mātrās (periods of time less than a second); the Madhyama is of twenty mātrās and the Uttama consists of thirty mātrās. A Prāṇāyāma with Japa and Dhyāna (contemplation) is called Sagarbha Prāṇāyāma, opposite of which is Agarbha Prāṇāyāma.

16. One shall conquer the various defects in the body by means of Prāṇāyāma. By Pūraka (inhalation), somnolence is to be conquered. By Kumbhaka (Retention of breath), one can conquer the shivering sensation. By Recaka (Exhalation), one can conquer the augmentation or excess of heat in the body.

17. Seated in a comfortable Yogic posture pressing the penis and the testicles with the heels one shall keep the Praṇava in the heart and practise Prāṇāyāma.

18. The function of the Tamoguṇa must be suppressed by means of Rajoguṇa and that of Rajoguṇa is to be suppressed

1. Inhaling the breath.
2. Retaining the breath.
3. Exhaling the breath.

by means of Sattvaguṇa and ultimately the practiser of Yoga should maintain himself in Niścalāvṛtti (unruffled serene state).

19. The sense organs, the vital air, and the mind should be withdrawn from the sensual objects. This complete abstraction is called Pratyāhāra which should be constantly practised.

20. Taking eight or ten Prāṇāyāmas is called Dhāraṇā. Persons who are able to see the truth have thus spoken of two types of Dhāraṇās.

21-22. There are ten points of concentration for the practice of Dhāraṇā. First in the Nāḍī (nerves) [or Nābhi the umbilicus] then in order in the heart, throat, mouth, tip of the nose, middle of the eyebrows, head and then finally in the supreme soul. After practising these ten Dhāraṇās successfully one attains the imperishable status.

23. As one fire gets merged in another fire, so the individual soul gets merged in the supreme soul. The single syllable Om, which is the symbol of Brahman and very holy should be repeated frequently.

24. The three letters A, U and M together constitute the mystic syllable Om which symbolises the imperishable Brahman.

25. I am Brahman the greatest effulgence divested of the gross body. I am Brahman the greatest effulgence devoid of old age and death.

26. I am Brahman the greatest effulgence untainted by the dirts of the Principle of Earth. I am Brahman the greatest effulgence free from the principles of Vāyu and Ether.

27. I am Brahman the greatest effulgence divested of the subtle body. I am Brahman the greatest effulgence unlimited by space or absence of space.

28. I am Brahman the greatest effulgence free from the essential principle of smell. I am Brahman the greatest effulgence free from the principles of ear and skin (sound and touch).

29. I am Brahman the greatest effulgence free from tongue and nose. I am Brahman the greatest effulgence free from Prāṇa and Apāna.

30. I am Brahman the greatest effulgence free from Vyāna and Udāna. I am Brahman the greatest effulgence devoid of the influence of Nescience.

31. I am Brahman the greatest effulgence, the greatest of the three Padas devoid of body, sense organs, mind, intellect, Prāṇa and the ego.

32. I am the Brahman the eternal, the pure, the enlightened, the conjoined, the bliss, the non-bifurcated. I am Brahman the greatest effulgence, of the form of supreme knowledge for salvation.

Sūta said :

33-34. O Śaunaka, I have thus explained to you the science of Yoga with its eight components, that yields salvation. Those who are bound by the fetters of Natural evolution are definitely reborn after the Nitya and Naimittika Layas (the permanent and the causal dissolutions). But not so after attaining the supreme soul. A man deludedly ignorant becomes free due to knowledge and emancipates himself.

35. Thereafter, he does not die. He is not miserable. He is not sick. He is not fettered. A truthful person is untainted by sins. He is never tortured in hell.

36. He has no misery of being in the womb. He becomes one with Nārāyaṇa the unchangeable. With single minded devotion alone he has to be attained, the Lord who accords worldly enjoyments and salvation.

37. By means of contemplation, worship, Japas, correctly sung songs of praise, duly performed rites, sacrifices and gifts the mind becomes pure and true knowledge is obtained thereby.

38-40. Brahmins (in days of yore) have attained salvation by repetitions of Praṇava and other Mantras. Indra attained the greatest region due to it. The Gandharvas, the celestial damsels and the Devas attained Deva-hood due to it. The sages gained their sagehood, the Gandharvas their Gandharvahood and the kings their kingship due to this alone.

CHAPTER TWO HUNDRED AND TWENTYSEVEN

Yoga and its Components

Sūta said :

1. I shall explain devotion to Viṣṇu whereby everything can be secured. Hari is not pleased by anything else so much as by devotion.

2. A regular remembrance of Hari is the root cause of great welfare, the source of origin of the stream of merits and the most tasteful fruit of life.

3-4. Intelligent scholars have mentioned that service unto God is the best of the various means of devotion. Those who shed tears of joy, with hair standing on their ends while the names of the Lord of the world are being sung along with His activities are the real devotees. The gain of feet of the great Lord, the support and creator of the universe, accords true wisdom.

5-6. Those who are affectionate and carry out the perpetual service of God are the real Vaiṣṇavas. Even without hearing the words of the Vedas or the discourse of the Lord (Theology and Philosophy) he who bows with great devotion and adores and commends the sympathy and favouritism of the Lord to His devotees is a real Vaiṣṇava.

7-8. If there is delight in hearing His stories, the ears become fruitful. He who has dedicated all his feelings unto God Viṣṇu with great devotion through a learned brahmin devoted to Lord Viśveśvara, is a Mahābhāgavata (a great devotee). He who himself worships the Lord by flower offerings, or he who takes to worship for sustenance is also a Bhāgavata.

9. There are eight types of devotion. Even a Mleccha (outcaste) who is a great devotee is on a par with the greatest of brahmins and sages. He attains the greatest of goals.

10. Exchange of articles with him is allowed. He can be worshipped like Lord Hari Himself. A Cāṇḍāla becoming a devotee casually sanctifies everything.

11. This is the rite of Lord Hari:—that he accords freedom from fear of all living beings to him who says 'Please

be merciful to me who have sought refuge in you. I am Thine."

12. A person who has mastered all the systems of vedānta is better than thousands of Mantrayājins (those who perform sacrifice reciting Mantras). A devotee of Lord Viṣṇu is better than ten millions of such Vedāntins.

13. Ekāntins (those who are single-minded in Lord's devotion) attain the greatest region even with their gross body. This unswerving faith in Viṣṇu makes them identical with Him and He is fondly attached to them also.

14. Those who are thus single-minded in their devotion to Lord are great favourites unto Him though he impartially loves everyone.

15-17. His Bhakti does not go astray even in times of danger. Remembering Lord Viṣṇu my great devotion does not go away from my heart (I am always attached to Him) as it is the greatest love that suffers no adverse effects from worldly objects. Even if a man has mastered the Vedas and Śāstras he should be considered the vilest among men if he is not devoted to Lord. Even if a man has not learned Vedas and Śāstras, even if he has not performed any sacrifice, it must be deemed that he has done everything if he is devoted to Lord Viṣṇu.

18. O great sages, even those who perform great sacrifices, even those who have learned the Vedas do not attain that goal which devotees attain.

19. A person reckless about his conduct of life and duties according to the stage of his life is able to sanctify the entire world if he becomes a Vaiṣṇava in the same way as the rising sun does.

20. Even ruthless wicked persons bent upon sinful activities attain the greatest region on being devoted to Lord Nārāyaṇa.

21. If there is firm and unflinching devotion to Lord Janārdana that alone will give one extreme pleasure. Heavenly bliss is nothing in comparison to it.

22. To those men who roam about the world that is impassable due to diversified actions, the sole support is Janārdana who is propitiated.

23. He who does not listen to the songs of praise of the divine qualities of the discus-bearing lord of lords (Viṣṇu), is no better than a deaf man. He is to be banished from all religious activities.

24. If any one's body is not thrilled with horripilation when the name of Viṣṇu is sung, it is no better than a corpse.

25. If there is annihilation of all sins when the mind is directed towards the Lord the devotion to Him will necessarily usher in salvation even long.

26. They say that Yama, on seeing his attendant with the noose in his hand whispers into his ears—'Avoid those men who have sought refuge in Madhusūdana (slayer of the demon Madhu). I am lord of other men not of Vaiṣṇavas.'

27. The lord has said—'Even if the vilest of persons were to be devoted to me to the exclusion of others he must be considered a saint. He is of the right and perfect enterprise.'

28. O Excellent brahmin, you can even swear that a devotee of Viṣṇu will become righteous quickly and attain permanent peace. He never perishes.

29. Not only virtue, wealth and love but even salvation is easily accessible to him whose devotion is firm towards Hari, the root cause of all worlds.

30. Hari's Māyā (Nescience, Illusion) is divine and insurmountable composed as it is of the three Guṇas. Only they who resort to Him can cross it.

31. If a person has his intellect concentrated on Hari of what use are sacrifices and worships to him ? Viṣṇu can be propitiated by devotion alone. There is no other cause thereof.

32. The noble-souled Janārdana cannot be so much propitiated by gifts of various kinds distributed by persons, or flowers or unguents as by single-minded devotion.

33. The worldly existence is a poisonous tree but two of its fruits are comparable even to nectar, one is devotion to Lord Keśava and the other is a chance association with His devotees.

34. Leaves, flowers, fruits and water are easily available always. Hence, by devotion alone the eternal being can be attained. Still people strive after salvation.

35. The manes jump with joy, the grandfathers dance in gaiety in view of the fact that 'A vaiṣṇava is born in our family. He is sure to enable us to surmount all difficulties.'

36. When such ignorant sinners cavilling at Indra and Lord Viṣṇu like Śiśupāla, Suyodhana and others have attained salvation shaking off their sins by means of constant memory (of the Lord) what doubt is there in the case of persons of great devotion ?

37. Even if they are devoid of contemplation and yogic practice people who have sought shelter in Him will cross the sea of death and attain the Vaiṣṇava region.

38. O Mādhava, he horse of my mind is bedevilled by hundreds of painful experiences arising from the world of existence. It is faltering in the pores of sense organs. May it be tethered to the peg of Thy foot with firm devotion as the cord.

39. Viṣṇu is the supreme Brahman, devoid of difference and differentiation. Although this is known from the Vedas, principles (enunciated by sages) and actual experience, those who are deluded know it not.

CHAPTER TWO HUNDRED AND TWENTYEIGHT

Devotion to Viṣṇu

Sūta said:

1. The man who bows to Aja (the Unborn deity) the cause of salvation, free from beginning and end, the unchangeable and the imperishable, becomes worthy of being revered by the whole world.

2. With great devotion for ever I bow down to Viṣṇu, Bliss personified, the unbifurcated, perfect knowledge, the omnipresent and the lord who resides in the hearts of men.

3. I bow down to the great lord Viṣṇu the immanent soul that sees the auspicious and the inauspicious in every one and bears witness to everything.

4. He who, though competent, does not bow down to Cakrapāṇi (the discus-wielding Lord Viṣṇu) is a mere destroyer of the grassy growth in the world (is a beast grazing grass).

5. Even a single bow firm and full of good feelings directed towards Kṛṣṇa handsomely dark in colour like the interior of the glistening cloud, the immeasurable overlord of all the worlds, is competent to sanctify immediately even a Cāṇḍāla who cooks dog's flesh.

6. Even by means of a hundred sacrifices it is impossible to attain that goal which a man who worships (Lord Viṣṇu) by means of a Namaskāra (kneeling down) done by falling down on the ground like a staff, attains.

7. A single Namaskāra directed towards Kṛṣṇa is conducive to save by according salvation to those who wander in the impassable woods of worldly existence which seems (to some) like a well in a pleasure grove.

8. Seated, lying down or standing whether it be here or there one shall always take refuge in the mantra 'Namo Nārāyaṇāya' (obeisance to Nārāyaṇa).

9. The word 'Nārāyaṇa' exists. The faculty of speech is under their control, still the ignorant fools fall into hell. How surprising is it?

10. A man may have four mouths or even a crore of them and he may be pure in mind. It may or may not be possible for him to narrate even a ten thousandth part of the good qualities of Viṣṇu the lord of deities.

11. Sages like Vyāsa and others in worshipping the slayer of Madhu stop in the middle because they have exhausted their mental faculties and not because the qualities of Govinda are exhausted.

12. Even if due to sheer helplessness a man calls out the name of the lord he is immediately freed from all sins like the deer saved from the claws of the lion. Surely, he has girt up his loins for his journey towards salvation.

13. If a man calls out the name of the lord even in his dream it destroys his all sins. Then what doubt is there that the sins will be removed when the name of Janārdana is openly repeated.

14. O Brahmin, they by whom the words 'Obeisance,

O Kṛṣṇa, Acyuta, Ananta, Vāsudeva' have been uttered with great feelings of devotion will never go to Yama's city.

15. Just as a blazing fire becomes dim or darkness is completely dispelled when the sun rises, so also the heap of sin is dissipated when Hari's name is sung.

16-17. Surely, a sojourn in heaven comes to an end. To persons who undertake a long journey with the memory of Kṛṣṇa filling their minds the food to be taken while in transit is the frequent repetition of the names of Puṇḍarīkākṣa (Lord Viṣṇu). The Vaiṣṇava name of Kṛṣṇa is the only panacea for the removal of the effects of the poisonous bite of the serpent of worldly existence. By reciting it the man becomes free.

18. What is obtained by means of contemplation in the Kṛta Yuga, reciting mantras in the Tretā Yuga and worshipping in Dvāpara is obtained in Kali Yuga by constantly remembering Lord Keśava.

19. He the tip of whose tongue bears the two syllables *Ha* and *ri* crosses the ocean of worldly existence and goes to the region of Viṣṇu.

20. A man who has realised thousands of wicked actions with which he is surrounded but who sincerely yearns for welfare and purity and therefore takes active interest in singing the praise of Nārāyaṇa does not see even in his dream a rebirth.

CHAPTER TWO HUNDRED AND TWENTYNINE

Devotion to Viṣṇu

Sūta said:

1-2. The propitiation of Hari the lord of the entire universe is essential. He who makes flower-offerings or libations of water after reciting the Puruṣa Sūkta has actually worshipped the entire universe consisting of the mobile and immobile beings. He who does not worship Lord Viṣṇu should be deemed to have committed the murder of a brahmin.

3. He who does not meditate upon Viṣṇu from whom the living beings take their origin and spread everywhere shall be reborn as a worm in the faeces.

4-5. A life undergoing tortures in the hell will be addressed thus by Yama:—"Hasn't the lord Keśava the destroyer of all pains been worshipped by you? Why is it that you have not worshipped the lord who gives residence in His region to the votary who offers even libations of water in the absence of other articles?

6. Neither one's own mother nor father nor other kinsmen can ever do unto one what Hṛṣīkeśa (Viṣṇu) does when propitiated and worshipped faithfully.

7. Viṣṇu the great Lord is to be worshipped by a person strictly adhering to the rules of conduct of life befitting his caste and stage of life. There is no other means of propitiating Him.

8. Neither by different kinds of gifts distributed (by the devotee) nor by flowers or unguents offered by him can the noble-souled Janārdana be propitiated as by devotion.

9. Salvation or identity (with the Supreme Soul) cannot be secured through riches, affluence or greatness or by a series of religious rites. The root cause for the same is the worship of Hari.

CHAPTER TWO HUNDRED AND THIRTY

Devotion to Viṣṇu

Sūta said :

1. After going through all sacred literature and deliberating frequently this is the only conclusion arrived at that Nārāyaṇa is to be meditated upon constantly.

2. If a man meditates on Lord Nārāyaṇa constantly with single-minded devotion, of what use to him are the making of gifts, pilgrimages, austerities and sacrifices ?

3. Sixty thousand holy centres and six thousand sacred rivers do not merit comparison with even a sixteenth part of the act of kneeling before the deity Nārāyaṇa.

4. Constant remembrance of Kṛṣṇa is far superior to all kinds of expiatory rites and practices of austerities.

5. If a person performing ordinary rites of expiation begins to love the sin committed, no other atonement is possible except hearty remembrance of Hari.

6. If a person meditates upon Nārāyaṇa even for a few minutes without any lassitude he attains heaven. What doubt is then about one who is always engrossed in it ?

7. The state of the mind of a Yogin in the various stages of walking, dreaming slumbering and trance is similar to that of the mind directed towards Acyuta.

8. It is the duty of the devotee to remember Govinda, the lord of Lakṣmī, whether standing, falling, prattling, entering the chamber, taking food or just waking up.

9. Assiduously engaged in one's own duty one shall fix one's mind in Janārdana. This statement is in accordance with the sacred literature. There is no use in talking much.

10. Meditation is the greatest virtue, meditation is the greatest penance, meditation is the greatest purificatory rite. Hence, one shall be devoted to meditation.

11. There is no greater object of meditation than Viṣṇu. There is no greater penance than fasting (on Ekādaśī day). Even more important than that is the constant thought of Vāsudeva.

12. Madhusūdana when meditated upon, gives the devotee, unsolicited, what is difficult to get and what cannot be even comprehended.

13. If inadvertently a slip occurs while one is performing a sacrifice a mere remembrance of Viṣṇu fills the void. This is what is laid down in the Vedas.

14. There is no other way of atoning for sins, comparable to meditation. The fire of Yogic practices (with the meditation on Viṣṇu) burns away the causes bringing about the birth of the future body.

15. A Yogin competent to practise the state of trance attains salvation in this very birth by burning all Karmans in the fire of Yoga without delay.

16. Just as a blazing fire with leaping flames consumes the heap of dried straw so also the fire of Yoga consumes all sins when Lord Viṣṇu is fixed in the mind.

17. Just as gold is freed of its impurities due to its contact with fire so also all the impurities of men are dispelled by Vāsudeva.

18. When Hari is remembered so much sin is quelled as can be quelled by thousands of ablutions in the Gangetic waters and the holy ablutions taken for millions of times in the holy tank of Puṣkara.

19. Within a moment after the contemplation of Hari so much sin is dissolved as is wiped off by means of thousands of Prāṇāyāmas.

20. Evil influence of the Kali age, wicked statements, vile utterances of heretics—none of these affect the mind of the person in whose mind Lord Keśava finds a place.

21. The moment in which Lord Hari is remembered has the auspicious properties of the holy Tithis (days of the lunar month), days, nights, beneficent lunar conjunctions and holy lagnas (units of time).

22. If a moment passes without remembering Vāsudeva, it is a great loss, a great void—a blindness, a sluggishness, a dumb-foundedness.

23. If Govinda is fixed in the mind, the vile Age of Kali is transformed into Kṛta. If Acyuta is not fixed in the mind even Kṛta Yuga is transformed into Kali age.

24. He, whose mind is fixed on Govinda while going ahead or retreating or standing alone, is always contented.

25. O Maitreya, even if there is any obstacle in Japa, Homa or worship, the desired fruits thereof as Devendrahood etc. can be attained if the mind is fixed in Vāsudeva.

26. A person with his mind dedicated to Keśava chops off the Māyā of the Puruṣa without forsaking the duties of a householder and without performing great penance.

27. If Govinda is stationed in the heart, people readily forgive angry persons and sympathise with fools. They are joyous in the company of virtuous people.

28. While performing the various holy rites of ablutions,

making gifts, etc., or expiatory rites especially after sinful actions, Lord Nārāyaṇa should be meditated upon.

29. They gain much, they achieve great success, they are not affected by failure, they in whose hearts is stationed Lord Janārdana dark in colour like the blue lotus.

30. Even worms, birds, etc., with their minds, fixed on Hari progress upwards. Then what doubt is there in the case of the wise ?

31. Why don't people seek refuge under the shade of the tree Vāsudeva which accords no excessive chillness or heat and which closes the doorway to hell ?

32. O friend, if Madhusūdana is fixed in the heart neither the curse of the sage Durvāsas nor the overlordship of Indra can effect the people.

33. Dhāraṇā (fixation of the heart) is perfect when the mind does not go astray (from Lord Viṣṇu), whether he is talking or standing or whether he is engaged in some activity of his choice.

34. One shall always meditate upon Nārāyaṇa, stationed in the middle of the solar zone, seated on the holy lotus seat, bedecked in bracelets, golden ear-rings, crown and necklaces, with a golden complexion and wielding Śaṅkha and Cakra.

35. There is nothing so holy as meditation. Even the sin of taking food from the hands of a Śvapaca (a Cāṇḍāla) does not taint him.

36. The mind of a wretch is always attached to worldly objects. If one's mind were that much attached to Nārāyaṇa how could he not be released from bondage?

Sūta said :

37. How can he who is devoted to Viṣṇu bow to anyone ? He can enable himself to cross the ocean of sins.

38. That is perfect knowledge where Govinda presides That is true holy discourse where Keśava is discussed. That is the holy rite which is performed for His sake. Of what use are other profuse discussions ?

39. That is the true tongue which utters the praise of Lord Hari. That is the true mind which is dedicated to Him.

Only those hands which perform His adoration are worthy of praise.

40. That head alone is fruitful which bows to the Lord. The success of hand lies in adoring the Lord stationed in heaven. The mind that always dwells on His qualities and exploits is successful. The speech extolling the qualities of Govinda is all-successful.

41. Sinful actions so huge as mountain Meru or the mountain Mandara are dissipated entirely by merely remembering Lord Keśava.

42. Whatever man does, good or bad, should be dedicated to Nārāyaṇa. Then he is not affected adversely.

43. The living beings beginning with a blade of grass and ending with Brahmā are fourfold. All the universe mobile or immobile lies asleep due to thy Māyā O Hari.

44. The person whose mind is dedicated to the Lord never goes to hell.; the person who thinks of the Lord attains heaven; if the mind rests in the Lord he is never faced with obstacles. The region of Brahmā is a mere trifle. The imperishable lord accords salvation to the sluggish minded persons if he is thought of. The fact that a person dissolves himself when the Lord Acyuta is sung is only a small matter.

45. Those who wish to cross the ocean of misery shall perform the rites in fire, Japa, ablution and meditation and adoration of Viṣṇu. They are sure to cross it.

46. The king is the refuge of the Nation, the parents that of the child, virtue is the refuge of all men and Lord Hari is the refuge of every one.

47. O excellent sage, there is no greater holy centre than those who bow to the eternal Vāsudeva, the source of the universe.

48. One can meditate on Govinda without lassitude with the same purpose in view as in observing the worship of valuable gems or the study of the Vedas.

49. I consider a Śūdra, Niṣāda, a Śvapaca or a brahmin equal to one another if they are devotees of the Lord. None of these goes to hell.

50. People praise a rich man with great respect wishing for some monetary benefit. If they were to praise the creator

of the world with the same zeal is there any doubt that they would be released from bondage ? (Who is not released from bondage ?)

51. A powerful forest fire burns even a wet fuel. Viṣṇu so stationed in the heart burns all sins of yogins.

52. Deer and other creatures never stay on in a mountain forest that burns. Similarly, all sorts of sins never stay on in a person engaged in yogic practice.

53. The benefit that accrues to one is in proportion to one's faith. If at all there is any limitation in the influence of Lord Kṛṣṇa, it is this.

54. Śiśupāla[1], the son of Damaghoṣa, remembering Lord Govinda with hatred attained salvation. What doubt is there about a person who is engrossed completely in Him ?

CHAPTER TWO HUNDRED AND THIRTYONE

Hymn to Narasiṁha

Sūta said :

1. O Śaunaka, I shall now mention the Hymn of prayer to Narasiṁha sung by Śiva. Formerly, the Mothers (Mātṛgaṇa)[2] told Śaṅkara thus :—

1. According to the Viṣṇu Purāṇa this monarch was, in a previous existence, the unrighteous Hiraṇyakaśipu, king of the *asuras*, who was killed by Viṣṇu in the form of Narasiṁha. He was next born as the ten-headed Rāvaṇa who was killed by Rāma. Then he was born as the son of Damaghoṣa and continued his enmity to Kṛṣṇa, the eighth incarnation of Viṣṇu, with even greater implacability. He denounced Kṛṣṇa when they met at the Rājasūya sacrifice of Yudhiṣṭhira, but his head was cut off by Kṛṣṇa with his discus. His death forms the subject of a celebrated poem by Māgha.

2. These appear to have been originally the female energies of the great gods, as Brahmāṇī of Brahmā, Māheśvarī of Śiva, Vaiṣṇavī of Viṣṇu, Indrāṇi or Aindrī of Indra, etc. The number of them was seven or eight or sixteen, but in the later mythology, they have increased out of number. They are connected with the Tantra-worship, and are represented as worshipping Śiva and attending upon his son Kārttikeya. [CDHM, p. 206].

2. O Lord, we wish to devour the entire universe along with deities, demons and human beings with your favour. Please permit us.

Śaṅkara said :

3. Certainly, all these people are to be protected by you all. Hence, this ruthless mentality may soon be diverted.

4. Disregarding the advice thus tendered by Śaṅkara, they began to devour the three worlds, inclusive of all mobile and immobile creatures, with impurity.

5. When the three worlds were being thus eaten by the Mothers, Lord Śiva meditated on the Lord in the form of Nṛsiṁha (the man-lion).

6-9. Lord Śaṅkara's conception of Nṛsiṁha was thus:—"He has no beginning or death; He is the originator of all living beings; His tongue blazes like lightning. He has great curved teeth; the manes blaze like a garland; He has bracelets studded with gems; He has a good crown; He is bedecked with golden manes; with His brilliance he pervades the whole Brahmāṇḍa (the Cosmic Egg); the hairs on His body are in curls in circlets. He is wearing a great garland consisting of many flowers of variegated colours."

10. As soon as He was meditated upon, the Lord appeared before Śaṅkara assuming the same form as was conceived by Rudra with great devotion.

11. In the same dazzling form unperceivable by the .evas He stood there. Śaṅkara thereupon knelt before the Lord and prayed.

Śaṅkara said :

12. Obeisance to Thee O Lord of the universe, having the body of a Man-Lion, shining with claws, resembling the oyster shell, with which the lord of demons (Hiraṇyakaśipu) was killed.

13. Thou hast the golden and tawny coloured body of the giant clinging to Thy lotus-like Nails (claws). Obeisance to Padmanābha; obeisance to the suspicious, O Preceptor of the world. Thou roarest like the rumbling cloud

at the end of the Kalpa, O deity shining with the lustre of ten million suns.

14. O deity terrifying like thousand Yamas, valorous like thousand Indras, affluent like thousand Dhanadas (Kuberas) O deity with a thousand lotus-like feet.

15. O deity resembling a thousand moons, thousand rayed, moving like a lion, resplendent like a thousand Rudras, sung in praise by a thousand Brahmās.

16. Remembered in Japas by a thousand Rudras, endowed with a thousand all perceiving eyes, progenitor and destroyer of thousands, untier of thousands of bondages.

17. O Fierce deity, having the velocity of a thousand winds, thousand eyes, O Compassionate One !'

Having thus sung the hymn to the lord of lords, Hari in the form of Man-lion, Śiva in all humility submitted thus :—

18. I had created the Mātṛs (the Mothers) for the destruction of the demon Andhaka. Disregarding my advice they are now devouring the wonderful created beings of the universe.

19. Having created them I am incompetent to kill them though unvanquished elsewhere. Having evolved them first how can I wish for their annihilation.

20-21. Thus addressed by Rudra, Hari in the form of the Man-lion created a thousand goddesses from the tip of his tongue. Hari the Vāgīśvara (Lord of speech) subdued the Mothers, protected the devas. He accorded peace and happiness to the world and vanished.

22. He who recites this Narasiṁha hymn in all purity and restraint of the sense organs shall be blessed with the realisation of all his desires like Rudra. There is no doubt in this.

23. One shall meditate on the deity Narasiṁha, with eyes shining like the midday sun (for the evil doers) and like white lotus (for the devotees), with his face beaming like the blazing fire, having neither beginning nor end, the eternal (the ancient), the unborn, lord of the great and the small, the receptacle of the Universe.

24-25. If anyone recites this hymn it quells all miseries like the sun dispelling the snow. When he wants to perform the worship of the Lord in the form of Narasiṁha, Lord Śiva, the destroyer of the Tripuras, prepares His idol along with the Mothers. Then the lord appears before him and stands near him. After propitiating the great lord and obtaining the boon he saved the universe from the Mothers.

CHAPTER TWO HUNDRED AND THIRTYTWO

Kulāmṛta or Jñānāmṛta Hymn

Sūta said:

1. When he was asked by Sri Nārada, Lord Hara mentioned this hymn called Kulāmṛta (otherwise known as Jñānāmṛta). Please listen to it.

Nārada said:

2. He who is fettered by Dvandvas (conflicting factors) —Lust and Anger, the auspicious and the inauspicious and the various objects of the sense organs, sound, etc., and is tortured by them is necessarily a wretch in this world.

3. O Lord, the slayer of Tripuras, I wish to hear from you the means whereby that creature can be saved quickly from the ocean of death and transmigration.

Maheśvara said:

4. On hearing these words of Nārada the three-eyed deity Śambhu (Hara) spoke unto the sage.

5. O, Excellent sage, I shall tell you the great secret mantra and hymn called 'Jñānāmṛta' that destroys all miseries and removes the fear of bondage of worldly existence.

6-7. The four types of living beings beginning with the blade of grass and ending with the four-faced deity Brahmā, consisting of the entire universe the mobile and the immobile, sleeps due to the Māyā of Viṣṇu. If due to the grace of Lord Viṣṇu any one among them wakes up, he will cross the ocean of worldly existence which is impassable even to the gods.

8-9. It is the person who is averse to the acquisition of real knowledge that becomes puffed up due to the enjoyments and prosperity he possesses. Inebriated creatures get entangled in their attachment to sons, wives and families like the wild elephants sinking below the surface of waters of deluge.

I do not find any means of salvation even after hundred crores of births for that wretch who shuts up his mouth [and does not sing the Lord's Prayer] like the silk worm in the cocoon.

10. Hence, O Nārada, one shall propitiate the imperishable lord of all gods. One shall take delight in meditating on Viṣṇu.

11. [The hymn begins here and ends in the eighteenth verse] He who meditates constantly on Lord Viṣṇu, the universe-formed, devoid of beginning and end, the unborn, stationed in His own self and the omniscient becomes free.

12. A person meditating constantly on Viṣṇu holding devas (and others) within Himself becomes free. He who perpetually meditates on Viṣṇu, devoid of bodies, the creator, possessed of all knowledge and mental proclivities, the immovable and all-pervading becomes free.

13. He who constantly meditates on Lord Viṣṇu, free from doubts and contradictions, devoid of specific manifestations, divested of the created groups, free from ailments and afflictions, Vāsudeva the preceptor of all, becomes free.

14. He who meditates on all manifestations of the sentient soul of the all pervading, on Viṣṇu the auspicious, the single, the imperishable, becomes free.

15. He who meditates constantly on Viṣṇu, who is beyond the pale of all statements, who knows the three uni s of time (the past, present and future) who is lord of the universe, who bears witness to everything and who is more excellent than all the others, becomes free.

16. He who constantly meditates on Viṣṇu served by

Brahmā and other gods, Gandharvas, Sages, Siddhas, Cāraṇas[1], and Yogins becomes free.

17. All the people wishing for release from the bondage of worldly existence become free on singing thus the prayer of Viṣṇu the granter of boons.

18. Whoever wishes to get release from the bondage of worldly existence shall with concentration meditate on Viṣṇu. He who contemplates on the endless, imperishable lord Viṣṇu, established in the universe, the unborn and the lord of worlds, becomes free.

Sūta said:

19. What the Bull-emblemed deity Śiva narrated to Nārada on being requested by him I have now told you.

20. My dear Sir, meditating on the supreme Brahman, the unwasting, the spotless, you shall obtain certainly the eternal and unchanging region.

21. Thousands of horse sacrifices, and hundreds of Vājapeya sacrifices do not merit even a sixteenth part of extremely concentrated devotion even for a moment.

22. After hearing the importance of Lord Viṣṇu from Śiva the divine sage propitiated Lord Viṣṇu devotedly and attained the status of achievement.

23. The sin committed in the course of millions of lives of the person who reads or hears this excellent hymn, perishes.

24. He who assiduously reads this hymn constantly of Lord Viṣṇu, recited by Lord Śiva at first, attains immortality.

CHAPTER TWO HUNDRED AND THIRTYTHREE

Mṛtyvaṣṭaka Hymn

Sūta said:

1. I shall mention the Hymn sung by Mārkaṇḍeya. (The hymn begins) I have sought refuge in Dāmodara. What can Mṛtyu (God of Death) do unto me ?

1. A wandering actor or singer: a bard.

2. I have sought refuge in the deity bearing Śaṅkha and Cakra, the unchanging, whose form is manifest and who is called Adhokṣaja. What can Mṛtyu do unto me?

3. I have sought refuge in the Divine Varāha (Boar), Vāmana (dwarf), Viṣṇu, Nārasiṁha, Janārdana and Mādhava. What can Mṛtyu do unto me?

4. I have sought refuge in the great Puruṣa, the seed of Puṣkarakṣetra, the holy lord of the universe and the master of the worlds. What can Mṛtyu do unto me?

5. I have sought refuge in the thousand-headed deity, the manifest and the unmanifest, the eternal and the great Yogī. What can Mṛtyu do unto me?

6. I have sought refuge in the deity who is the inner soul of all living beings, the noble soul, the source of sacrifices, not born of any womb, and the multi-formed. What can Mṛtyu do unto me? (The hymn ends).

7. On hearing this hymn sung by the noble soul (Mārkaṇḍeya), the god of Death left the place repulsed by the emissaries of Viṣṇu.

8. Thus, the god of Death was conquered by Mārkaṇḍeya the intelligent. There is nothing impossible of realisation if the lotus-eyed Nṛsiṁha is delighted.

9. These eight stanzas are of holy potentialities and quell death. For the sake of the benefit of Mārkaṇḍeya, Viṣṇu Himself mentioned this.

10. He who reads this hymn thrice a day, with great devotion regularly and pure-minded will never have a premature death. His mind is fixed in Acyuta.

11. That Yogin defied Mṛtyu by contemplating within himself in the lotus of his heart the ancient Puruṣa Nārāyaṇa, the permanent and the immeasurable.

CHAPTER TWO HUNDRED AND THIRTYFOUR

Acyuta or Cakradhara Hymn

Sūta said:

1. O Śaunaka, please listen. I shall narrate the hymn of Acyuta which Brahmā had narrated to Nārada on being requested by him.

Nārada said:

2. Be pleased to tell me how the imperishable and unchanging Viṣṇu has to be eulogised by me, Viṣṇu the granter of boons, every day at the time of adoration.

3. Those who eulogise Acyuta constantly are the blessed. Their life is excellent. They enjoy all happiness. Their life is fruitful.

Brahmā said:

4. O Sage, I shall tell you the hymn of Vāsudeva, that yields salvation. At the time of worship, if the lord is eulogised with this hymn He will be propitiated.

5-10. OM, obeisance to lord Vāsudeva, obeisance to the dissipater of all sins. Obeisance to Him who is of pure body, knowledge embodied, Lord of all deities, bearing Śrīvatsa, having sword in his hand, bearing garland of lotuses, the base of the entire world, wearing yellow garment Nṛsiṁha, Vaikuṇṭha, lotus-navelled, lying in the ocean of milk, having thousand heads, lying upon the serpent, bearing axe in his hand, destroying the warriors, of true vows, unconquerable, lord of the three worlds, bearing discus, beneficent, the minutest, the oldest, usurper of Bali's kingdom as Vāmana.

11. Obeisance to the sacrificial Boar. Obeisance, obeisance to Govinda. Obeisance to Thee, O Blissful one, obeisance to Thee the great Imperishable.

12. Obeisance to Thee the Knowledge-Existence; Obeisance to Thee the dispenser of knowledge; Obeisance to Thee the great unbifurcated; Obeisance to Thee the best among men.

13. Obeisance to Thee the creator-deity of the universe:

Obeisance to Thee the conceiver of the universe; obeisance to Thee the lord of the universe; obeisance to Thee the cause of the universe.

14. Obeisance to Thee the slayer of the demon Madhu;[1] obeisance to Thee the slayer of Rāvaṇa; obeisance to Thee the slayer of Kaṁsa and Keśin;[2] obeisance to Thee the suppressor of Kaiṭabha.[3]

15. Obeisance to Thee the lotus-eyed, obeisance to Thee, the Garuḍa-emblemed, obeisance to Thee the slayer of Kālanemi[4], obeisance to Thee, seated on Garuḍa.

1. Madhu and Kaiṭabha were two horrible demons, who, according to the Mahābhārata and the Purāṇas, sprang from the ear of Viṣṇu while he was asleep at the end of a *kalpa,* and were about to kill Brahmā, who was lying on the lotus springing from Viṣṇu's navel. Viṣṇu killed them, and hence he obtained the names of Kaiṭabhajit and Madhusūdana. The Mārkaṇḍeya-Purāṇa attributes the death of Kaiṭabha to Umā, and she bears the title of Kaiṭabhā. The Hari-vaṁśa states that the earth received its name of Medinī from the marrow (*medas*) of these demons. In one passage it says that their bodies, being thrown into the sea, produced an immense quantity of marrow or fat, which Nārāyaṇa used in forming the earth. In another place it says that the *medas* quite covered the earth, and so gave it the name of Medinī. [*CDHM*, p. 139].

2. In the Mahābhārata, a demon who fought with and was defeated by Indra. In the Purāṇas a *daitya* who took the form of a horse and attacked Kṛṣna, but was killed by that hero's thrusting his arm into his jaws and rending him asunder [*CDHM*, p. 156).

3. See fn. 1.

4. (1) In the Rāmāyaṇa, a demon, uncle of Rāvaṇa. At the solicitation of Rāvaṇa, and with the promise of half his kingdom, he endeavoured to kill Hanumān. Assuming the form of a hermit-devotee, he went to the Gandhamādana mountain and when Hanumān proceeded thither in search of the medicinal drugs, the disguised demon invited him to his hermitage and offered him food. Hanumān refused, but went to bathe in the neighbouring pond. Upon his placing his foot in the water it was seized by a crocodile. but he dragged the creature out and killed it. From the dead body there arose a lovely *apsaras* who had been cursed by Dakṣa to live as a crocodile till she should be released by Hanumān. She told her deliverer to be beware of Kālanemi, so Hanumān went back to that deceiver, told him that he knew him, and taking him by the feet, sent him whirling through the air to Laṅkā, where he fell before the throne of Rāvaṇa in the council-room. (2) In the Purāṇas a great demon, son of Virocana, the grandson of Hiraṇyakaśipu. He was killed by Viṣṇu [*CDHM*, p. 141].

16-17. Obeisance to Thee, son of Devakī; obeisance to Thee, scion of the family of Vṛṣṇis; obeisance to Thee, Lord of Rukmiṇī;[1] obeisance to Thee son of Aditi; obeisance to Thee, resident of cowherds' colony; obeisance to Thee fond of cowherds' colony.

18. Victory to Kṛṣṇa of the form of a cowherd; Victory to the beloved of cowherd classes; Victory to the supporter of Govardhana;[2] Victory to the promoter of cowherds' colony.

19. Hail Thee, the slayer of the powerful Rāvaṇa; Hail thee the slayer of Cāṇūra[3], Hail Thee the illuminater of the family of Vṛṣṇis; Hail Thee, the suppressor of Kāliya[4] serpent.

20. Hail Thee, the true witness of the universe; Hail Thee the achiever of all riches; Hail Thee the comprehensible to the knowers of Vedānta; Hail Thee the giver of every thing Mādhava.

1. Daughter of Bhīṣmaka, king of Vidarbha. According to the Harivaṁśa she was sought in marriage by Kṛṣṇa, with whom she fell in love. But her brother Rukmin was a friend of Kaṁsa whom Kṛṣṇa had killed. He, therefore, opposed him and thwarted the match. Rukmiṇī was then betrothed to Śiśupāla, king of Cedi, but on her wedding day, as she was going to the temple, Kṛṣṇa saw her, took her by the hand, and carried her away in his chariot. They were pursued by her intended husband and by her brother Rukmin, but Kṛṣṇa defeated them both, and took her safe to Dvārakā, where he married her. She was his principal wife who bore him a son Pradyumna. By him also she had nine other sons and one daughter. [*CDHM* p. 270].

2. A mountain in Vṛndāvana, which Kṛṣṇa induced the cowherds and cowherdesses to worship instead of Indra. This enraged the god, who sent a deluge of rain to wash away the mountain and all the people of the country, but Kṛṣṇa held up the mountain on his little finger for seven days to shelter the people of Vṛndāvana. Indra retired baffled. [*CDHM*, p. 114].

3. A wrestler in the service of Kaṁsa who was killed by Kṛṣṇa.

4. A serpent king who had five heads, and dwelt in the deep pool of Yamunā, with numerous attendant serpents. His mouths vomited fire and smoke, and he laid waste all the country round. Kṛṣṇa, while yet a child, jumped into his pool, when he was quickly laced and entwined in the coils of the snakes. His companions and friends were horrified, but Balarāma called upon him to exercise his divine power. He did so and the serpents were soon overcome. Placing his foot on the mundane head of Kāliya he compelled him and his followers to implore mercy. He spared them, but bade Kaliya and his followers to free the earth from their presence, and to move to the ocean. [*CDHM*, p. 144].

21. Hail Thee, the supporter of all, the unmanifest. Hail Thee, the giver of everything O Mādhava; Hail Thee, the unsullied in the mind.

22. Victory be thine, the unsupported; Be victorious O quiescent eternal. Be victorious O Lord, the nourisher of the universe, Be victorions O Viṣṇu; obeisance to Thee.

23. Thou art the preceptor O Hari, thou art the disciple. Thou art the initiation and the group of mantras. Thou art the Nyāsa, the Mudrā (gestures). Thou art the School of theology. Thou art the flowers and other ingredients.

24. Thou art the base; Thou art Ananta (the serpent); Thou art the tortoise; Thou art the earth and the lotus; Thou art virtue, knowledge etc. Thou art the potentialities of the altar and mystic diagrams.

25. O Lord, thou art Rāma the wielder of ploughshare Thou art the destroyer of Śambara;[1] Thou art the Brahmanical Sage; Thou art the lord Viṣṇu. Thou art true of exploits.

26. Thou art Nṛsiṁha, the ultimate bliss, lord of the earth Suparṇa, discus, club and conch.

27. Thou art Śrī, Thou art Puṣṭi (nourishment). Thou art the permanent Māyā, Thou art Śrīvatsa, Kaustubha; Thou art Śārṅgī and the quiver.

28. Thou art the sword along with the leather buckler; Thou art the guardian deity; O Lord, Thou art the lord of Rākṣasas; Thou art Sādhya; Thou art the wind and the moon.

29. Thou art the lord of wealth, Īśāna, Indra, Varuṇa, lord of the demons, Sādhya, Vāyu, and the man.

30. Thou art the Ādityas, Vasus, Rudras, the Aśvins, the Maruts; Thou art the Daityas, Dānavas, Nāgas; Thou art Yakṣas and the Khagas (Skyroamers).

1. In the Vedas a demon, also called a *dasyu*, who fought against king Divodāsa, but was defeated and had his many castles destroyed by Indra. He appears to be a mythical personification of drought, of a kindred character to Vṛtra, or identical with him. In the Purāṇas a *daitya* who carried off Pradyumna and threw him into the well.

31. Thou art the Gandharvas, Apsaras, Siddhas, Pitṛs; thou art the great immortal devas: Thou art the living beings, thou art the objects of the sense-organs; thou art the Avyakta (the unmanifest) to the sense-organs.

32. Thou art the mind, the intellect, the ego, the soul, Thou art the lord in the heart. Thou art the sacrifice, Thou art the Vaṣaṭkāra. Thou art Oṅkāra, the sacrificial twig and the Kuśa grass.

33. Thou art the altar, O Hari, Thou art the initiation; Thou art the sacrificial post; Thou art the sacrificial fire, Thou art the Hotṛ (the priest making the offerings in fire), Thou art the Yajamāna (the officiating priest); Thou art the grain. Thou art the sacrificial animal, the Yājaka (the householder requesting the priests to perform the sacrifice).

34. Thou art the Adhyaryu (the presiding priest), Thou art the Udgātā (the singer of Sāman hymns). Thou art the sacrifice. Thou art the Puruṣottama (the best among men). Thou art the quarters, the nether worlds, the earth, the sky, the heaven, Thou art the creator of Stars.

35-37. Whatever mobile or immobile in the universe is seen among the Devas, beasts or mankind, O Lord, the Cosmic egg, the entire universe—all these are only Thy forms, they are manifest to the eyes, O Lord, the supreme Brahman, you are inaccessible even to gods.

38. Who is competent to comprehend that pure imperishable Puruṣa, accessible to Yogins, the unmanifest, the unborn, the unchanging ?

39. He is devoid of annihilation and origin. He is all-pervading, he is the lord, he is omniscient, he is divested of three Guṇas, he is pure Bliss, he is unageing, he is the greatest.

40-42. O Lord, Thou art Consciousness, the permanent, the quiescent, the complete, the unbifurcated, the unwasting. In Thy incarnations many of Thy forms are seen, but unable to comprehend Thy real greatness the heaven-dwellers go on adoring thee (in whatever manner they conceive). O Puruṣottama, how can I know such a subtle being as Thou art.

43-45. Thy vibhūtis (the various manifestations) such as saṅkarṣaṇa, etc. have been adored by me by means of flowers, incense, etc. If there is any defect in it, be pleased to forgive my omissions and commissions. I am incompetent to perform Thy Pūjā as laid down (in śāstras) in an orderly manner.

46. Whatever Japa, homa, etc, have been performed by me, O Puruṣottama, cannot be successfully concluded with true devotion. Hence, I crave Thy pardon.

47. By day or night, during dusk and dawn, in all states, whatever I do, may my devotion be steady, O Hari in Thy feet.

48. I have no such love towards the physical body or ritualistic activities as I have, in an exclusive form, towards Thee, O Lord of the Universe.

49. What sacred rite conducive to Heaven and salvation has not been performed by him who has firm devotion towards Viṣṇu, the dispenser of fruits of all cherished desires.

50. O Acyuta, who is capable of performing Thy worship or eulogising Thee properly ? (Anyhow) I have eulogised and adored you. Please forgive. Obeisance to Thee.

51. Thus I have narrated to you the hymn of Cakradhara. O sage, if you wish to attain the great status, eulogise Viṣṇu with devotion.

52. He who eulogises the preceptor of the universe by means of this hymn at the time of adoration attains salvation ere long breaking off the fetters of worldly existence.

53. Even in the age of Kali, he who recites this hymn with great devotion thrice every day with physical and mental purity shall realise all his desires.

54. The devotee desirous of sons shall beget sons, the imprisoned shall be freed from bondage, the sick devotee shall be cured of his ailments; the indigent shall be affluent.

55. The seeker of learning shall acquire knowledge, fame and renown. The intelligent shall be able to remember his previous birth and shall get whatever he thinks of.

56. He who eulogises Puruṣottama shall be truthful in his statements, pure and liberal-minded. The unblessed shall turn out to be omniscient and intelligent; the indecent shall be transformed into one who performs all holy rites.

57. Those who do not engage themselves in holy rites with Hari as the object of devotion can never be pure in conduct. They are to be banished from all religious rites.

58. He who has no unflinching devotion to Viṣṇu who grants all riches shall never benefit from purificatory rites of mind and speech. He is wicked.

59. A man who propitiates the lord Hari duly, who grants all happiness, shall obtain whatever he wishes for.

60. He is the Primordial deity the Siddha (who has achieved everything) who is meditated upon by all sages. He is the witness into all who knows whatever there is in any heart. He is unborn. He is nectar. He is free from fear and death. He is eternal. He is Bliss. I bow unto that Vāsudeva.

61. I adore with the flowers of mental conception the lord of all worlds, the eternal, the delighted, the pure, the untarnished, devoid of the three Guṇas and the delighter of every one. May the Sentient Soul, the witness of everything enter the lotus of my heart, the inner feelings of my soul.

62. Thus I have narrated the greatness of the Supreme Viṣṇu who has neither beginning nor end. Hence, the great lord is to be duly meditated upon by a man on the way to salvation.

63. Who is the Yogin who does not merge himself (in the Supreme Brahman) after meditating upon Viṣṇu without a parallel, the consciousness in form, the ancient Puruṣa, resplendent like the sun, the unsullied, the Pure ?

64. The man who constantly reads this hymn and remains pure and quiet can wash off his sins and shall attain the extensive region of the Lord with his influence spreading all round.

65. He who seeks wealth, unlimited pleasure, virtue, love and salvation can cast off everything and seek refuge in Viṣṇu the ancient, the excellent.

66. He who has abjured all association (with worldly objects) and seeks refuge in Vāsudeva the pure, the allpervading, the lord, the supporter of the universe, the pure and the cause of the destruction of all worldly objects.

CHAPTER TWO HUNDRED AND THIRTYFIVE

Vedānta and Sāṅkhya

Sūta said :

1-4. I shall expound the mode of knowing the Brahman in accordance with the tenets of the schools of philosophy—Vedānta and Sāṅkhya. Just as the self same principle of Jyoti (Brilliance) appears in three different forms of Fire, Sun and Moon so also Viṣṇu appears as Aham (I, the individual self), Brahman (God, Īśvara) and Paraṁ Jyotiḥ (the supreme Brilliance or soul). This must be meditated upon. The butter is actually present in the body of the cows. But it does not add to the strength of the cows. When the milk is taken out from the body and churned and the ghee is administered to the cows it gives them additional strength. So also the all pervading Viṣṇu though present in the body too does not grant any special benefit to men without being propitiated. The devotee desirous of ascending the tree of Yoga must have recourse to Karma and Jñāna as the steps to achieve the goal.

5. Those who have already climbed the tree of Yoga must also resort to Jñāna and renunciation. If a person begins to experience sound, etc., he becomes affected by Rāga and Dveṣa (Desire and Hatred).

6. From them spring Lobha (greed), Moha (delusion) and Krodha (anger). A man affected by all these commits sin.

7. The hands, the generative organ, the belly and speech (are at the root of all sins). If they are brought under control a man becomes a wise brahmin.

8. Hands can be brought under control by desisting from taking another man's wealth, refraining from injuring others and not playing at the game of dice.

9. If a man avoids other women his genitals are brought under control. If he is neither gluttonous nor craves for delicacies, his belly is brought under control.

10. If he speaks limited, wholesome and truthful words his speech is under control. Of what use are the austerities and sacrifices to the person who has controlled these four ?

11. Unity of intellect, mind and the organs, with seed or without seed is called meditation.

12-13. A life in the state of Jāgrat (waking) employs his intellect which is situated between the eyebrows, in the direction of objects of sense. Scholars say so.

14-15. When the life (soul) comes to the heart and is enveloped by Tamas (darkness) he experiences neither delusion nor false perception. In fact, he does not know 'where' he is or 'wherefrom' he has come. That state is called Suṣupti (Slumber). He is not aware of even his wife nearby. He does not perceive the objects of sense organs like a man who has controlled his senses.

16-18. [The Turīya (fourth) state is now described]. The sense organs and the mind are diverted (consciously) from the objects by means of intellect. The intellect and the ego are diverted by means of Prakṛti (nature). The Prakṛti is abstracted by means of Cicchakti (the psychic force). He then stations himself in the pure Self alone and sees only the soul which is consciousness pure and simple, pure and inert, all pervasive and auspicious. Now the soul is in the Turīya (fourth) state undoubtedly.

19-20. Of the lotus called Puryaṣṭaka (the heart) these are the petals [i.e. sound, touch, taste, colour, smell and the three Guṇas i.e. Sattva, Rajas and Tamas]. Their equilibrium is maintained by the three Guṇas. Prakṛti is the pericarp (Karṇikā) of the lotus. The Lord Cidrūpa (the conscious principle) is stationed in the pericarp. If the life leaves off the Puryaṣṭaka and the Prakṛti consisting of the three Guṇas, it is called Mukti (absolution, salvation).

21. The six ancillary factors assisting Yogic practice are Prāṇāyāma, Japa, Pratyāhāra (Diversion of sense organs), Dhāraṇa (Retention), Dhyāna (meditation) and Samādhi (Trance).

22-24. A perfect control of the sense organs brings about the destruction of sins and the favour of gods. A Prāṇāyāma accompanied by Japa and Dhyāna is called Sagarbha and the opposite is called Agarbha.

The excellent Prāṇāyāma consists of thirtysix mātrās; the

middle one of twentyfour mātrās; and the last one of twelve mātrās, Oṅkāra is to be added to all Japas.

25. If the Vācaka (that which signifies) Praṇava is understood the Vācya (that which is connoted) Brahman is delighted. The six syllabled Mantra 'Oṁ Namo Viṣṇave' (obeisance to Viṣṇu) must be constantly repeated, along with Gāyatrī and the twelve syllabled mantra 'Om Namo Bhagavate Vāsudevāya'.

26. The natural urge of the sense organs is towards the objects. Their diversion from them along with that of the mind is called Pratyāhāra.

27. A Yogin who thus diverts the sense organs from the objects consciously along with his intellect is said to be in Pratyāhāra state (state of abstraction).

28-29. The mind must be fixed in Brahman for as much time as is necessary to perform twelve Prāṇāyāmas, each of twelve mātrās. If the Yogin feels sublime bliss in this state and continues in it, it is called Samādhi (Trance).

30-31. While meditating one must not stir at all. The mind is energetically engaged in it. As long as the mind is in its grips the Dhāraṇā (retention) must be maintained. The mind is fixed in the object of Dhyāna. It sees it alone, nothing else. That is called the (perfect) Dhyāna (meditation).

32. When the mind is inert in its grasp of the Dhyeya (the object) it is called the perfect Dhyāna by the sages who have thought over Dhyāna.

33. The Yogin identifies himself with the Dhyeya and sees it alone everywhere without any second object. This state is called Samādhi.

34. The mind is without any special conception. The objects of the sense organs are not thought of. If it is merged thus completely in Brahman it is called being in Samādhi.

35. If the Yogin's mind thinking of Brahman is fixed in It and identifies itself with It he is called a person in Samādhi.

36. The defects causing obstacles in the practice of Yoga are—the unsteadiness of the mind of the Yogin, false notions, mental dejection and elatedness.

37. In order to steady the mind, the practiser of Yoga shall first think of gross objects. This practice coming to be concentrated on the sun (solar plexus) steadies the mind.

38. There is nothing existing in the world except the Paramātman. It is this alone that takes all forms. A person who knows this gets release.

39. Oṅkāra and the Brahman (supreme) shall be meditated upon. The lord shall be meditated upon as stationed in the lotus (heart) without the distinction of Kṣetra (body) and Kṣetrajña (soul). The two Mantras Oṅkāra and the six-syllabled one (Supra Verse 25) must be repeated.

40-43. At the outset the practiser of Yoga must meditate upon Pradhāna (Principle of nature) as stationed in the lotus. Above it are the zones of Tamas, Rajas and Sattva in order. Over that is the Puruṣa (appearing) black, red and white (due to the Guṇas) called Jīva (the individual soul). Over that is located the mystic lotus with the eight petals of Guṇa, etc. Knowledge is the pericarp, the Śāstraic knowledge is the filament. Allergy to worldliness is the stem; the Vaiṣṇava cult is its bulb. The Jīva must be then meditated upon as stationed in the pericarp motionless and conjoined to Oṅkāra in the heart. This meditation is an aid to salvation.

44. If a Yogin dies while meditating he is sure to attain Brahman. A Yogin meditating on Hari after placing Him in the lotus of the heart attains devotion.

45. Some Yogins see the Ātman through the eye of meditation; others through Sāṁkhya knowledge and others by means of Yoga.

46. Knowledge clarifying the Brahman chops off the fetters of worldly existence. Yoga which is singleminded concentration in Brahman yields salvation undoubtedly.

47. He who is satiated in knowledge and who has conquered the sense organs and the Karaṇas (limbs) is said to be a liberated soul. The Paramātman is stationed there like one blind (i.e. passively).

48. Āsanas (postures), Sthānas (particular places) and Viṣayas (objects) cannot be called auxiliaries of Yoga. These

superfluous things actually delay the successful conclusion of yogic practice.

49. Even Śiśupāla attained salvation on account of constant remembrance. Those who practice Yoga see the soul through their own souls.

50. A Yogin who is compassionate towards all living beings, who is averse to those who hinder his progress and who has subjugated the genitals and the belly becomes liberated.

51. If he does not come into contact with the objects of sense organs through them, if he has merged himself completely in Brahman and appears senseless like a log of wood he is a liberated soul.

52. Annihilating everything — all the castes, all women (objects of sense organs) and all sins by means of the fire of meditation the intelligent Yogins attain the highest goal.

53. By churning, fire is manifested. Similarly, Hari manifests Himself through meditations. The highest Yoga is the identity of Brahman and Ātman.

54. There is no salvation through external forms. Through the internal Yama (restraint) etc. it can be made possible. The realization of the Ātman through Sāṅkhya, Yoga and Vedānta is called salvation. The bondage is the perception of non soul as soul and the non existent as existent.

CHAPTER TWO HUNDRED AND THIRTYSIX

Vedānta and Sāṅkhya

The Lord said :

1. O Nārada, I shall explain the knowledge of the soul in the proper perspective. Please listen. The Advaita (the unbifurcated) itself is called Sāṅkhya and Yoga is the concentration on it.

2. Those who are endowed with Advaita Yoga are released from the bondage. The Karmans (results of actions) whether

past or beginning to fructify or those yet to come become quelled through knowledge.

3. He who has cut down the tree of worldly existence by the axe of right conception and has taken his plunge in the sacred river of Jñāna (knowledge) and Vairāgya (non attachment) attains the status of Viṣṇu.

4. Māyā is called Tripura inasmuch as the three states of waking, dreaming and slumbering are brought about by Māyā. This is included in the nondual Brahman.

5. The great status of Brahman is free from name, form and action. After creating the boundless universe, Īśvara entered it Himself.

6. 'I know this Puruṣa, who is in the form of Cit (consciousness) and who is beyond darkness. I am He'. This knowledge is conducive to salvation. There is no other means to that.

7. Śravaṇa (listening to noble tenets) Manana (deliberation) and Dhyāna (meditation) are the means of knowledge. Salvation cannot be secured through sacrifices, gifts, austerities, pilgrimages and Vedic recitation.

8. By some, Dhyāna is secured by renunciation as by means of worship and sacred rites in the case of others. Vedic injunctions are twofold : 'Do the rites' and 'renounce the rites in the supreme deity.'

9. Sacrifices etc. are not for the liberation of those who cherish no desire. They are for the sake of purification of the mind of those who are not liberated. This is what some say.

10. Those who fancy a twofold existence cannot gain salvation in the course of a single life even, due to perfect knowledge. Those who err from Yogic practices or those who do not practise Yoga properly are born again as brahmins in the families of Yogins.

11. Man is fettered through actions. He is saved from worldly existence through knowledge. One shall resort to the knowledge of the Soul. What is opposed to this is ignorance.

12. When all passions stationed in the heart leave one off, one becomes liberated undoubtedly even as one lives.

13. Since the soul is all pervasive how can he go? Who is it that goes ? Where does he go ? Since he is unlimited there

is no place for him to go. How can there be any movement since he is disembodied ?

14. Since he is without a second there is none for him to go to. Since he is knowledge itself how can there be sluggishness ? Others' going or coming or standing is with some one in view.

15. It is like the firmament and hence its movement is like the movement of the firmament i.e. it is stationary. The three states of waking, dreaming and slumbering are fancied through ignorance.

16. The indivisible constituents of the individual soul are the very constituents of the universal soul. That is why each and every individual is attracted to his or her own soul.

17. O Nārada, that is why the mind of each and every individual is inclined towards his or her own self.

18-19. It is the soul, not intellect, that passes through the four states of consciousness. It is the soul, not intellect that being omniscient knows past, present and future.

20. If there were no soul in the body of a person he would not feel the thrill of pleasure nor the pang of the pain in the different states of consciousness.

21-22. It is the soul, the witness of all activities which is truth, intelligence, eternal principle, not distinct from intellect and which is bliss itself.

23-24. By knowing Brahman one knows every thing, just as on knowing a jar of clay one knows all the jars or on knowing gold one knows all that is made of gold.

25-26. Just as in darkness one cannot cognize the rope, similarly through ignorance we cannot perceive the soul. We super-impose a snake on what is in fact a rope, we superimpose the elements, ether, etc. on what is in reality the soul.

27-28. Even the evident reality assumes a different form. The rope becomes a snake; the mother-of-pearls becomes silver. A deer cannot quench its thirst in the mirage; similarly, a man cannot satisfy his desire by indulging in the false pleasures of the senses.

29-30. So long a man has the sense of pleasure, he is called a possessor. But when possession is lost he remains his true self. The individual soul associated with Māyā identifies himself with the body but when māyā withdraws he realizes his reality as Brahman.

31. Just as a noble person is not effected by the loss of possession, similarly, the withdrawal of Māyā does not effect a person who has realized Self.

32. Reality and illusion are both eternal. But Reality is an unassailable truth while illusion is a mirage.

33. Though declared to be unborn he passes through a series of birth and death. Though one, he becomes many in the form of husband, wife, pleasure, universe, etc.

34-35. The three Guṇas multiplied by twenty-eight become eighty-four and these contribute to the formation of bodies, male and female and the universe with all its parts, names, forms, and actions from beginningless time to the endless one.

36-37. The existence of forms, names, etc is assumed and not real just as the chariot, etc which exist in the state of dream are not real. Similarly, things or objects which exist in the state of wakefulness do not exist in reality.

38-39. By his association with Māyā born of ignorance, Brahma appears to be dual, while by the withdrawal of Māyā through knowledge he remains non-dual.

40-41. Thus the non-dual Brahman is as the refulgent sun, Reality, Truth, Existence, Knowledge. It is eternal, complete, inward bliss. As eternal it is unborn, as non-doer it is nectar, as the light of an earthen lamp, it is an inward light. The realization that the individual soul is identical with the Supreme Soul leads one to release.

CHAPTER TWO HUNDRED AND THIRTYSEVEN

Essence of the Gītā

The Lord said:

1. I shall narrate to you the gist of Gītā mentioned to Arjuna formerly. A person who practises Yoga with its eight components has mastered Vedāntic lore.

2. The realization of Ātman is the only great asset, nothing else. The Ātman is devoid of physical body. It is also divested of form, colour and of the gross body, mind, eyes and the rest.

3. The Prāṇa is devoid of knowledge. In deep slumber 'I' (the knowledge of the self) is seen. This cannot be the real Ātman, since the existing man is in conjunction with misery and worldly bondage.

4. Just like a smokeless blazing fire, just like the lightning in the sky, the Ātman shines in the inner heart.

5. The ears, etc, cannot see themselves or the Ātman. But the soul the omniscient, the onlooker of all sees them.

6. The Ātman is self luminary. Due to its contact the sin is dissipated and knowledge arises in the individual soul in the manner of the screen that appears to be blazing when a light burns nearby.

7-10. Like the objects reflected in a mirror the soul sees things reflected in itself such as the sense organs, the objects, the great elements, the mind, the intellect, the ego, the unmanifest and the Puruṣa. By pervading the cluster of sense organs with the mind and by fixing the mind in the ego, O Pāṇḍava, the ego in the intellect and the intellect in Prakṛti, the Prakṛti in the Puruṣa and the Puruṣa in Brahman, one realises 'I am Brahman the great Light' and realising this one becomes liberated.

11. The body is a house with nine door ways (the external apertures), three presiding deities (the three Guṇas) and five witnesses (the five sense organs). The supreme presiding officer is the Kṣetrajña (the soul). He who knows this thoroughly is the excellent poet (Kavi or Krāntadarśin i.e. a seer).

12. Thousands of horse sacrifices, and hundreds of Vājapeya sacrifices do not merit even a sixteenth part of Jñāna yajña (the sacrifice of knowledge).

CHAPTER TWO HUNDRED AND THIRTYEIGHT

Essence of the Gītā

The Lord said:

1. O Pārtha, the eight components of Yoga are Yama (restraint), Niyama (ritualistic observances), Āsana (the Yogic Posture), Prāṇāyāma (breath-control), Pratyāhāra (abstraction), Dhyāna (meditation), Dhāraṇā (retention) and Samādhi (trance). These are conducive to salvation.

2. Ahiṁsā (non-violence) is the virtue of refraining from inflicting injury upon living beings by actions, thoughts and speech at all times. It accords happiness.

3. Even an injury inflicted in accordance with Vedic injunctions is also Ahiṁsā. The eternal virtue is the telling of truth, the telling of the pleasant. One shall not tell even truths which are unpleasant and untruths which may be pleasant.

4. Seizing of another man's wealth by stealth or by force is called Steya (theft). Not doing it is called Asteya. It is a righteous thing.

5. Abjuring sexual intercourse by actions, thoughts and speech in all states, at all times and everywhere is called Brahmacarya (celibacy).

6. Acceptance of wealth must be avoided carefully. Non acceptance of the same willingly even in danger is called Aparigraha.

7. Śauca or purification is of two varieties : the external one by means of earth and water and the internal one by means of good feelings and thoughts. Santoṣa (contentment) is the sense of satiety over what is casually secured. It gives everlasting happiness.

8. Tapas or austerity is the concentration of mind and the sense organs. It is also the voluntary withering up of the body by holy rites-Kṛcchra, Cāndrāyaṇa, etc.

9. Learned men call the recital of Vedic passages, Śatarudrīya, Praṇava, etc which purify the soul Svādhyāya.

10. Īśvaracintana is the unflinching devotion to Hari

by means of eulogy, remembrance and adoration as well as by speeches, thoughts and actions.

11. Āsana is the posture such as Svastika, Padma and Ardhāsana. Prāṇa is the air within the body. Āyāma is the suppression of the same.

12. O Pāṇḍava, the restraint and diversion of the sense organs that stray into evil objects, is called Pratyāhāra.

13. Dhyāna (meditation) is the contemplation of the embodied or disembodied Brahman, At the beginning of the practice of Yoga, Hari can be meditated upon in the embodied or disembodied form.

14. The deity of Vāyu must be contemplated upon as stationed in the middle of the zone of Agni. The four armed deity (Viṣṇu) must be meditated upon as bearing Śaṅkha, Cakra, Gadā and Padma and also as having Kaustubha.

15. I, endowed with Kaustubha and known as Brahman and Vanamālin shall be meditated upon as such. This is called Dhāraṇā because the deity is retained in the mind.

16. The state in which one is conscious 'I am Brahman' is called Samādhi. Men get salvation through the knowledge generated by the Vedic statement 'I am Brahman'.

The two words 'I' and 'Brahman' must be taken to mean the implied sense and the feeling of identity realised.

CHAPTER TWO HUNDRED AND THIRTYNINE

Brahmā said :

1. I shall now tell you of Brahmagītā, the knowledge of which will release you from the bond of activities. The knowledge derived from the aupaniṣadic text *I am Brahma* releases one from the tangle (of the senses).

2. The knowledge of *aham* and *Brahma* leads to the knowledge of the meaning of *aham* and *Brahma* and it leads to the knowledge of the sentence *aham Brahmāsmi*. The sense of the two words : aham and Brahma is twofold : denotative and indicative.

3. The denotative sense of the sentence *aham Brahmāsmi* is not so clear as the indicative one. The relationship between the two is like that between the body and the soul.

4. The śruti declares that denotatively the word *aham* refers to the personal self while indicatively it refers to the non-dual Brahman.

5. Indeclinable, blissful and unmanifested consciousness is denotated by the word Brahma while the personal self manifested in the body is denotated by the word aham.

6. Indicatively the word *aham* refers to Brahma, while the word *Brahma* refers to the soul in the body. (The two are identical).

7-10. The word *aham* refers to the perceptible entity (*Jīvātman*) and the word *Brahma* refers to the imperceptible (*Brahma*). By adopting the Indicatory process (lakṣaṇā) the person arrives at the meaning of *ahaṁ Brahma* which leads him to realize the non-dual supreme Self. The knowledge of the meaning of the Mahāvākya *ahaṁ Brahmāsmi* removes ignorance, enlightens the path and effects release.

Lord Hari said :

11-16. From the eternal Brahmā was originated the ether, from ether the fire, from fire the earth. The subtle body consisting of seventeen parts came into being; viz the five organs of action, viz. hands, feet, mouth, the generating organ, the organ of evacuation, five organs of intellect, viz. ears, skin, eyes, tongue, organ of smell, and five winds viz Prāṇa, Apāna, Samāna, Vyāna, Udāna, and mind of which the nature is doubting and intellect of which the nature is ascertainment. This is the subtle creation. Hiraṇyagarbha is an individual soul which is ascertainable only by its actions. From the five subtle elements originated the five gross elements : earth, water, fire, wind and ether, from the five gross elements originated the universe.

17. The body consists of feet, hands, etc is known as the gross body. It originates from five elements and functions as the base of all activities.

18. The body consisting of organs of action is called gross but has its basis in the Supreme Self.

19. The individual self pervades the subtle as well as the gross body; as the Śrutis declare, the very Brahma has entered the bodies.

20. Like the Sun in the water, the higher self reflected in the intellect is called Jīva (the personal self) which sustains life and functions as the witness of three states, viz, the state of wakefulness, of dream and sound sleep.

21-22. The supreme self is not associated with attributes, is distinct from three states of consciousness, viz, the state of wakefulness, dream and sound sleep. It is not divided in parts, is non-dual, is of eternally pure nature. Seated inside the body and characterized by three states of consciousness, the individual self is no other than the higher self.

63. A person who is ever intent on three states, viz., the state of wakefulness, of dream and of sound sleep can never realize Brahma. I shall now tell you something about those activities which are undertaken for the attainment of fruits and about the three states of consciousness jāgrat etc.

24-25. The knowledge of an object through the organ of senses is called jāgrat. The seeker for the knowledge of an object goes in contact with that very object through the medium of senses. The same is repeated in dream (svapna). In sound sleep there is a total withdrawal of senses. The mind and intellect are concentrated in Brahman.

26-31. Serially or non-serially, the individual soul passes through the three states. In the preliminary state of meditation he is aware of the objective world. As soon as the desire for liberation is created in him he withdraws his senses from the outside world which being emanated from the creator himself appears to be distinct as the jar appears distinct from clay. The universe constituted of the five-fold elements is nothing but an aggregate of five subtle elements which again are nothing but the indivisible Brahma itself.

The earth as the substratum of all stationary and living beings has also a substratum in Brahma. There is no fire without wind, no wind without ether, no ether without Brahma and no Brahma without ether.

32-34. In pure consciousness there is no awareness of the states jagrat, svapna etc. and no sense of separateness. The personal soul loses its identity and merges into the eternally pure, intelligent, awakened and non-dual Brahma. Then 'thou' and 'that' are dropped and what remains is pure Brahma (indicated by *asi*).

Just as in Om, the syllables *a*, *u*, *m*, are merged, losing their identity, similarly all appendages that create a feeling of separateness are merged into the Brahman. The expressions *Brahmāhamasmi*, *aham Brahma* serve merely to create confusion.

35. The self is the supreme light, supreme consciousness, supreme joy, supreme truth, eternal knowledge, expressed by the word *tvam*. So declares the Śruti.

36. I am Brahma, pure and simple. I am omniscient. That one is seen in the orb of the sun, that one I am, eternally. The lord conveyed this essence of Gītā to Arjuna who realized the Self.

CHAPTER TWO HUNDRED AND FORTY

Lord Hari said :

1. O Rudra, I have narrated to you the Garuḍa Purāṇa, the essence of all knowledge. It brings joy to the listener and brings about his release.

2. It confers learning, fame, glory, wealth, victory and health. O Rudra, he who reads or hears the Purāṇa becomes omniscient and goes to heaven.

Brahmā said :

3. O Vyāsa, I have heard this Purāṇa from the mouth of Viṣṇu. It surely brings about liberation to the hearer.

Vyāsa said :

Thus Brahmā who had heard the Purāṇa from the mouth of Viṣṇu related it to Dakṣa, Nārada and others including myself.

4. I had gone to Viṣṇu-loka with my mind set on Brahman. I heard this Purāṇa and later on, imparted the same to Sūta. Now you have heard the same from the mouth of Sūta.

5. On hearing the Purāṇa the person attains omniscience satiates his desire, reaps the fruits in the form of realizing the self. This Purāṇa, the essence of all knowledge, Viṣṇu related to Garuḍa.

Sūta said :

6. This Purāṇa contains the essence of all knowledge and confers Dharma, Artha, Kāma and Mokṣa.

7. In olden days, Vyāsa narrated to me this Purāṇa which he had heard from Brahmā—Vyāsa who had divided a single Veda into four Vedas.

8. He divided the single Purāṇa saṁhitā into eighteen saṁhitās. Śuka, the son of Vyāsa, has narrated to me this fact. And I have related to you this Purāṇa O Śaunaka.

9-11. Since you have asked me to narrate the Purāṇa to the sages (I have done so). One who reads or hears or hires the services of a Paṇḍit to recite it to others, or writes it himself or hires the services of a scribe to write it out or keeps the Purāṇa at home, attains Dharma, Artha, Kāma or Mokṣa, whatever may be the choice. He satiates his desire by listening to this Purāṇa.

12. If he is a Brāhmaṇa he attains the knowledge of the Vedas; if a Kṣatriya he is conferred the strength of protection.

13. None of the other classes (Vaiśya or Śūdra) is authorized to hear the Purāṇa. If, by mistake, he narrates it to an unworthy person, he becomes the object of censure.

14. But, if he narrates the Purāṇa from behind the screen, then both the deserving and the undeserving person become worthy to hear.

15. As Viṣṇu is a celebrated deity, Garuḍa is a venerable celebrity. In praising Garuḍa we praise Viṣṇu. By singing praise for Garuḍa, formerly King Vasu satiated his desires.

King Vasu said :

16. Homage to Garuḍa, of irresistible might, the Vehicle

of Viṣṇu, the emblem in the banner of Viṣṇu and a terror to the Asuras.

17. Homage to you, the destroyer of the pride of the Nāgas, the nourisher of joy to his mother Vinata, possessed of beautiful wings, guileless, refuge of the piteous asuras.

18. [Now listen to a story]. Once Supratīka and Vibhāvasu, the two brothers, cursed each other and as a result of curses they were born as the elephant and tortoise.

19-20. They had immense bodily height as well as breadth. In their struggle for superiority over each other, you acted as a judge. You released them from the accursed curse which they had inflicted upon each other.

21. You swallowed the Niśādas in large proportion. When by mistake you swallowed a pious Brāhmaṇa, you vomited him alive, immediately on knowing that he was a brāhmaṇa.

22. You broke the bough of a Banian tree spread over a hundred yojanas, regardless of the fact that it supported the Bālakhilyas.

23. With mighty effort you seized the elephant and the tortoise, put them in the navel of your thumb, while they were fighting in the supportless sky.

24. You conquered the gods, together with their leader Indra. O son of Kaśyapa, you extinguished the sacrificial fire and carried away the Soma forcibly.

25. There were two poisonous serpents who could inject poison by their very sight. You made them sightless by your magical skill.

26. Out of devotion for Viṣṇu you brought Soma from heaven. You did not partake of it yourself. You therefore got a place of honour in the banner of Viṣṇu and became his vehicle.

27. You concealed Soma in the Darbha grass and deceived the Nāgas. You carried nectar to the abode of Brahmā [and distributed the same among the gods].

28. O best of birds, by you the tonque of the Nāgas was split into two. You released your mother from Kadrū, the mother of the Nāgas who had made her a slave.

29-31. They say that the horse Uccaiḥśravas is white in complexion but I believe he is dark (for his glory is diminished). In the interest of your mother you had cut off his wings with the stroke of Indra's thunderbolt. When god Indra saw your mighty deed he bestowed upon you the title of honour—Suparṇa.

32. By merely meditating on you, one destroys the effect of poison of whatsoever sort. One who hears or reads the purāṇa gets sensuous pleasure and release.

Sūta said :

33. King Vasu heard the Garuḍa Purāṇa and satiated his desire. The venerable Garuḍa meditated on Viṣṇu and obtained the objects of his desire.

Sūta said :

34. I have narrated to you the sacred treatise, viz, the Garuḍa Purāṇa. He who reads this Purāṇa achieves the objects of his desire, and ultimately reaches the supreme goal.

35. By reciting even a quarter of verse, one destroys sins. He who keeps the treatise at home obtains everything in this world.

36. He who possesses this Purāṇa attains all that is just. He who reads and hears this Purāṇa enjoys sensuous pleasures and gets also release.

37-38 By listening to this Purāṇa he attains Dharma, Artha, Kāma and Mokṣa. Desiring a son, he obtains son. Desiring an object he obtains the object. Desiring knowledge he obtains knowledge. Desiring Victory he obtains Victory. If he has killed a brahmin he is absolved of that sin.

39. A barren woman obtains Son; a girl a good husband. Desiring welfare he obtains welfare. Seeking pleassure he obtains pleasure.

40. Desiring auspiciousness, he obtains auspiciousness. Desiring merit, he receives merit. Desiring to be a poet, he becomes a poet. Desiring to learn the secret of knowledge he obtains the secret of knowledge.

41. Desirous of knowledge, he obtains knowledge that puts an end to his cycle of birth. This auspicious narrative of the Garuḍa Purāṇa narrated by Garuḍa himself is associated with bliss.

42. By reading even a single verse one escapes an untimely death. If he reads half a verse he achieves the end of his wicked foes.

43. At Naimiṣa, at the Sacrifice of sages, Śaunaka heard the Purāṇa from Sūta. He meditated upon Brahman identifying his self with the Supreme Self and got release.

DHARMA (PRETA) KĀṆḌA

CHAPTER ONE

Garuḍa's query

1. One should begin the recital of Jaya (this holy Purāṇa) after bowing to *Nārāyaṇa*, Nara the most excellent among men, Goddess Sarasvatī and Vyāsa. The renowned Viṣṇu shines victoriously like the wish-giving Kalpa tree with Dharma (virtue) for its firmly fixed roots; the Vedas for its main stem, the Purāṇas for its branches, the sacrifice for its flames and salvation for its fruits.

2. In Naimiṣa forest, the solitary region, the sages Śaunaka and others asked Sūta who was sitting comfortably on his seat after going through his daily rites.

3. O Sūta, you possess perfect knowledge (of the Purāṇic lore) through sage Vyāsa's favour. Hence, you can clear off our doubts we have in our mind.

4-5. Following the maxim of caterpillar, some sages say that the soul attains another body after leaving the previous one. Others hold that the soul enters another body after going through Yama's torture. What is true ?

Sūta said :

6. Gentlemen, you have put the right question. Now hear. To allay your doubts.

7. I shall take recourse to a dialogue between Kṛṣṇa and Garuḍa. I shall try to remove your doubts thereby.

8. Obeisance to sage Kṛṣṇa. They who take recourse to him can easily cross the ocean of the world as it were a small river.

9. Once upon a time, Garuḍa desired to go round the world. He started on journey, wandered all over, muttering the the name Hari.

10. He wandered over the earth, in hell and heaven but could not get peace. He returned to Vaikuṇṭha, more distressed by the sight of people's sorrows.

11. There in Vaikuṇṭha, neither *Rajas* exists, nor *Tamas*, nor *Sattva* mixed with either of these two. *Sattva* alone exists there.

12. Neither Māyā nor destruction nor the evils like anger, attachment etc. exist there.

13. There dwell glorious Viṣṇu's *gaṇas* dark and fair, bright, lotus-eyed, worshipped by deities and demons, clad in tawny robes and adorned with ornaments, bedecked with garlands of gold coins set up with jewels.

14. Possessed of four arms and tufts of hair, wearing earrings and garland, they shone by the rows of resplendent aerial cars.

15. There Lakṣmī gladly adorns Lord Viṣṇu's feet by offering many precious gems. Herself surrounded by the rows of beautiful damsels and friendly associates she sits in a moving swing and praises Hari.

16-21. There he saw Hari All-powerful, Lord of Lakṣmī, Lord of the good, Lord of the world, lord of the sacrifices, surrounded by the courtiers : Sunanda, Nanda, Prabalārhaṇa, chief among them possessing a face delightful to the servants, possessing big reddish eyes, bearing crest and ear-rings, being looked at the chest by Lakṣmī, wearing yellow garment; possessing four arms, and a delightful smiling face, sitting on a costly seat surrounded by the powers, Pradhāna[1], Puruṣa,[2] Mahat,[3] Aham[4], the eleven organs, the five elements and delighting in Self. Garuḍa was pleased to see the Lord. His hair thrilled with joy and with tears coming out of his eyes he bowed to him with the feeling of love.

1. The first evolver, originator, or source of the material world, the primary germ out of which all material appearances are evolved, according to the *Sāṅkhya* philosophy.

2. The soul. According to the *Sāṅkhya* it is neither a production nor productive: it is passive and a looker-on of the Prakṛti.

3. The great principle, the intellect. The second of the twenty five elements or *tattvas* recognised by the *Sāṅkhyas*.

4. In *Sāṅkhya*-philosophy, the third of the eight producers or elements of creation, i.e., conceit or conception of individuality. In *Vedānta*-philosophy egotism is considered to be spiritual ignorance.

22. Viṣṇu spoke to Garuḍa who had come to see him and who had bowed to him: "O Garuḍa, tell us how much of this earth you have wandered over and within such a short time."

Garuḍa said :

23. My Lord, by your grace, I have visited the three worlds and seen all beings — the movable and the immovable.

24. From bhūloka[1] to satyaloka, I have visited all regions, except the region of Yama, O my lord.

25. Among all the worlds, the bhūloka is thickly populated by various kinds of creatures. This region is the most auspicious of all inasmuch as it affords a place of enjoyment to all and is celebrated as the place where they can strive for salvation.

26. A region better than this for those who perform good actions has neither been before nor will there ever be.

27. It seems that the gods sing songs to this purport. Those who live in this part of the world called *Bhārata* are in fact blessed. In order to enjoy the fruits of heaven and salvation they are born as human beings, casting off their deity-hood.

28. Why is the corpse tied to the bamboo-sticks ? Why are the five jewels kept in the mouth ? Why is the grass placed beneath ? Why are the feet kept southward ?

29. Why do the sons and grandsons walk ahead ? Why are the gifts given, including the gift of a cow, O Keśava ?

30-31. Why do the relatives, the friends, and even the foes forgive him. Why are the gingelly seeds, iron, gold, cotton, salt, seven types of grains, land (or house) and cow are given ? How does a creature die ? Having died, where does he go ?

1. Hindu mythology accepts fourteen *lokas* or worlds. Seven higher regions rising from the earth one above the other are, *bhūrloka*, *bhuvarloka*, *svarloka*, *maharloka*, *janaoka*, *tapoloka* and *Satyaloka* or *brahmaloka*; and seven lower regions, descending from the earth one below the other are *atala*, *vitala*, *sutala*, *rasātala*, *talātala*, and *mahātala* or *pātāla*.

32. How does he take shelter in the body being carried? Why does the son carry the corpse on his shoulders and the grandson lights the fire?

33. Why is the anointment done with the butter? Wherefrom is the *ekāhuti-kriyā*? Why is *Vasudhārā* performed and wherefrom the lamentations from women?

34. Why is the *Yama-sūkta* recited? Why is water carried to the north? Why is the sun looked through a cloth?

35. Why barley, mustard-seed, dūrvā, the two stones, the leaves of margosa? Why do men and women wear one lower and one upper garment.

36. Why should the meals, etc. be not taken alongwith other persons after returning home? Why do the sons give nine piṇḍas[1]

37. Why is the milk in an earthern pot placed on *catvara*?[2] Why are the three wooden sticks tied together and placed on the cross-roads in the night?

38. Why is a lamp placed every night for one year? Why should the water be offered in the name of the deceased by the relatives and other people?

39. Why should the nine piṇḍas be offered? How is the gift to be given to the manes? Why is the call for the bearers of the corpse?

40. When this is done, O lord! then why is the rite of piṇḍa repeated? What should be given next after the gift of piṇḍa is made?

41. Why are the bones collected? Why is the earthen pot broken? Why is a bath taken on the second day? Why on the fourth day?

42. Why is it taken on the tenth day alongwith the other mourners? Why the anointment with oil?

43-44. The *piṇḍa* given on the tenth day is done so with meat, why? Why is the piṇḍa on the eleventh day given after releasing the bull?

1. Balls of rice offered to the Manes at obsequial ceremonies.
2. , A quadrangular place or courtyard : a place where many roads meet.

45-46. Why are vessels, shoes, umbrella, clothes and ring given on the thirteenth day. Why the sixteen śrāddhas ?[1] Why are food, water, etc. given everyday for three-hundred and sixty days of the year ? Why is the food put in a vessel for satiating the deceased ?

47-48. O lord, the mortal man dies at the appointed time. I do not see an outlet, then from where does the soul go away ? From where do the elements—earth, water, mind, fire, air and sky pass away; tell me, O lord ?

49. From where do the five organs of action, the five organs of perception and the five vital airs go away and how ?

50. From where do the five thieves of the body—greed affection, desire, love and pride go away, O Janārdana ?

51. Whatever little action has been done, whether good or bad or whatever gifts have been tendered which procure merit where do these go away after the body has decayed ?

52. Why is the rite of sapiṇḍana[2] done within the year of death ? With whom is the union of the deceased sought and how ?

53-54. What does in the end happen to the people who pass away, in conscious or unconscious state, burnt or unburnt or who have been sinners or bad-charactered.

55-56. O lord, what is the end of those who commit suicide, murder a brāhmaṇa, or happen to be thieves or deceivers by nature ? What happens to that Śūdra who drinks the milk of a kapilā cow, who reads the scriptures, who wears the sacred thread or who possesses a brahmin wife ?

57. O lord, you tell me all this, for I am terribly afraid of the sinner. Hear something more, O soul of the universe. While wandering with curiosity, I saw the entire world.

58-59. After seeing people merged in sorrows, a great pain arose in my heart. The affliction on the earth caused by

1. Funeral rites performed in honour of the departed spirits of dead relatives.

2. The performance of a particular *Śrāddha* in honour of the deceased's relatives is called *Sapiṇḍa,* to be performed at the end of full one year after the death of a relative, but now usually performed on the 12th day after death as part of the funeral rite.

death and disease is greater than affliction from the sight of asuras in paradise.

60. I had the fear of losing my desired object in hell. There is no other place safer than your feet, O Lord.

61. Time has consumed the unreality as it has consumed the dream-world. Still, I saw a number of people suffering from sorrows in the land of Bharata.

62-63. They were merged deep in attachment, envy, affection, etc. Some were blind, some squint-eyed, some dumb, some lame, some one-eyed, some deaf, some suffering from leprosy and other diseases and some from pride as false as the sky-flower.[1]

64. After seeing the strangeness of their faults in the face of death. I have come to you with a mind to ask what is death ? Why is this strangeness ?

65. How does death occur ? How is it that even after death, if rites are performed for one year one does not fall in the bad state ?

66. Formerly, I had heard from the sages in general; now I ask you specifically on these points, O lord.

67. O Viṣṇu, what shall a dying man do? What shall he give in charity? After death, what is the method of cremation?

68. Does he languish or obtain another body? When he lives in Yama's city, what are the rites to be performed by his descendants in the year of his death?

69-70. What are the rites of propitiation for the common ignorant deceased? For one dead in *pañcaka* ? Be pleased, dispel my ignorance. I have asked all that I wanted to ask only for the welfare of the world. Please answer my queries.

1. Used figuratively to denote anything impossible.

CHAPTER TWO

Results of actions

Lord Kṛṣṇa said:

1. O gentle one, you have put up the right question, that too for the general good of the people. Now hear attentively. I shall tell you about the rite to be performed after death.

2. It is without any controversy quoted by Śrutis and smṛtis. It has not been heard by the gods including Indra, nor by yogins absorbed in yoga. Being the secret of secrets, it has not been conveyed to anyone, anywhere.

3. O Garuḍa of great accomplishment, I shall tell you about this since you are my devotee.

4. There is no place for a sonless person. The heaven is not for him. One must have a son by any means whatsoever.

5. The son can take his father out of hell, if he cannot get him salvation. The son puts his shoulder to coffin and the grandson lights the fire.

6. A woman in her menses shall stay in the hut and lie on the bed bestrewed with sesame and darbha grass, on the ground. She shall put five gems in the mouth. Thus her foetus attains growth.

7-8. If the seed[1] is destroyed then whereat the conception? Hence, for the protection of the foetus she shall lie on the ground, as enjoined in the Śāstras. Similarly, in regard to the dying person he is laid on the ground besmeared with cowdung and bestrewed with the *darbha* grass. Thus the ailing person is released of sins which do not cling to him any more.

9. A bunch of *darbha* for his bed takes him to heaven no doubt. Darbha should be thrown off after the corpse is removed from the place.

10. Where there is no besmearing, the ground remains impure. Where the earth is already besmeared it should be smeared again for the sake of purification.

1. Menstrual discharge.

11. If the corpse is kept on the unsmeared ground, the foul spirits enter the corpse.

12. A circle[1] should be drawn around the corpse (to fix up the circumference) ; Śrāddha shall be performed where the feet of the Brāhmaṇas should be washed. All these would not serve the corpse, if the same is not placed on the ground.

13. Brahmā, Viṣṇu, Rudra, Lakṣmī and Fire stay within the circle. Hence a circle is drawn around the corpse.

14. If a circle is not drawn, the deceased person whether a child, youth or old does not get a womb[2] but remains in the air, O Garuḍa !

15. He may not be born soon but live in the air for some time. He receives no *śrāddha,* no libation of water from his relatives.

16. O Garuḍa ! Sesame is held sacred, for it is produced from my perspiration. The sesame can destroy the evil spirits.

17. The sesame is white, black or of the colour of the cow's urine. They can burn all sins committed by the deceased.

18. A single grain of sesame offered with the libation of water to the deceased or an article given in charity or a sacrifice held for his welfare becomes fruitful as droṇa-kalaśa does in rewards.

19. Darbhas are born from my hair and sesame from my perspiration. By performing *śrāddha* one can please deities, asuras and the manes.

20. The Universe and the creator of the universe live by the ceremonial form. By wearing the secred thread over the right shoulder, one can please the creator, the manes and the deities.

21-23. When the sacred thread is worn over the right shoulder the manes are pleased. Brahmā stays at the root of darbha, Janārdana in its middle and Śaṅkara at the point of darbha. Thus the three deities are said to be stationed in darbha. The brāhmaṇas, mantras, sacred grass, fire and Tulasī are

1. A kind of a mystical diagram.
2. Form of existence.

never spoiled though used again and again. Tulasī, brāhmaṇa, Cows, Viṣṇu and Ekādaśī—

24. These five are the protection boats for the people drowning in the ocean of worldly existence. Viṣṇu, Ekādaśī, Gītā, Tulasī, Brāhmaṇa, and the Cow—

25. These are the six steps to salvation in this universal fortress of little use. Sesame and darbhas are sacred and so is Tulasī.

26. These guard the deceased against misfortune. Darbhas should be taken out with hands. The earth should be sprinkled over with water.

27. As the hour of death approaches, darbhas should be placed in the hands of the deceased. He whose body is spread over by darbhas goes to Viṣṇu-loka, no matter if he is not initiated in the Vedic lore.

28-29. The feet of the deceased person are kept on the ground and the toe raised upward. In this ocean of universal existence, which is practically of little use, the atonement of the sin is made by sacrificing the body in the holy fire. Having smeared the ground with the cowdung, they should spread the mattress of darbha for the dying person.

30-31. Salt is very much effective for the destruction of sins. Let them donate salt for the manes, for it suits their taste and takes them to heaven. As for the men in general, it fulfils their desires.

32. Salt has come out from the body of Viṣṇu, hence yogins recommend a gift of salt placing the same over other gifts.

33-34. When at the time of death, the soul does not depart but lingers on to the body, no matter whether the dying person is a brāhmaṇa, kṣatriya, vaiśya or śūdra of either sex, they should donate salt for him whereby the soul leaves the mortal body and enters the doors of heaven which open immediately for him. O king of birds, now hear from me in detail, the various forms of death.

35. It is Kāla which detaches soul from body. It causes death of the person, at the appointed hour, without a single exception.

36. Just as the wind scatters clouds here and there, just like that Kāla, the Destroyer, floats people from one end of the shore to another.

37. Whether they be sāttvika or rājasa or tāmasa—all these *bhāvas* operate in man due to the influence of Kāla.

38-39. Sun, Moon, Śiva, water, air, Indra, fire, sky, earth, herbs, Vasus, rivers, seas, existent or non-existent, O Garuḍa, all these are created and destroyed by Kāla in due course of time.

40. Indeed, O Garuḍa, when the hour of death approaches, then by chance, a certain disease raises up its head.

41. The Organs grow weak. Troubles start showing their powers, as if all of a sudden, millions of scorpions have stung the person.

42. O bird, then the person begins to feel the pang of death. At the very hour his consciousness is replaced by unconsciousness.

43. The breath is pushed by Yama's messengers standing nearby. The person assumes a terrible form and the breath lingers to stay in the throat.

44-45. Froth comes out of the mouth full of saliva. Just at the moment when every body is lamenting, the soul, as big as a thumb, is carried away by Yama's messengers, even as it looks towards its home. Now hear about the state of death.

46. The heat in the body is disturbed due to sudden commotion of winds. Though without fuel, it breaks up the vital points.

47. The Udāna-wind moves upward. It stops the downward movement of the deceased who in his life-time had full devotion for the lord but no desire in return.

48. He who has never spoken falsehood, nor has any partiality in devotion but believes in God, obtains death peacefully.

49. He who does not stray from Dharma, due to pleasure, wrath or envy but does what he says and is gentle obtains death peacefully.

50-52. Those who preach ignorance pass through darkness. Those who are false witnesses, liers and deceitful obtain death unconsciously, just as those who abuse the Vedas.

The ferocious, foul-smelling messengers of Yama, with clubs and sticks in their hands, come and seize this wicked person. Having reached a ferocious path he begins to shiver.

53. He cries for his father, mother and sons. His indistinct voice, spoken with effort, appears to be single-lettered.

54. Due to terrible suffering his looks waver and his mouth gets dry due to hard breath. Then wrapped up in suffering, the Jīva departs from the body.

55. Since that very moment the body becomes untouchable and despicable.

Thus I have spoken to you about the form of death of the mortal man.

56. Now I shall answer your query about the peculiarities of form the body takes in different births.

57-58. Due to different actions performed in the previous births, the wandering *jivas* attain different forms, as of a deity, a demon, a yakṣa, man, beast bird, etc. O lord of birds, these are due to the chain of actions, performed in different ages.

59. Now, I shall tell you about the results of actions which a person obtains, so that the strangeness involved is explained clearly.

60. When the sinners have exhausted the fruits of their actions in dreadful hells, they are born on the earth.

61. Now, hear about their characteristics. The killer of a brāhmaṇa attains the form of a deer, horse, pig or camel.

62. The stealer of gold becomes a worm or a germ or a fly. He who lies on the bed of a teacher becomes grass, plant or vine.

63. The slayer of a brāhmaṇa suffers from consumption. A drunkard possesses brown teeth. A gold stealer has bad nails. The defiler of the teacher's bed possesses bad skin.

64. That very thing becomes his mark with which he was associated in the previous birth. If he moves with the wretched people he himself becomes wretched within a year.

65. The sins of the people spread by talk, touch, breathing, going together, eating together, sitting together, worshipping together, by teaching and sexual union.

66. After having sexual intercourse with the wives of other men or after killing a brāhmaṇa, one becomes a brahma-rākṣasa, in a lonely place.

67. The stealer of a jewel is born in a low caste. A man who steals plants becomes a shrew.

68. The thief of corn becomes a rat; that of vehicle, a camel and that of fruit a monkey. He who takes meals un-invited becomes a crow. He who steals utensils becomes a vulture.

69. The stealer of fruit becomes a honey-bee; that of a cow, a vulture; that of a woman's clothes, a white leper and that of juice, possesses no taste at all.

70. The stealer of bronze becomes a swan; so also the stealer of other's possessions. The slayer of his teacher becomes epileptic and the performer of cruel deeds becomes a dwarf.

71-72. He who discards his wife becomes an animal to be killed by a hunter. He who snatches the possessions of a deity or a brāhmaṇa suffers from jaundice. He who eats meat becomes a leper. He who does not return the deposit becomes one-eyed. He who lives on the earning of his wife becames lame.

73. He who discards progeny and wife encounters ill-luck. He who eats sweets only becomes rheumatic. He who has sexual union with a brāhmaṇa's wife becomes a jackal.

74. A stealer of bed becomes kṣapaṇaka[1], and that of clothes becomes a moth. He who envies is born blind. He who steals a lamp becomes a beggar.

75. He who kills a friend becomes an owl. He who abuses the ancestors suffers from consumption. He who speaks lies cannot speak properly. He who gives false witness suffers from dropsy.

76. He who disturbs a marriage is born as a mosquito. He who eases himself on crossroads is born as a bull.

77. He who spoils a young girl becomes a eunuch. He who sells the Vedas becomes a leopard. He who performs a sacrifice but not in the prescribed manner becomes a pig.

1. A Baddha or Jain mendicant.

78. He who eats here and there becomes a cat. He who sets fire to a forest becomes a glow-worm. He who eats the stale food becomes a worm. He who envies others becomes a bee.

79. He who sets fire becomes a leper. He who does not give gifts becomes a bull. A stealer of cows becomes a serpent; that of food suffers from dyspepsia.

80. A stealer of water becomes a fish, that of milk a crane. He who gives stale food to a brāhmaṇa becomes hunch-backed.

81. If he steals fruits, his progeny dies, O bird. If he eats alone without giving a morsel of it to anyone else, he becomes issueless.

82. If he does not opt for Sannyāsa he becomes an evil spirit in the desert. A stealer of water becomes a *Cātaka*; that of book is born blind.

83. He who promises but does not give it to the *brāhmaṇas* becomes a jackal. He who earns the blame of the people becomes a tortoise.

84. A seller of fruits meets with bad luck. He who marries a Śūdra woman, becomes a wolf. He who touches fire with foot becomes a cat. He who eats another's meat suffers from diseases.

85. He who breaks a water-reservoir becomes a fish. He who hears neither Hari's tale, nor the praise of the good suffers from ear disease.

86-87. He who takes out a morsel from another's mouth becomes a blockhead. He who steals the deity's utensils suffers from *gaṇḍamālā*[1]. He who observes religion without sincerity suffers from a skin disease.

88. A treacherous fellow suffers from head-ache. He who is against Śiva suffers from the disease of genital organ.

89. And the women too who commit these sins suffer in the similar way or they become wives of persons suffering in the aforesaid manner.

90. After their present life they reach hell. Know that I have told you all this in short, O bird ! Just as there are many kinds of disease so also there are many kinds of man.

1. Inflammation of the glands of the neck.

91. In this way, due to the variety of their actions, men attain happiness or grief. Thus, I have told you about the strangeness of human nature. Good actions give good results and bad actions give bad results.

92. In this way your queries are answered completely.

CHAPTER THREE

Description of Hell

Sūta said:

1. Thus encouraged, Garuḍa asked about the description of Hells, being curious to know about their nature and function.

Garuḍa said:

2. O Lord, tell me about the nature and division of hells where the evil-doers are thrown mercilessly.

Lord Kṛṣṇa said:

3. O younger brother of Aruṇa, there are thousands of hells. It is not possible to describe all of them in detail. I shall tell you about the principal hells thoroughly.

4. The principal hell is *Raurava*. The person who tells lies and gives false evidence goes to this hell.

5. Raurava is two thousand yojanas in measurement. There is a knee-deep pit, difficult to cross.

6. It is levelled upto the ground by a heap of burning coal. And the ground there is well-heated by fire.

7. The servants of Yama leave the sinner there in the middle. Burnt by burning fire he runs helter-skelter.

8. At every step his foot is burnt. Day and night he moves here and there lifting and putting his feet.

9. There he is left along a thousand Yojanas. Then for the purgation of remaining sins he goes to other hells.

10. Thus I have told you about the first hell named *Raurava*. Now, O bird, hear about the hell called *Mahāraurava*.

11. It is five thousand Yojanas in measurement. It has copper-coloured earth scorched below.

12. When heated by it, the earth shines like lightning. It appears extremely fierce to the sinner.

13. The servants of Yama tie hands and feet of the sinner and throw him in this hell where he goes down rolling.

14. While rolling down in the way he is bit by fearful crows, cranes, ants, mosquitoes and scorpions.

15. Thus being burnt, he loses his wits and cries restlessly, 'O father, O father,' again and again, but attains no peace.

16. The persons who have committed sins with bad intentions are thrown into this hell and get release from there only from myriads of years.

17. Then there is another hell by name and nature *Atiśita* (very cold). It is as big as Mahāraurava and full of dense darkness.

18. There in the fierce darkness, the sinners are tied and left, suffering from cold. Meeting each other they clasp lightly.

19. Shivering with cold their teeth sound loudly. Even there the overpowering trouble of hunger and thirst exists, O Garuḍa.

20. The fierce wind blowing over the blocks of ice pierces the bones. The hungry men consume decayed marrow, blood and bones.

21. Meeting together and clasping each other they wander here and there. The persons who had been hoarding wealth suffer too much in that darkness, O the best of birds.

22. Then there is another hell called *Nṛkṛntana*.

23. A series of potter's wheel is moving round and round there, O bird. There the sinners, whose feet and head are tied by a string are held by Yama's servants in their fingers.

24-25. O bird, their life is not destroyed but their organs are cut into hundred pieces and restored again to their original position. Thus for thousands of years, the sinners rotate till their sins are exhausted completely.

26-27. Now hear, I shall tell you about the hell named Apratiṣṭha. The people who go to this hell suffer intensely. There too the potter's wheels and the ghaṭīyantra operate constantly.

28. Those sinners who had caused untold sufferings to men are placed there on the potter's wheels and rotate incessantly.

29. They remain there for thousands of years, tied as they are to *ghaṭīyantra*[1] like the water-pots.

30. The sinners rotate there vomitting blood again and again. Their intestines come out through mouth and their eyes are suspended by intestines.

31. Now hear about another hell named Asipatravana, where the sinners suffer unbearable miseries.

32-33. There over a thousand *Yojanas* a fierce fire burns with seven fierce rays. The sinners thrown in this hell feel burnt without recess. In the midst is seen a tree with a big trunk, overgrown with cool and smooth leaves which are torn here and there, O Garuḍa.

34-36. There powerful dogs roam about, always eager to eat meat. They have fierce jaws, fierce mouths and are powerful like tigers. Then seeing in front, the forest with cool shade, the miserable sinners suffer from hunger and heat, run to it, crying 'O mother, O brother, O father.'

37-38. Then their feet burn by the ground-fire. Still then, a very cool wind blows forcefully which makes those sharp blades fall upon them. Cut into pieces they fall in the burning fire.

39-40. Then the licking dogs tear their bodies into pieces even as they weep woefully. Thus I have told you about the *Asipatravana*.

41. Now hear about a more fierce hell called Taptakumbha, where all around are kept heated pitchers full of burning flames.

42. The pitchers are full of burning fire, hot oil and iron filings. Therein are thrown the sinners by the attendants of Yama.

1. A machine for raising water.

43. They (the attendants of Yama) boil their bodies disintegrating, marrow flowing out, heads, eyes and bones breaking.

44. Fierce vultures tear them taking them out and again throwing them in. They boil there till they are merged into oil.

45. When their head, limbs, sinews, flesh, skin and bones are liquefied, then Yama's servants stir them with a ladle.

46. The sinners are boiled in oil in Yama's abode. Thus I have narrated to you in detail about Tapta-Kumbha, O bird.

47-48. So the first hell is *Raurava*, the second *Mahāraurava*, the third *Atiśīta*, the fourth *Niṣkṛntana*, the fifth *Apratiṣṭha* and the sixth *Asitapatravana* and the seventh *Taptakumbha*. These are the seven hells.

49. We hear about some other hells also where the sinners fall according to their sins.

50-53. They are *Rodha*, *Śūkara*, *Tāla*, *Taptakumbha*, *Mahājvāla*, *Śabala*, *Vimohana*, *Krimi*, *Kṛmibhakṣa*, *Lālābhakṣa*, *Viṣāñjana*, *Adhaḥśiras*, *Pūyavaha*, *Rudhirāndha*, *Viḍbhuj*, *Vaitaraṇi*, *Suma*, *Asipatra Vana*, *Agnijvāla*, *Mahāghora*, *Sandaṁśa*, *Abhojana*, *Tamas*, *Kālasūtra*, *Loha*, *Abhida*, *Apratiṣṭha*, *Avīci*.

54. These dark hells are situated in Yama's country. Herein fall the sinners in the order of their sins.

55. These hells, Raurava, etc, lie below the earth. Now hear about the sins which drive the sinners to particular hells.

56. A man who kills a cow, a foetus or indulges in arson, falls in Rodha. A killer of brāhmaṇa falls in Śūkara. So also a drunkard, a stealer of gold, a killer of kṣatriya or vaiśya falls in Tāla.

57. He who kills a brāhmaṇa or defiles his teacher's bed or has sexual union with his sister falls in Taptakumbha. So also a soldier who speaks lies.

58. In the similar way, he who sells liquor or he who discards a devotee also falls there.

59. He who co-habits with his daughter or daughter-in-law, he who sells Veda, or he who blames the Vedas falls into Mahājvāla.

60. He who insults his teacher or abuses him or he who co-habits with an unworthy woman falls into Śabala.

61. He who transgresses codes of moral conduct prescribed for the conduct of war falls into Vimohana. He who does an undesirable act falls into Kṛmibhakṣa.

62-63. He who holds no honour for deities or the twice-born brāhmaṇas falls into Lālābhakṣa. A potter who digs pits or a physician who flouts trust or a person who sets fire to parks, falls into Viṣāñjana. So also a brāhmaṇa who receives prohibited gifts or performs sacrifice for a wrong person.

64-65. Or a Kṣatriya who does not live by valour falls into Adhomukha. He who sells milk, liquor, meat or cuts wood or deals in scents, juices, gingelly seeds, falls into fierce Pūyavaha. He who catches cocks, eats pigs, birds, deer and goats falls into this hell.

66-67. He who deals in buffaloes, or a juggler or he who sells liquor, an actor, or brāhmaṇa who is a bird-hunter or a village-priest who indulges in arson or he who administers poison or he who is a pump or he who sells soma, or a drunkard, a meat-eater or a killer of animals—

68. All these fall into Rudhirāndha. Those who administer poison to their guests, sitting in a row, fall into the fierce hell Viḍbhuj. There is no doubt in this.

69. He who drinks wine falls into Vaitaraṇī. He who calls others by bad names falls into Mūtra.

70. He who has not lived a pious life falls into Asitapatravana. So also he who is hot-tempered. A deer-hunter falls into Agnijvāla where he is eaten by the crows.

71. The person who breaks his vow during the course of sacrifice falls into Sandaṁśa. So also brahmacārins who discharge their semen in dream.

72. The fathers who are taught by their sons or who receive orders from them fall into Abhojana.

73. Those who perform acts violating the rules of their Varṇa and Āśrama, on account of anger or pleasure go to hell.

74. There is the hot Raurava above and the cold Tāmasa below.

75. In this way, the hells are situated one below the other. The climax of misery is due to bad acts.

76. And the climax of joy accrues from good acts. The gods look down and see the fierce hells.

77. The sinners of hell also look up and see the gods above. There are thus hundreds of hells, O bird.

78-79. Daily in the hell, the sinners are cooked, burnt, torn, broken, pounded, moistened, boiled, heated and blown by winds. A day in hell is equal to one hundred years of the mortal.

80-82. Having crossed these, the sinner is reborn as a worm, a germ, a fly, a one-hoofed creature, a wild elephant, a cow, an ass, a horse, a mule, a buffalo, śarabha, a camarī, a six-hoofed animal or one having five nails. In these and other *yonis* he takes birth.

83. If born as a human being he becomes hunch-backed or a dwarf or a cāṇḍāla in wretched yonis.

84. The sinner is born again and again and dies again and again till he has exhausted his sin and acquired virtue.

85. Then some time he steps into the yoni of Śūdra or Vaiśya or Kṣatriya or Brāhmaṇa or a deity.

86. Thus I have told you how a sinner falls into hell. Now I shall tell you how and where the virtuous go after death.

87. The virtuous obtain good yonis as directed by Yama. Immediately after the soul leaves the body, the Gandharvas come singing and dancing, adorned with garlands and anklets.

88. And then appear splendid aerial cars decorated with sweet smelling garlands (which take the virtuous souls to heaven).

89-90. When their merits are exhausted, the virtuous souls fall from heaven and are born in the houses of kings or nobles of illustrious character, where they enjoy various pleasures. Thus men go up and down the ladder as stated before.

91. Death is certain for the mortals who are born on this earth. The soul of the sinner leaves the body from the downward path, undoubtedly.

92. Earth mingles with earth, water with water, fire with fire, air with air.

93. Sky mingles with sky, pervading all around. In the body there exist love, anger and five organs.

94. O Garuḍa, there abide thieves in the body in the form of love, anger and pride. Mind is the leader of all these.

95. Death is temporal. The *jiva* along with sins, virtues and five subtle organs enters into new body just as a householder enters into a new house when the old one is burnt.

96-98. In the body exist seven elements and seven Kośas. All these exist in the body—urine, waste, allied matter, bile, cough, marrow, flesh, fat, bones, semen, sinews which are destroyed along with the body (when the soul departs).

99. Thus I have told you, O bird, about the end of all bodies. Now I shall tell you, O bird, how their body looks like.

100-102. It is a shrub of sinews adorned with three trunks, combined with organs and having nine openings. Full of sensual pleasures, love, anger, desire and envy, possessing a high way robber in the form of greed, caught in the net of avarice and covered by the cloth of affection. It is bound by illusion and inhabited by greed.

103. These qualities inhere in the bodies of all creatures. Those who do not realize their self are nothing more than beasts.

104. Thus I have told you about the fourfold body. Formerly, eightyfour yonis were created [for the jīva to pass through].

105. While narrating about the hell I told you about all these—that are born from the earth, from the sweat, from the eggs and from the embryo.

106. I shall tell you more as and when necessary or do you possess a desire to ask more?

CHAPTER FOUR

Lord Kṛṣṇa said:

1. Whatever sin a man commits consciously or unconsciously stands in need of purification by means of atonement.

2. The wise one should first perform ten types of baths

beginning with *bhasma*. These should be observed as far as possible for six years repeatedly.

3. Or half of that or half of that or half of the half of that. Then as far as he can he should donate ten gifts. Now hear about them.

4. Cow, earth, gingelly seeds, gold, butter, cloth, grains, sugar, silver and salt—these are known as ten gifts.

5. He should make these gifts to those who have come during atonement. Then to cross the river *Vaitaraṇī*[1] full of pus and blood, at Yama's door he should donate the Vaitaraṇī cow.

6. A black cow with black udders is called Vaitaraṇī.

7-8. Gingelly seeds, iron, gold, cotton, salt, seven grains, earth and cow—these are all pure. These eight precious gifts should be given to a learned brāhmaṇa by the dying person. I shall now tell you about the form of *pada*.

9. Umbrella, shoes, clothes, ring, gourd, seat, vessel and food—these are the eight kinds of pada.

10. A vessel full of gingelly seeds or butter and a bed with all its epuipment should be gifted or all those articles which are liked by the donor.

11. Horse, chariot, she-buffalo, fan and cloth—all these should be given to the brāhmaṇas.

12-14. O Lord, these gifts and others should be given as far as possible. He who has done atonement, given ten gifts on this earth, or the gift of Vaitaraṇī cow or eight gifts or the gifts of a vessel full of gingelly seeds or clarified butter or the gift of bed or of *pada*, as prescribed in the Śāstras does not go hell. The wise have prescribed the gift of salt to be given freely.

15. The salt is produced from the body of Viṣṇu. When the soul of the dying person does not leave the body but lingers on, the salt should be gifted as it opens the door of the heaven.

16. Whatever gifts a man has given himself they all stand in his favour (at the hour of death).

17. O bird, the man who has completed atonement in all its parts is placed in heaven, after all his sins are washed away.

1. Name of the river of hell.

18. O noble bird, since the cow's milk is nectar, whosoever gifts a cow attains immortality.

19. Whosoever gives the eight gifts lives in the abode of the Gandharvas.

20. He gets shelter even in the tortuous hell named Raudra where the sinners are burnt. If he gifts an umbrella, he encounters the comforting shade in the way.

21. So also he passes comfortably through the fierce Asipatravana. If he gifts shoes he moves there too mounting a horse.

22. If he gifts food and seat he eats sitting comfortably in the way. If he gifts a water-jar he feels comfortable even in the waterless region.

23. He who gifts clothes and ornaments liberally is not tortured by the fierce messengers of Yama who are black and yellow in colour.

24. O bird, if a vessel full of gingelly seeds is donated to a Brāhmaṇa it destroys all the three types of sins born out of his voice, body and mind.

25-26. If he gifts a vessel full of clarified butter he stays in Rudraloka. If he gifts a bed along with all its equipment he rides an aerial car in the company of fairies and enjoys in the abode of Indra for sixty-thousand years.

27-28. After falling down from Indraloka he becomes a monarch in this world. He who gifts a young faultless horse along with all equipment to a Brāhmaṇa lives in heaven, O bird, for years, equal to the number of hair on the body of a horse.

29-30. If he gifts a chariot drawn by four horses along with the contiguous equipment to a learned Brāhmaṇa he reaps the benefit of performing a Rājasūya.[1]

31. If he donates to a Brāhmaṇa a milk-yielding buffalo with her plump hind parts, and a golden ornament on her forehead, accompanied by her satiated calf, what wonder is there that he attains heaven.

1. A great sacrifice performed by a universal monarch (in which the tributary princes also took part) at the time of his coronation as a mark of his undisputed sovereignty.

32. If he donates a fan (*Tālavṛnta*), he is fanned by air in the way. If he donates cloth he becomes full of lustre, wealth and prosperity.

33. If he donates a horse along with salt, food and other ingredients to a Brāhmaṇa, his family does not suffer a break and he goes to heaven after death.

34. O bird, there is a difference in result according to faith and gifts.

35. He who donates water and salt gets enjoyment in distress.

36. He who donates food with a heart purified by faith is satiated even without food.

37. If he accepts sannyāsa as prescribed in the sacred texts he is not reborn but is merged into Brahma itself.

38. If he dies at a sacred place he attains *mokṣa* (release from re-birth) after dying there. If he dies in the way, each and every step he has taken in reaching this place procures for him the fruit of performing a sacrifice. There is no doubt in this.

39. If he undertakes a fast unto death he does not return to this world, O bird.

40. I have given the answer to your queries about gifts. Now, I shall tell you about the obsequies and the funeral rites of the deceased.

41. When it is ascertained that life has gone out of the body, the son should bathe and wash the corpse with pure water without delay.

42. Having clothed it afresh they should smear the body with the sandal-paste. The son or the successor should perform the *ekoddiṣṭa*[1] rite afterwards.

43. Then the arrangement for cremating the corpse should be made as far as the means allow.

44. The following four should not be undertaken in the cremation rite: āvāhana, arcana, patrālambha and avagāhana.

1. Funeral rite performed for one definite individual deceased, not including other ancestors.

Let there be saṅkalpa for each gift and let there be a piṇḍadāna.

45. The five articles common to every sacrifice should not be there. The libation of water should be given but not the trio :

46. Svadhā-Vācana, Āśiṣ and Tilaka, O bird. A vessel full of mustard should be given. Iron should also be gifted.

47. The piṇḍa-cālana rite is followed but not the following three, pracchādana, visarga and svastivācana.

48-49. Procedure has been laid down for six śrāddhas, at six places; at the place of death, at the door, at the crossroads, at the place of rest, on the wood-pile and at the collection rite. The dead body is called Śava at the place of death. The deity Earth is pleased thereby.

50. It is called pāntha at the door; the deity Vāstu is pleased. It is called khecara at the crossroads; the deity Bhūta is pleased.

51. It is called bhūta in the resting place. The ten quarters are satisfied thereby. It is called sādhaka on the pyre and preta at the collection-rite.

52. Holding gingelly seeds, darbha, clarified butter, the sons and other relatives go round the pyre reciting gāthā or the sūkta of Yama.

53. Taking cow, horse, man and bull everyday Yama is not satiated just as a wicked person is not satiated with wine.

54. They should recite the *gāthā*[1] or the hymn *apeta*[2] in the way. The relatives accompany the corpse to a forest in the southern direction.

55. O bird, in the aforesaid manner the two śrāddhas should be performed in the way.

56. Then the corpse should be laid lightly on the earth with its head to the south and the aforesaid śrāddha should be performed. The sons should fetch dry grass, dry pieces of wood and gingelly seeds.

57. If these are fetched by a Śūdra each and every act done in favour of the deceased would go futile. The performer of the funeral rite should wear the sacred thread over the right

1. A religious verse but not belonging to any one of the Vedas.
2. RV. 10. 14. 9.

shoulder and should sit, along with the mourners, facing the south.

58. O bird, an altar should be made there as prescribed. The cloth for the corpse should be torn into twofold pieces and the corpse should be covered with the one-half.

59. The other half should be spread over the earth. The piṇḍa should be kept in the hand of the deceased as stated before.

60. The corpse should be anointed with the clarified butter. Now hear about the *piṇḍa-vidhi* for the deceased prior to his cremation.

61. By virtue of the aforesaid five piṇḍas, the departed soul attains fitness for becoming a mane (*pitar*). Or else, it attains the form of a demon.

62. Having cleansed and smeared the ground at the altar, the fire should be lit as prescribed.

63-64. Having worshipped the deity named *Kravyāda* with flowers and grains of rice, the wise man should lighten fire according to the Vedic rites, but avoid cāṇḍāla, citā or patita fires.

65. "You are the creator of creatures, the birth-place of the world, the protector of the people. Please therefore, consume the corpse and carry the soul to the heaven"—having thus worshipped the deity *Kravyāda*—the meat-devouring fire-god, he should set fire to the corpse.

66-68. When the body is half-burnt, a quantity of clarified butter should be poured over it with the mantra: 'You are born from it, you be born again. Let this be for heaven, Svāhā'. He should recite this mantra announcing the name of the deceased and pour forth butter along with the gingelly seeds while the relatives weep loudly. This gives comfort to the departed soul (still wandering in the air). After cremating the corpse the rite of collection should be done there.

69-70. O bird, Preta-piṇḍa is given in order to comfort the deceased. Then having circumambulated the pyre and casting a mournful look at it, the mourners should go for bath muttering the hymn, with the youth marching ahead.

71. Then having reached water and washed cloth, they should wear the same saying for the deceased—we are taking bath.

72-73. Then they all, each wearing one cloth only, with shaven heads, wearing the sacred thread over the right shoulder should enter water silently.

74-76. The bathers should not agitate water. Then coming out of the water to the bank, tying their Śikhā (knot of hair in the centre of the head) they should take in their right hand Kuśas and water with the gingelly seeds and offer the same in the southern direction, pouring it from the paitṛka-tīrtha over the earth silently once, thrice or ten times.

77. 'Be gratified, be gratified with this piṇḍa, O preta of such and such gotra. Let this water reach you,' reciting this formula he should let the water go down.

78. After giving the water offerings he should cleanse his teeth, O bird. The water-offering shall be done regularly for nine days by all his kith and kin.

79. Then coming out of water, they wear the same clothes as before, while they wrinse the bathing dress which they spread over the clean earth (for drying).

80. They should abstain from shedding tears while giving the water-offerings after cremation. But if they shed tears and vomit cough, the departed spirit consumes the same helplessly.

81. Hence, they should neither weep nor cough. The entire ritual should be performed according to the means.

82-85. And when they have sat quietly, a learned person well versed in the Purāṇa should alleviate their sorrow discoursing on the temporality of time and the unsubstantial nature of the universe. He should tell them about the hollowness of life and if anybody searches substance inside the human body resembling the trunk of a banana plant he is a perfect fool; for it is like the water bubble. The body is constituted of five elements and if it goes back to the elements by virtue of bodily actions what is there to be lamented for ? The earth, ocean and even deities are bound to be destroyed. The same fate awaits the universe which has arisen like a bubble. How it can escape destruction ? Thus, he should speak to them about the transient nature of life, while they all sit on the soft grass in the courtyard of the cremation ground.

86-87. Having heard this, the mourners should return home with the youngsters walking in front. At the door of their house they should chew the margosa leaves, wrinse their mouths with water and touching cowdung, gingelly seeds, durvā grass, coral, bull or any other auspicious thing and keeping their feet lightly on the stone should enter the house.

88-90. Āhitāgni[1] should kindle the sacred fire according to the Vedic rites. He should not dig up the earth for less than two years. The water-offering should be made (on return to the house).

A woman who has been chaste and faithful to her husband should mount on the pyre after bowing to her (deceased) husband before the funeral rites start. One who gets away from the pyre due to fainting should observe the vow named prājāpatya.

91. One who ascends the pyre and follows up her husband stays in heaven for a period equal to the number of hair on the body, three and a half crore.

92. Just as the snake-charmer takes out the snake from the hole so also she takes out her husband from hell and enjoys with him in paradise.

93. She who ascends the pyre goes to heaven. She is praised by the celestial nymphs and enjoys with her husband so long as the fourteen Indras rule in heaven successively.

94. Even if the man has killed a brāhmaṇa or a friend or any other person of noble conduct he is purified of sins by his wife who ascends his pyre.

95. A woman who enters fire after the death of her husband prospers in the heaven like Arundhatī.

96. Until and unless the woman burns herself after her husband's death she is never released from the bond of her sex.

97. A woman who follows her husband purifies the three families on her mother's side, the three families on her father's side and the three families on her husband's side.

98-100. That woman is chaste who is sad when her husband is sad, who is glad when her husband is glad and who pines when he is out of station and dies when he is dead. Common rites are enjoined for all women right from brāhmaṇī

1. A twice-born who consecrates the sacred fire.

to Cāṇḍālī except for those who are pregnant or who have young children.

101. O bird, I have told you in general about the method of cremating the corpse. Do you want to hear something more with reference to it.

Garuḍa said:

102. If a man dies out of station and his bones too are destroyed, then how should the rite of cremation be performed. Tell me, O lord of the world!

Lord Kṛṣṇa said:

103. If the bones of a person who died abroad are not available, I shall tell you about the procedure of rites of his death.

104-109. O Garuḍa, hear. I shall now tell you the great secret about the rite of death for those who die through serpent, tiger, toothed, head-breaking horned animals, disease, stone, water, brāhmaṇa, dog, nails, iron; those who die of hunger, poison, fire and cholerá; those who are killed by a bull, a thief, a cāṇḍāla, a woman in her menses, śunakī, śūdra, washerman; those who commit suicide or die by fall from a tree, hill, wall or precipice; those who die in water, on cot, in firmament, in bondage; those who are killed by Ūrdhvocchiṣṭa, Ardhocchiṣṭha or Ubhayocchiṣṭa; those who die of wounds by weapon on horseback.

110-112. All these deaths are known as bad deaths where no rite of Aurdhvadehika or piṇḍa-dāna is performed. If the same is done by mistake it is all destroyed in the air.

113. But desiring welfare of the deceased and out of fear of the people's reproach his sons or grandsons or sapiṇḍas should perform *Nārāyaṇa Bali*, O bird.

114. By that the relatives of the deceased are purified. This is stated by Yama. There are no other means. When Nārāyaṇa Bali is performed they become fit for aurdhvadehika.

115-116. Except Nārāyaṇa Bali, there is no rite for their purification. The Nārāyaṇa Bali should be performed in some holy place, through the Brāhmaṇas, preferably in the temple of lord Kṛṣṇa for the sake of purification. At first, water-offering should be made by the Brāhmaṇas well versed in the Veda and the Purāṇa.

117. This should be done for lord Viṣṇu with herbs and akṣatas mingled with water by reciting the Puruṣa-sūkta or the mantras of Viṣṇu, facing south and remembering Viṣṇu as well as the deceased.

118. Viṣṇu should be thought of as beginningless, bearing conch, discus and mace, who is immortal, who has eyes as lovely as a lotus and who renders mokṣa to the preta.

119. At the end of water-offering he should remain calm, desireless and free from envy.

120. Having controlled his sense-organs and mind and being full of devotion he should devoutly perform the eleven śrāddhas.

121. Performing all rites with concentrated mind he should give water, rice, barley, wheat and long pepper.

122. He should give ablation, coins, umbrella, turban, milk with honey.

123. Eight types of pada should also be given along with clothes and shoes. These should be given essentially for all sins without break.

124. The piṇḍas should be placed on the earth together with incense, flowers aud akṣata and be gifted to Brāhmaṇas as prescribed for the ritual.

125. Water-offering should be made by conch, sword, or copper, by each separately.

126. He should meditate while kneeling on the earth on Brahmā, Viṣṇu, Rudra, Yama and the deceased who is the fifth.

127. Then in separate pitchers he should keep five jewels, cloth, sacred thread and *Mudga*.

128. Five śrāddhas should be done for deities as prescribed in the ritual. Then on each piṇḍa, separately, water should be poured.

129. In conch or in a vessel of copper and if that is not available, in an earthen pitcher he should keep water full of gingelly seeds[1] and containing specified herbs.

1. Water with sesamum seed offered to the dead as libation.

130-132. The copper-vessel with gold and *dakṣiṇā* should be given to a learned brāhmaṇa. For Yama iron with gingelly seeds should be given together with dakṣiṇā.

Thus by giving Viṣṇu-bali according to the procedure and his means he can secure the release of the deceased very quickly. There is no doubt in this. If a person dies of snake-bite, there is a specific rite to be performed for him.

133. A serpent made of gold and a milch cow should be given to a brāhmaṇa in the prescribed way. Thereby he becomes free from the debt which he owes to the manes.

134. By giving snake-ablation thus, he becomes free from *Sarpadoṣa*.

135. Then he should make an effigy of the deceased out of Oṣadhis[1] and the stalks of palāśa. O bird, I shall now tell you about the details: Black-deer-skin should be spread and the effigy should be made of grass.

136. Three hundred and sixty stalks should be spread over his limbs separately.

137. Forty represent the bones on the head, ten on neck, twenty on chest, twenty on stomach.

138. A hundred on both the hands, twenty on waist, a hundred on both thighs, three hundred on both shanks.

139. Four on the generating organ, six on both scrotums, ten on the toes.

140. Coconut on the head, tumba for palate, five jewels for mouth and plantain for tongue.

141. Nālikā for intestine, vālukā for nose, earth for marrow, so for all haritāla and manśśilā.

142. Mercury for semen, brass for the waist, Manaśśilā for all limbs, tilapakva for the joints.

143. Yava-piṣṭa for meat, honey for blood, jaṭā-jūṣa for hair and deer-skin for skin.

144-146. Tālapatra for ears, guñjas for breasts, śatapatra for nose, lotus for navel, Bṛñjala for scrotums, gṛñjana for penis, clarified butter for the navel and trapu for kaupīna,

1. Herbs or plants in general.

pearls (mauktika) for the breasts, saffron, camphor, aguru, incense for the forehead and scented garlands for the neck.

147-148. Thus the garment and the silk-thread on the chest, ṛddhi-vṛddhi for the arms, Kapardikas for eyes, seeds of pomegranate for teeth, campaka for fingers, sindhūra for eye-corners and tāmbūla for the gift.

149. Thus the effigy of the deceased should be made of Oṣadhis. Worship should be performed as prescribed, before the sacrificial fire with the sacrificial vessels if the deceased person kept fire in the house.

150. Reciting the mantra *Śriyaḥ punantu me śiraḥ* or *imam me Varuṇa*[1] he should sprinkle water made pure by contact with the Śālagrāma śilā. He should gift a gentle milch cow to a Brāhmaṇa for the propitiation of god Viṣṇu.

151-252. Gingelly seeds, iron, gold, cotton, salt, seven grains, earth,—all these are called purificatory. Then a vessel full of gingelly seeds should be given as also the gift of pada.

153. A Vaiṣṇava śrāddha should be performed for the release of the deceased from pretahood. Thus thinking about Viṣṇu in the heart one can get the deceased released immediately from Pretahood.

154. Having made the effigy of the deceased in this way, he should burn the same in the prescribed way. As for the purification of the deceased he should observe atonement.

155. Three kṛcchras should be performed, or six, or twelve, or fifteen, for the sake of atonement as prescribed for a Brāhmaṇa.

156. If one cannot do so, one should donate a milch cow or gold. If he cannot do that, he should perform a sort of purification.

157. That which is performed without purification, does not stay. It is all destroyed in the air.

158-161. After purification the rite of aurdhvadehika should be performed for the deceased.

If a person performs obsequies without doing atonement consciously or unconsciously in favour of the deceased, he incurs

1. ṚV. 1.25.19.

sin. I shall now tell you how he can eliminate the sins of omission and commission. If one has set fire to the corpse or taken bath in water, touched or carried the corpse, cut the ropes binding the corpse, or shed tears after cremation or delivered funeral ovation, he is purified by taptakṛcchra. Anyone of those who carry the corpse or cremate the dead may do kaṭodaka-kriyā[1] and perform kṛcchra sāntapana. A little should be done if the cause be small and much should be done if the cause be big.

Garuḍa said :

162. O lord observing good vows, please explain to me the details of kṛcchra, Tapta-kṛcchra and Sāntapana.

Lord Kṛṣṇa said :

163-164. O bird, hear. If he eats for three days in the morning and for three days in the evening and observes fast for three days, the Vrata is called Kṛcchra. If he drinks hot milk, clarified butter and once water in a day and observes fast for one night, the Vrata is called Taptakṛcchra.

165. For one day, each one should take cow's urine, cow-dung, milk, curd, clarified butter and water purified by the holy grass and observe fast the next day, the Vrata is called Kṛcchra sāntapana.

166. O bird, thus I have told you the rites to be performed for durmṛta[2]. He is known mṛta if they perform for him the rite of dīpa-nirvāṇa.

167. Then they should perform cremation and observe impurity for three days. Then for ten days the rite of garta-piṇḍa should be performed for the deceased.

168. All these rites should be performed for the person who died abroad. However, if the person concerned returns home, after his effigy has been burnt thinking him to be dead.

1. Offering water for a funeral libation.
2. One dying an unnatural death.

169. Then the person thought to be dead should take bath in the ghṛtakuṇḍa and go through all the rites from *Jātakarman* onward.

170-71. He should marry his wife again, O bird. If one remains out of station for fifteen or twelve years and his whereabouts remain unknown, his effigy should be burnt. Now hear specially about the death of rajasvalā[1] and sūtikā.[2]

172. When a ṣūtikā is dead, the performers of obsequy do thus: Water is taken in the pitcher. So also pañcagavya[3].

173. Then water is purified by reciting *puṇyāha mantras*. Then the bathing is done by the water cooled by hundred winnowing fans.

174. When the bathing is done they should start the rite of cremation, O lord of birds. The deceased *rajasvalā* is bathed by pañcagavya.

175. Her worn clothes are changed for the fresh ones and the cremation is done as prescribed. Now hear, I shall tell you about the rites to be performed for those who die during the pañcaka.

176-177. The five constellations from Dhaniṣṭhā to Revatī are always inauspicious. Cremation should not be done on these days. It is tortuous to all creatures. Water-offering should also be avoided, for it is inauspicious on these days.

178. All rites should be performed after the Pañcaka is over. If done otherwise, sons or close relatives are affected thereby.

179. If one dies during these constellations and his cremation is performed during this period his family suffers tremendously.

180. Cremation is harmless during the period if the following injunctions are observed strictly. Brāhmaṇas should perform sacrifice along with āhuti mantras.

181-182. Close to the place of corpse, four effigies made of grass should be raised and then thrown into the pyre while the Brāhmaṇas recite the mantras of constellations. Then after

1. A woman during menses.
2. A woman recently delivered, a lying-in woman.
3. The five products of cow taken together—milk, curd, *ghī*, urine and cowdung.

completing the days ef impurity, the rite *śāntikapauṣṭika* should be performed by the sons of the deceased.

183. For the deceased to obtain heaven, cow, gold, butter and gingelly seeds should be gifted.

184. To the Brāhmaṇas should be given gifts to quell all obstacles. Food, shoes, umbrella, gold-coin and clothes should be given as gifts to get release from sin.

185. Thus I have told you all about the rites for the deceased, how the dead goes to Yama's abode and what are the post-death rites over a year for him.

CHAPTER FIVE

The Annual Rite

The lord said :

1. Thus having burnt the corpse, having taken bath and offered sesame-water, they should return home, with woman-folk proceeding ahead.

2. In the way, they should consume leaves of margosa tree and rinse their mouths while sitting on stone.

3. Then having entered the house, the sons and relatives of the deceased should observe *āśauca* for ten nights.

4-5. Having brought food from the market, they should take meals. During the days of impurity, they should not take saline and pungent food. They should take bath thrice a day and abstain from taking meat. The couples should observe celibacy and sleep on the ground separately without touching each other. They should abstain from study as well charity.

6-7. They should wear dirty clothes, move with downward faces and avoid all pleasures. They should leave shampooing of body, hair, etc. They should eat in earthen pots or in those made of dry leaves. They should observe fast on the cremation day or for more number of days during impurity.

Garuḍa said:

8. Sir, you have just stated that they should observe āśāuca. Now please tell us what is this āśauca ? What is its period ?

Lord Kṛṣṇa said:

9-10. The ten-day-period of āṣauca is prescribed for the relatives of the deceased on the father's side. This commences from the hour of birth, also with a view to obtain purity.

11. Since the time of birth, purity can be had after three nights. After death, purity is attained after three days.

12. After teething immediately, after caula overnight, after Vratādeśa for three nights, and for ten nights in other cases.

13. Thus I have told you about *āśauca*[1]. Now I shall tell you in brief how purity is achievable. Water in the open and milk in an earthen pot should be kept for three days.

14. 'Bathe here, drink here', this mantra should be recited, O Kāśyapa. The sticks bound with a string should be placed on the crossroads in the night in order to propitiate the dead person.

15. Bones should be gathered on the first, third, seventh or the ninth day by the relatives.

16. The relatives[2] should touch the body of one another as prescribed, perform actions as far as they can and share in the common water-offerings.

17. Preta-piṇḍa (an offering to the mane) should be given outside, leaving aside grass. Curu[3] should be given in the north-eastern direction, after bath and with calm mind.

18. For the non-purified on the ground, for the purified on the kuśa grass, he should offer nine piṇḍas in nine days i.e. one piṇḍa on each day.

19. After giving the tenth piṇḍa, one becomes pure after

1. Impurity.

2. Kinsmen of the same family, connected by funeral oblations of food and water.

3. An oblation of rice, barley and pulse boiled for presentation to the deities and manes.

the night expires. One may be asagotra (indirect relation), sagotra (direct relation), man or woman.

20. That which is given on the first day should be continued for ten days. It may be rice, saktu[1] or śāka[2].

21. So far as there is *āśauca*, a gift of one añjali should be made, i.e. so much of gift as joined hands can contain.

22. Or else, the number should be equal to the number of days on which the gift is given, O bird, and the number on the last day should be fifty-five.

23. Or these doubled shall be hundred anjalis. When there is *āśauca* for three days anjalis shall be ten.

24. These shall be three on the first day, four on the second day and three on the third day.

25. If one hundred añjalis are given, then thirty should be given on the first day, forty on the second day and thirty on the third day.

26. O bird, thus the water-offering is divided. For performing the rites of the manes, the son is the proper person.

27. *Piṇḍa-praseka* shall be done in silence and with flowers, incense, etc. On the tenth day, bath should be taken outside the village.

28-29. Then they should leave their old clothes, hair, beard and nails. Brāhmaṇa is purified by touching water, Kṣatriya by touching Vehicle, Vaiśya by touching a goad (or a whip) or reins, and Śūdra by touching stick after performing the rites. The relatives, younger in age, should undergo shave.

30. Ṣoḍaśī should be performed by offering sixteen piṇḍas.

31. O bird, the piṇḍas given for ten days—one piṇḍa on each day regularly, by sons, etc. are divided, each one into four.

32. Two parts for the body, the third one for Yama's servants and by the fourth he lives.

33. During nine days and nights, the body is formed. By offering the first piṇḍa, the head of the Preta is formed.

1. The flour of barley first fried and then ground.
2. Any edible leaf, fruit or root used as a vegetable.

34. By the second, ears, eyes and nose. By the third, neck, shoulder, arms and chest.

35. By the fourth piṇḍa, navel and private parts. By the fifth thighs, calves.

36. By the sixth all vital organs, by the seventh nerves, by the eighth teeth and hair, by the ninth semen.

37. By the tenth fulness is achieved, hunger is satisfied. Now, I shall tell you, O Garuḍa, about Madhya-ṣoḍaśī.

38. The eleven beginning with Viṣṇu and ending with Viṣṇu. Then five śrāddhas for the deities. This is called madhya-ṣoḍaśī, O bird.

39. If Nārāyaṇa-bali is to be performed for the atonement of bad death, it should be done on the eleventh day. Vṛṣotsarga[1] rite is also prescribed for such a deceased.

40. If the bull is not released on the eleventh day in favour of the deceased he remains ghost eternally, even if hundred śrāddhas are performed for his sake.

41. If the rite of *piṇḍa*-pālana is done without Vṛṣotsarga then all rites will go in vain.

42. No rite is superior to Vṛṣotsarga. It is prescribed for the deceased and performed by his son, wife, grandson, father or daughter.

43. Vṛṣotsarga is performed only after death. If the bull is released along with four she-calves duly decorated the deceased does not turn into ghost.

44. If the actual bull is not available on the eleventh day, a bull of darbhas and piṣṭa should be made.

45-46. If that too is not available, a bull made of mud and grass should be released. If an alive bull is desired to be released, it should be done on the eleventh day.

47. They should give bed, cow, etc. to the brāhmaṇas in favour of the deceased. Brāhmaṇas should be fed to satisfy the hunger of the departed soul.

48. Now, O Vainateya, I shall tell you about the third Soḍaśī. Twelve for the twelve months and the half yearly one, and sapiṇḍīkaraṇa[2]. These are called third ṣoḍaśī.

1. Setting free a bull on the occasion of a funeral rite.
2. A rite the performance of which qualifies the deceased to share offerings with the Pitṛs.

49. On the twelfth day for the three fortnights, half-yearly, monthly and yearly.

50. This too is called third ṣoḍaśī according to another opinion. If these sixteen preta-śrāddhas are not given,

51. Then his ghosthood becomes permanent, even if hundred śrāddhas are performed for his benefit.

52-53. Śrāddhas are performed on the eleventh or twelfth day, at the beginning of the month, every month, on the date of death, one day or three days, O son of Vinatā, every month, every six months, yearly, or on three fortnights. The rite of sāpiṇḍa[1] is performed after a year or six months.

54. Or after three fortnights, at the rise of a planet or within twelve days, for, the family traditions are many and human life is short.

55. Human life is transitory. It is better therefore to perform the rite of sapiṇḍī-karaṇa within twelve days. O bird, now, I shall tell you about the method of spiṇḍīkaraṇa.

56. O Kāśyapa, it should be done by the process of ekoddiṣṭa. Four vessels should be made ready along with sesame, incense and water.

57. Out of these one is the vessel for the preta, the other three are for the manes. O bird, the performer should sprinkle the three pitṛpātras with the water from the pretapātra.

58. Then four piṇḍas should be offered and libations be made. Thereafter, the preta becomes one with the manes.

59. Then, O bird, when the preta has become one with the manes, the manes should be worshipped along with him.

60. If the woman ascends the pyre of her husband on the same day, then no separate sāpiṇḍya is prescribed for her.

61. If husband and wife are cremated together, there is one *pāka*[2], one *kāla*[3] and one *kartṛ*[4] O bird, you need not entertain any doubt in this.

62. If she ascends the pyre on a different date, she should be offered a separate piṇḍa on the separate date of death.

1. Connection by the offering of rice-balls to the same manes.
2. Cooking.
3. Time.
4. Performer.

63. Every year, nine śrāddhas should be performed together.

64. If the sapiṇḍīkaraṇa is done before a year has passed, then a monthly offering of a water-jar should be made for one year.

65. Nine śrāddhas, sapiṇḍīkaraṇa and sixteen śrāddhas should be done by the eldest son, even though the inheritors have divided property.

66. Women's sāpiṇḍya may be done with the paternal grandmother, or maternal grandmother or with husband, according to the tradition prevailing in different regions.

67. Now, I shall tell you about the time of nine śrāddhas O Kāśyapa bird. The first Śrāddha should be performed on the day of death near the corpse.

68. The second on the same date on the way to cemetery where the mourners take rest; the third on the day at the place when or where they collect the bones.

69. The rest of the śrāddhas on the fifth, seventh, eighth ninth, tenth and eleventh day. These are nine śrāddhas, O bird.

70. The third one is called ṣoḍaśī wherein the procedure is the same as in ekoddiṣṭa.

71. The six śrāddhas are performed on the first, third, fifth, seventh, ninth and eleventh day.

72. These six are told but they may be nine by addition. I have stated six according to different traditions of the sages.

73. I have preferred tradition but practice is not altogether ruled out. On each of the first and second days a sacred thread should be gifted.

74. So, when the brāhmaṇas are feasting, piṇḍa should be offered to the preta. Then the host and the brāhmaṇa should indulge in question-answer dialogue.

75. When the same is completed then "such and such (N. of the preta) should become perennial" is to be uttered. The *ekoddiṣṭa* is perennial, please note.

76. The sixteen śrāddhas after sapiṇḍīkaraṇa should be ekoddiṣṭa except those performed on festival days.

77. He who performs them annually should perform them in that manner. The preta eats twice in a day on the eleventh and the twelfth day.

78. To each—husband and wife—a piṇḍa should be offered. Once sāpiṇḍya is completed, the pretahood ends.

79. For one year, a lamp should be kept burning at the door of the house. Food, lamp, water, cloth, or whatever else is given, the same gives satisfaction to the preta.

80. In brief, I have told you the period of sapiṇḍīkaraṇa as one year.

81-82. Now, I shall tell you how people go to Yama's abode. On the thirteenth day, after śravaṇā-karma, he is captured by Yama's attendents, just as you capture the serpents by neck, O Garuḍa. He is led in the way like the caught-up monkey.

83. The body attains a form like air. Born out of piṇḍa it assumes a shape different from the one born from the womb of the mother.

84-89. According to age, state, etc it differs. Eightysix thousand yojanas long is the distance between the mortal's and Yama's worlds. Two hundred and a half yojanas and forty-seven krośas he covers daily. So in forty-eight and thirty days he reaches Yama's city, being dragged by Yama's servants. Thus when the way is being covered by the sinner, what happens then, you hear, O Garuḍa. For thirteen days, he is tied with fierce nooses, by Yama's servants with goad in hand, with looks frowning and the hand engaged in striking with sticks. Thus, he is dragged towards the south.

90. There, on the fierce way, full of thorny grass, thorns, anthills, sharp stones, which contains burning fires as well as hundreds of charms.

91. Which is heated by a burning sun, is infested by dogs or flies, which echoes with the howling sounds of jackals, he is dragged by Yama's messengers.

92. The sinner perishes when his body is burnt in Yama's abode.

93. Thus as his body is eaten, torn asunder, pierced, he suffers immensely.

94. On account of his own deeds, though he is dead. There are sixteen cities in this way. Now hear about them.

95. Yāmya, Sauripura, Nagendrabhavana, Gandharva, Ṣạilāgama, Krauñca, Krūrapura, Vicitra-bhavana, Bahvāpada, Duḥkhada, Nānākrandapura, Sutaptabhavana, Raudra, Payovarṣaṇa, Śītāḍhya, and Bahubhīti — these are the sixteen cities not seen by you.

96. Then he goes to Yāmya saying, 'O son, O son' he cries painfully remembering his own misdeeds.

97. He reaches that city on the eighteenth day, O Tārkhya. There is Puṣpabhadrā river and a good-looking tree.

98. He wants to take rest there but Yama's servants do not bid him do so.

99. Here, on the earth, whatever is given by his sons every month, rice-ball, etc. due to affection or kindness he eats the same and then he goes to Sauripura. As he goes he cries being beaten with clubs.

100. "I did not construct a tank for satiating thirsty people, beasts and birds. I did not make a pasture for satisfying cattle. Now, O body, suffer for whatever you have done".

101. King Jaṅgama rules in that city who can assume any shape at will. Out of fear of that king's frowns he eats the rice-ball.

102. Whatever is offered to him in the three fortnights together with the oblation of water, he eats and drinks. He is then struck with clubs.

103. Neither daily gifts were given nor pastures made, nor the sacred books such as the Vedas and Dharma-śāstras offered in charity nor Purāṇas heard. Now, O body, you suffer for your acts of omission.

104. Having reached Nagendra nagar and having eaten the riceballs offered by the relatives in the second month, he moves further.

105. As he goes onward he laments being struck with the sword. "A fool that I am, I have lost everything. to others.

106. I obtained manhood by virtue of accumulated merit" Then he reaches Gandhamādana in the third month.

107. There he eats the rice-ball. Then he goes further. As he goes further he laments being beaten by Yama's emissary

108. I neither gave gifts nor poured oblations into fire nor undertook penance in the caves of the Himālayas nor bathed into Gaṅgā's water. Hence, O body, suffer for whatever you have done.

109. He reaches Śailāgama in the fourth month. There stones rain upon him continuously, O bird.

110. Having eaten the fourth monthly oblation he moves. As he moves, he is struck again with the stones by the messengers.

111. "I followed neither Jñānamārga[1] nor Yogamārga[2] nor Karma-mārga[3] nor Bhaktimārga[4]. Nor did I remain in the company of saints. O body, now suffer for whatever you have done".

112. Then in the fifth month, he goes to Krūrapura, O Kāśyapa. Having eaten the rice-ball and drunk water by his relatives he goes to Krūrapura.

113. As he goes, he laments, being struck with spears. "O mother, O father, O brother, O sons, O my wives.

114. I was not advised by you. I have reached this state." As he laments thus Yama's messengers say to him.

115. "Where is the mother? Where the father? O fool, Where is the wife ? Where the sons ? Where the friends ? O fool. Now suffer the results of your evil activities. All sinners go by this ancient path".

116. As you know, the provisions are the only strength of the traveller. So none without provision can venture to travel over this path. For the path is such where no selling and purchasing system exists.

117. In less than six months he reaches Krauñca and having eaten the rice-ball and drunk water he rests there for a while and then leaves for Vicitra nagara.

1. Path of knowledge.
2. Path of meditation.
3. Path of action.
4. Path of devotion.

118. As he goes, he laments being struck off with spear-heads by Yama's emissaries.

119. "Where do I go, O my life, a dead man cannot revive again. Thus lamenting he goes in the way, his body being captured by tortures".

120. Vicitranagara is ruled by king Vicitra. Being satiated with the six monthly rice-ball he moves further.

121. As he goes, he laments being struck with the club.

122. "Do my brother, son, parents or any one exist who may take out a sinner like me falling in the ocean of distress.

123. As he goes, there in the way is Vaitaraṇī' hundred yojanas long, full of pus and blood.

124. There are seen boatmen, fishermen. They say, if he has gifted Vaitaraṇī cow, he can get into the boat and cross the river.

125. But if he has not gifted the cow, he is brushed aside by the boatmen.

126. He is bit by the birds with sharp beaks, like crows, cranes, ants, etc., O bird, the gift of cow at the time of death serves for the relief of the deceased.

127. The gift of cow destroys all sins and affords all facilities. The deceased goes to Bahvāpada in the seventh month.

128. After partaking the seventh-monthly offering made by the relatives he reaches Bahvāpada, where he laments being struck with the iron club.

129. Neither you offered gifts nor gave oblations nor performed penance nor undertook bath nor rendered a good act. So O foolish creature, now suffer for whatever act you have done.

130. In the eighth month, after eating the rice-ball and drunk water, he goes to Nānākrandapura, O Tārkhya.

131-132. Being struck with pebbles there, he says : "Where are those sweet dishes offered with sweet tit-tat by my wife, and where this beating with the pestles." In the ninth month he eats his rice-ball in Nānākrandapura.

133. Then he laments in many ways. In the tenth month he reaches Sutaptabhavana.

1. A river in the way to Pitṛloka.

134-135. Thus moving, he laments in the way being struck with ploughs. 'Where the massaging of my feet by my sons and where the dragging of my legs by the thunderlike hands of messengers". He then eats the rice-ball given in the tenth month together with the offerings of water-oblation.

136. At the end of the eleventh month he goes to Raudra-pura. As he goes to Raudrapura he laments being struck in the back.

137. "Where the cotton-bed I used to roll in and where this rigid place where I am beaten by the messengers".

138. There he eats the rice-ball etc. given by his relatives and then he goes to the city called Payo-Varṣaṇa.

139. While going he laments, as he is struck at the head. "Where the servants who with soft hands used to massage oil in my head.

140. Where my head being struck by Yama's servants". At the end of the year he eats the annual śrāddha offered by his relatives.

141. Then at the end of the year he goes to Śrotriya. He weeps while his tongue is cut out with the knife.

142. "Where that sweet feeling of *rasa* and where this cutting of my tongue with the knife."

143. Having partaken of the annual *śrāddha* there, he goes to Bahubhūti. He has assumed by this time a body composed of the essence of his merit accruing from the gift of rice-balls.

144. The sinner abuses his own self. He also abuses his wife and thus laments in the way.

145. Then he reaches the city of Yama nearby. It is forty yojanas in measurement.

146. There are fourteen door-keepers called *Śravaṇas*. They are pleased with the *Śravāṇā* karma performed by his relatives or else they get angry.

147-149. There very soon among Death, Time, etc he sees Yama with red eyes, looking fierce and dark like a heap of collyrium, with fierce jaws and frowning fiercely, chosen as their lord by many ugly, fierce-faced hundreds of diseases, possessing an iron-rod in his hand and also a noose. The creature goes either to good or to bad state as directed by him.

150. A sinner goes to bad state, as I have told you before.

151. Those who give umbrella, shoes and shelter see Yama as gentle-faced with ear-rings and a shining crest.

152. In the Śrāddha of the eleventh or twelfth month many brāhmaṇas should be feasted because then the deceased is very hungry.

153. He who does not perform the needful while alive being instructed by sons, wife and others suffers afterwards.

154. Thus I have told you how one goes to Yama's abode; what shall be done in his favour for one year by his relatives. Do you wish to ask anything more.

CHAPTER SIX

The glory of Vṛṣotsarga

Garuḍa said :

1. Even if he has the means and is fond of pilgrimage and offering gifts he cannot reach the splendid world if he does not perform a Vṛṣotsarga.

2-3. Hence, Vṛṣotsarga shall be performed, O Kṛṣṇa; this I have heard. Now tell me what type of bull shall be chosen. At what time shall the bull be released. What is the method ? Please tell me everything.

4. O lord of birds, I shall tell you the past history which was told to king Vīravāhana by Nārada, the son of Brahmā.

5. A king, Vīravāhana by name, reigned in the Virādha city. He was pious, truthful, generous as well as heroic. He used to satiate the brāhmaṇas with sumptuous meals.

6. With a mind to satisfy his curiosity he went to Vasiṣṭha's hermitage.

7. He saw the sage surrounded by the munis, bowed to him putting his problems before him.

The King said :

8-9. O sage, I have performed religious duties to the best of my capacity. I am terribly afraid in my heart, O ocean of mercy. Now tell me the way that I may not see Yama and his fierce-looking messengers.

Vasiṣṭha said :

10. O king, the sages who are well versed in scriptures have prescribed many religious rites. But due to their subtlety people attached to Karma-yoga do not know them.

11. Gifts, pilgrimage, penance, sacrifice, saṁnyāsa and pitṛyajña—all these come under religion, specially the Vṛṣotsarga.

12. A man should desire many sons, because even if one of them goes to Gayā, he may perform a horse sacrifice or release a bull.

13. All heinous sins like the Brāhmaṇa slaughter, done knowingly, or unknowingly, are purified by releasing a bull or by swimming in the ocean.

14. O king, if the bull is not released on the eleventh day, the ghosthood of the deceased person becomes eternal. Then what is the use of performing a śrāddha ?

15. Somehow or other, in the holy place or in the town, a Vṛṣa-yajña should be done, O bird.

16-17. A young Pañca-kalyāṇa bull, moving among the cows should be wedded to the four she-calves or two or even one, reciting the wedding *mantras* accompanied by the auspicious rites.

18. An offering should be made to God Fire reciting the six ṛks *Iha ratiḥ* etc. It is specially recommended on the full moon day of Kārttika, Māgha, Vaiśākha or on Saṅkrānti days or on Sampāta days, in the Pitṛ-tīrtha or on Akṣaya day[1].

19-21. A bull red in colour, white in the tail, yellow in hoofs and horns is called Nīla, that of white colour is Vipra, that of red colour is Kṣatra, that of yellow is Vaiśya, and that of black is Śūdra, just as the colours of four castes have been prescribed by the wise ones.

22-26. A bull of red colour is preferred. Father, grandfather, and great-grandfather hope that the son will perform a Vṛṣotsarga. "You are Dharma in the form of a bull, the

1. Perhaps the same as Akṣaya tṛtiyā, i.e., the third day of the bright half of Vaiśākha.

delighter of the whole world. You are aṣṭa-mūrti[1], hence, give me peace. Drink and eat grass in the *antarvedi* of Gaṅgā and Yamunā. O bull, you should speak about my good deeds, before Dharma rāja." Thus praising and marking him with the sign of *Triśūla* in the right shoulder and with the sign of Cakra in the left thighs and worshipping the bull with incense, flowers, uncooked rice, etc., he should release the same along with the she-calf.

27. Hence, O king, perform Vṛṣotsarga as prescribed in the Dharma-śāstras. You possess all the virtues for under taking the rite. There is no other way for you.

28-29. Long, long ago, in the Tretāyuga, there lived a brāhmaṇa Dharma-vatsa by name, in the city of Vaideha. He was learned, dutiful, lustrous and devoted to Viṣṇu. He remained satisfied with whatever he could get. When the pitṛ-pakṣa came he went to the forest for collecting the Kuśa grass.

30. When he was moving here and there, picking the sacred grass and leaves, four good-looking persons came all of a sudden.

31-33 They caught hold of him while he was perplexed. They carried him forcibly into the sky. Crossing fierce mountains and forests, rivers and rivulets, they reached a city of huge dimension, with *gopura* doors, adorned with palaces, cross-roads, markets and shops crowded with men and women, resounding with the noise of trumpets, lutes and drums.

34-36. There he saw persons—some poor, some rich, some hungry, some good, some bad some ill clad, some dressed in golden clothes like the deities. He thought within himself. Is this a dream or an illusion or a fancy.

37-38. They took the surprised Brāhmaṇa to the king. There he saw in a golden palace a divine throne fanned with Cāmara and Chatra and the king sitting there with a shining golden crest.

39-40. The king possessed great lustre and was praised by the singing bards. On seeing that brāhmaṇa come, the king

1. The eight-formed one. The eight forms being: the five elements (earth, water, fire, air, and ether), the sun and the moon, and the sacrificial priest.

stood up with folded hands, honoured him in the traditionally prescribed way with Madhuparka, seat, etc. Then with joy and delight he praised the Brāhmaṇa who was fully satisfied.

41. To-day, my birth has been successful and my family purified, O lord, as I see today a religious devotee of Viṣṇu.

42. Having bowed to the Brāhmaṇa and praised him in many ways, the king said: "you will be taken back to the place whence you have come here."

43-44. On hearing the king's words the Brāhmaṇa said : "What is this land ? Who are the people ? the noble, the middle, and the base ones ? By what good deeds have you obtained the lordship of this region ? What for was I brought here and why am I being carried away ?"

45. "I see many things unseen before. To me everything seems to be a dream."

The king said :

46. "As you have been always devoted to religion and have been a devotee of Viṣṇu disinterested in any other thing I respect you. You have always been on the pilgrimage and have performed Vṛṣotsarga to the deserving.

47. As you always speak truth and give gifts, you are bowed to by the deities. O Parantapa, you have been brought for a glimpse of this land, as you are worthy of this honour.

48. Be pleased with me, O Lord, and excuse my rash act." Having said thus he presented his ministers by name by hint of brows.

49. "He will tell you everything. It is not proper for me to speak more." Thus he introduced Sāmanta who knew the Vedas, and understood their meaning, and asked him to speak. The Sāmanta spoke:

50. "This man was a Vaiśya, Viśvambhara by name, in his previous birth, in the city named Virādha, adored by Brāhmaṇas and deities.

51. He lived by the profession of his caste and maintained his family. He served the cows and worshipped the Brāhmaṇas.

52. He offered gifts to the deserving, welcomed the guests and poured oblations into the fire. He performed the duties of his profession together with this truthful wife.

53-54. By his righteous conduct he won his people; by his gifts of oblations he won the deities. Once, when after completing his pilgrimage together with his relatives, he was returning home, he saw Sage Lomaśa in the way. He bowed to him immediately, fell prostrate and then stood up with joined hands.

55-57. The pious sage who was the ocean of pity said to him :

The Sage said:

Gentleman, from where do you come together with your relatives and Brāhmaṇas. On seeing you, a religious person that you are, my heart has melted.

Viśvambhara said :

After seeing the decaying body and the death standing before, I went to pilgrimage together with my wife.

58-76. I am returning home when I happen to see you just now.

Lomaśa said :

There are many holy places in this sacred region. Tell me those which you have visited now.

Vaiśya said :

I have visited Gaṅgā, the daughter of the sun[1], holy Sarasvatī where Brahmā performed ten horse-sacrifices; Kāśī, the best of holy places where the kind Mahādeva recites *Tāraka* in the ears of dead creatures; the holy hermitage of Pulaha; Phalgutīrtha; Gaṇḍakī[2]; Cakratīrtha; Naimiṣa; Śivatīrtha; Gopratāraka; Nāgeśa; Ayodhyā where the lotus-eyed Rāma lived to confer *mukti* (salvation); Madhurā where Hari always stayed; Puṣkara; Satyatīrtha; Jvālā-tīrtha; Dineśvara; Indra-

1. The Yamunā.
2. Gaṇḍaka in Uttara Pradesh.

tīrtha; Kurukṣetra where flows the ancient Sarasvatī; Tāpī[1]; Payoṣṇī[2]; Nirvindhyā; Malaya; Kṛṣṇā-Veṇikā[3]; Godāvarī; Daṇḍaka; Tāmracūḍa; Sadodaka; Dyāvābhūmīśvara; Śrīśaila[4], the best of mountains where many Liṅgatīrthas exist; Veṅkaṭa, a mountain where god Hari Śrīraṅga, lives, and also the goddess Veṅkaṭi, the slayer of Mahiṣa lives, Candratīrtha, Bhadravaṭa, Kāverī; Kulilācala; Avatodā; Tāmraparṇī, Trikūṭa; Kollaka mount; Vāsiṣṭha Brāhmatīrtha and Jñānatīrtha ocean;[5] Hṛṣīkeśa; Virāja; the huge Nīla mountain; Bhīma Kūṭa; Śveta-giri; Rudra-tīrtha; Umāvana where Goddess Girijā obtained Śaṅkara by performing penance; Vāruṇa; Sūrya-tīrtha; Haṁsa tīrtha; Mahodaya[6] where ravens become royal geese after having a dip and where the demons became deities after bathing; Viśvarūpa; Bandī-tīrtha; Ratneśa; Kuhakācala where one is released from crores of sins after seeing Nara-Nārāyaṇa; Sarasvatī; Dṛṣadvatī; Narmadā that grants happiness to kings; Nīlakaṇṭha; Mahākāla;[7] holy Amarakaṇṭaka; Candrabhāgā; Vetravatī[8]; Vīrabhadra; Gaṇeśvara; Gokarṇa, Vilvatīrtha; Satāraka[9]; Karmakuṇḍa where one is immedialely released from the bondage of Karmas by taking a dip; and so many other holy places I have visited by your grace.

77. Whenever the saints take pity there dawn upon the visitor so many good thoughts. Hence, all sacred places are on the one side and the compassionate saints on the other.

78. These men of character are moved to pity all creatures. By knowledge and by age you are the instructor of all Varṇas.

79. Hence, I shall ask you the secret about the spiritual eternal. What shall I do and whom shall I approach ? Tell me O sage, my mind is wavering.

1. Modern Tāptī.
2. Modern Pūrṇā in Central India.
3. The rivers Kṛṣṇā and Veṇṇā.
4. A mount near Karnool in South India.
5. The modern Tirupati in Andhra.
6. Modern Kannauj in Uttara Pradesh.
7. At Ujjayinī.
8. Betwa in Central India.
9. Perhaps modern Satara in Maharashtra.

80. It has no desire for attaining Brahma. It is very much fond of worldly objects and it cannot stand their separation even for a moment, nor can it consider them to be illusory.

81. Infatuated by various bhāvas it thinks the field of Karmas to be the best. O Brāhmaṇa, now tell me how it may obtain peace.

82. How it may incline towards good thought and how it may become pure. Now enlighten me on this point, please.

The Sage said :

83. The mind is always very powerful and naturally inclined to error.

84-85. As the elephant keepers can bring under control even an uncontrollable elephant, similarly by association with the saints, by constant application of proper means, by adopting the path of devotion and virtue, the mind can be controlled. I shall now tell you an old history to make you believe it.

86-87. Now, hear what Nārada had told me about the history of his previous life.

Nārada said :

In my previous birth, I was the maid's son of a Brāhmaṇa. In my childhood, I was taught continuously and I remained in the company of pious people who stayed by good luck, in my house during the rainy season. Once, interested in their talk and wholesome precepts I was greatly delighted. I approached them with extreme politeness and due reverence and addressed them thus:

88. I said : O noble sages, be pleased to purify my thoughts so that my intellect may get pure and seek the good only, seeing everything full of Viṣṇu.

The Sages said :

89-92. O child, hear. We shall tell you something for your benefit, by understanding which you will achieve happiness here and hereafter. Different types of creatures of the world—deities, animals, men are tied with the noose of *Karmas* and experience different types of enjoyment. By *sattva* they attain deityhood; by *rajas* they attain manhood; by tamas they attain animalhood. A creature is led by desires and is ignorant. He is born again and again out of the womb of his mother and dies again and again in different births.

93-94. They pass through several births as the result of their activities. Sometimes, they are born as men by virtue of their previous actions. It happens that they come in contact with the pious people and by their good will and blessing they come to realize the Supreme Self and achieve liberation.

95-96. This vast ocean of Existence abounds in crocodiles, overspread with the network of illusions. Any person who wishes to cross this ocean has no means other than the recitation of the name Rāma.

97-98. As we get butter by churning the curd, fire by rubbing the two pieces of wood, so by constant and concentrated meditation we can realize the Self and obtain peace. The Self is eternal, indeclinable, truth, omnipresent, all-supporting, great, non-comprehensible, self-refulgent, non-apprehensible even to the mind. In the form of Existence, Consciousness and Bliss, the self is stationed in the heart of all creatures. While all other things are mortal, the Self alone is immortal. The Self is present in all beings as the ether in fire and water.

99. The Supreme Self, like the fire, is not attached to any one. It is compassionate to the devotees and for their protection it assumes human form but the ignorant regard it as man.

100. If a person, possessed of differential knowledge meditates on him in the heart, the Unborn Self is pleased by his devotion and appears to him in his true form.

101. It makes the seeker ever gratified when all sorts of desires forsake him for ever.

102. Hence, leaving your ego and attachment for this mortal frame you should move all alone in this dream land without imbibing any sense of desire.

103. Where is stability in dream, truth in magic, eternity in the autumnal cloud and reality in the body.

104. Knowing that the world is born of ignorance, you should restrain your senses and control your mind, thereby you will obtain peace.

105. Having said thus the affectionate saints went away and I followed the path shown by them.

106. Then very soon, I saw within myself a wonderful ever-joyful *Ātman* pure like the autumnal moon.

107. Sprinkling me with happiness and making me more inclined, the dazzling light hid itself inside like lightning in the sky.

108. Realizing the same in my mind through devotion, I left my mortal coil in due course and went to the eternal abode of Hari.

109. Then by His desire, O Brāhmaṇa, I was born again through the grace of God. I had no attachment in the world.

110. Playing on my lute and singing I moved from place to place. Thus telling me his experience, the self-willed sage went away.

111-114. I was surprised and satisfied. Thus, indeed, in the company of virtuous men and by God's grace, a person becomes pure and calm in mind and attains perfect peace. O Knower of Virtue, even the sin inherited from previous births disappears immediately in the company of good men like the water of the autumnal clouds.

Vaiśya said:

Drinking the nectar of your words, my soul has obtained peace. I have received the fruit of all pilgrimages at the very sight of yours. Having heard the words of the king the sage said unto him.

115. O mighty monarch, who desire the result of Trivarga[1], this is for your benefit. Whatever good you have done is, in my opinion, rendered fruitless because it is done without Vṛṣotsarga.

116. Hence, it is like a dew-drop. There is no other means of accomplishment in this world except the performance of Vṛṣotsarga.

117. Know that the two can easily obtain the status of pious persons—One who performs Vṛṣotsarga and the other who performs the horse-sacrifice.

1. The three objects of worldly existence, i.e., *dharma*, *artha* and *kāma*.

118. I have seen the two standing side by side near the Great God Indra. Hence, go to Puṣkara and perform a Vṛṣotsarga.

119. Then go home, O gentleman, and do the needful. For what is to be done should be done immediately.

Vipaścit said:

120. Then in the month of Kārttika come to the Puṣkara lake where god in the form of boar himself performs a sacrifice. Thus told he performed Vṛṣotsarga as prescribed by the best of the sages.

121-122. He visited holy places in the company of Lomaśa and his merit was increased by performing Vṛṣotsarga. After death he went to heaven, enjoyed heavenly pleasures, travelling in magnificent cars (and after the exhaustion of merit) was born in the royal family of Vīrasena.

123-130. He was known as Vīrapañcānana. When he performed Vṛṣotsarga that obtains for the performer the fruits of Trivarga he was assisted by a number of attendants. These were sprinkled over by the drops of water from the bull's tail and as a result got divine forms. These were the persons who looked strong, stout and beautiful. Then there were the persons who out of jealousy did not cherish the performance of Vṛṣotsarga. They were born lean, remained naked and dirty. This, in brief, is the record of the past life of the king. This strange story I have heard from Parāśara. Having heard this story you may go home immediately.

On hearing the words of Vipaścit the Brāhmaṇa was very much surprised. He went home escorted by the King's servants.

Vasiṣṭha said:

Therefore, O king, perform Vṛṣotsarga, the best of all pious acts, if you are afraid of Yama.

There is no other means better than Vṛṣotsarga, O King, I have told you the secret of Dharma to-day.

131-132. If a woman whose husband and son are alive dies in the presence of her husband, Vṛṣotsarga should not be performed and as an alternative a milch cow should be given to a Brāhmaṇa

The lord said :

133. On hearing the words of Vasiṣṭha, the king went to Madhupurī and performed Vṛṣotsarga and was gratified at heart. When in due course of time he passed away he was carried by Yama's messengers.

134-135. He passed by the city of Yama in the way. He asked the escorting messengers about the city of Śrāddhadeva where the sinners were let down by Yama's servants for the purgation of their soul, and where the lord who knows dharma and adharma resides.

136. Thereupon the messengers told him that they had passed by the city of Sinners which was not to be seen by persons like him. They then escorted him to the city of Dharmarāja and standing before Dharma-rāja informed Him about the history of the monarch.

137-140. The lord who stood along with the deities and gandharvas showed His divine form. The king bowed prostrate and then stood with hands joined in reverence. Delighted in mind, he praised the lord in many ways. Then Dharmarāja praised the king and asked the messengers to take him to Devaloka where many delights exist.

Vīravāhana was surprised. He asked Dharmarāja to tell him what merit he had performed in life that he was brought to heaven by the messengers.

Dharmarāja said :

141. You have done several pious deeds, given gifts and performed sacrifices and accomplished Vṛṣotsarga in Mathurā at the instance of Vasiṣṭha.

142. O King, even a little *dharma* if done properly multiplies, due to the favour of brāhmaṇas and deities.

143. Having said thus, Yama disappeared at once. Vīrabāhu went to heaven and enjoyed there in the company of deities.

The lord said :

144. O bird, I have told you in detail all about Vṛṣotsarga. On hearing this, the people get released from sins which they incur as the result of their bad activities.

CHAPTER SEVEN

The story of five ghosts

Garuḍa said :

1. I have heard the story relating to the rite of Vṛṣotsarga. I wish to be enlightened further upon this topic, for your knowledge is very great.

The lord said :

2. Now I shall tell you a wonderful dialogue between Santapana and the ghosts on this very point.

3. There was a brāhmaṇa Santapana by name whose sins had been destroyed by penance. Knowing the futility of the world he left home and went to the forest.

4. Whenever Vaikhānasas, sages and Vrātas saw him they bowed to him with respect. Once he went on a pilgrimage.

5. Though he controlled the outer senses and acted in the prescribed way, he was still dragged by the organs and he slipped in his path.

6-7. Once in the morn while he was taking bath, he opened his eyes and looked around. He saw a forest full of shrubs, creepers, trees, barks, branches, etc.

8-9. He saw tālas[1], tamālas[2], priyālas[3], panasas[4], śūparṇī[5], sālas[6], śākhoṭas[7], syandanas[8], tindukas[9], sarjas[10],

1. Borassus Flabellifer.
2. Cinnamemum tamāla.
3. Buchanania lanzan.
4. Artocarpus heterophyllus.
5. Gmelina arborea.
6. Shorea robusta.
7. Streblus asper.
8. Ougcinia dalbergioides.
9. Diospyros tomentosa.
10. Vateria indica.

arjunas[1], āmras[2], śleṣmātakas[3], bibhītakas[4], picumardas[5], Ciñcimas, Karkandhus[6] and Karaṁkaras[7].

10. All these and other trees were there among which the way could not be seen even by the birds, not to say of men.

11-12. There in that fierce forest, full of lions, tigers, hyenas, wild oxen, bears, buffaloes, elephants, deer, cobras, monkeys and other animals and also demons and goblins,

13. Santapana was terrified in his heart and could not decide where to go. Then thinking 'Come what may', he went further.

14. Hearing the singing of crickets and the hooting of owls, he moved forward about five steps.

15. There he saw a corpse tied to a banyan tree and five fierce ghosts eating the same.

16-17. They were rejoicing over their feast by relishing the head-bones, stomach attached to the back, fallen bones of the body, marrow, brain, etc.

18. Seeing the ghosts who were loudly cracking the bones with their fierce jaws, he was awe-struck in his heart and stopped at once.

19. When they saw that brāhmaṇa in that lonely forest, they ran towards him saying 'I first, I first'.

20. Two of them caught hold of his two arms, two caught hold of his legs and the fifth one caught hold of his head.

21. Speaking loudly in their own language, 'I shall eat first, I shall eat first', they got busy in dragging him.

1. Terminalia arjuna.
2. Mangifera indica.
3. Cordia mixa.
4. Terminalia belerica.
5. Azadirachta indica.
6. Zizyphus nummularia.
7. Cassia fistula.

22. Then, all of a sudden, they went up in the sky. From there they looked down how much flesh was left in the corpse.

23. They saw the corpse bitten by their jaws. Then they got down and caught hold of the corpse by legs.

24-26. Thus taking hold of the body cut by themselves, they went up again in the sky. Then seeing himself being borne in the heaven, the brāhmaṇa praised the lord in his mind. "I bow to lord Viṣṇu, the holder of discus who is supreme consciousness, who kept away the crocodile by throwing his discus and released the elephant from the noose of crocodile. May he release me from the noose of my actions.

27. When the kings were captured by Māgadha Bhīma, the lord got them released so that they might visit Bharga's sacrifice. May he release me from the noose of my activities."

28. He praised me in his mind and being praised I got up all of a sudden and I went to the place where he was being carried by the ghosts.

29. Seeing him thus carried away by the ghosts I was surprised and without speaking anything I followed them a while.

30. Simply by the dint of my presence, O bird, that Brāhmaṇa felt the pleasure of riding a palanquin.

31. Then in the way, I saw Maṇibhadra going to Meru and winking at him I took the king of Yakṣas by my side.

32. I said to the lord of Yakṣas to be active and destroy the ghosts and take away the corpse.

33. Being instructed thus he took the form of a ghost terrific even to those ghosts.

34. He stretched his arms besmeared with blood and appeared before the ghosts challenging them.

35. He struck two with arms, two with legs and one with head and beat the ghosts with severe blows.

36. They held that corpse bound by hands and legs and began to fight.

37. They attacked the Yakṣa lord with nails, feet and jaws.

38. But avoiding their attacks, the Yakṣa-lord snatched the corpse, as death takes away the breath.

39. When the corpse was snatched by Yakṣa they ran towards him.

40. As soon as they reached the Yakṣa moving in air, the Yakṣa vanished immediately. In utter dejection they went to the Brāhmaṇa.

41. As they were goiny to kill that Brāhmaṇa on the mountain they remembered their previous birth. It happened by the glory of my position and by the nobility of the brāhmaṇa.

42. Then they encircled the brāhmaṇa and spoke to him reverentially.

43. Please excuse us to day. They spoke like the echo of the mountain or the turmoil of the stormy sea.

44. Hearing their words he asked : 'Who are you ? Is it simply an illusion, a dream, or a fancy ?

The Chief ghost said :

45. Hear, O brāhmaṇa, we shall tell you what you have asked us, O Mahāyogin. We are absolved of our sins by seeing you. My name is Paryuṣita. He is Sūcīmukha.

46. The third one is Śīghra and the fourth one is Rodha and the fifth one is Lekhaka.

The Brāhmaṇa said :

47-48. Why are these meaningless names borne out by you ? Can they be derived from actions performed by you ? O ghosts, now tell us the meanings of these names.

The lord said :

49. Being thus addressed by the brāhmaṇa, they replied separately.

Paryuṣita said :

50. Once, in a month, when Śrāddha is performed for the manes, I invited a brāhmaṇa to my house. He arrived after I had eaten the part of food out of hunger.

51-52. Then I gave stale food to that Brāhmaṇa when he came. On account of that sin, when I died I became a ghost and got the name Paryuṣita since I had given him the stale food.

Sūcīmukha said :

53. Once an aged woman of the Brāhmaṇa caste went to the holy place Bhadravaṭa.

54-56. The old woman lived with her son aged five years. I being a kṣatriya pretender stopped her in wilderness, became a wayside robber and I took her viaticum with clothes along with the dress of her son. I wrapped them around my head and wanted to leave.

57. I saw the little boy drinking water from a jar. In that wilderness, only that much water was there. I frightened the boy from drinking water and being thirsty myself began to drink from the jar.

58. The boy died of thirst and the mother who was struck with grief died too, bythrowing herself into a dry well.

59. O Brāhmaṇa, by that sin I became a ghost with mouth as small as the hole of a needle and body as huge as a mountain.

60. Although I get food I cannot eat. Although I burn with hunger my mouth is contracted.

61. Since in my mouth I have a hole equal to that of a needle I am known as Sūcīmukha.

Śighra said :

62. Formerly I was a rich Vaiśya and went to a distant country for business.

63. I was accompanied by a friend who was a partner in business. He was rich but greedy. Then due to bad luck we fared badly in business to the extent that even our capital was lost.

64. Then we started from there, travelling in a boat. Just as the sun reddened, we began to cross the river.

65. My friend was tired due to labour, slept in my lap. Then a cruel thought entered into my mind.

66. I threw my friend sleeping in my lap into the river. Nobody in the boat knew anything about my act.

67. I got hold of his belongings, jewels, rubies, gold, etc. and returned home.

68. I kept that all in my house and told his wife: "My

brother has been taken away by robbers in the way and robbed of his wealth.

69-71. I ran away and escaped. Do not weep." She was overwhelmed with grief and burnt herself into the fire. Then seeing my path was without obstruction I returned home gladly. I enjoyed my friend's wealth to my heart's content. Since throwing my friend into the river I returned home quickly, I am called Śīghraga.

Rodhaka said :

72-73. O Brāhmaṇa, formerly I was a Śūdra. By the king's favour I owned a hundred villages. I had old parents and a young brother.

74. Very soon my brother was estranged from me by a greedy person. I stopped giving him food and clothes. He suffered too much at my hands.

75-79. My parents gave him something secretly. Whatever they gave him I learnt from my close confidants. Then I bound my parents with iron chains in a deserted temple. Being miserable they ended their life by drinking poison. The boy who was left all alone wandered here and there and expired ultimately. By this sin, O Brāhmaṇa I have become ghost. Since I chained my parents I was called Rodhaka.

Lekhaka said:

80. Formerly I was a brāhmaṇa in Avanti. I was authorised to worship the deities of Bhadra king. There were many images with different names.

81. On their bodies they wore gold and jewels. While worshipping them an evil thought entered me.

82. Piercing their bodies with an iron-rod I took out jewels from their eyes.

83. When the king saw the images in that state and their eyes without jewels, he became inflamed like fire.

84. Then he vowed, O Brāhmaṇa and said : "Whosoever has stolen gold and jewels from these images, if known will be killed".

85-86. Knowing all that, one night, with a sword in hand, I entered the king's palace and struck him dead. I then took jewels and gold and went away at midnight.

87-88. Then in the deep forest, a tiger put on me his nails. Since I had incised the images with iron-rod I was known as Lekhaka.

The Brāhmaṇa said :

89. You have told us facts about your names; now let us know about your way of life as ghosts as well as your food.

The Ghosts said:

90-91. We stay where people do not follow the Vedas, where there is no feeling of shame for falsehood, no faith in religion, no sense of discipline, no inclination for forgiveness, no patience and no knowledge.

92-95. We trouble the person who does not perform Śrāddha or Tarpaṇa.

We eat his flesh and suck his blood. Now hear about our food which is most despicable in the world. Something of this you have already seen. We shall now tell you something unknown to you. Vomiting, waste, cough, urine, and tears—these we eat and drink. Do not ask us further, O Brāhmaṇa, we are ashamed to tell you about our food. We are ignorant, in dark, fools and puzzled. Suddenly have we remembered about our previous births.

96. We are neither humble, nor wild and we know nothing.

The lord said :

97. When the ghosts were speaking thus and the Brāhmaṇa was hearing.

98-99. I showed my form, O Tārkhya. When that Brāhmaṇa saw before him the Puruṣa of his heart, he praised me with hymns and fell prostrate before me. Those ghosts too trembled with eyes wide open in surprise.

100. Their voice muttered with affection, still they could not speak. "Bow to you who release the cruel from *rajas* and the stupid from *tamas*." This being uttered by the

brāhmaṇa that mountain was adorned with six shining aerial cars moving at my will and attended by celestial beings.

101. By that Vimāna the Brāhmaṇa went to my abode along with the five ghosts. The ghosts went to heaven by virtue of their association with the Brāhmaṇa.

102. Living in heaven along with the ghosts that Brāhmaṇa Santapana became my famous gaṇa called Viṣvaksena. Thus I have told you everything, O bird. Whoever tells or hears this narrative, O bird, does not become a ghost.

CHAPTER EIGHT

Person authorised to perform obsequies

Garuḍa said :

1. O Lord, now tell me who are authorised to perform obsequies and what are the methods of performance prescribed in the Śāstras.

The lord said :

2. Son, grandson, great-grand-son, his brother and brother's progeny, so also sapiṇḍa-progeny—all these are authorized to perform the obsequies. In their absence, samānodaka-progeny of all these can perform the rite.

3-4. If both the families are maleless, the women should perform the obsequies. Or the king may perform all the rites—the preliminary, the middling and the final. O bird, the Ekoddiṣṭa śrāddha should be performed every year.

5-6. Now hear about the fruit accruing from the performance of this sacrifice.

7. When Brahmā, Indra, Rudra, Nāsatyās, Sūrya, Agni, Vasu, Maruts, Viśvedevas, manes, birds, men, animals, serpents, the Mother deities and other divine beings are given Śrāddha with faith, there is rejoicing in the whole world.

8. When they are satisfied they satisfy the performer with sons, wife and wealth. Thus I have told you, in brief, about the rites and the persons authorized to perform them.

Garuḍa said :

9. O Lord, now tell me when no authorized person is alive, who should conduct the obsequious rites.

The Lord said :

10. If no authorized person is alive to conduct the obsequious rites after death, one should perform the rites in his life time.

11. After fasting and bathing he should along with his wife worship Viṣṇu, the lord of all, the Creator as well as the Enjoyer.

12. With Svadhā he should offer *Jaladhenus* to the manes along with Dakṣiṇā and gingelly seeds.

13. Reciting the mantra *Agnaye Kavyavāhanāya svadhā, namaḥ, Somāya tvā pitṛmate svadhā namaḥ.*

14. With right hand he should donate the third one with dakṣiṇā reciting *Yamāyāṅgirase cātha svadhā namaḥ.*

15-16. In between he should invite the brāhmaṇas and feast them. The first should be stationed in north and the second one in the south, the third one in the middle. Before he invokes the other deities, he should worship the Viśvedevas.

17. He should then tell the Brāhmaṇa. "O Brāhmaṇa, I am feeding you for the propitiation of Vasus, Rudras and Sūryas." He should thus tell all the Brāhmaṇas.

18. He should then perform *āvāhana* (invocation), etc, as it is performed in the case of manes. He should give Saumyā cow to the Brāhmaṇa for the propitiation of Vasus.

19. He should give Agneyā cow for the propitiation of Rudra and Yāmyā cow for the propitiation of Sūrya. He should give a vessel full of gingelly seeds for the propitiation of Viśvedevas.

20. Then uttering *svasti* and giving sacred water (as that of the Ganges) he should dismiss the Brāhmaṇas (i.e. ask them to go away as they liked), while he himself should set his heart on the eight-syllabled Viṣṇu.

21. Then he should think of Kāma, Kuleśānī, Śiva and Nārāyaṇa. He should go to the nearest river on Caturdaśī.

22. Muttering the mantra *Vastrāṇi lohakhaṇḍāni jitaṁ te* he should light fire facing the south.

23. Then making a Brāhmī image with fifty Kuśas he should burn the same in fire. He should perform the sacrifice usually done in the crematorium and offer the final oblation (Pūrṇāhuti).

24. Or he should not kindle fire but simply propitiate Earth, Yama and Rudra. He should invoke each one of them separately and give offering at the appropriate place.

25. He should sacrifice caru mixed with mudga into the fire. He should offer sacred thread, rice and gingelly seeds to a Brāhmaṇa.

26. He should say; 'Oṁ homage to Earth', Oṁ homage to Yama.

27. Oṁ homage to Rudra, lord of cemetery. Then in the fire lit on the earth

28-29. He should give handful of water to Yama, one to each of the seven names of Yama, viz, Yama, Dharma-rāja, Mṛtyu, Antaka, Vaivasvata, Kāla, Sarva-prāṇahara, muttering *svadhā, namaḥ* and *Om* seven times, i.e. with each of the seven names of Yama.

30-31. O you of such and such gotra, this water with gingelly seeds is for you. Ten piṇḍas (rice-balls) should be given along with argha, flowers, incense, lamp, bali and gandha. He should then say: Let everyone be prosperous. After giving the ten piṇḍas he should remember the gentle face of Viṣṇu.

32-33. He should perform this rite spread over for a month. He should do *sapiṇḍikaraṇa* for himself or others at the end of āśauca within a month but not later than that knowing fully well the transitoriness of vitality, health, wealth and age. Thus I have told you all about Jīvat-śrāddha, O bird.

CHAPTER NINE

The king authorized to perform rites

Garuḍa said :

1. O sinless one, you have just said that a king may also perform the aforesaid rites. Did any king in the past perform such rites for any one?

The Lord said :

2. Hear, O bird, I shall tell you how a king performed such rites (for an issueless deceased). In the Kṛtayuga, there was a king Babhruvāhana by name, in the country of Aṅgas.[1]

3. O King of birds, He protected the earth on all sides. Following the laws of the land, he enjoyed the earth, having four divisions.[2]

4-6. During his reign, there was no sinner. Fear of thieves or evil-doers did not exist. During his reign there was no fear of any epidemic : He followed the path of religion for the welfare of his people. In lustre he resembled the sun, the earth in stability and the mountain in forbearance. Once, he of long arms, with his ample army and armaments went to a great forest.

7. He was surrounded by hundreds of horses, roars of warriors, sounding of conches and beating of drums.

8. As the king proceeded on journey he was praised by the brāhmaṇas and other learned people on the way.

9. He went to the forest with great pleasure for hunting. He was delighted to see the forest which resembled the *Nandana*[3] garden of Indra.

10. It was full of Bilva, Khadira, and Kapithadhvaja. It was surrounded by the mountains on all sides.

1. *Aṅgas*—a country and the people inhabiting it, identifiable with the region about the modern Bhagalpur in Bengal.

2. *four divisions*—comprising elephants, chariots, cavalry and infantry. These make a complete army capable of subjugating the entire world : चतुरङ्गबलो राजा जगतीं वशमानयेत् ।

3. *Nandana*—A divine park in the world of gods.

11. It was devoid of water, devoid of human beings. It spread over many yojanas and abounded in deer, lion, and other fierce wild animals.

12. Accompanied by his attendants and surrounded by his army he walked into the interior of the forest, killing different animals.

13. Leisurely, he struck a deer in the stomach with his arrow. The deer ran helter-skelter with pain, followed by the monarch.

14. While his army was left behind, he wandered all alone, hungry and thirsty and entered another forest.

15. Then suffering from thirst and seeking for water here and there, he got the indication of a lake from the noise of geese and cranes.

16-17. At last he found a lake where he immersed for bath together with his horse. Mixed with the filament of the lotuses, the water was fragrant, clear and cool. As he was tired of travelling a long way he rested beneath a fig tree on the bank of the lake.

18. He fastened his horse to the branches of the tree, spread the coverlet and used the clubs as pillows.

19-20. He slept there for a moment being fanned by air. Even as he slept for a moment a certain kingly ghost came there along with hundreds of attendant ghosts. It was a remnant of bones, skin and sinews.

21. He was moving here and there, in search of food and drink. He did not rest even for a while. On seeing such a terrible ghost, the king put an arrow on his bow.

22-24. The ghost looked at the king for a long time and stood before him like a branchless post. The king got curious at the sight of the ghost and put the question to him thus : Who are you ? How did you get this deformity ? The ghost replied : I have just left my ghosthood and attained a different form, just at the sight of you, O long-armed one. None is more fortunate than myself.

Babhruvāhana said :

25-26. In this fierce forest, shaken with wind and cyclone, full of flies and mosquitoes, trunks and head, fish, tortoise, lizards, scorpions, bees, serpents are seen with their mouth bent downwards and their feet raised upwards.

27. Dry winds are blowing ; lightning is flashing ; grass is scattered here and there.

28. I see many creatures — Nāgas and Śalabhas. I hear many sounds at some places and at some places I have no sounds at all. At the sight of all this deformity my heart trembles overwhelmingly.

The ghost said :

29-32. Those for whom the rites of cremation, funeral offering, such as the offering of rice-ball, gingelly-water are not performed nor the rites of daśa-piṇḍas, daśagātras nor sapiṇḍīkaraṇa, who during their life were ungrateful, drunkards gold-stealers. who died by accident, who were envious, without atonement, attached to women of ill repute, take the form of ghost and suffer for their bad actions through want of food and water.

33. O king, please perform their funeral rites since they do not have mother, father, sons and relations.

34-35. O king, you perform this good deed for their welfare, so that theymay be released from misery and may cross the ocean of distress. Of what avail are the brothers and sons ? One should not rely on women for they are expert in selfishness.

36. A person reaps what he sows. All objects or belongings remain at home. The relatives turn back from the cemetery.

37. Body is consumed by fire; good and evil deeds alone accompany the deceased.

38. Therefore, for your welfare, you perform immediately the funeral rites of the kinless deceased, as you are mortal yourself.

The king said :

39. With your emaciated form and fierce book, you seem to be a ghost. O king of ghosts, now tell me all about yourself in order to relieve my anxiety.

Thus asked, the king of ghosts began to tell all about himself.

The Ghost said:

40. O best of kings, I shall tell you all about myself from the very start. After hearing the causes that obtained ghosthood for me, you will have sympathy for me.

41. There is a city Vidiśā[1] by name, full of pleasure and prosperity. It has many *janapadas* and abounds in abundant treasure.

42. It has forests of flowers where dwell the holy sages. I too lived there, O king, engaged in the worship of gods.

43. I belong to the Vaiśya caste, and my name is Sudeva. I propitiated the deities with oblations and the manes with śrāddhas.

44. I presented gifts to the Brāhmaṇas and donated food.

45. I gave money and precious articles to the poor and the needy. But by bad luck all that went in vain.

46. I had no progeny, no friends, no kins and no friends who could perform my funeral rites.

47-49. For that reason, my ghosthood became perpetual. Now hear, O king, there are sixteen principal Śrāddhas — the eleventh day, monthly, half-quarterly, six-monthly, etc. The dead who do not receive these Śrāddhas turn into ghosts perpetually even though hundreds of other Śrāddhas are performed for them. Knowing this, O king, you perform Śrāddhas and release me from ghosthood.

50. For, a king is the relative of all castes. Therefore, I request you to release me from ghosthood. I give you the best of jewels in my custody.

51 Taking pity on me, O king, you act in such a way that I may be released from ghosthood.

52-53. (Moreover, I may tell you why I became a ghost). My kins being disinterested in me did not perform Vṛṣotsarga[2] in my favour. Hence, I was transformed into ghost. I feel con-

1. *Vidiśā*—the capital of the district called Daśārṇa in Mālava : Cp. Meghadūta I. 24 :

2. *Vṛṣotsarga*—setting free a bull on the occasion of a funeral rite or a religious act generally.

stantly hungry and thirsty, for want of food and drink. Hence, this deformity and leanness without food.

54. I suffer pain due to hunger and thirst, for this ghost-hood is malevolent.

55. I, therefore, pray you, O king, for, you are the ocean of pity.

The king said :

56. Tell me, O ghost, how one is released from ghosthood.

The ghost said :

The people can infer about the present of a ghost at home by signs and tormentations.

57. I shall now tell you about tormentations given by the ghost to the people on earth. When the menses of the women go in vain and the family does not multiply.

58-62. When men die young it is tormentation by ghost. Sudden loss in profession and insult among the people, sudden setting of house on fire, permanent quarrelling at home, false praise, suffering from consumption and foul diseases are due to tormentation by ghost. When the money invested in the customary way bears no fruit but is destroyed, it is due to tormentation by ghost. When crops are ruined even after proper rains, when commerce is unsuccessful, when wife creates tension, it is due to tormentation by ghosts. By these tormentations, O king, people can know about the presence of ghost at home.

63. If Vṛṣotsarga is done properly, one is released from ghosthood. Hence, O king, I pray you to perform Vṛṣotsarga in my favour.

64 I authorize you to perform this rite for me. Once, I killed a certain prince and as a result thereof I became ghost.

65. O king please take this precious-gem from me and with the money received through it, perform Vṛṣotsarga for me on the fullmoon day in the month of Kārttika or Āśvayuj or on the day conjunct with Revatī[1]. For perfoming Vṛṣotsarga you invite the learned brāhmaṇas and set up fire as prescribed in the Śāstras.

1. *Revatī*—One of the 27 constellations which contains 32 stars.

66-67. Then perform sacrifice, reciting the prescribed mantras. You shall feast the brāhmaṇas, spending the money obtained by the sale of this jewel. When this is done, I shall be released from ghosthood, O king.

The lord said :

68. The king took the jewel, saying, 'be it so'.

69-71. He had no atternative but to perform the rite, for he had taken the gem from the ghost. When the ghost and the king were talking together, there was heard a resounding noise of bells and trumpets. At the indication that the king's caturaṅga army was close by, the ghost disappeared. The king too left the forest for the capital.

72. Then on the Kārttikī Pūrṇimā with the money realized from the sale of the jewel, the king performed Vṛṣotsarga for the ghost.

73. The ghost obtained a new body as splendid as gold, at the end of the rite. He approached the king in the new splendid body and eulogized him. Attributing his release from ghosthood to the pious deed of the king he was grateful to him for the obsequies he had made in his favour.

74. Thus, I have told you how the ghost was released. What else do you desire to hear ?

CHAPTER TEN

The Gratifying Nature of Śrāddha

Garuḍa said :

1. After sapiṇḍīkaraṇa[1] has been done and the annual rites performed, the deceased may obtain godhood, manhood or birdhood as the case may be.

1. *Sapiṇḍīkaraṇa*—A rite of establishing kinship by offering libations of water, rice-ball etc. to the manes. This relationship extends from the seventh or the eleventh to the thirteenth or the fourteenth degree. Cf. M.S. 5.60. According to certain smṛtikāras it is performed at the end of a year after the death of a relative but now usually performed on the twelfth day as part of the funeral obsequies.

2. But they eat different types of food. How can *śrāddha* satiate them ? The *śrāddha* food is eaten by the brāhmaṇas or given as oblation into the fire.

3. The *piṇḍa* is given by the good as well as the bad relative. How can the ghost discriminate ? Why should the śrāddha be performed on a particular day ?

The Lord said :

4. O bird, hear, *śrāddha* is gratifying to ghosts. There is no restriction on a person if he becomes a deity or a man or an animal according to the actions of his previous life.

5-7. If he becomes a deity, the *śrāddha* food turns into nectar ; an article of enjoyment if he becomes a gandharva; a grass if he becomes an animal ; an air if he becomes a nāga ; fruit in case of a bird ; meat in case of a demon; blood in case of a ghost ; grain in case of a man and an article of enjoyment in case of a child.

Garuḍa said :

8. How kavya[1] and havya[2] given by men reach pitṛloka and devaloka and who takes them there ?

9. How can a śrāddha gratify the dead ? Can oil in a blown-out lamp light the wick ?

10. Tell me, O Lord ! How does the deceased enjoy the fruits of the deeds such as rites of obsequy performed by his son.

The lord said :

11. The validity of tradition, O lord, is more powerful than the validity of direct perception. The Śruti declares that the food served to the brāhmaṇas in the Śrāddha turns into nectar, etc. for the departed souls.

12. By their names and gotras the manes receive the offerings made by the relatives. The mantras carry the same when they are recited with devotion and faith.

13. How the articles reach the manes should not be doubted, O bird. I tell you how the articles of gift can reach the manes.

1. *Kavya*—an oblation of food to deceased ancestors.
2. *Havya*—an offering to the gods or oblation in general.

14-15. The Agnisvātta pitṛs (the manes who are cremated in fire) remain in charge of the departed. When food is offered to the departed souls in the appropriate manner, at the appropriate time and place, as prescribed in the Śāstras, they carry the same to the manes in their path.

16. Even though they assume different species and reach different worlds, with different names and gotras, they receive the offering made in their favour by their kins.

17. The three piṇḍas given on Darbha or spread over the earth, by the nearest relative of the deceased, with his sacred thread worne over the left shoulder, gratify the manes even in their ghosthood.

18-19. Those who have been pious on the earth in all ways do not go to the torture-place. These as well as others who have assumed multifarious forms and those who are born in low species obtain whatever food they eat in those species.

20. Just as when the cow is lost in the herd of cattle, the calf searches for her and ultimately finds her, so the śrāddha food searches the deceased person, though he is set on journey (or has, assumed a different form).

21-22. The manes consume the srāddha victuals in the company of Vaiśvedevas, Vasus, Rudras, Ādityas, ancestors, Śrāddha devas. When gratified they gratify the deceased person.

23. Just as a pregnant woman gratifies herself and her foetus by satiating her desire, so also the deities gratify themselves and the manes by partaking the śrāddhas.

24. They feel elated at the approach of śrāddha time. Thus thinking in their mind they reach the śrāddha-place with the spread of imagination.

25. Staying in the horizen they eat with the brāhmaṇas. In their aerial form they eat with pleasure.

26. Whosoever be the brāhmaṇa invited for the feast, they enter his body, eat and return to their abode.

27-30. If the performer of Śrāddha (such as the son of the deceased) has invited a single brāhmaṇa for śrāddha, the father stays in his stomach, the grandfather on his left side, the greatgrandfather on the right and the consumer of piṇḍa at the back. During the period of śrāddha Yama releases even the ghosts and the manes staying in hell who being hungry run to the world of mortals to receive the offering made by their relatives. They repent for their misdeeds while they desire to be served with the milk-rice mixed with honey by their sons and grandsons. Therefore, the descendent should gratify them with the milk-rice.

Garuḍa said :

31. O Lord, now tell me, has any one seen the manes descending from the other world and partaking śrāddha on this earth ?

The lord said :

32. Hear, O Garuḍa, I shall tell you how once Sītā saw in the body of a brāhmaṇa the manes, the father-in-law, grand-father-in-law and the great-grand-father-in-law.

33-34. At the behest of his father, Rāma went to the forest. When he reached Puṣkara, the holy centre, together with his consort Sītā he performed śrāddha with the ripe fruits Sītā collected from the trees.

35-36. When the sun reached the middle of the sky the sages who had been invited by Rāma presented themselves. When Sītā saw the sages she was extremely delighted.

37. By the instructions of Rāma she served them with food. Then, all of a sudden, she got away from among the brāhmaṇas.

38-40. Covering herself behind the bushes she hid herself. Then having learnt that Sītā had gone all alone, Rāma was anxious and lost in thought. He wondered why she had gone away so soon without feasting the brāhmaṇas. He thought to himself. May be she felt shy. I shall search for her. Thinking this way or that he himself feasted the brāhmaṇas.

41. When the brāhmaṇas went away Sītā returned. Then Rāma spoke to her : "Why did you leave when the sages came here to the forest. Let me know the reason of your abrupt departure.

42. Then addressed by the lord, Sītā stood with her face cast dawn. With tears flowing down from her eyes she spoke thus to her lord.

Sītā said :

43-44. O lord, hear, I saw a wonder here. I saw your father in front of the brāhmaṇas, dressed in royal costume. I saw two elderly folk doning the similar garb.

45-46. On seeing your father I moved away from his presence. Attired in bark and hide, how could I serve him with food ?

47. How could I offer him food in a vessel of grass in which even slaves would not eat ?

48. How could I, full of perspiration and dirt, go before him knowing that he had never seen me before in that miserable state. I felt shy and moved away from his presence, O Rāma.

49. On hearing these words of his beloved, Rāma was surprised at heart, thinking that it was a miracle never witnessed before.

50-51. Thus I have told you how Sītā saw the manes. Now, here in short is another account of Śrāddha. On the day of Amāvāsyā, the airy manes stand at the threshold of their decendants in order to receive śrāddha.

52-53. They remain there till Sun-set. When they do not receive śrāddha they fall in despair and out of suffering heave long sighs and go back cursing the descendents.

54-55. Therefore, one should carefully perform śrāddha on the amāvāsyā day. If sons or relatives perform śrāddha at Gayā, they uplift their ancestors from lower regions and themselves enjoy brahmaloka together with the manes. They never suffer from thirst and hunger.

56-58. Therefore, the wise should perform śrāddha imperatively. If no other article of food is available even vegetable if offered with devotion would suffice. If śrāddha is done in time the family would never perish. Age, sons, fame, heaven, glory, health, strength, splendour, cattle, happiness, wealth and grain — all these can be procured by worshipping the manes. The rites performed in favour of the manes are more beneficial than the rites performed for the deities.

59-65. Gratification of the manes in proportion to that of the deities is more beneficial. Those who worship manes, deities, brāhmaṇas and fire, in fact, worship me who am the soul of all beings. By performing śrāddha according to the means and method, the man pleases the universe as far above as brahmaloka. Whatever food is spread over the earth by the performer, the same gratifies them, though they have become ghosts. Whatever water falls on the ground dripping from the bathing clothes of the performer the same gratifies them, though they may have become trees. Whatever scents fall on the ground the same gratifies them though they may have obtained deity-hood. Those who are outside the caste groups, unfit for rites or averse to rites, consume water scattered after washing.

66. Whatever water is revised in the day by the brāhmaṇas and others, the same gratifies those who have become piśāca, worms and germs.

67. Whatever piṇḍas are left on the earth the same gratify those who have become men.

68-69. Thus when all this is being done by the twice-born, whatever water and food is left, good or bad, the same gratifies those who have opted for another caste, in case the śrāddha is done properly.

70. When men perform śrāddha with ill-gotten wealth, the same gratifies caṇḍālas and others of low species.

71. Thus, O bird, whatever is given to the manes, by their relatives while doing śrāddha, they receive the same and remain gratified with food, water and vegetable.

72-73. Thus, I have told you all what you had asked me for. Now that you have queried me whether the soul obtains body immediately or after some time I shall tell you about the same in short. Body is obtained both immediately and late.

74. How the soul gets a new body, hear from me. The soul without body is like a flame without fire. It is about a thumb in size[1].

75-77. After leaving the earthly body, the soul obtains an airy body. Like a caterpillar who lifts up the back feet only when the position of the front feet becomes firm. the soul leaves the previous body only when the airy body is available to enjoy.

78. In that actionless body he moves in air only. Whatever body he has obtained, the same he himself leaves.

1. *Puruṣa*—According to Vedic Tradition, *Puruṣa* (the personal soul) s of the size of thumb : *aṅguṣṭhamātraḥ Puruṣaḥ*—Ta. 10.38.1.

79. He leaves the body just as the child leaves the womb. He may come out, stay and enjoy.

80. The fools do not see him, only those who possess the vision of knowledge can see him in that state.

81. O bird, this type of body the deceased can have out of the piṇḍa (rice-ball) offered to him.

82. Whatever piṇḍa the sons or kins give him during the ten days, the same unites the Vāyuja body with the piṇḍaja body.

83. If the piṇḍaja body be not there, the Vāyuja body suffers. Just as in his body a man has childhood, youth and old age, so also he obtains another body[1], this you already know, O king of birds.

84. Just as men wear new clothes casting off old ones, so also the soul obtains another body leaving the old one.[2]

85. Neither the weapons cut it nor the fire burns it nor the water wets it nor the wind dries it.[3]

86. Just now, I have told you that it obtains the airy body immediately. Now, hear about the body it obtains belatedly.

87. After sometime, the Jīva when he reaches Yamaloka. obtains the piṇḍaja body.

88-89. As directed by Citragupta, he suffers in hell. Having suffered tortures there, he is born in the low species as an animal, a bird, etc. There too, very full of attachment, he suffers from the result of good and bad actions, O king of birds.

Garuḍa said :

90. O Treasure of pity, please tell me how even though full of sins, a Jīva may obtain you, after crossing the occean of worldly existence.

91. Please also tell me, O lord, how a man can avoid suffering ?

Tho lord said :

92. Man obtains success being busy in the performance of assigned acts. Now, hear how he can get success while he is engaged in doing acts.

1. *Bh. Gītā* II. 13.
2. *Ibid.*, II. 22.
3. *Ibid.*, II. 23.

93-96. By taking shelter in Vāsudeva, possessing pure intellect, controlling the self with fortitude, discarding the objects of enjoyment and leaving attachment and envy, serving without expecting reward, controlling speech, body and mind, practising meditation and Yoga, taking recourse to detachment, leaving pride, force, desire, anger, thus calm and serene he attains brahma. After this, he has to do nothing, O son of Kaśyapa.

CHAPTER ELEVEN

Doors for Departure :

Guruḍa said :

1. How does a person obtain manhood and how does he attain death ? O best of deities, when he dies where does his body go ?

2. Where do the organs of sense repair ? How does the body become untouchable ? How and where does he suffer the fruits of his actions ?

3. Be pleased, for you alone can remove my ignorance. O best of deities, I am Garuḍa, son of Kaśyapa from Vinatā. Please tell me how do men go to Yamaloka or Viṣṇuloka.

The Lord said :

4-5. By kidnapping another man's wife and stealing the property of a brāhmaṇa, one becomes brahmarākṣasa in wilderness. The thief of jewels is born in a low caste.

6. Whatsoever one desires one is born, having the symbol of the same. The weapons do not cut his soul nor fire can burn it.

7-8. Nor water wets it nor wind dries it.[1] Mouth, eyes, nose, ears, anus and penis—these are the holes in all animals born of egg, etc. There are eight upper holes from navel up to the head.

9-10. If men have done good deeds, they depart from the upper holes, O bird. Whatever rites are prescribed for the deceased from the day of his death to the end of the year (of his death) shall be performed even by the poor. As for the

1. *Bh. Gītā* II. 23.

place of enjoyment in whatever body the jīva has entered he reaps the fruits of his actions therein, no matter whether the actions be good or bad.

11. In this way, O king of birds, a person suffers from the faults of body, mind and speech. After his death, he obtains happiness when he has suffered the results of his actions. He is released from the noose of Māyā and he is not likely to be born again to indulge in evil acts.

CHAPTER TWELVE

Importance of Dharma

The lord said :

1. O Garuḍa I have thus explained to you the various proclivities of life for the benefit of men and to ward off the stalemate in which the dead may find themselves.

2. There are eight million four hundred thousand species of creatures divided into four main classes. They are (1) *aṇḍajas* (born of egg), (2) *svedajas* (sweat-born like bugs, etc. (3) *udbhijjas* (born of seeds), (4) *Jarāyujas* (the viviparous.)

3-4. The *aṇḍajas* are of two million one hundred thousand varieties. Similarly, the Svedajas, Udbhijjas and the Jarāyujas in the last of which are included human beings are also enumerated. It is very difficult for the lower animals to get manhood.

5. The receptacle of the set of five sense-organs can be acquired through great merits. Mankind is divided into four varṇas—Brahmins, Kṣatriyas, Vaiśyas, Śūdras and also Antyajas (the lowest class).

6. The Antyajas are divided into seven groups Viz, — Washermen, Cobblers, Actors, *Varuḍas*, *Kaivartas*, *Bhedas* and *Bhillas*.

7. Adding the Mlecchas and *Dumbas* there are thirteen groups of people. The species of lower strata of animals are thousands.

8. Taking food, indulging in sexual intercourse, sleeping, fearing and becoming angry—these are found in all living beings. Here the distinction is impossible.

9. Bodies are of ten varieties in view of the divisions such as single-footed, etc. Where the deer *Kṛṣṇasāra*[1] is found in plenty that region is called *Dharmadeśa* (the land of virtue)

10. O Bird, the deities *Brahmā* and others, the sages and the Pitṛs, virtue, truthfulness and learning are always present in that land of virtue.

11. Among living beings, the animals are the best ; among the animals, the intelligent are the best; among the intelligent, men are the best and among men, the brahmins are the best.

12. Among the brahmins the scholars, among the scholars those who cultivate Vedic studies, among them those who act according to the injunction and among them the Brahmavādins[2] are the best.

13. One is guilty of self-deception who does not strive to gain either heaven or salvation after being born as a man whereby he could gain either.

14. A man who has hundred (silver pieces) craves for a thousand; a man who has a thousand, yearns for a lac; a person who has a lac, wishes to rule over a kingdom; a man who rules over a kingdom pines away to become an emperor.

15. An emperor wishes to become a *deva* (god) and on getting godhood he wishes to be the lord of gods. The lord of gods wishes to go still further and still his thirst for power does not recede.

16. A person afflicted by covetous thirst falls into hell. Those who are freed of undue thirst secure a residence in heaven.

17. A man depending upon his own self is sure to be happy. The qualities of sound, touch, colour, taste and smell make one dependent on the objects of sense and hence one is sure to be unhappy.

18. The deer, the elephant, the moth, the honey bee and

1. *Kṛṣṇasāra*—a spotted antelope. The idea is found in M.S. II. 23.
2. *Brahmavādins*—those who discuss and deliberate on Vedic topics.

the fish — these five are destroyed due to addiction to their five sense-organs[1].

19. In infancy one is extremely obsessed with one's parents ; in youth, one is obsessed with one's wife ; later in life one becomes obsessed with one's sons and grandsons. Never is one obsessed with the *Ātman*.

20. It is easy for one bound with iron fetters to wooden pegs to get oneself released. But one bound with the nooses of children and wives is never released.

21. It is impossible to escape death whether one is a fool or a scholar, a child or an old man, young (or old and infirm), extremely happy or excessively dejected. He comes and goes. (He dies and is born again.)

22. Man is born alone; man dies alone; he enjoys his merits by himself; he reaps the bitter fruits of his sins by himself.

23-25. Even as every one is watching, one leaves off everything and dies. Casting off the dead body along with logs of wood or clods of earth the kinsmen turn away (from the cremation or burial ground) but the dead man's virtue or evil definitely follows him. His riches recede from him in the house itself and his kinsmen turn away at the cremation grounds with friends.

26-27. The fire consumes the body but the merit and demerit accompany him. The body is burnt by fire but the actions perpetrated by him keep his company.

28-33. Auspicious or otherwise, a man has to experience the fruits of his action. If before sunset wealth is not distributed among the suppliants, I do not know to whom it will go in the morning that follows. If some wealth is not handed over to

1. The following table will elucidate the point very clearly.

Victim	Sense-Organ	Object
Deer	Ear	Listens to sweet music aud gets caught by the hunter.
Elephant	Sense of touch	It is caught through she-elephants.
Moth	Eyes	It is attracted by the colour of the flame and is burnt.
Honey bee	Nose	Attracted by the fragrance of lotus it gets caught within.
Fish	Sense of taste	It nibbles at the bait and gets caught.

Even one of the sense-organs is destructive. How is it possible that man who uses all the five will excape destruction ?

brahmins and friends or spent in holy rites or pilgrimages, the wealth begins to cry 'who shall be my lord ?' Whether plentiful or scanty whatever wealth one has, is due to one's previous merits. Realizing this, one has to spend it away in virtuous rites. It is by wealth that virtue is sustained if the mind is sanctified by faith. A sacred rite devoid of faith is neither fruitful here nor there. It does not flourish. Virtue is the cause of wealth, love and salvation. Hence, one shall be virtuous. It is by faith that virtue is sustained and not by heaps of riches. Indigent sages endowed with faith have attained heaven. *Homas*, gifts, penances and actions without faith are base, O bird, and they are not found fruitful, here or in the life after death.

CHAPTER THIRTEEN

Obsequial Rites

Garuḍa said :

1. O Lord of gods, please tell me by means of what rite can one prevent a stalemate after death. (What are the rites that men should do in the world to forestall the state of being a ghost for ever ?)

The lord said :

2. Please listen, I shall explain briefly the obsequious rites. If one desires to attain salvation, one has to perform them oneself.

3-4. Even in regard to women, and children above the age of five, this is specially insisted on. The rites of *Vṛṣotsarga* (gifting away a bull calf) are for forestalling the continuance of ghosthood. There is no other rite in the world except *Vṛṣotsarga* (for that purpose). While during his life or after death if *Vṛṣotsarga* is performed he will never continue for long as a ghost. There is no necessity for other gifts or sacrifices.

Garuḍa said :

5-6. If *Vṛṣotsarga* is to the performed during life or after death, at what time has it to be performed, O foremost among gods, *Madhusūdana*, please tell me. If the sixteen types of *Śrāddha* are performed what are their effects on the dead man ?

The lord said :

7. If *Piṇḍas* are offered without performing *Vṛṣotsarga* no benefit accrues. Every thing given unto the dead is fruitless.

8. If *Vṛṣotsarga* is not carried out on the eleventh day after death, the ghosthood of the dead becomes eternal even if hundreds of *Śrāddhas* are performed in his favour.

Garuḍa said :

9-10. If a person dies of snake-bite, no funeral rite, such as cremation takes place. Similarly, if he dies by drowning or being struck by a horned animal or through weapons or an accident for how many days do the relatives remain impure ? O lord, please remove my doubts on this point.

The lord said :

11. If he is a Brahmin, impurity lasts for six months; if a Kṣatriya, two months and a half; if a Vaiśya, one month and a half, and if a Śūdra it lasts for a month.

12. If a person has gifted some precious articles of different sorts to a worthy receiver and has lived a celibate life when alive, he does not go to a wretched state (even if he dies an unnatural death).

13. If a person has performed the rite of Vṛṣotsarga and has lived a celibate life, he goes to Brahmaloka, even if he dies an unnatural death.

14. If a person has lived an unrighteous life devoid of good conduct, but has performed Vṛṣotsarga, he does not go to the world of Yama after death.

15. When a person dies, his son, brother, grandson, relative, caste-man or the successor should perform Vṛṣotsarga.

16. If there be no son, the wife can perform Vṛṣotsarga; if no wife, the daughter's son or the daughter herself can do the same. But, in case, he has sons, none else should perform Vṛṣotsarga.

Garuḍa said :

17. If one has no kinsmen such as sons, mother, relatives, wife or husband, how are the obsequial rites to be performed? By what rite are men and women to attain salvation warding off miseries. O lord, please dispel this doubt of mine entirely.

The lord said :

18. There is no salvation for a man without a son. He can never hope to attain heaven. Hence, somehow a man must strive to get a son.

19. Whatever gifts are made by one during the life time, become beneficial later.

20. Different sorts of delicacies and foodstuff given by one's hand stand in good stead after death.

21. Cows, plots of land, gold, clothes, foodstuffs, good posts (positions), etc. offered to the needy succour a man wherever he is.

22. One shall perform sacred rites as long as the body is hale and hearty. Falling sick, one may not feel enthusiastic to do anything even if prompted by others.

23. Until the rites of obsequies are performed the dead man, ever hungry, roams about day and night in the form of airy matter.

24. He is likely to be born again, a worm or an insect or a locust or in the womb of an evil-minded base woman. He may die immediately after rebirth.

25. As long as the body is healthy, free from sickness, as long as old age has not set in, as long as the power of sense-organs is not impaired, as long as there is no risk to life, an intelligent man should endeavour for the welfare of the soul. It is foolishness to begin to dig a well when the house has caught fire.

CHAPTER FOURTEEN

Merits of gifts

Garuḍa said :

1. O lord, please tell me what is the effect if one offers things oneself or through others, if one offers things when one is hale and hearty or when one is sick ; or if things are offered when one is unconscious or without reference to the injunctions in the sacred texts ?

The lord said :

2-3. One cow, offered when one's mind is at rest and peaceful, is on a par with hundred cows offered when it is not, or a thousand cows given at the time of his death when it is doubtful whether he is conscious of it at all, or a hundred thousand cows after his death. If it is given without reference to the injunctions in the sacred texts it is fruitless. Even a single cow offered to a deserving person at a holy centre is on a par with a gift of a hundred thousand cows elsewhere in yielding merit.

4-5. O foremost among birds, anything given to a deserving person flourishes day by day. A gift wipes off the sin of the giver and the acceptance of the same by a person of good wisdom does not affect him. The mantra quells person and the fire chillness. Are they affected by the same ?

6. Every day something must be given to deserving persons, particularly so on special occasions. If one wishes for one's own weal, one shall be sane enough not to give anything to the undeserving.

7. A cow gifted to an undeserving causes the downfall of the giver into hell. The receiver too falls into hell along with the members of his family for twenty one generations. If on being born again he performs some meritorious deeds, the effect there-of is also wiped off.

8. O lord of birds, I affirm that just as seeds and other valuable things invested or sown in the ground offer fruitful

results so also things offered by one's own hands yield fruitful results.

9. Particularly, a man having no son shall perform the funeral rites in his life-time and the same is true with those who crave for salvation and even indigent persons.

10. Any sacred rite performed by ourselves even with very little wealth accords undying results, just like drops of clarified butter offered into the fire with sacred *mantras*.

11. A gift of a single bed, a virgin, and a cow, if sold or shared burns the members of the family till the seventh generation.

12. Therefore, life being unsteady it is incumbent on everyone to do every thing beforehand. With the food for the journey in the form of gifts offered to the deserving, one is able to travel with comfort in the Great Highway in the journey after death.

13. Otherwise, the wretch undergoes great hardships without the food to subsist on, on the way. O foremost among birds, after realising this, one shall perform *Vṛṣayajña*.

14. Even a man having sons, dying without the performance of these rites, does not attain salvation. A man without sons by doing these rites beforehand shall have a happy journey on the Great Highway.

15. The goal that is reached by *Vṛṣotsarga* cannot be attained by the performance of sacrifices like *Agnihotra*, etc. or by various kinds of gifts.

16. Among all sacrifices the *Vṛṣayajña* is the best. Hence, it must be performed with redoubled efforts.

Garuḍa said :

17. Please tell me the details of *Vṛṣayajña* when, on what *Tithi*, by what rites shall it be performed ?

18. What is the fruit that he reaps after performing the same ? Now please tell me this.

The lord said :

19-21. When the sun is in *uttarāyaṇa* (northern Transit i.e. proceeding away from the tropic of capricorn) in the months of *Kārttika*, etc., on the twelfth day of either the bright or dark lunar fortnight, on an auspicious hour, in a clean place, he shall perform the rites of *Japa* and *Homa* after inviting a pious brahmin conversant with the rites.

22. On a holy day in conjunction with an auspicious star he shall worship the planets and deities. He shall perform *Homa* according to his capacity with various auspicious *mantras*.

23. He shall fix the planets mystically and worship, O lord of birds. He shall then perform the worship of the Mothers and *Vasudhārā* (offerings of gold or other coins in a stream).

24. After kindling the fire he shall perform the *Pūrṇa Homa*. Then he shall instal *Śālagrāma* and perform *Vaiṣṇava Śrāddha*.

25. The *Vṛṣa* (bull calf) must be bedecked with good clothes and ornaments. Four heifers must be kept in front.

26. At the end of the *Homa* the householder shall circumambulate the bull and let it loose reciting the following mantra and facing the north.

27. "O Bull, thou art *Dharma* (virtue) created by *Brahmā* in the form of a bull. Please raise one up from the ocean of worldly existence by means of the power of this setting free."

28. With this *mantra* and along with the holy water from *Rudrakumbha* (the water pot sanctified by Rudra mantras) poured over its head, the *Visarga*[1] rite is performed. The water pot is then placed on *Darbha* grass.

29-30. After duly pouring the water with due recital of mantras in accordance with the injunctions in the sacred texts, he recites the mantra *Tena Krīda* etc and finally releases the bull. He shall then perform *Ātmaśrāddha* and feed a pious brahmin and offer water unto him.

31. What he liked most in his life-time must be made over as a gift in accordance with one's capacity. Then after death he shall be able to go along the rugged path (to the city of Yama) without any difficulty.

1. The rite of setting the bull at liberty. Usually, it is called *visarjana*.

32. If the *Śrāddha* is not performed on the eleventh day, neither what is offered by himself here nor what is offered by others reaches him in the other world.

33. He shall then make over *Padadānas* thirteen, seven, five or three with great faith.

34. Three, five or seven pots of gingelly seeds shall be gifted away and brahmins must be fed. He shall then offer a cow as a gift.

35-36. If a bull calf is gifted a *Cakra* shall be placed on its left side, a trident on its right and a garland round its neck.

37. The eleventh day rites are to be performed like the *Ekoddiṣṭa* rite and the twelfth day rites are performed with *Svāhākāra*.

38. Before the *Sapiṇḍīkaraṇa*, sixteen *Śrāddhas* have to be performed. After feeding the brahmins *Padadāna* must be made.

39. A cloth is spread on the ground and a copper vessel is kept over it. The idol of *Acyuta* is kept in it and covered with a cloth. This is given along with *Arghya* and good fruits as gifts.

40. A boat is to be made with sugar cane stems and covered with a cloth. Clarified butter is kept in a bell metal vessel. This is the symbolic offering to enable him to cross the *Vaitaraṇī* river.

41. The boat is offered for crossing. *Garuḍadhvaja*[1] is then worshipped. In accordance with one's own wealth many such gifts can be given.

42. *Janārdana* is the god who saves people who are sunk in the ocean of worldly existence, who are dejected due to its waves of sorrow and distress and who are devoid of the boat of *Dharma* (virtue).

43. Gingelly seeds, metallic substances, gold, cloth, salt, seven grains, plots of land and cows—any of these can be given as *Dāna*. It is holy.

44. Vessels full of gingelly seeds or beds can be gifted. According to one's capacity, *Dakṣiṇā* can be given to poor people, orphans or noble and pious persons.

1. A flag staff, bearing the portrait of Garuḍa painted on it.

45. O *Tārkṣya* he who performs thus, whether he has a son or no son, obtains great *siddhis* (achievements) like one who has realised *Brahma*.

46. As long as one lives, one shall perform *Nitya* and *Naimittika* rites. Whatever one does righteously shall yield him good results.

47-49. In the rites concerning pilgrimages to holy centres, in the annual *śrāddha*, etc, and in those of gods, preceptors, mother or father, gifts made thus are holy. He who makes gifts in this *yajña*, O bird, flourishes every day.

50-51. It yields undying results as the rites performed in altars. Just as *Brahmacārins* are worthy of worship those who give gifts are also worshipped. I grant boon unto them. Similarly, the fourfaced god *Brahmā* and *Śiva* too grant boons.

52. Wherever in the tank, the offered bull drinks water or digs the earth with horns, there enough food and water for the manes exist.

53-54. This is my affirmed truth that they go to great regions. On full moon days or in conjunction with *Revatī* star a blue calf is to be set free. In setting free a blue bull calf, the merit accrued is the same as in performing thousands of *Saṁkrānti* rites or hundreds of rites of solar eclipse.

55. Heifer must be given to a brahmin. *Padas*, vessels of gingelly seeds, etc. must be given to the brahmin devotees of Śiva.

56-57. After worshipping *Umā* and *Maheśvara*, *Acyuta*, dark as the *Atasī* flower and robed in yellow garments, must be worshipped. Those who do so need not be afraid of anyone. Those who desire to escape ghosthood shall perform their respective rites.

58-59. I have thus mentioned everything connected with the rites of obsequies. On hearing this, one freed from sins goes to *Viṣṇu's* region. On hearing this glory of performing rites and the merits of gifts expounded by the lord, *Garuḍa* was delighted. He bowed his head down and asked the lord again.

CHAPTER FIFTEEN

Observances immediate after death

Garuḍa said

1. O lord, please give me a decisive description of *Yama's* region, its dimension, extent and greatness.

The lord said :

2. O *Tārkṣya*, listen. I shall describe the region of *Yama*. All the sixteen worlds are very extensive.

3. The distance between the Earth and *Yama's* region is more than a million and thirtytwo thousand kilometers.

4. O bird, after enjoying the fruits of his merits and demerits in the world, a man falls sick due to the effect of some previous action.

5. This sickness is due to a chance cause. Death occurs to a man in accordance with his actions taking their own definite course.

6. The individual casts off his body and dies due to the effects of his actions. His dead body must be kept on the ground after purifying it with cowdung.

7. Gingelly seeds and *Kuśa* grass must be scattered. A piece of gold is placed in the mouth of the dead man. *Tulasī* leaves and the *Śālagrāma* rock are placed near it.

8. *Sāmasūktas* are recited near him. This is conducive to his salvation. Rods or pieces of gold are to be placed for the benefit of the dead man in his vital opertures.

9. One piece in the mouth, one in each of the nostrils, eyes and ears are to be placed in this order of enumeration.

10. One piece in the operture of the genitals and one piece in the rectum. *Tulasī* leaves are placed in both the hands and the neck.

11. The dead body is to be covered with two clothes. Saffron and raw rice grains are strewn. It is then decorated with flower garlands. The body is to be taken out through the back doorway.

12-13. The son with his relatives and the Brāhmaṇas of the town should carry the corpse on the shoulder to the cremation ground. The corpse should be placed on the pyre with the face of the dead to the North, while the son should sit on the ground with his face turned to the east. The pyre should be made on the ground on which no other dead body has been cremated presently.

14-15. The pyre should be made of woods of sandal, Tulasī, and Palāśa. When the organs lose their functioning power, consciousness is benumbed and the messengers of Yama are near at hand, the breath leaves the body. The departed soul attains divine vision and can see the universe at a glance.

16-17. He observes the dreadful form of Yama even when he is on the verge of death. He sees Yama's servants beating the wicked with the cane. He sees the attendants of Viṣṇu cheering the good.

18-19. The path of Yamaloka is hard to pass. The sinners traverse the path in discomfort. Yama assumes a form of body with four arms, holding conch, discus, bow and mace. He treats the pious with amity and accord and chastises the sinful with the rod of iron.

20-24. He thunders like clouds[1] at the time of dissolution. He looks as dreadful and dark as a mount of collyrium. He is seated on a buffalo[2]. He can be easily propitiated or appeased by the devotee. His body shines as the lustre of lightning. It is as long as the three Yojanas in dimension. He is terrible to look at, wields an iron-rod and noose in his hands. His bodily appearance and eyes are dreadful to the sinners.

1. The cloud Saṁvarta or Saṁvartaka or the rest are extremely dark as they are thick with water at the dissolution of the universe.

2. A popular mantra whereby Yama is invoked in a rite has reference to Mahiṣa (buffalo) as his vehicle.

Mahiṣastha Yamāgaccha
daṇḍahasta mahābala /
rakṣa tvaṁ dakṣiṇa-dvāraṁ
Vaivasvata namostu te //

Mahiṣa-Vāhana is an oft-occurring epithet of Yama.

The soul in human body is of the size of a thumb.[1] When it is dragged out of the body by the messengers of Yama, it cries painfully looking wistfully at his erstwhile home. The disgustful body without life and breath becomes untouchable suddenly, smells foul and is disliked by all.

The body suffers in three ways : Either it is eaten by worms or transformed to feces or reduced to ashes.

25-29. O Garuḍa, Body is liable to destruction in an instant. How can a man boast of it ?

The purpose of wealth is charity, that of speech is truth, that of life is fame and spirituality, that of body is benevolence. In this way, one can gain something substantial out of the things unsubstantial.

When the departed soul is being carried away, the messengers chastise him in the way. They describe the dreadful fate that awaits him in hell.

They tell him thus : "O wicked soul, walk quickly. You are being taken to hell. We carry you to *Kumbhīpāka*[2] and kindred hells. Make haste and do not delay."

Thus hearing the words of messengers and the lamentations of his relatives he cries aloud and is carried by Yama's messengers.

30-31. The son should perform Śrāddha at the appropriate place. He should offer six piṇḍas, on the day of death in the serial order : (1) at the place where the person breathes his last (2) at the door-way, (3) at the courtyard, (4) at the resting place, (5) by the pyre and (6) at the collection of bones.

O Garuḍa, I shall now tell you the purpose why the six piṇḍas are offered to the dead.

32-33. The piṇḍa that is offered to the dead at the place of death pleases the household deities. This piṇḍa satiates

1. *Aṅguṣṭhamātraḥ puruṣaḥ* This śruti citation recurs in treatises on philosophy and is corroborated by the statement of the Mahābhārata when Yama is said to have forcibly dragged the thumb-sized soul out of the body of Satyavān.

Aṅguṣṭhamātram puruṣaṁ niścakarṣa balād Yamaḥ ||

2. *Kumbhīpāka*—a hell. The cruel folk who kill animals and birds for food are roasted in Kumbhi fire. For details see *Devī Bhāgavata, Skandha* 8

both—the earth and the presiding deity. The doorway piṇḍa should be given addressing the departed soul as pāntha (passenger).

34. The gift of this piṇḍa pleases the household deities that abide at the door. In the courtyard lives the Khecara. A piṇḍa should be given in his name.

35. At the resting place, he should offer a piṇḍa to the Bhūta categorized as Deva. This piṇḍa is, therefore, called *bhūta*. The gift of this piṇḍa to the Bhūta makes him genial to the dead.

36. Piśācas, Rākṣasas, Yakṣas and the rest preserve the sanctity of the body which is sacrificed in the fire.

37. When the Piṇḍa is offered by the side of the pyre, the dead is designated as preta. But, O Garuḍa, instead of calling him preta, some call him Sādhaka.

38. But, generally, he is called preta. Henceforth, the offerings are made to him in the name of preta.

39. By gifting away the five piṇḍas, the body achieves sanctity and fitness to be sacrificed in the fire. Otherwise, the presiding deities, as stated above, cause large-scale destruction.

40. Three piṇḍas are necessary : (1) one at the time of death, (2) another in the half-way from the place of death to the cremation ground and still another by the side of the pyre.

41. The piṇḍas are associated in their serial order with their presiding deities, viz., Brahmā, Viṣṇu, and the messengers of Yama.

42. When the third piṇḍa is offered, the dead body is relieved of impurity. The son or the nearest relative should set fire to the pyre.

43. He should cleanse, besmear, dig up, extract the place of altar and after sprinkling the same with water, he should arrange sticks in the prescribed way and light the fire.

44-45. After worshipping the deity Kravyāda[1] with flowers and rice he should recite the following formula : "O Kravyāda, the originator of beings, the source of the universe,

1 *Kravyāda*—a messenger of Yama, so called because he eats raw flesh.

thou art the originator, saviour and the destroyer of the people. Take this dead person to heaven." Thus worshipping the deity Kravyāda, he should sacrifice the dead body.

46. When the body is half-burnt he should pour ghee into the pyre reciting the formula : *Lomabhyaḥ svāhā.*

47. Putting dead body on the pyre he should pour ghee over the pyre with the formula : *Yamāya Antakāya Svāhā.*

48. A single offering should be made to each of the deities—Mṛtyu, Brahmā, Jātavedas (fire) as well as in the mouth of the *preta.* Then he should light the fire from the eastern direction.

49. He should recite the mantra (addressed to the dead); thou art born of this fire; (addressed to the fire) : May he be born of you again. May thou take him to the world of heaven, please.

50. Reciting this mantra he should pour ghee mixed with gingelly seeds. Thus, he should cremate the body as dictated by the funeral code (*antyeṣṭi paddhati*).

51. He should weep aloud at this juncture. For this would assuredly give pleasure to the deceased. The rite of cremation is followed by the rite of collecting bones.

52. The preta-piṇḍa forestalls the pain due to cremation. The Bhūtas (who share the piṇḍa with the deceased) allow the preta to wait till he receives the piṇḍa from his relatives.

53. After the corpse is cremated, the sons or the descendents should bathe in dress. They should offer libations of water mixed with gingelly seeds by his personal name or by the appellation of his lineage.

54. The people of the town who have assembled for morning should applaud the dead by reciting the formula *Viṣṇu, Viṣṇu.* They should accompany the relatives back to the house (as a token of sympathy for the relatives).

55-56. At the southern part of the house he should put cow-dung and the white mustard. He should set up an icon of Varuṇa in the house, eat the leaves of the Nimba[1] and partake of the ghee.

1. *Nimba*—a tree with bitter fruits.

57. O lord of birds, some sprinkle milk over the pyre. He should not shed tears but offer libations of water to the dead.

58. They should not weep. If they weep and spit phlegm the soul of the dead person is compelled to eat that.

59. The son should perform the obsequial rites as his means can afford. O Garuḍa, he should pour milk or water by the earthern jar, in favour of the deceased, over the sloping roof or the courtyard.

60. The soul of the deceased held fast by his previous actions and terribly bewildered, desires for another body. While he is being taken to the abode of Yama by his messengers he casts a mournful look at the cemetery and the courtyard of his house.

61-62. For ten days, without intermittence, the son should offer piṇḍa in the pit and pour handful of water in favour of the deceased. If he has no son, his wife should perform the obsequial rites.

63. If he has no wife, his disciple should perform the same. If no disciple, his brother should do that. The libations of piṇḍa and water should be given either at the cremation ground or at the place of pilgrimage.

64. Whatever the descendent offers—boiled rice, barley-meal, vegetables, fruits, etc.—on the day of death, he should partake of the same on successive days.

65. The son or the descendent offers Piṇḍa for ten days consecutively. The piṇḍa is divided every day into four parts, O lord of birds.

66. Two parts of the piṇḍa go to the building of new body. The third part goes to the messengers of Yama. The fourth he partakes of himself.

67. Within three days and nights the soul assumes a new body. On the tenth day the embodied soul longs for food.

68. No procedure, no mantra and no rites are prescribed. He should offer gifts to the deceased just by his personal name or by the appellation of his lineage.

69-71. O bird, when the dead body is cremated, the soul that has gone out of the body takes a new body.[1] With

1. A popular idea contained in the Bhagavad gītā, II. 22

the piṇḍa of the first day his head comes into being; with the piṇḍa of the second day his neck and shoulders; with that on the third day his heart; with that on the fourth day his back; with that on the fifth day his navel; with those on the sixth and seventh days his waist and private parts; with that on the eighth his thighs; with that on the ninth his palate and feet; with that on the tenth a feeling of hunger comes into being.

72. Having assumed a new body tormented by hunger he stands at the threshold of his house. The tenth day piṇḍa should be accompanied with the offering of flesh.

73. The soul of the deceased when he had assumed a new body feels extremely hungry. His hunger is not appeased if an offering without flesh is made to him.

74-75. On the eleventh day and the twelfth, the soul of the dead eats to his fill. While offering gifts of lamp, food, water etc. to the male or the female deceased one should mutter the name *preta*. Whatever is offered to the deceased, should be done by the name preta, for, doing so gives delight to the deceased.

76. On the thirteenth day, the soul of the dead is taken to the High Way. Now, he assumes a body born of the piṇḍa and feels hungry by day and night.

77. The sinners travel by the path of extreme cold and heat—the path which is beset with nails, infested with demons and spread over with fire. Hunger and thirst await the sinner but the good escape torments.

78. In the path beset with trees, with their leaves as sharp as swords, such tortures are usual. He suffers from hunger and thirst, tortured by the messengers of Yama.

79. The departed soul traverses two hundred and forty-seven Yojanas in twentyfour hours.

80. He is bound by the noose of Yama. He weeps as he leaves the house for the city of Yama.

81. The departed soul goes to the city of Yama which the pious souls find comfortable and where the sinners feel distressed.

82-83. In his upward journey he passes over the best of cities viz, Yāmya, Sauripura, Nagendrabhavana, Gandharva,

Śailāgama, Kraunca, Krūrapura, Vicitrabhavana, Bahvāpada, Duḥkhada, Nānākrandapura, Sutaptabhavana, Raudra, Payovarṣaṇa, Śītāḍhya and Bahubhīti. Yama's city heads the list.

84. On the thirteenth day seized by the servants of Yama, and all alone, the departed soul traverses the path like a monkey led by the juggler.

85-86. As he goes along the path, he cries aloud repeating: "O my son, O my son, I am undone, alas, I am undone. I did not act well." He laments, crying over and over again : Human body is rare to get. I got it by my accumulated merit.

87-88. I earned sufficient wealth but gave nothing to the poor. Alas ! that wealth has gone to others (in spite of hoarding it). Thus he speaks in the choked voice. He is severely tortured by the servants of Yama while he remembers his past.

89. None gives him pleasure or pain. This is wrong to presume that pleasures or pains are caused by others. The soul suffers for all that he performs in his life. O soul, now suffer the consequences of your past activities.

90. [He laments :] I neither gave gifts to the needy nor poured oblations into the fire. I neither practised penance in the caves of the Himālayas nor bathed in the Ganges. O soul, now suffer the cousequences of your activities.

91. I neither gave regular gifts nor made any pastures nor offered sacred books : the Vedas and the Dharmaśāstras to the learned Brahmins in charity nor heard the Purāṇas. Now, O soul, suffer for your activities.

92. I did not construct a tank for satiating thirsty people, beasts or birds. I did not make a pasture for the cattle to graze. Now, O soul, suffer for your activities.

93. I neither enjoyed the pleasures of my husband's company, nor did I enter the pyre of my husband. Nor did I observe the vow of charity after his death. O soul, now suffer for your activities.

94. I did not reduce my body by keeping monthly fasts or Cāndrāyaṇa vow or observances of like nature. I derived

womanhood—the cause of multiple sorrows, from unholy activities of my former life.

95. O bird, you think attentively on what I have said about the lamentations of men and women for their acts of omission and commission done in their previous life.

CHAPTER SIXTEEN

Life after Death

The lord said :

1-2. O lord of birds, when the departed soul laments thus, he cries being struck by Yama's servants who drag him for seventeen days in the firmament. On the eighteenth day he reaches the city of Yama.

3. In that beautiful city there abides a group of departed souls. The river *Puṣpabhadrā* flows there and a big fig tree grows up there.

4-6. There in that city, the servants of Yama bid him take rest. In utter distress he remembers pleasures he enjoyed in the company of his wife and sons. Thirsty and distressed he weeps bitterly and laments over the erstwhile comforts of his wealth, wife, house, sons, servants, friends and comforts of life. He is extremely distressed with hunger. As he laments the servants of Yama speak to him.

The servants of Yama said :

7. Where is your wealth ? Where are your sons ? Where is your wife ? Where are you in this wretched state ? Now suffer for your past evil actions and go by this ancient path.

8. O traveller in this foreign world, do you not know the power of Yama who is the lord of us all—his messengers. Assuredly, you have to travel over that path where there is no provision for barter in virtue or vice.

9. O bird, hear attentively what the messengers of Yama speak to the departed soul. They strike him with the rod of iron.

10. Here, on the earth, whatever is given by his sons every month, rice-ball, etc., due to affection or kindness, he eats the same and then he goes to Sauripura.

11. King Jaṅgama rules in that city who can assume any shape at will. He is frightened by his looks. He feels the urge of taking rest.

12-13. Whatever is offered to him in the three fortnights together with the oblations of water he eats and drinks. He passes over that city and reaches the beautiful town Nagendra by name. He has to travel day and night for two months for reaching that city. He passes over dreadful forests in the way and cries aloud.

14-15. He is beaten by the cruel and merciless messengers of Yama and weeps over and over again. Having eaten the rice-balls and drunk the libation of water offered by the relatives in the second month, he moves further. He is tied with the noose and dragged by the messengers of Yama.

16. He reaches Gandharva nagara (or Gandha-mādana) in the third month. Here, he eats the quarterly rice-ball offered by the relations. Then he moves further.

17. He reaches the city Śailāgama in the fourth month. The stones rain upon him continuously, O lord.

18. There he eats the fourth monthly oblation and feels satisfied.

19. In the fifth month, he goes to Krūrapura. There he eats the rice ball offered by his relatives. In the sixth month he reaches the Krauñcapura.

20. There he feeds upon the rice-ball offered by his relatives in the sixth month. He takes rest for a while but all the time he remains frightened and distressed.

21. He passes over that town being struck and dragged by the messengers of Yama. He reaches Citranagara where rules King Vicitra.

22-23. He is the younger brother of Yama. There he eats the sixth monthly rice-ball but is not satiated fully. Then he moves further; he suffers again and again for want of food.

24. "Do my sons, brothers, parents or relatives exist who may take me out of the ocean of distress wherein I have fallen."

25-28. He laments in the way and is warned by the messengers of Yama. He then, reaches the Vaitaraṇī[1] that flows over hundred Yojanas. It is full of pus and blood, abounds in fish and vultures. Here the fishermen approach him saying, "O traveller, give us liberal fee; we shall row you across the river."

If he has gifted the Vaitaraṇī cow he is rowed across the river. The gift of a cow at the time of death is called Vaitaraṇī which gives relief to the departed soul.

29. The gift of Vaitaraṇī cow destroys his sins and takes him to the region of Viṣṇu. O best of birds, if the Vaitaraṇī cow is not gifted, the departed soul is drowned in that stream.

30. When a person is in good health he should gift a cow to a learned person.

31-32. While drowning he reproaches himself : 'I gave no food to a brahmin traveller nor poured oblations in the fire nor performed *Japa* nor undertook bath nor prayed to the gods. Now, let me suffer for the acts I did in my life.

33. The messengers of Yama strike him again. He repeats those words but in silence this time.

34. He eats the sixth monthly offering made by the relatives and proceeds further. O Garuḍa, the gift of food to the pious brahmins gives relief to the donor in distress.

35. O bird, the departed soul covers two hundred and forty seven Yojanas every day. Thereafter he is completely exhausted.

36. In the seventh month he reaches the city Bahvāpada. He eats the rice-ball offered by his relatives.

37. In the eighth month he reaches Nānākrandapura. There he sees people crying bitterly aloud.

38. Himself in utter distress, he cries in pain. He eats the eighth-monthly rice-ball and feels comfortable.

39. He, then, leaves for Taptapura. Having reached Taptapura in the ninth month he eats the rice-ball and the *Śrāddha* which his son or relatives have gifted in his favour.

40. In the tenth month he reaches Raudrapura. He eats whatever his son or relatives give in his favour.

1. *Vaitaraṇī* : Name of a river in hell.

41. After eating the tenth monthly rice-ball in Raudrapura he goes to Payovarṣaṇa where the clouds rain heavily and cause distress to the departed.

42. Then suffering from heat and thirst he partakes of the eleventh-monthly meal gifted by his relatives.

43. A little before a year has passed or at the end of eleven and a half month he reaches a Śītapura—city of extreme cold and distress.

44. Tormented by cold and hunger he looks in all directions and speeks : "I wish I had a relative who would have removed my distress."

45. The attendants of Yama speak to him thus : "Where is thy holy merit that it may give relief to thee." On hearing their words he cries : 'O my fate.'

46. Fate is nothing but a result of accumulated merit or sin. 'I did no good acts, hence this trouble'—pondering over the matter thus, he takes up courage for the time being.

47. At the distance of forty four Yojanas from Śītapura, there is a beautiful city of Dharmarāja (Yama) where live the celestial musicians and the heavenly nymphs.

48. There live eightyfour lacs of people in human and divine forms. The guards are put at the thirteen gates of the city.

49-52. There abide honourable and respectable Śravaṇas, the sons of Brahmā who know and report to Citragupta whatever good or bad actions are performed by the mortals.

The Śravaṇas are eight in number. They move about in heaven, hell and on earth. They can see and hear from afar. Their women are known as Śravaṇīs who are identifiable by their individual names. They are the presiding deities of mortals and have full knowledge of their activities.

53. A mortal should worship them with vows, gifts and prayers. They become cordial to him and cause death in an easy manner.

CHAPTER SEVENTEEN

Glory of Śravaṇas

Garuḍa said :

1-2. O lord, I want to know about the parentage of Śravaṇas. How are they stationed in the city of Yama ? How do they know about the activities of mortals ? How do they hear what the people talk about among themselves ? From what source is that knowledge derived by them ?

3. O lord, where do they eat ? Favour me with your answers to my queries. On hearing the words of the king of birds, the lord spoke.

The lord said :

4. Now hear, what I am going to speak about Śravaṇas is both truthful and pleasant. I shall tell you about the activities of Śravaṇas.

5. When the entire world of moveables and immoveables became one uniform whole and I, the lord of beings, was reposing in sleep in the milky ocean.

6-7. The self-born Brahmā seated in my navel-lotus practised penance for many years. The universe consisting of fourfold creation was reduced to a single entity—the universe which is created by Brahmā, preserved by Viṣṇu and annihilated by Rudra.

8. Brahmā created the all-pervading wind. He created the refulgent sun. He created Yama along with Citragupta.

9. He created the universe afterwards, and practised penance for many years, sitting in the navel-lotus of Viṣṇu.

10-11. He created the universe and assigned duties. The gods were anxious to know what time the creator created the universe, how Rudra, Viṣṇu and Dharma ruled over the earth.

12. Thus lost in anxiety, the gods pondered over the problem. They discussed the matter with Brahmā.

13-14. Brahmā who was urged by the gods created twelve sons[1] by the chemical process out of flowers and leaves.

They possess lustrous, wide eyes. At the behest of Brahmā, they carry all tidings of Man's activities whether good or bad to the ears of Brahmā.

15. They can hear from afar and see far-off things. O bird, they are, therefore, called Śravaṇas.

16. They roam about in the firmament and watch the activities of the people which they reveal to Yama at the time of their death.

17. They also declare on the fitness of the departed soul for a particular goal, due to his activities.

18. There are four paths in man's life, viz, paths of Dharma, Artha, Kāma and Mokṣa. O son of Vinatā,[2] a man can go by any one of these paths, superior or inferior.

19. One who bestows riches goes by a celestial car. One who fulfils wishes rides the horse. One who desires liberation travels by swan-vehicles.

20. A sinful person walks bare-footed on rows of sword-edged leaves. He is struck with stones, pierced with thorns and bound by nooses.

21-22. He who in the world of mortals propitiates Śravaṇas, offering them water from a jar and food cooked in a vessel, worships Śravaṇas and me.

O lord of birds, I shall grant him that position which is inaccessible even to the immortals.

23. With devotion he should feed eleven Brāhmaṇas who are pious and virtuous and the twelfth together with his wife, just for my propitiation.

24. Men should worship Śravaṇas together with the gods. By doing so, they who seek for pleasure can get to heaven. By worshipping Śravaṇas they propitiate me, Citragupta and Yama.

1. Another tradition ascribes 12 sons to Kaśyapa and his wife Aditi who are known as the twelve Ādityas.

2. *Vinatā*—wife of Kaśyapa and daughter of Dakṣa. Two sons Aruṇa and Garuḍa and a daughter Sumati were born to her. For details see Purāṇic Encyclopaedia, under Garuḍa.

25-26. With Śravaṇas pleased, the pious people go to Viṣṇuloka. O best of birds, whosoever hears about the glory of Śravaṇas, their origin and pious activities is not covered up by sins. He enjoys pleasures of this world and attains glory hereafter.

CHAPTER EIGHTEEN

Life after Death

The lord said :

1-2. On hearing the words of Śravaṇas and thinking about the problem for a while, Citragupta informs about all those actions pious or impious performed by the people. He repeats them also to the person concerned.

3. Whatever action a person undertakes, by word of mouth, body or mind, whether good or bad, he reaps the fruits thereof.

4. O lord, thus I have told you about the path which the departed soul has to traverse. I have also told you about the places of rest for the departed soul.

5. If food is gifted in his favour he travels in comfort on the High Way. To illuminate the path, an earthen lamp should be kindled, put in the appropriate place and kept burning by day and night.

6. The path, though dark, dreadful, dog-infested and void of resting-place, becomes luminous and pleasant for those who have gifted an earthen lamp.

7. If an earthen jar is gifted on the fourteenth day or the month of Kārttika, it gives comfort to the deceased. Now, I shall tell you in brief about the path of Yama for the departed soul.

8. He goes to the world of manes as a result of the merit accruing from the performance of Vṛṣotsarga. By the rice-ball offered on the eleventh, he attains physical purity.

9. The servants of Yama are satiated by the gift of water-jar.

10. By gifting bed the deceased goes to heaven by the aerial car. The gift of bed can be made on any day or on the twelfth day from death.

11. On the 13th day he should give precious articles of different varieties in favour of the deceased or the person himself, when alive, should gift these articles for himself.

12-13. O Garuḍa, by the merit accruing from these gifts he goes comfortably on that path. O lord of birds, there prevails a uniform law for all : the higher, lower and the middling classes. O bird, you should know that a person reaps the fruits, sour or sweet, in proportion to the nature and extent of actions done by him.

14. Whatever gifts he or his relatives make in his favour stand in good stead while he is on journey to the world of Yama.

Garuḍa said :

15. O lord, why should they give *padas* and of what nature. Who shall receive the gifts ? O god of gods, let me know the facts.

The lord said :

16. An umbrella, shoes, clothes, a ring, a water-jar, a chair or stool and a vessel—these seven are called *padas*.

17. There is a terrible heat in the way which scorches the departed soul. By the gift of umbrella, the deceased receives shelter of shade and feels comfortable.

18. By the gift of shoes the deceased passes over the sword-edged forest, mounted on the horse.

19. By the gift of a seat (*āsana*) to a Brahmin, the deceased obtains tasty meals in the interval of time while he walks over the path at his leisure.

20. By the gift of a water-jar, he gets enough water on the way which is full of heat, devoid of air and water.

21. A person, gifting a water-jar made of copper, receives, assuredly, the merit of constructing a thousand wells.

22. The messengers of Yama are dreadful to look at, dark and yellow is appearance. They are courteous too, if propitiated by the gift of clothes and ornaments. When satisfied they do not torment the deceased.

23. They wield terrible weapons, run here and there. By the gift of a ring they vanish from the presence of the deceased.

24. The *pada* is completed by the gift of a vessel, a seat, raw food, clarified butter and a sacred thread.

25. Tired and thirsty, the traveller feels comfortable if he has gifted the buffalo's milk in his life-time.

Garuḍa said :

26. O lord, things are gifted by the relatives at home in favour of the deceased. How do they reach the deceased and who receives them ?

The lord said :

27. God Varuṇa receives those gifts and hands them over to me. I give them to god Bhāskara (the sun), from Bhāskara the deceased person obtains them.

28. As a result of sinful activities when no descendant is left on the earth, the deceased person goes to hell until his sin is exhausted.

29-33. After his term has expired, the pious soul is allowed by Yama, the lord of eightyfour lacs of hells, to have a look at hells and hear the cries of pretas (the departed souls). In the midst of hells, there are 21 notorious hells, viz. Tāmisra, Lohaśaṅku, Mahāraurava, Śālmali, Raurava, Kudvala, Kālasūtraka, Pūtimṛttikā, Saugatā, Lohatoda, Saviṣa, Pretāpana, Mahānaraka, Kālola, Sajīvana, Mahāpatha, Avīci, Andhatāmisra, Kumbhīpāka, Asipatravana and Patana.

34. Those who have passed several years in the dreadful hell and have no descendants (to offer gifts) in their favour become messengers of Yama.

35. Yama sends them on errand and they share with the dead the food and drink which their relatives offer them from time to time.

36-37. Being extremely hungry they seize the dead man's gifts on the way and eat them. A rice-ball gifted as food to the dead at the end of a month satiates them for a year.

38. By such deeds of merit, gradually he reaches Sauripura. Then by the end of a year, he reaches the vicinity of dreadful Yamaloka.

39. Here, he gives up his dreadful body, of the measure of arm, which he derived within ten days from the ten piṇḍas gifted to him by his descendants. His spirits droop at the sight of Yama as the spirit of Paraśurāma at the sight of Rāma (Dāśarathi).

40. He gives up his previous body for the one derived from his actions. He receives an airy body of the size of a thumb and reaches the sword-edged hell.

41. Here, he walks on single foot bound helplessly by his actions as a caterpillar by reeds.

42. Just as a person casts off his old dress and puts on a new one, so the soul gives up his old body and assumes a new one.[1]

CHAPTER NINETEEN

Life after Death

The lord said :

1. Assuming an airy form derived from his previous actions and suffering from hunger he moves along with Yama.

2. There is a town of Citragupta covering twenty yojanas. There the embodied beings observe their virtue and sin all around.

3. If he had made substantial gifts in his life-time he derives pleasure therefrom. From here Vaivasvata town of Yama is situated at the distance of twentyfovr Yojanas.

4. The residents of Vaivasvatapura are satiated by the gifts of iron, salt, cotton and a vessel of gingelly seeds, offered by the relatives of the deceased.

1. A popular theme occurring in the *Bhagavad gītā*, II. 22.

5. The dead repair to Vaivasvata town and inform Dharmadhvaja, the keeper at Yama's gate (about the gifts). Dharmadhvaja is always present at the gate of Yama.

6. Dharmadhvaja is pleased with the gift of seven grains. Propitiated by that, he tells the dead about their virtues and sins.

7. Holy and pious people see Dharmarāja as a god of noble countenance, while the sinful and the wicked see him as a god of dreadful and terrible aspect.

8. The deceased person is terribly afraid at his sight and laments bitterly. Those who have offered gifts in their life-time should entertain no fear.

9. Yama moves from his seat as soon as he sees a holy man. He thinks that he will supersede him in status and reach Brahmaloka.

10. Virtue can easily be procured by offering gifts. The path to Yama's region can easily be traversed by acts of Charity. This High Way cannot be easily covered otherwise. O dear, none can reach the city of Yama without doing charitable acts.

11. That dreadful path is full of terror-striking servants of Yama. Each of the cities is guarded by a thousand of these servants.

12. The messengers of Yama torture the sinner in (hot) waters and take off his skin till he becomes a skeleton.

13. The deceased for whom no obsequial rites have been made traverse the path with great difficulty. They are led like animals bound with ropes.

14-15. The person may become a god, a mare, a man of low species, or as Yama ordains he may attain salvation or be born as a human being as a son to his father.

16. He obtains birth according to his activities. He passes through a series of births in this world.

17. Knowing that even the highest happiness is non eternal, he should perform acts of righteousness when he has received a human body.

18. Human body is either reduced to worms, ashes, or feces. Though he carries a lantern in hand, he may fall in a dreadful hell full of darkness.

19. He can acquire human body as a result of his pious

acts. He who performs holy deeds in human body acquires supreme position.

20. If he neglects Dharma, he comes to grief.

21. The soul obtains human body after passing through series of births. O bird, in human body too, his birth as a Brāhmaṇa is a rare event. He who observes vows natural to his caste becomes immortal after death by the blessing of God.

CHAPTER TWENTY

Functions of the Departed Soul

Garuḍa said :

1. Having obtained a new body where does a preta shelter ? Released from pretahood, where does he go to live in?

2-3. Passing through torments in hells which number eighty four lacs and guarded by Yama and his thousand attendants how do the pretas get release and how do they roam about in this mortal world ?

The lord said :

4. O king of birds, hear. I shall tell you about the region where the pretas live. Men attain pretahood by stealing other man's riches, by indulging in sexual intercourse with other man's wife or by doing acts of treachery.

5. Having incurred sins, they seek for redemption in their progeny. Being bodiless as well as suffering from hunger and thirst they roam about here and there.

6. Even the captives released from prison are frightened at their sight. They seek for means to kill their kith and kin.

7. They bolt doors on their ancestors, put obstacles in the way of manes. Like thieves, they snatch the mane's food in the way before it reaches them.

8. They return home, stay on the roof and watch the activities of their kins. They cause disease and grief to their relatives.

9-11. Having assumed the form of tertian and such-like fevers they cause diseases due to cold or wind like head-ache or cholera. They stay at the place of leavings or refuse, in the company of other ghosts and partake of food and drink left over by their relatives.

12. In this way, the sinning pretas move about freely.

Garuḍa said :

13-14. How do the pretas behave and in what form ? How is it possible to know their attitude, since the pretas do not speak to us ? If you are pleased to do me a favour, you clear off my doubts. O lord, I hear that in the Kali Age many people become ghosts.

Garuḍa said :

15. The ghost torments his family people through the enemy. While he was in human body he was affectionate to his people, now that he is dead he becomes hostile to them.

16. He who is devoted to Rudra, follows the path of righteousness, propitiates gods, satiates guests, speaks truth and pleasant words, is not tormented by the pretas.

17. He who does not observe rites, has no faith in the sanctity of the Vedas, hates righteous acts and indulges in falsehood, is tormented by the pretas. By doing unrighteous acts, O Garuḍa, he becomes a preta in this Kali age.

18. From the beginning of Śatya yuga to the end of Dvāpara, nobody became a preta and nobody suffered from preta.

19-20. It is observed that of the many children born of one and the same mother, one is happy, one is addicted to bad habits, one is blessed with progeny, one is tormented by pretas, one abounds in wealth, one gets sons who die young, one is burdened with the offspring of daughters, one is at daggers-drawn with his relatives. This all is due to the bad intentions of the preta, O Garuḍa.

21. A woman becomes barren in life or if she gives birth to children they die at an early age. There is a loss of wealth and cattle. These sufferings are caused by preta.

22. If there is a sudden change in his nature or an enmity with his relatives or an unexpected calamity, the suffering is due to preta.

23. If a person loses faith in religion or if he loses the means of his livelihood or if he feels greedy in excess or if there is a regular quarrel at home, that suffering is due to preta.

24-25. If he slays his parents or reproaches gods and Brahmins and is found guilty of murder that suffering is due to preta.

26. When crops do not grow up, though the rains are abundant; when the expenditure goes up and income is reduced; when quarrels rise in gravity, that suffering is due to preta.

27. When, on travel to a foreign land, he is distressed by the onrush of wind, O lord of birds, that suffering is due to preta.

28. When he associates with the people of low caste or when he performs disreputable acts or when he is interested in acts of unrighteousness, that suffering is due to preta.

29. When the hoarded wealth is destroyed by misfortune or when the work in operation bears no fruit or when there is loss of wealth due to undue taxation or due to fire or theft, that suffering is due to preta.

30. When an incurable disease sets in, or when children suffer from pain or when wife suffers immensely, that suffering is due to preta.

31. When one loses faith in the Vedas, Smṛtis, Purāṇas, and Dharmaśāstras, that suffering is due to preta.

32. When one abuses gods, gurus and Brahmins in their presence or absence, that aberration of nature is due to preta.

33. This is due to preta and to no other course when a person suffers from loss of livelihood or break in social position or break in the continuity of lineage.

34. When women suffer from abortion or do not conceive or when children die at an early age that suffering is due to preta.

35. When he does not perform the annual śrāddha in sincerity and has no inclination either—that suffering is due to preta.

36. When on pilgrimage he indulges in sexual intercourse or neglects his duties or when he fails to prosper though

he has done acts of piety—that suffering is due to preta.

37. When both husband and wife quarrel at meals, when there is a strong inclination to harm others that suffering is due to preta.

38. When trade does not prosper though he has gone abroad where he lives in separation from wife, that suffering is due to preta.

39. When he lives in foreign lands or when he loses position at home, that suffering is due to preta.

40. When he is inimical to his people, regards his son as his enemy, when he has no interest in home and feels uncomfortable there, that suffering is due to preta.

41. When he refuses to obey his parents and has no love for his wife, is of cruel nature, is lost in his own affairs, that suffering is due to preta

42. If the funeral rites are not performed in the prescribed way, the soul of the deceased (in rebirth) deviates from the righteous path and falls in the company of the wicked. Then Vṛṣotsarga is the only rite to redeem him.

43. O Garuḍa, a person becomes a ghost and undergoes sufferings if he dies an accidental death or if his body is not crema+ed properly.

44. O best of birds, when the descendent knows all this, he should conduct those rites which may release the deceased from ghosthood. If he does not perform rites for the ghost he himself turns a ghost after death.

45. The person whose house is haunted by a ghost does not feel happy or comfortable. He loses faith, pleasure, devotion, discrimination as well as wealth.

46. His lineage breaks either at the third or at the fifth generation. In each and every birth he lives a wretched, poor and sinful life.

47. There are people who have fierce, dreadful, disfigured and ghostly appearance, who have no regard or honour for their caste, progeny, parents, or womanfolk, who put on fashions, go an unpleasant way and talk loosely. Alas, it is painful to see them suffer, under the force of fate, from the recollection of their past sinful deeds.